MAYBE I SHOULD'VE STAYED IN BED?

The Flip Side of the Rock'n'Roll Dream

DEKE LEONARD

First Published in 2000 by
NORTHDOWN PUBLISHING LIMITED
PO Box 49, Bordon
Hants GU35 0AF

email: enquiries@northdown.demon.co.uk
website: www.northdown.demon.co.uk

This work is Copyright © Deke Leonard 2000

The rights of Deke Leonard to be identified as the author of this work has been asserted by them in accordance with the Copyright, Designs and Patents Act, 1988

All Rights Reserved

This book is sold subject to the condition that it shall not, by way of trade or otherwise, be lent, re-sold, hired out or otherwise circulated without the publisher's prior consent in any form of binding or cover other than that in which it is published and without a similar condition being imposed on the subsequent purchaser.

No part of this publication may be reproduced, stored in a retrieval system, or transmitted in any form or by any means, electronic, mechanical, photocopying, recording or otherwise, without the prior permission of the copyright owner.

British Library Cataloguing-in-Publication Data
A catalogue for this book is available from the British Library

ISBN 1900711 09 5

Designed by Mary Hodge.

Also by this author
Rhinos Winos & Lunatics
ISBN 1900711 00 1
(Currently reprinting, contact publishers for details)

contents

1	intro	5
2	the welcome death of a fascist	8
3	5X	21
4	a gathering of eagles	27
5	be-bop-a-lula	37
6	the problems of being too sexy	40
7	the years of bondage	47
8	the L-club	53
9	swashbuckling	61
10	call an ambulance	65
11	what could be more pointless than playing a banjo?	71
12	more, roger, more!	74
13	the committee-man cometh	78
14	a perfect right-hook	84
15	i am forced to write a song	89
16	the blackjacks	92
17	the jet set	120
18	taking london by storm	129
19	what a show! what a show!	133
20	a few swansea stories	147
21	the hottest ticket in K-town	159
22	the decline and fall of a sky-blue shark	180
23	cool hand plum – stealing by finding	184
24	'lectric, is it?	192
25	here come the drugs	198
26	the biggest freak-out to hit south wales	204
27	'you will arrive!'	221
28	the end of a perfect dream	225
29	outro	229

acknowledgements

I would like to thank the following people: All the staff at Northdown Publishing – Ian Welch, Alan Kinsman, Simon Joslin. Once again they have proved to be immaculate in conception.

Mike Rees, Geoff Griffiths, Keith Hodge, Mary Hodge, Alan 'Lewie' Lewis, Tony 'Plum' Hollis, Martin Ace, Stuart Hickman, Pete James, Christine Corvette and Mike Brewer, for allowing me access to their memories. which were always better than mine.

Ron Bevan, for allowing me to plunder his photographic archives. Where his work appears, he is duly credited.

Jenny Evans, for providing me with a photo of Billy Doc. The book wouldn't be complete without it.

Phil & Eve Wilson, for their boundless generosity.

Mary Hodge, a diamond on the tiara of life, for being the most beautiful sounding-board in the world. And for being the oxygen to my nitrogen. And for resisting the temptation to murder me in my sleep. And for designing the book.

Michael Heatley, for boldly going where no publisher has gone before. History will judge him, in the wisdom department, as the equal of Solomon. Thank you, Michael.

1
intro

I was dripping with sweat, my throat was parched, my legs were trembling, and I wanted to go to the toilet. I had hot and cold flushes, blurred vision, and pins and needles in my extremities, which I presumed were the initial symptoms of a heart attack. I was petrified and I wasn't alone. Mike and Geoff were in the same state. We were 'Lucifer and the Corncrackers' and this was our first gig.

We sat on a row of chairs at the side of the stage, eyes cast down, like condemned men waiting for the hangman to arrive. I wracked my addled brain for an excuse to run. I prayed that somebody would rush in and inform me of a death in the family – unlikely, since I come from a line of long-livers; I longed for a power cut – next to impossible, I would have thought, given that we were playing in a power station; and I yearned for an earthquake – the thought of the earth opening up and swallowing me was curiously comforting but the San Dafydd Fault had been depressingly inert for some years. But nobody rushed in, the lights didn't flicker, and bloody terra remained bloody firma. There was no escape. Suddenly I understood how Custer must have felt.

It was Saturday, the 17th of March 1962, and we were at the Car Bay Club, the social club of the Carmarthen Bay Power Station in Burry Port, just down the coast from Llanelly. The place was packed and the average age of the audience was about sixty. In the run-up to the gig, ignorance about what was to come had made us somewhat cocky but that cockiness disappeared completely in the face of the public. We took one look at them and had a small, collective nervous breakdown.

It was billed as a talent contest. There were six acts and we were the third on. We were told that there was a big agent in the audience. He was easy to spot. He sat at a table directly in front of the stage. He was a lumpy, balding man in a crumpled suit and he shared the table with his wife, who looked just as you'd expect an agent's wife to look – like a down-market bookie's wife. She sat in morose silence while he talked loudly to her about show business, name-dropping furiously. He mentioned Shirley Bassey at least four times.

The first act was a Cliff Richard look-alike who sang 'The Young Ones' in a key far too high for him.

'He'll never make the middle-eight,' I said to Mike.

As expected, he broke down halfway through the song and, red-faced with embarrassment, returned to his seat on a wave of sympathy from his mates. We, who thought Cliff Richard was a disgrace to civilisation, were rather pleased. Much to our delight the agent ignored him and continued talking loudly to his wife, who'd obviously heard it all before.

maybe i should've stayed in bed?

The second act was a genial, semi-famous, ex-rugby player who sang 'Do Not Forsake Me, Oh My Darling' in a tremulous baritone voice. It was excruciating because he was a little sharp all the way through, but it was obvious that the audience had heard him sing it a million times before because he received warm, indulgent applause. He failed, however, to make any impression on the agent, although he clearly affected his wife, who was knocking back gin & tonics at an alarming rate.

Then the compere, an elderly committee-man holding a sheet of paper, shuffled on to the stage. He stood in front of the microphone and blew into it. It whistled derisively. He cleared his throat.

'Ladies and gentlemen,' he said, 'it's their first booking so give them a big hand...' He rummaged around in his pockets until he found his glasses. Then, holding the sheet of paper at arm's length, he began to read, '...Loose Ivor and the Prawn Crackers.'

My bowels went into spasm. There was no backing out now. We walked on to the stage like pall-bearers. We passed the committee-man coming off.

'You got our name wrong,' I hissed. 'It's not the Prawn Crackers. It's the Corncrackers. We're a group, not a Chinese aperitif. And who the fuck is Loose Ivor?'

'There's no need for that kind of language.' he said, 'and, anyway, I didn't say that.'

'Yes, you did,' I said.

'No, I bloody didn't,' he said.

'Yes, you bloody did,' I insisted. with white-knuckled nonchalance.

'Well, it's a stupid name for a group, isn't it?' he said. 'You want to get yourself a proper name, boy.'

'It is a proper name,' I said. 'Just because...'

I was about to give him a lecture on the lack of imagination exhibited by the musical community in the choosing of band names, when I noticed the audience. Any applause we might have received had long-since died away and they were sitting in deathly silence, waiting for us to start.

'Get on with it,' shouted a voice from the back.

So we got on with it. We'd had no rehearsals as such. We'd just played through a few songs in each others' front rooms. There was no plugging in because we had acoustic guitars – our first mistake, because once we started all you could hear were Geoff's drums. We opened up with Eddie Cochran's '20 Flight Rock', which Mike sang. I counted it in. I was rigid with fear. I dared not look at the audience so I looked at my feet and waited for the first bottle to be thrown. I abandoned all hope and gritted my teeth, swearing that I'd never put myself through this kind of ordeal again. I just wasn't cut out to be a musician. I would have to resign myself to a tedious and unremarkable life in the building trade. Then out of the corner of my eye I saw movement. I risked a glance. It was Mike. He was leaping all over the stage. He'd put down his guitar, grabbed the microphone, and assumed the mantle of front-man. The audience were on their feet, laughing and clapping, and the agent had stopped talking to his wife, which was just as well because she was lying back in her chair, head thrown back, eyes closed and mouth open.

We were going down a storm. Mike got more outrageous as the set progressed. Teetering on the edge of the stage, he swivelled his hips suggestively at a couple of matrons in the front row and they dissolved into giggles. He rubbed the microphone against his groin and the matrons covered their eyes with shame. He finished the set by taking his jacket off and waving it above his head, just like we'd seen Joey Dee and the Starliters do in a recent film. The agent stared at the stage, mesmerised. Everybody stared at the stage. Except, of course, the agent's wife.

It was then I learnt my first lesson in stagecraft. It didn't matter if the drums were too loud. It didn't matter if you couldn't hear the guitar. It didn't even matter if you couldn't hear the vocals. As long as somebody was jumping up and down in the middle of the stage then all was well with the world.

We left the stage with rapturous applause ringing in our ears. The agent pulled out a notebook and started scribbling. We assumed he was working out how much money he was going to offer us for the forthcoming world tour he was arranging on our behalf. We gathered at the side of the stage and congratulated each other. We were on our way. Success was a foregone conclusion. Fame and fortune were just around the corner. Then the next act came on.

She was a portly woman about sixty years-old dressed in a floral pinafore and carpet-slippers. She was carrying a metal drinks tray. She shuffled to the centre of the stage, took out her false teeth with a flourish and sang 'She'll Be Coming Round The Mountain When She Comes', accenting the off-beat by hitting herself over the head with the tray. And, as a bonus, every time the tray hit her head she went squint; I have no way of knowing whether this was intentional or a by-product of cerebral pummelling but, by God, it was effective. As the song drew to a close she gave up all pretence of timing and beat herself randomly about the head, ending with a savage skull-crushing staccato. The tray was mangled beyond recognition and she was suffering from severe concussion but she had the audience in the palm of her hand. The agent was on his knees in front of her, begging her to sign a lifetime contract for a million pounds. Even the agent's wife had woken up, jarred back to consciousness, no doubt, by the sound of unforgiving metal on splintering bone. The agent ignored the last two acts and spent the rest of the evening deep in conversation with his new find. He appeared to have forgotten about us.

At the end of the evening we were paid ten bob each. I remember thinking I could make a living at this. There was a complaint from the committee that some of Mike's bumping and grinding had been a little on the lewd side, but we brushed it aside. We forgot about being upstaged by a geriatric sado-masochist and remembered the sweet sound of applause.

2
the welcome death of a fascist

At first there were two of us – Mike Rees and me. We passed the 11-plus at the same time and found ourselves sitting next to each other in 1B2, the class for those deemed the least promising of the year's intake at Llanelly Boys' Grammar School. I didn't realise it at the time but we were cousins. My first memory of him was during our first rugby training, when I put him in hospital. Mike, a bantamweight, was arbitrarily selected as hooker for the A team while I, a light-heavy, was chosen on equally flimsy grounds as prop-forward for the B team. As the first scrum went down I made my presence felt by head-butting Mike, who collapsed in a heap. He was stretchered off and taken to Llanelly General. The following day he was back in school, none the worse for my thuggery. I bumped into him in the toilets during the mid-morning break and apologised. That's when he told me we were cousins. He'd known since the first day at school but did not deem the subject worthy of mention. We'd met before, he said, at the Odeon Cinema two years ago. His parents had taken him to see 'The Robe' and so had mine. We'd found ourselves standing next to each other in the queue and Winston, my father, and George, his father, old friends as well as cousins, had introduced us. Mike remembered it in detail but I didn't remember it at all. Our kinship now firmly established, I felt it was time to move on to the next stage.

'Do you want a fight?' I asked.

'OK,' said Mike.

We went out to the playing fields and wrestled until it was time for our next lesson. When the dinner-break came, we wolfed down our food and headed back to the playing fields where we wrestled until the afternoon bell. And when the final bell rang, we had a quick wrestle before we went home. During that first year we were inseparable but at the start of the second, Mike, who was far more conscientious than I about matters educational, moved up into the A-stream. I was now his social inferior. A member of a lower educational caste. But despite the social stigma we continued to wrestle at break times. We had no idea that we were about to be swept away by the glorious tidal wave of rock'n'roll that was rapidly engulfing the world.

I was twelve years old when I first heard rock'n'roll. I was staying with my grandparents at Nathan Street in the Seaside district of Llanelly. I was out playing on the street – probably pretending to be a Spitfire pilot just scrambled from Tangmere taking on the might of Goering's Luftwaffe over the South Downs – when the sky darkened. The real sky. I looked up. It was John Phelps, my cousin by marriage. He was my Auntie Nan's stepson and lived with her and Uncle Tom three doors down from my grandparents. He was four years older than me and

the welcome death of a fascist

something of a hero because he was a Teddy Boy and, as such, regarded as the black sheep of the family. He was always being brought home drunk in the early hours of the morning by the police. I'd sit on the top of the stairs in my pyjamas, listening to the late-night screaming matches that always spilled over into our house.

'Come with me,' said John. the sunlight glinting off his Brylcreemed quiff. He put his arm around me and steered me toward his house. (I was vaguely irritated by the interruption because I was about to send a Focke Wulf 190 into the English Channel, but I knew it would still be there when I got back. That's the beauty of fantasies – they always do what you tell them; I could have Brigitte Bardot flying the damn plane if I wanted to.) We went through the back door and into his living room. There were three Teddy Boys waiting in there, in magnificent repose, wearing drape jackets, drainpipe trousers, brothel-creepers and ducktail haircuts. They were all pulling heavily on roll-ups and the room was thick with smoke.

'Listen to this,' said John, slouching over to the record player and putting on a record.

'Well, it's a-one for the money...'

I jumped at the volume.

'Two for the show...'

John was watching me.

'Three to get ready...'

I was aware of four pairs of eyes watching me.

'Now, go cat, go...'

I froze, not sure how to react, while the Teddy Boys sneered in time to the music. When the song ended there was silence. Then John spoke.

'That was Elvis Presley singing "Blue Suede Shoes",' he said. 'What d'you think?'

They all leaned forward, waiting for my response.

'It was very nice,' I said politely.

'You didn't like it?' said John, shaking his head sadly.

'Er, not really, John,' I said.

I liked Eric Coates marches: 'The Dam Busters', 'Reach For The Sky'; stuff like that.

'There's not much of a tune,' I added, feeling I was expected to say something. They all put their heads in their hands and groaned.

'He's too young,' said one of them.

'He's too stupid,' said another.

I didn't know which was the worse insult, presumably because I was too young and stupid to judge. Whatever I was, I was now surplus to requirements. One of the Teddy Boys put 'Blue Suede Shoes' on again and John, with his arm around my shoulder, showed me out.

'See you later,' he said. In a perfect world he would have tousled my hair.

I went back to that damned Focke Wulf 190. It was still there. I told you it would be. Brigitte Bardot wasn't the pilot so I sent it to oblivion.

maybe i should've stayed in bed?

I have no idea why John hauled me in off the street like that. Was I being tested? Did they have a bet going? Would the idiot-child like Elvis Presley? Whatever the reason, they impressed the hell out of me. It was years before it occurred to me that they might have been wise men trying to show me the star in the east; or the west, as it turned out.

Then I forgot all about them and pursued my military ambitions. I wanted to be Douglas Bader, the legless World War Two flying ace, so I adopted a rolling gait, as if had tin legs, and joined the Air Training Corps. At school I tried to persuade Mike to join too but he just laughed.

It is a theory of mine that every child starts out as a fascist. Then, provided they have a vestige of intelligence, they move, with the onset of adulthood, to the left. Those without any intelligence whatsoever join the Conservative Party, which Lloyd George accurately called 'the Stupid Party'. Lloyd George was Welsh. Did you know that?

The ATC, recognising my unbridled fascism, promoted me to the rank of corporal and put me in charge of parades, mainly because I had a loud voice. This meant I was responsible for ensuring that the squadron was well-drilled and immaculately turned-out at all times, particularly on public occasions. It was an uphill task. My squad were not the flint-eyed, whipchord-muscled, fighting clay of my dreams – they were split fairly evenly between unrepentant endomorphs and uncoordinated ectomorphs. We did have one cadet of normal build but he was seriously flawed. He couldn't stop farting on parade. I tried to think of ways to stop him. Ten minutes before we were due to start he would, under orders, sit on the toilet and force-fart, in the hope that by the time he got to the drill hall he would have expended at least some of what appeared to be infinite resources of methane-like gas. At rest, the problem was manageable. He would occasionally let go the odd plaintive whisper but the squad held fast. The trouble started when he began to march. Then he truly came into his own. Tuba-like drones of inordinate length, some lasting five or six marching beats, resonated through the rafters. By the second circuit of the drill hall, the squad were reduced to tears and totally unresponsive to orders. I had to face the facts – a man with a militant bowel disorder could reduce my fighting machine to ashes with a random twitch of his sphincter. It was intolerable. What if it happened under enemy fire? In the interest of squad morale, mainly mine, I tried to get him transferred to desk duties but his uncle, the commanding officer, wouldn't have it, insisting that one day his nephew would become the first Welsh Marshall of the Royal Air Force – yeah, dream away, uncle. As the offence of 'farting without leave' is not covered by military regulations, my hands were tied. I spent most of my waking hours inventing erroneous errands on which to send him.

'Nip into town and get a bag of sugar, Alwyn.'

'But there's some sugar in the mess, corporal.'

'Ours not to reason why, Alwyn bach…'

I took my duties seriously, obsessively even, and in the run-up to a public parade I had the squad marching up and down the drill hall until their feet started

the welcome death of a fascist

to smoke. I quickly earned the nickname 'Corporal Punishment', of which I was absurdly proud.

The Remembrance Sunday parade loomed. This was the big one. All the local paramilitary organisations would be there: the Boy Scouts, the Sea Scouts, the Girl Guides, the Brownies, the St John's Ambulance, the Boys' Brigade, the Real Boys' Brigade (a hardline splinter-group from the Boys' Brigade), the Army Cadet Corps (the less said about them the better), and the Coleshill Girls' Secondary Modern School Netball Team (a fearsome platoon of Amazons who the previous year had paraded in black balaclavas). The music was provided by the Band of the Territorial Army of Wales, plus goat. There was a ten o'clock kick-off.

We mustered in front of the Town Hall at nine-thirty, a colourful riot of military-drab. Watched by an ever-growing crowd of townsfolk, which by now included my mother and father, the officers on parade, of which I was one, did their best to shepherd their wayward charges into a single unit. It took some doing. Several times I'd get close, but just when I'd think I had them all in one place, I'd notice one was missing. Ordering the rest, on pain of death, to stay put, I'd go on a recce. I'd return with the missing cadet only to discover that during my absence another one had wandered off. There's some dozy fuckers about, aren't there? When all the squads were finally mustered, each took it in turns to form into marching order. It was a shambles. None of the units present were up to the task, substituting semi-organised jostling for parade ground discipline. The Brownies, in particular, disgraced themselves. giggling like fools and getting completely out-of-step as they danced around the fairy toadstool. We were the last to go. By now, the Town Hall square was packed. My squad lined up in front of the municipal railings and I marched out and took up a prominent position in the square. I did a razor-sharp about-turn to face my squad and snapped noisily to attention. Out of the corner of my eye I saw my mother snapping away with her Brownie 127, recording this proud moment in our family history. A hush fell on the assembled company. I became conscious of the rustling of the trees. A baby cried briefly before being stifled. I waited for total silence. When I got it, I shattered it.

'RIGHT, MARKER!' I bellowed.

There is no mystery here – the marker is the tallest member of the squad and he stands on the right. On the order, he comes to attention and marches toward the officer on parade, stopping in front of him and coming to attention. He now becomes the foundation stone on which the squad is built and the pivot for their exertions. Unfortunately the tallest man in the squad isn't always the brightest. Lofty, bless his heart, six-foot three at the age of fourteen, meant well. He marched across the Town Hall square toward me. But something was wrong. Was he limping? Was he having some sort of sexual crisis? He minced across the open square. The crowd began to snigger. He knew something was wrong but he didn't know what it was. His face flushed and his eyes darted back and forth as if seeking some escape hatch. Then I sussed it. He was swinging his right arm with his right leg and his left arm with his left leg. Lofty sussed it about the same time I did but he couldn't correct it. He gave a couple of skips but he still came out the wrong way. The crowd were now hysterical, although I did detect a growing swell of sympathetic murmurs. The last few paces must have been hell for him and his bottom lip was quivering uncontrollably when he mercifully reached me.

'Sorry, corporal,' he said, avoiding eye-contact.

'That's all right, Lofty,' I should have said. 'It's only a parade. In years to come we'll look back on all this with an equanimity born of distance and laugh at the imbecilities of adolescence.' That's what I should have said, but I didn't.

'You long streak of piss,' I growled. 'When this is over I'm going hunt down all your relatives and kill them – slowly. And then, and only then, it'll be your turn.'

Lofty began to whimper.

'SQUADRON – ON PARADE,' I shouted.

The squad marched toward me, their footfalls echoing in the still, morning air. Then the bloody farting started. Even the regimental goat looked around. I looked at Alwyn. He seemed to be straining every sinew of his body in a futile attempt to control his capricious fundament. The crowd fell apart and amid sustained and cruel laughter I got the squad into marching order. The band started up and marched off. In prearranged order we followed. Mercifully, the sound of the band covered up the farting – what is one tuba amongst many? – and we got round the parade route without further mishap although the squad, skittish and spooked by the disastrous start, had to be severely bullied in order to maintain their lines. The end of the parade was a relief. I issued threats of future punishment to everybody in the vicinity and stomped off home.

My mother and father were waiting for me. To be fair to them, they didn't laugh openly in my face, preferring to lurk together in the kitchen, sniggering. The final humiliation came with the development of my mother's photographs. The squad looked fine, ramrod-straight and marching as one, but I seemed to have adopted a simian lope, as if I was a gorilla seconded from the Rwanda squadron of the ATC. This was a legacy of my Douglas Bader rolling gait. I'd tried to get rid of it, but I'd obviously over-compensated.

One day the commanding officer called all the non-coms into his office. He stood with his back to us, puffing reflectively on his pipe, looking out of the window at the summer twilight

'I'm sending you all on an NCO training course at St Athan,' he said, turning around and banging his pipe on the corner of his desk. 'You'll be gone for three days and you'll leave on Friday.'

St Athan was an RAF base near Cardiff. 'Lovely,' we thought, 'a nice weekend break.'

The first thing we were required to do upon arrival at St Athan was a five-mile, cross-country jog, followed by an hour of intense drill under the instruction of an RAF drill sergeant, a psychopath of diminished stature, who had a deep and abiding hatred of all things human. He lined us up in three ranks and we stood to attention while he gave us the once-over. I was in the front rank. He strolled along, stopping occasionally to make deeply hurtful remarks about someone's physical shortcomings. As he approached I held my breath and tried very hard to become invisible. He passed by me without comment and I breathed again. Then I heard

the welcome death of a fascist 13

him coming up the second rank. I heard his footsteps stop behind me. I held my breath again. Then I heard his voice, seemingly in my ear.

'And where are you from, laddie?' he said gently.

I went hot and cold. I was about to answer when another voice behind me spoke up.

'Trimsaran, sergeant.'

Oh, glory of glories, he wasn't talking to me.

'Trimsaran?' said the drill sergeant. 'Nice place, is it?'

'Yes, sergeant,' said the cadet, perking up.

'And do you want to see Trimsaran again, alive?' said the sergeant slowly.

'Yes, sergeant,' said the cadet, now unsure.

'THEN YOU'D BETTER SMARTEN YOURSELF UP BEFORE I SEE YOU AGAIN OR YOU'LL SPEND THE REST OF THE WEEKEND POLISHING THE CANTEEN FLOOR WITH A TOOTHBRUSH. IS THAT CLEAR? DO YOU HEAR ME?'

It would have been difficult not to hear him, even if you were standing at the South Pole. It was the loudest voice I'd ever heard.

When he'd finished inspection he stood in front of us, shaking his head.

'I've seen some rubbish in my time,' he said, 'but you lot take the biscuit. I must have been a sinner in a previous life and you must be God's punishment. You are a shambles. A complete and utter shambles. But by the end of this weekend you will not be a shambles. You will be Airmen. Do I make myself clear?'

'Yes, sergeant,' we chorused.

'Right!' he said, snapping to attention. 'Let's see what you're made of.'

He drilled us into the ground. Marching at full pace, we covered every inch of an extremely large parade ground for half-an-hour without pause while he kept up a constant stream of satirical abuse. When he finally called a halt we were breathing hard and dripping with sweat.

'Stand at ease,' he said. 'Five minutes break. Stand easy.'

Five minutes break? You mean the nightmare isn't over? We milled around, trying to get our breath back. Some required nicotine. One of the braver souls walked over to the drill sergeant who stood apart, with his back to us. staring into the far distance.

'Please, sergeant,' said the cadet, 'can we smoke?'

'You can burst into flames for all I care, laddie,' said the drill sergeant, without turning around.

Five minutes later, we were hurtling around the parade ground again. When we were finally dismissed my lungs were on fire, I had a stitch, and my feet were bleeding. Well, they weren't actually bleeding but they were very red. I was in bed by seven and asleep by five-past. I dreamt I was marching across a vast, featureless desert, knowing I had an extremely urgent task to perform but, for the life of me, unable to remember what it was? I was woken at six in the morning by somebody playing the trumpet.

maybe i should've stayed in bed?

'You talk in your sleep,' said the cadet in the next bed.

'What did I say?' I asked.

'You said "Left-right-left-right" all night. Corporal Becket from the Ammanford squadron put a pillow over your face for a bit but it didn't stop you. He wanted to kill you but we stopped him. He didn't sleep all night.'

'The poor lamb,' I said.

I remembered Corporal Becket from yesterday's drill. It was hard not to. Well over six-foot tall and pencil-thin, he had a massive, bulbous nose and no chin to speak of. Like all tall people he had co-ordination problems. When marching he could eat up the ground but any order demanding a change of direction resulted in a hideous tangle of limbs. He was surly of demeanour and appeared to lack most of the social graces. And he obviously didn't know it was against military regulations to murder someone of equal rank.

I lay on my bunk and tried to think of an excuse to get out of the day's upcoming exertions. This wasn't what I'd expected at all. It was supposed to be an NCO training course. I'd expected lessons in giving orders. I thought they'd teach us how to shout properly. I'd expected to be inculcated in the black arts of military sarcasm. I was a corporal, for god's sake. Surely marching was for the lower orders.

We had a communal wash in ice cold water, collected our 'mug and irons' and headed for the canteen. Corporal Becket made a point of standing next to me in the food queue.

'Oi, wuss,' he said, 'if you start chopsing in your sleep tonight I'm going to piss in your fucking mouth.'

I looked up, but all I could see were a huge pair of nostrils. I leant to one side and, looking around the side of his nose, caught his eye.

'How does fuck off sound?' I enquired politely.

Social equilibrium now established, we queued in silence and took our food to opposite ends of the canteen to eat. Every time I caught his eye, he glared back. Apart from blowing him the occasional kiss, I ignored him.

After breakfast we reluctantly formed up outside the barracks, dreading another day of square-bashing but to our utter relief we were marched down to the rifle range.

'Today you will be taught how to shoot a rifle,' said the drill sergeant, as we marched along, 'although in my opinion they'd be better off giving guns to a bunch of chimpanzees. Try not to shoot each other.'

Shoot each other, Sarge? The thought never crossed our minds. But accidents will happen. Wouldn't it be terrible if somebody shot Corporal Becket by mistake?

This was more like it. Weapons training. The sharp end. Not before time we were going to be taught how to shoot the enemies of the Queen of England. I was far too blinkered to see the colossal irony involved. We marched down to the range with a spring in our step. An RAF squad marched toward us on the opposite side of the road. We stiffened into precision, wanting to show them that a cadet squad was easily the equal of the real thing. As they passed us they sniggered and some

the welcome death of a fascist

made uncalled-for remarks. Our sergeant did a sharp about-turn and marched alongside them. As we marched away we could hear him bellowing at them.

'YOU OVERGROWN SPERM,' he screamed, 'SWING YOUR ARMS OR I'LL TEAR 'EM OFF AND BEAT YOU TO DEATH WITH THE SOGGY ENDS.'

This is what I aspired to. To be able to control people by shouting at them. It was so obvious. So elemental. Government of the loudest voice, by the loudest voice, for the loudest voice.

The rifle range was a large field. At one end was a raised, tarpaulin-covered, firing platform and at the other an artificial sand-dune, in front of which were five targets on poles. It was here I caught a fleeting glimpse of transitory glory.

The drill-sergeant, having delivered us, went for a cup of tea.

'When I come back,' he said, 'it'd be nice if some of you were still alive.'

We were given concise but thorough instruction on the mechanics of the Lee Enfield .303 rifle – loading and firing of. In groups of five we were ordered to lie down on the firing platform and fire at individual targets. They were an awful long way off in the distance and with my dodgy eyesight I could barely see them, let alone be able to tell whether I'd hit one. I was in the first batch. I lay down, loaded the rifle, and sighted my target. I'd never fired a proper rifle before. I was looking forward to it.

'Fire at will,' barked the gunnery sergeant.

We each fired our first shot. The volley was ear-shattering. I jumped with surprise and my glasses fell off. I began to hear a high-pitched whistle.

'Good shot!' said the gunnery sergeant, looking through binoculars.

He couldn't have been talking about me. Even though I couldn't see the target, I knew I'd missed. I'd seen my bullet kick up a good two-foot high in the sand beyond. I adjusted my aim lower and fired again. This time the sand kicked up directly behind the target. That's better, I thought.

'Ah, it was just a fluke,' said the gunnery sergeant

Again he couldn't have been talking about me. I continued firing low and the sand kicked up satisfyingly behind the target. After the sixth shot we all got up and the next lot lay down. As I passed the gunnery sergeant, he stopped me.

'I thought for a minute you were a hot-shot,' he said. 'Your first shot hit the bull but the rest were too low.'

'But it hit the sand behind about two-foot high,' I said.

'No, it didn't,' he said. 'It just looked as if it did from your prone position.'

I explained my optical problems. My first shot had been properly aimed but, I'd assumed from the final impact point of the bullet, too high. From then on I was compensating.

'Were you now?' he said. 'Well, have another go at the end. We're always on the look out for marksman for the ATC Rifle Team.'

'OK,' I said.

The ATC Rifle Team? In my mind's eye I saw the Earps and Doc Holliday walking four-abreast through the deserted streets of Tombstone on their way down to the OK Corral.

'Leave Ringo to me, Wyatt,' said Holliday.

'And leave the McLowerys to me,' I said quietly.

A faint smile played on the deadly dentist's lips. It was a smile that said, 'You are now one of us. A brother in everything but blood. An equal in whose charge I would place my life. Welcome to the ATC Rifle Team.'

Then my stomach churned. What if I missed? What if that first shot had just been beginner's luck? I began to think of excuses. Then I ran out of time.

'Corporal Leonard,' shouted the gunnery sergeant. 'Corporal Leonard to the firing platform.'

I trudged up to the firing platform. The gunnery sergeant, smiling, handed me a .303, and patted me on the back. I lay down and sighted my target, conscious of the presence of every non-com in the Welsh ATC. The potential for humiliation was boundless.

'Fire at will,' said the gunnery sergeant quietly.

I fired six shots. There were non-committal murmurings. Apart from my fellow Llanelly non-coms everybody else, coming from rival squadrons, was willing me to fail. When I'd finished there was silence. I put the rifle down and got up. The gunnery sergeant lowered his binoculars.

'Five bulls and one inner,' he said.

I remembered that inner shot well. I was distracted. My nose was itching.

'Well done!' said the gunnery sergeant. 'Bloody well done!'

I acknowledged the grudging applause but noticed that Corporal Becket didn't join in, preferring to examine his cap-badge, as if seeing it for the first time, I tried to behave with modesty and decorum but I felt like Matt Braddock, VC and bar. My fellow Llanelly non-coms gathered around me, slapping me on the back.

'It was easy,' I said. 'I just imagined I was shooting at Corporal Becket.'

The gunnery sergeant took down my details and said he would get in touch with my CO to set the wheels in motion for my induction to the ATC Rifle Team. I swaggered off the range. I felt invincible. Which was just as well because the next thing on the agenda was two hours of unbelievably brisk square-bashing.

'Come on, Annie Oakley,' said the drill sergeant. 'Just because you can shoot a rifle doesn't mean you're not a chimpanzee.'

Bed by seven, asleep by five-past. Another marching dream, this time carrying a fifty-pound pack. Halfway through the long march I experienced difficulty in breathing but I assumed it was Corporal Becket, back in the real world, trying to smother me again.

Once again I was woken at six-thirty by that bloody trumpet. It really was a most inconsiderate time to practice. To paraphrase Oscar Wilde: a civilised man is one who *can* play the trumpet but chooses not to do so. Oscar had the accordion in mind, but I think the trumpet works just as well.

On the last day, as a treat, they took everybody up in a Handley Page Hastings, a huge transport aircraft. Everybody except me. There were seventy-five seats in the Hastings and seventy-six cadets. Because I was the last to board – last minute bladder problems – I was the unlucky one. As the Hastings taxied on to the

the welcome death of a fascist

runway I saw Corporal Becket making grotesque faces at me through a cabin window. At least I think he was making faces. It was hard to tell.

I allowed myself a little reverie. The Hastings would develop engine trouble over the Bristol Channel and, despite the valiant efforts of the pilot to return to base, it would ditch in the drink. After a few days everybody would be saved by Air Sea Rescue, except for Corporal Becket, who would be reported missing, presumed drowned. But he would still be alive. During the second night, in the throes of ungovernable panic, he would swim off into the darkness. At first light, he would find himself floating on an empty sea. Lacking moral fibre, he would start to whimper. Then he would spot a fin circling him, getting ever closer (a shark in the Bristol Channel, I hear you ask? It's feasible. It could be a navigationally-challenged Great White who, having taken a wrong turning at the Great Barrier Reef, was now cruising up the Bristol Channel, feeling a little peckish). Corporal Becket's screams of despair would evaporate in the indifferent dawn. Suddenly, he would see the fin turn sharply and come scything through the water toward him. On the first pass the shark would take away Corporal Becket's legs and lower torso, leaving him in unimaginable agony but still conscious. I broke off here and, leaving Corporal Becket bobbing about in the sea, opened the packed lunch, kindly provided for me by the catering corps. Munching on a chopped ham sandwich, I returned to the Bristol Channel. There wasn't much left of Corporal Becket by the time I got back – just a bulbous nose floating in the water. Two weeks later, the nose, now officially designated a danger to shipping, would be towed into Milford Haven by the Coastguard.

I spent the afternoon sunbathing on the airfield, thinking of different ways to kill Corporal Becket. I should have shot him when I had the chance. Then I heard the distant hum of the returning Hastings. He was still alive. Won't somebody rid me of this turbulent corporal?

Everybody was elated as they came down the aircraft steps, with the blush of adventure still on their cheeks. My eye couldn't help but be drawn to Corporal Becket. He looked so unbearably happy I almost vomited. We were driven back to our barracks to pack our kit, ready for departure. Corporal Becket and I said our goodbyes.

'If I ever see you in civvy street,' he said, 'I'll beat your fucking brains out.'

'I'd offer to do the same,' I said, 'but I doubt whether you've got any brains to beat out.'

'Piss off!' he said.

'Piss off, yourself,' I said.

Well. what's the point of these weekends if it's not to make friends with people of different, and it appears alien, cultures?

The drill sergeant hadn't said goodbye as such. After our final drill he'd just walked off, shaking his head,

I arrived back in Llanelly in buoyant mood. I was going to travel the world shooting at bits of cardboard. A noble calling, I thought.

But it all changed at the annual ATC Christmas Dance. An out-of-town skiffle

maybe i should've stayed in bed?

group had been booked for the occasion. I wasn't looking forward to it. ATC Christmas Dances were a painful experience. The girls stood on one side of the hall and the boys on the other. It took immense courage to walk across the empty dance floor and ask a girl to dance. Every eye in the place followed you, wondering who your target would be, and the girls, as you approached them, backed away, writhing with embarrassment. When it became clear who your intended was, her friends formed a protective cordon around her and she, giggling hysterically but safe behind the oestrogen barricade, would shout 'No!'. Then you'd have to make the long trek back across the empty dance floor to the safety of your own gender, who were split fifty-fifty in their reaction; some were sympathetic, others were consumed by barely-suppressed glee. But it could have been worse. She could have said yes. Then you'd have to dance on an empty dance floor in front of your peer group. It wasn't worth the emotional turmoil. Either way you lost. So we stayed put, thank you very much.

While I and my fellow crypto-fascists stood around in edgy, little groups, the skiffle group came on and tore the place apart. The only song I remember them playing was 'I Traced Her Little Footsteps In The Snow'. They obviously held us military types in some contempt and made lots of jokes about us; the ones about our wispy, handlebar moustaches were particularly hurtful. The girls, who up till now had been self-conscious virgins, suddenly turned into predatory amazons and rushed to the front of the stage, from where they pointed at various members of the band and whispered to each other. The band leered back at them and made suggestive gestures.

My first reaction was outrage. How dare these out-of-towners come down here and proposition our women. But it soon faded because I found myself fascinated by the mechanics of guitar playing. I watched the guitarist all night, trying to equate what was he was doing with the sound that was coming out. After they finished playing I talked to him and he showed me a few licks.

The following day I issued instructions to all my relations that I was to be given money instead of socks for Christmas. With any luck I'd have enough money to buy a guitar. I ended up with twelve quid.

The first day the shops were open I went to the Falcon Music Shop. I had no idea what I was looking for. There were two guitars in the window amid the trumpets and trombones. One was a solid-body electric guitar that seemed to be made of silver lurex and the other was a Boosey & Hawkes F-hole acoustic guitar with a sunburst finish. The electric guitar was £18 and the acoustic was £14. £18 was a fortune but £14 wasn't far away so I went home and asked my mother to lend me two quid. After a prolonged and occasionally savage discussion she grudgingly agreed.

'I'm not going to regret this, am I?' she said.

'Don't be silly, Mam,' I said. 'You can trust me. You have brought me up to realise the value of honesty and responsibility. More than that, you have succeeded in producing a well-rounded citizen, dripping with integrity. I think you can congratulate yourself on a job well done.'

the welcome death of a fascist

'I'm making a terrible mistake,' she said. 'Give me my two pounds back,'

I assumed this was matriarchal humour and rushed back down to the Falcon Music Shop. I bought the acoustic, which was just as well because I didn't realise you needed an amplifier with the electric guitar so I'd have just plugged it straight into the wall-socket and the world of the performing arts would have been robbed of the career of Deke Leonard – or spared, depending on your point of view.

I took the guitar home and we locked horns in my bedroom. I tried to remember the licks the skiffle group's guitarist had shown me but they sounded awful. After a week I was convinced there was something wrong with the guitar. I toyed with the idea of guitar lessons but not for long; the last thing I needed in my life was another bloody teacher. But I obviously needed help, so I bought 'Elementary Guitar Chords' by Mel Bay and set about it with some gusto. I still sounded awful but I kept going and soon I sounded semi-awful. I needed some sort of path to follow. I needed greater access to music. I needed a record-player. I asked my Mum and Dad to buy me a Dansette. They said no. I was expecting this. So, using tactics developed by Richard Coeur de Lion at the siege of Acre during the Third Crusade, I embarked on a campaign of unrelenting attrition. It took a while, believe me, but eventually they reached breaking point and, just to shut me up, they succumbed.

The first record I bought was 'A Date With Elvis'. With great expectations I put it on. By the time it had finished I was a different person. It was a sublime moment that has stayed with me to this day. Suddenly I understood why John Phelps had dragged me in off the street to listen to 'Blue Suede Shoes'. I felt the fascism drain from my body. I resolved, there and then, to resign from the ATC and grow sideburns – two of them. Of course, it meant the end of my aspirations to become a sharpshooter but, given my faulty eyesight, it would only have been a matter of time before I shot somebody, probably myself.

Why is it only in retrospect that we see those moments when life changes course. That sublime moment, always accompanied by the whiff of burning boats, when fate gently tips you off your bearings. The new experience is pleasant. It desires repetition. With repetition comes ability. With ability comes confidence. Confidence leads to action. Action results in change. It is most inconvenient. But inconvenience matters little to the young. Nothing matters to the young. Back in school I told Mike about my change of heart.

'I've bought a guitar,' I said. 'I'm going to be a rock'n'roll star.'

'Thank goodness,' he said, 'I thought you were never going to grow up.'

'Why don't you buy a guitar too,' I said.

'OK,' he said. And he did.

I spent the next two years practising in my bedroom, I bought every Elvis record I could lay my hands on and tried to learn every note Scotty Moore played. Scotty Moore, Elvis's guitarist, was the man who invented rock'n'roll guitar. All Presley's early records are illuminated by huge wedges of abstract guitar that never quite go where you think they're going to. Mike had been practising too. His timing wasn't all it could have been but when we'd play a song we'd start and finish together so it wasn't all bad. We took it for granted that this was the start of a rock'n'roll band. We'd need a drummer. We didn't know of one, but we assumed one would come along in due course. And a bass-player. But that wasn't so important. Bass-players were optional extras.

We did have one major bone of contention. I thought Elvis was the greatest rock'n'roll singer and Mike thought Gene Vincent was. This could have been because he was a dead-ringer for Gene. I, on the other hand, didn't look anything like Elvis, although, in suspect lighting conditions, I looked a little like Eddie Cochran; not much, but enough to keep me warm in the cold, dark watches of the night.

3
5x

We sat our GCEs. Mike sailed through with eight passes but I only got three: Art, English and Geography. Art can't be taught. It is a matter of genetic chance. You can either draw or you can't. I can, so I walked it – 85%. English was a close call. You'd have thought I'd be good at it, given that I spoke the damn language every day, but no. The rigid inconsistencies of grammar, which now seem to govern my every waking moment, were far too esoteric for my literal mind, and I couldn't see the point of precis at all until I started writing for a living. I just made it – 56%

Geography was even closer and I couldn't have passed without the help of Anthony Quinn. I had to answer five questions out of eight on offer. I could manage four but a fifth was beyond me. One of the remaining questions was about Canada so I decided to have a go at it because a week earlier I had seen the film 'The Savage Innocents', in which Anthony Quinn played an Eskimo. Eskimo? Canada? The link was tenuous but workable so I wrote a harrowing little piece, a straight synopsis of the film, about the threat posed to the Eskimo way of life by the encroaching barbarism of civilisation, and I scraped through – 51%.

Naturally I failed music. I was doomed to 5X.

5X was the class for fifth-formers too dumb to move on to the sixth-form, the minimum qualification being six O Levels. We were the dimwits of the school. We redressed the balance by being highly aggressive and wearing our badge of stupidity with pride. We weren't just the stupidest people in the school – we were the stupidest people in the world! We used more Brylcreem than the rest of the school put together and our classes were like out-takes from 'Blackboard Jungle'. There was no attempt to teach us, the governing body having apparently settled for a policy of containment.

The school itself was in a state of upheaval because it had been split in two. The original school, on top of Bigyn Hill, was falling apart so a new school was built at an out-of-town site in Pwll. As the new school expanded, more and more pupils were transferred from the old. While I was in 5X the transfer was completed and an official opening ceremony was planned. The Duke of Edinburgh was booked for the occasion. He was scheduled to arrive by helicopter at three in the afternoon. The whole school – eight-hundred boys – were turned out to meet him. We were to stand in orderly lines either side of a long, red carpet which stretched from the main entrance of the school to a makeshift helicopter pad on the front lawn – perish the thought that the Greek parasite should soil his royal feet by walking on common grass. The operation started two hours before he was due to

maybe i should've stayed in bed? 22

arrive. Class by class we were shepherded into our places by a team of teachers. As you would expect, it was chaos. When the dust finally settled we, 5X, were surprised to find ourselves in the front line, right next to the helicopter pad. The first thing the Duke would see upon arrival would be us.

The headmaster reviewed the assembled company, checking for last minute blips. Then he spotted us. The colour drained from his face. He called a teacher over and a heated discussion took place.

'We can't have this lot standing there,' he said, sweeping a derisive arm in our general direction. 'The Duke'll take one look at them and get straight back on the helicopter. Move them.'

The teacher herded us back toward the school while we made sheep noises. The rest of the school shuffled up to fill our place.

'I'm going to put you in the staff-room until I can find a new place for you,' said the teacher.

The staff-room? Why the staff-room? It was on the other side of the school and there were more convenient places in which to put us. But ours not to reason why... We had long-since given up trying to find any logic in the thought processes of the teaching profession.

The staff-room was huge. There were nigh-on forty teachers at the school and they all had to have somewhere secluded to pick their noses and read Tit-Bits. We passed the time until the Duke's arrival by opening every drawer and cupboard in the place and trying to break into the staff lockers, looking for some little piece of evidence of character defect in those set above us. To be used for the purposes of... blackmail's too strong a word... influence, perhaps... edge, certainly. After half-an-hour we began to get suspicious. We tried the door. It was locked.

'That's why they put us in the staff-room,' said Douglas Alistair Campbell McKay, our token Scot. 'It's the only lockable room in the school.'

We heard the helicopter land. We heard cheering. We heard a voice, presumably the Duke's, giving a little speech on the school's tinny tannoy system. 5X turned nasty. We ransacked the room, searching for crowbar-like instruments with which to prise the door open. Then we hit pay dirt.

'Look at this,' said Michael Creel, the school's star footballer. 'I think I've found the button that controls the school bell.'

There were electric bells dotted around the school. He gave the button a tentative push. A loud clang reverberated through the empty corridors.

'It works,' said Creel joyfully. He jabbed his thumb down on the button and kept it there. The Duke's speech was drowned out, no doubt depriving the school of some priceless right-wing drivel. We all took it in turns to press the button. Some refused to give way to the next man and had to be forcibly removed from the vicinity. Almost immediately, a master started banging on the staff-room door, shouting for us to stop and threatening us with eternal detention. But he wouldn't come in. Not even a teacher is that dumb. We stopped ringing the bell when we heard the Duke's helicopter taking off. Pupils started filing back into the school and we heard the murmur of adult voices just outside the door. A key turned in the lock and the door swung open. A semi-circle of teachers stood, canes in hand, waiting for us to emerge. We strolled out, hands-in-pockets, smiling serenely.

We were sentenced to a week's detention. An hour every day. It was the first time in the school's history that a whole class had been sentenced to detention. The headmaster noted this landmark in a speech delivered to the school assembly the next morning. It was meant to shame us but we loved every minute of it. Well, records, we were constantly told by the headmaster himself, were made to be broken.

One of the teachers waiting for us outside the staff-room was our gym teacher, a mean-spirited bully called Tommy Dap. Dap is Welsh colloquialism for gym-shoe. He got his nickname because his favourite instrument of torture was a gym-shoe on a long piece of string, and his idea of a good time was to stand in the middle of the gym swinging the gym-shoe round and round on an ever-increasing length of string while the boys cowered in the corners. Of course he only did this with the younger boys. He didn't dare do it to the older boys, for fear of having the gym-shoe stuffed down his throat. He was a heavy-set, slovenly man, always dressed in a crumpled track-suit with a permanent meg-end hanging out of the corner of his mouth. In a typical lesson he would line us up, shout 'Running on the spot – go!' and retire to his cubby-hole to read the Daily Mail. 'Running on the spot – go!' became a school catch-phrase, uttered whenever anybody appeared to warrant punishment. And Tommy Dap became the most mimicked teacher in the school.

His favourite game was British Bulldog. For the benefit of my feminine readership I will explain the game because it is played exclusively in boys' schools. You have netball, we have British Bulldog.

British Bulldog is organised ferocity. All the class line up at one end of the gym, except for one boy, selected by Tommy Dap, who has to stand in the middle. On the shout 'British Bulldog!' the entire class charge down to the other end of the gym. The objective for the solitary boy is to bring down one of the on-rushing horde of teenage hooligans and hold him down until the tide passes. The objective for the on-rushing horde of teenage hooligans is to wipe the solitary boy, and his shadow, off the face of the earth. But with a little application the solitary boy can bring someone to ground. Then there are two. On the shout 'British Bulldog!' the class charge back down the gym. Then the two boys may become three, or even four. The carnage continues until halfway through the game, when the balance tips and instead of the many charging the few, it becomes the few charging the many. Ideally it ends with a solitary boy charging a salivating horde of teenage hooligans. I rather enjoyed it.

Another of Tommy Dap's favourite lessons was boxing, because it enabled him, on the pretence of teaching the noble art of self-defence, to beat up children of all shapes and sizes. But one of 5X refused to fight him. Phil Charles was an old friend. He had been one of my fellow non-coms in the ATC. He was a much-liked, genial lad who happened to be ATC Boxing Champion, middle-weight division. Tommy Dap knew this and was always trying to goad him into a fight. Phil always politely declined but Tommy Dap wouldn't let go. He kept on chipping away and one day Phil snapped.

'OK,' he said, 'Let's get the gloves on.'

We settled back, rubbing our hands with glee. It's not every day you get the chance to see a despised teacher beaten to a pulp. We were confidently predicting a Phil Charles victory and we weren't disappointed. Phil beat the fuck out of him. Punch after punch thudded into Tommy Dap's head and body and he reeled around the gym, gulping for air. To be fair to him, he did attempt a few roundhouse swings, which Phil effortlessly avoided, before dropping to his knees and raising a glove.

'That's enough for today,' he gasped. He shut himself away in his cubby-hole and we didn't see him for the rest of the lesson. We gathered around Phil and took it in turns to shake his hand. But if we thought that this was happiness, we didn't know the half. We would soon be ecstatic. The gods were about to present us with a priceless gift.

Tommy Dap was caught wanking in the boot room by two juniors. The news spread through the school like bushfire. The following morning at assembly the whole school, buzzing with expectancy, waited for the teaching staff to arrive. As was customary, they walked in through a door at the back of the hall in single file, in order of seniority, with the headmaster in the lead. In silence, they trooped down the central aisle to the stage. Tommy Dap was way down the line and his appearance was greeted by the sound of eight hundred sniggers. When he was about halfway down the aisle, Tony Charles, one of the more urbane members of my peer group, piped up.

'Wanking on the spot – go! One-two-three, change hands. One-two-three, change hands...'

The whole assembly burst out laughing, except for the teachers, who looked mystified. Tommy Dap's face reddened and he lowered his head. We had him. He was never the same again.

Tommy Dap may have been the most detested teacher in the school but it was a close-run thing. He wasn't short of rivals. Rolf, the senior chemistry master, was an elderly dunghill of a man, who seemed vaguely irritated by everything in life. I never heard him utter a civil word to either boy or fellow teacher, and all he required from his class was total submission. His moment of truth arrived on a blustery summer day, The windows of his classroom were open and a gentle breeze ruffled the exercise books on our desks. He was droning on about the physical properties of manganese (Mn), while we perfected the art of dozing off with our eyes open. Suddenly the wind caught the blackboard behind him, tipping it forward out of its wall bracket. It crashed onto Rolf's head with a sickening thwack. His knees buckled and he fell forward onto his bench, scattering retorts and bunsen burners in all directions. He slumped to the floor. We sat in stunned silence. Then, suppressing our giggles, we went to pick him up. He was unconscious and the back of his bald head was covered with blood.

'Maybe he's dead?' said Gimlet.

'No such luck,' said Vic Bowles.

Somebody strolled off to report the incident to the headmaster. Rolf, unfortunately, wasn't dead but he did have a few days off sick. When he came back, a delightful scab had formed on the back of his bald head, in the shape of a life-size butterfly. We tried to persuade some of the younger boys that it was a real butterfly, worthy of inclusion in their collections, fervently hoping that one of them would creep up behind Rolf and jam a butterfly net over his head, but none of them rose to the bait.

Then there was Froggy, so-called because he looked like a frog. His principal subject was Welsh but he also took us in cricket and managed to instil in me a hatred for the game that took years to overcome. He was a good batsman and insisted on opening the batting for whichever team batted first. He would occupy the crease for the whole lesson while we ran around like headless chickens retrieving the ball from the remotest corners of the playing field. Not even my devious leg-spin could remove him. In the whole three years he taught us, not once can I remember him being out. Close LBW appeals were refused with a sad shake of the head by the umpire, who was, invariably, Froggy himself.

Into each life, we are told, a little rain must fall. If that's true then Froggy was swept away by a monsoon. His son was a pupil at the school and, like all teachers sons, he was despised. A leper would have been more welcome in our social circle. We dropped our voices in his presence because we assumed the little stoolie would run straight back to Dad and spill the beans. Had we been in Stalag Luft 99 we would, one night, have dressed him in someone else's clothes and thrown him into the nearest searchlight beam. On the boy's seventeenth birthday, Dad bought him a car. He duly passed his test and was soon on the road. A couple of months later he had a crash. It didn't seem like a serious one; he merely demolished a traffic light outside Stanley Pearce, the grocers. When he got out of the car he appeared to be fine but, unnoticed in the gathering crowd, he wandered off. The following morning the headmaster told us he was missing and asked everybody to keep an eye out for him. We were given the day off to search for him. We went down the beach because it was a sunny day. We searched for a good ten seconds and spent the rest of the day swimming and sunbathing. We cared little and, with the callousness of the young, made ever-more tasteless jokes. Naturally I was among the worst offenders.

Three days later he was found floating in the Lliedi River. The Lliedi is hardly the Nile and, where he was found, the river is a foot-deep in full flood. The headmaster announced his death at the next assembly. Still, we didn't care. 'Good riddance to bad rubbish', we probably said.

It was only years later I began to feel the odd pang of guilt. In an attempt to exorcise my remorse I wrote a song about it called 'A Hard Way To Die'. It didn't work, but it was the best I could do.

Incidentally, Stanley Pearce's son was called Warren. His nickname was Tolstoy.

I may have given the impression that the teaching staff of Llanelly Boys' Grammar School were a bunch of social misfits with severe behavioural difficulties, and while that might be something of an exaggeration, the evidence was impossible to ignore. But even if they were flecks of excrement on the anus of the world, they were nothing compared to the viper that lurked within our own bosom. Among the pupils was a pestilence that would one day walk the land. A right-wing zealot intent on destroying constitutional freedoms our forefathers had fought and died for. As Yeats might have said: 'And what rough beast, its hour come round at last, slouches toward Llanelly to be born?' I was in school with Michael Howard.

Howard went on to become the most hated man in Britain. His tenure as Home Secretary, in fact his whole political career, was an unqualified disaster, causing incalculable damage to the fabric of this country. A slippery creature, unencumbered by principle and crippled by incompetence, he vandalised everything he touched, shamelessly playing to the dimwit gallery and avoiding responsibility at every turn. He was four years ahead of me at school so we had no contact, but I can remember a vague feeling of unease whenever he walked past. If I'd known then what I know now, I'd have killed him. If I'd done it then, it would have been just another schoolboy murder, but if I'd killed him in, say, 1996, it would have been justifiable homicide and I would have been made a Hero of Socialism. He isn't worth killing anymore. He's finished. One of the undead. This country should celebrate his passing with champagne and bunting.

Of course, he's not as bad as Thatcher. Who is?

We were all entered for the November handicap, a second chance to sit the O Levels we had failed the first time around. This time I got one pass. Maths – 51%. This, I was told, was excellent news because I could now get a job as a trainee metallurgist at Trostre, the huge steelworks just outside the town.

'Hooray,' I said.

We all went to see the careers officer.

'I want to be a rock'n'roll star,' I said.

'I don't think we have any vacancies for pop singers at the moment,' he said frostily. 'Have you got anything more realistic in mind?'

'How about archaeology?' I said. I'd always fancied myself as a bit of a Howard Carter, discovering, to international acclaim, the long-lost tomb of Rameses 94th. 'Got anything in that line?'

He sighed deeply and rummaged through his papers

'I can offer you a job as a trainee metallurgist in Trostre,' he said.

'But that's what you offer everybody,' I said. 'I sometimes think that Llanelly Boys' Grammar School only exists to provide staff for Trostre. I want to do something different. Something rewarding. There's more to life than metallurgy.'

'Well,' he said, as if he hadn't heard a word I'd said, 'it's a secure job with good prospects. I'd think about it, if I were you.'

4
a gathering of eagles

Back in the real world our hormones were singing the Hallelujah Chorus. Mike and I stalked Llanelly, looking for action. There wasn't much going on during the week so we went to the pictures. There were five cinemas in Llanelly so we were spoilt for choice. But on the weekend we went drinking and dancing. There were loads of pubs that weren't too fussy about underage drinking, and after an illegal skinful we went dancing. There were plenty of places to go and we got thrown out of most of them, usually for unruly behaviour, which covered everything from excessive jostling to puking on the dance floor. Our favourites were the Presbyterian Youth Club, where we danced to records until we were thrown out, or the Ritz Ballroom, where we danced to local bands until forcibly ejected. Mike was a great dancer and, with Bethan Vaughan as his partner, always won the twist competitions. When we were at a loose end, we hung around Rabiotti's Cafe, looking mean,

We bought black leather jackets, winkle-picker shoes, flat caps (worn pulled down menacingly over the eyes), and blue jeans. I prided myself on my six-inch turn-ups; the biggest in Llanelly. We began to fancy ourselves as hardcases. Although we still wrestled each other at every opportunity, we were forced to cut down after a costly mishap. Our favourite place to wrestle was the front room of my house. It was a big room and ideal for fighting. We'd push the furniture back and set to. We had to fight quietly so my mother wouldn't hear. One day Mike threw me through the bay window into the front garden. Amazingly, my mother didn't hear a thing, so we just drew the curtains over the broken window and said nothing. Two days later she discovered it and all hell broke loose. My father went to do some work on the car, as he always did when Mum and I went head to head, and I was told, in no uncertain terms, to grow up. I was also informed that my pocket money would be suspended until the new window was paid for. Robbed of our chosen arena, Mike and I were at a loss. So we turned our attention to innocent passers-by.

We fell in with bad company. We met Flash. He was part of the aristocracy of terror that preyed on teenage Llanelly; hard-nuts who were spoken of in hushed whispers. If you ever saw any of them coming you crossed the street. Flash was a psychopath in embryo who spent most of his waking hours stripping the copper off church roofs. He could tell, just by looking, whether a car was locked or not. If it wasn't, he'd help himself to the contents. This was done at a leisurely pace in the hope that the owner would return so Flash could have, at least, an argument and, at most, a scrap. He was lethal in a fight and he was always arranging showdowns.

'Seven o'clock outside the New Dock Cinema,' he'd say. 'I'm fighting the Morfa boys.'

We would be expected to back him up but we rarely had a chance to do anything. He was so fast and destructive we hardly had time to take our hands out of our pockets before it was all over. He encouraged us to pick fights and when we did, far from joining in, he would stand on the sidelines and shout advice. As a result of his constant goading I did the most appalling things. One of the worst involved Stewart, who was in the same year as me at school. We had a nodding acquaintance.

One Saturday night Flash, Mike and I were walking, mob-handed, down Station Road – the Sunset Strip of Llanelly – when ahead of us we saw Stewart and his mates walking toward us. Seeing us coming they stepped off the pavement to allow us to pass. Suddenly Flash turned to me.

'Go on,' he said. 'Nut him!'

I didn't know who he meant but Stewart was the closest so I stepped into the road and head-butted him. He staggered back, holding his bloody nose.

'What did you do that for, Leonard?' he said. 'There's something wrong with you.'

Laughing and joking we swaggered on. From then on every time I saw Stewart in school he shook his head sadly and gave me a quizzical look which, if I hadn't had the skin and the brains of a rhino, would have stopped me in my tracks. I haven't seen Stewart since school but I would like to apologise unreservedly to him for my mindless, unprovoked thuggery.

But my comeuppance was at hand. At a dance at the Ritz I bumped into one of the Bynea Boys. We looked hard at each other and I went for him. I beat the fuck out of him, or would have if my mates hadn't pulled me off. At the end of the night I waited outside for him. When he came out I confronted him.

'Come on,' I said. 'Let's go over to Peoples' Park and finish it off.'

He didn't want to know, but I insisted and, in front of his mates, he couldn't refuse. We walked over to Peoples' Park, just across the road from the Ritz, climbed over the railings and found a nice, grassy bit between the flower beds. All the way over he kept trying to wriggle out of it, suggesting we shake hands and forget about it.

'Too late,' I said, taking my jacket off.

Then we got down to it. Fighting in total darkness, he beat seven kinds of shit out of me. Each punch was an explosion of light in my head (until then I'd thought that 'seeing stars' was a rhetorical device). At one point he knocked me into a rhododendron bush. I came out fighting but he knocked me straight back in. I should've stayed there. After a couple of minutes I'd had enough and dropped to my knees.

'You're all mouth,' he said, picking me up.

By the time we got back to the Ritz everybody'd gone. We were going in the same direction so we walked home together along the High Street. I looked at my face in a shop window. It was all mashed up. My bottom lip was split, I had a black eye, and one side of my face was so swollen I thought at first that the glass must be distorting it. I moved quickly on to the next window but, terrifyingly, it was the same. I looked down. I was covered in mud and all the buttons had come off my shirt. The Bynea Boy, seeing my distress, was sympathetic.

'Sorry,' he said, 'but you asked for it.'

'That's all right, pal,' I said. 'It's nothing to what's coming next. Now I've got to explain this to my mother.

I knew she'd still be up when I got home because she was wallpapering the front room. She loved wallpapering, especially at night. While Dad slept she worked through the house using the Forth Bridge principle – as soon as it was finished, it was time to start again. The house was subject to perpetual redecoration. There was always a trestle table set up somewhere awkward and I couldn't remember a time when there wasn't a whiff of wallpaper paste in the air. Some mornings Dad would wake up in what appeared to be a strange house. For years he worried that it might be encroaching senility until one night he was woken by a fearful crash. He rushed downstairs, fists clenched, ready for a burglar, only to find my mother, covered in paste and tangled up in a step-ladder, unconscious on the floor of the living room. She soon came round and, dismissing him with an airy wave of the hand, resumed wallpapering. Dad went back to bed in high spirits. He wasn't going ga-ga.

'Good luck,' said the Bynea Boy, as I eased my key into the front door.

I sneaked in and tried to tip-toe upstairs but Mum heard me.

'Is that you, Roger?' she whispered loudly. 'Put the kettle on and I'll have five minutes break.'

I went into the kitchen and put the kettle on. She followed me in, complaining about the difference between the shade of lavender in the wallpaper brochure and the shade of lavender now going up on the wall. When she saw me she stopped dead. Taking advantage of the lull, I told her I'd walked into a door. She didn't believe me. She slapped me hard across the face and I stumbled back, more in shock than in pain. 'If you want to fight anyone,' she hissed, 'fight me.' Now I may be stupid, but I'm not that stupid. I may have considered myself a hardcase but I knew I wouldn't last two seconds against 'The Beast of Frondeg Terrace'. Besides, I'd already been beaten up once today, thank you. But I had to say something. I opened my mouth to speak, but that's as far as I got. She tore me to shreds although, given my dishevelled condition, she didn't have far to go. Then her maternal instincts got the better of her and she calmed down and dressed my wounds.

'You're an intelligent boy,' she said, dabbing my face with Dettol. 'Haven't you got anything better to do than get drunk and go brawling around town?'

'It won't happen again,' I said. 'I promise.'

And it didn't, mainly because Flash, our agent provocateur, got himself thrown in jail for five years, deemed guilty by the law of the land of GBH. That's the last I saw of him. Years later he got a life sentence for murder. He escaped and went on the lam. The national press branded him 'the most dangerous man in Britain' and warned the public that he should not be approached under any circumstances. Too fuckin' right! After two weeks he was recaptured and returned to jail where for all I know he still is.

'Serves you right,' said Mike at school the following Monday.

'Thanks for the sympathy,' I said.

'You don't deserve any,' he said, examining my face with a what-a-twat-you-are expression on his face.

'I've had enough of this,' I said, 'I'm knocking it on the head. I've had my last fight. I thought I was a hard-nut but I turned out to be a cream puff. I'm just going to have to be satisfied with looking hard.'

'Me too,' said Mike, probably thinking that there, but for the grace of God...

Not long after I renounced the Devil and all his works, I was stopped in the school playing fields by a handsome, blonde boy, some three years my junior. Social intercourse with juniors rarely went beyond clipping them 'round the ear as you passed them in the corridor, but this was a junior with form. He was well-known in the school because he was the Welsh Junior Tennis Doubles Champion, as well as being Dyfed Junior Singles Champion for as long as anyone could remember.

'My name's Geoff Griffiths,' he said, 'and I'm a drummer, I hear you play guitar. Fancy coming over to my house for a jam session?'

'Yeah, OK,' I said, resisting the temptation to clip him 'round the ear. 'When?'

'Tonight?'

'Where?'

'The Newmarket House in Gilbert Crescent. My parents keep it.'

'The Noggin?' I said. The Noggin was the nickname for the Newmarket House. It was famous locally because the landlord, presumably Geoff's father, rang a school bell whenever a policeman was spotted in the vicinity, thereby warning the underage drinkers that it was time to slip out the back.

'That's it,' he said. 'About seven o'clock?'

'See you at seven,' I said.

I went to find Mike.

'Rehearsal tonight in the Noggin at seven,' I said. 'I think we've got a drummer.'

'I can't,' he said. 'I've got exams coming up and I've got some revising to do.'

'I've got exams coming up too but you don't see me revising.'

'I know,' he said, 'and that's why I'll pass and you'll fail.'

'There's more to life than passing exams,' I said, grudgingly accepting his point.

'Not at the moment,' he said. 'You go ahead and I'll catch up after the exams,'

That night at seven on the dot I arrived at the Noggin carrying my guitar. Geoff showed me upstairs to a back room where a full drum-kit was set up. It must have been the oldest drum-kit in the world. It had once been champagne-sparkle but now it was a dull beige. It had a twenty-eight inch bass-drum and when Geoff sat behind it you could only just see the top of his head. The kit pre-dated the invention of the hi-hat but it had a lo-hat, which was exactly like a hi-hat but only a foot-high, so you could 'chick' it with your foot but you couldn't hit it with a stick without risking severe intestinal difficulties. We ran through a few songs but, because I didn't have an amp, all you could hear was Geoff. He surprised me. I wasn't expecting much but he was a proper drummer with an immaculate snare-drum technique which came to the fore on numbers like 'His Latest Flame', which he played with brushes.

'My uncle taught me,' he said. 'He used to play with a danceband in Caernarvon. When he retired he gave me his drum-kit and a few lessons.' He played a little roll on the snare-drum as if to confirm that the kit actually existed. We agreed to form a band.

'Now all we need is a bass-player and some gigs,' he said.

'They'll turn up,' I said, with all the confidence of the truly simple-minded. I suggested regular rehearsals and Geoff agreed. 'Next Monday?'

'Ah, I can't,' he said. 'I'm playing tennis on Monday. I'm in training. I've got a big tournament coming up. Tuesday's OK.'

'Tuesday it is,' I said.

He showed me out.

'What shall we call the band?' he said.

'No idea,' I said. 'Something'll turn up.'

Then we met Hugo. He was two years ahead of us at school, which made him a semi-adult. He was the coolest guy in town. He had an Elvis Presley ducktail, complete with sideburns, which filled Mike and me with envy because we spent every waking moment trying to grow a decent set of sideburns. Outside school, where uniforms were compulsory, Hugo wore Western-style suits with half-moon pockets and 13-inch trouser bottoms. We knew him by sight. Everybody did. We met him at the Bullring, a circular car park in the centre of Llanelly which was a regular after-school hangout for all the ne'er-do-wells in town. We got talking to him and the talk soon turned to rock'n'roll. He let it slip that he had a complete collection of Elvis singles on 78. This was unusual because 78s were already becoming obsolete. Most people had switched to 45s.

'Haven't you got any 45s?' I asked him.

'Nah,' he said, '45s are just a fad. They'll never catch on. 78s are here to stay.'

During the conversation he kept looking at Mike and frowning.

'You remind me of somebody,' he said, 'but I can't work out who? Let me think for a minute.' We let him think for a minute. 'I know,' he said, clicking his fingers. 'Gene Vincent. You look like Gene Vincent.'

Mike glowed. The coolest guy in town had just told him he looked like Gene Vincent. What more could a man want from life? Hugo invited us over to his house to listen to his records and hang out. We accepted immediately. It was like being granted an audience with the Dalai Lama.

Hugo had commandeered the entire front room of his house. His mother was not allowed to enter, even for cleaning purposes.

'Especially for cleaning purposes,' said Hugo.

His collection of 78s were laid out like soldiers along one wall, either side of a massive radiogram. He gave us the guided tour. Not only was there a complete collection of Elvis, there were complete collections of Gene Vincent, Eddie Cochran, Buddy Holly, the Everly Brothers, Freddy Cannon, Gary US Bonds, Bobby Darin, Dion and the Belmonts, Duane Eddy, and his all-time favourites, Johnny And The Hurricanes. We were impressed. He also had a sunburst, semi-acoustic guitar.

'Do you play?' I enquired.

'A bit,' he said, picking up the guitar and playing a few chords. He wasn't bad.

'Do you want to join our group?' I said.

'What group?' he said, surprised. 'Who's in it?'

'Me and Mike on guitar and Geoff Griffiths on drums. We need a bass-player. Can you play bass?'

'No,' he said.

'Never mind,' I said, 'just play guitar and see what happens.'

'What are you called?'

'We haven't got a name yet.'

'I've got one,' said Hugo. 'The Corncrackers.'

'The Corncrackers?' we said.

'Jimmy crack corn and I don't care'. He sang Johnny And The Hurricanes' 'Beatnik Fly.'

We didn't like to say no, and the Corncrackers it was.

We started to meet after school at Hugo's. Now and again Geoff wouldn't be able to make it because he was training for some bloody tournament or other but his absenteeism was tolerated; if you're a great drummer you can get away with murder. It was here I received the first setback of my musical life. I heard my own voice for the first time. Hugo had a Grundig tape-recorder. He rigged it up and I sang a song. Then he played it back. It was awful. In my head I sounded uncannily like Elvis but on Hugo's Grundig I sounded like a Penclawdd cockle-woman with a pronounced lisp. I was mortified. I decided to give up singing. The boys couldn't see what all the fuss was about. .

'Do I always sound like that?' I asked.

'Yes,' they chorused, nonplussed. My misery was complete. It was all made worse by the fact that Hugo and Mike sounded fine on the Grundig. Of course they didn't like the way they sounded either but I thought they were making a fuss about nothing.

It was in Hugo's front room I received my education. My record collection was limited; just Elvis and Ricky Nelson. Nelson wasn't the greatest singer in the world but his guitarist, James Burton, was a revelation. With Hugo's 78s at my fingertips I drenched my brain in rock'n'roll. The more I heard, the more I wanted. Mike and I pored over Hugo's lists of mail-order, specialist records and ordered all the records we couldn't get at Falcon Music. We ordered on reputation, having no idea what we'd be getting. Chuck Berry, Bo Diddley, *a gathering of eagles* 33

Little Richard and Fats Domino all arrived through the post, lighting up our life.

We started hanging out together. We went up to Cardiff Arms Park to see Wales v Scotland. We always went up to Cardiff for the Internationals but this was the first time we'd gone as a band and I think we excelled ourselves. We were thrown out of the Arms Park for running on the pitch – twice. Not during the match – we were, after all, civilised men – but during half-time. If you could elude the stewards and reach the band of the Royal Regiment of Wales you could dodge in and out of them for hours. The first time we did it, the stewards genially ushered us back to the North Stand but the second time they threw us out. Mike went straight back in because, thanks to a mix-up at the entry turnstiles, he still had his ticket. The rest of us stood outside and listened to the cheering for a while but it was torture so we went to the Queens Bar, which was empty except for a lone barman watching the match on a portable TV. Well, at least we'd see the match. Scotland won 9-3. We didn't mind losing to the Scots or the Irish as long as we beat the English, and the French of course. Well, we did mind. We felt sick. It's a matter of degree.

The Queens Bar started to fill up and the place was soon jam-packed and the noise was deafening. Mike, fighting his way through the boisterous throng, found us and we got down to some serious sackcloth and ashes. Then we spotted Tommy Titch, one of our chemistry masters, but we didn't think he'd seen us. If he had, we'd really be in the shit.

Tommy Titch got his nickname because he was a borderline dwarf. He was a pig of a man; a perfect amalgam of petty vindictiveness and unbridled sadism. He believed it was a teacher's inalienable right to twist the ears of any boy put in his charge. There had been several unsuccessful attempts to assassinate him. I myself was a party to many, including hammering a potato into the exhaust-pipe of his car in the vain hope that the subsequent build-up of pressure would blow the little Nazi swine into the next world. But luck was with him and he escaped with superficial burns. One day, with nothing to do during a physics lesson, I wrote a parody of Jimmy Dean's song 'Big, Bad John', then riding high in the charts and dedicated it to Tommy Titch. I can still remember it:

In the mornin' at school you would see him arrive,
He stood four-foot four and weighed five-stone five,
Narrow at the shoulder, kinda broad at the hip,
And everybody couldn't stop giving lip to Small Tom,
Small Tom.
Small, sad Tom.

When my back was turned, somebody took it and pinned it up on the school notice-board. The following day at assembly Stan Rees, the headmaster, brought the matter to the school's attention. He said that whoever had written the poem about one of the teaching faculty had undoubted literary talent but should put some serious thought into alternative ways in which to channel it. But, he warned, if any more poems appeared the author would be hunted down and sentenced to fifty lashes. He didn't actually say that, but that was the gist of it. This, I thought, was rather a good review and my colleagues agreed. A bit of chest-puffing was called for. Tommy Titch, having no sense of humour whatsoever, was livid and became pathologically strict, punishing even the slightest transgression of the amorphous visigothic disciplinary code he carried in his tiny, little head, presumably on the grounds that if he punished every boy in the school, sooner or later, by the law of averages, he would get to the author of the poem. If anybody reading this book knows Tommy Titch please tell him it was me. If he's still alive. I'd like to think he's dead by now.

At assembly on the Monday morning after the match the headmaster drew our attention to a serious matter. Certain boys, he said, had been seen underage drinking in a Cardiff pub by a master. This was disgraceful behaviour and the following boys were to report to his office after assembly. He read out a list of names:

'Hugh Griffiths, Roger Leonard, Michael Rees, and Geoffrey Griffiths.'

'Blinkin' heck!' said Mike. Mike was unusual in our company in that, alone among us, he didn't swear. 'Blinkin' heck!' meant that things were going seriously wrong.

I was distracted. It was the first time I'd heard the band names read out loud. It didn't sound right. Roger? Roger? I couldn't be a rock'n'roll star with a name like Roger. I decided to change it. To what I didn't know. The matter needed some thought.

We reported for punishment. With much solemnity we were ushered into Stan Rees's office by grave-faced teachers. He gave us a stern lecture on moral turpitude and suspended us for two weeks. He was particularly upset about Geoff, who he regarded as an innocent lamb led astray by older, more worldly, sheep. On the grounds of diminished responsibility due to age, he reduced Geoff's sentence to four days. The rest of us got the full whack. We were sent home with a note for our parents requesting a meeting at the earliest convenience. I was the last to leave his office and he called me back.

'Leonard,' he said, dropping his voice confidentially, 'if you leave, I'll give you a good reference.'

'No thank you, sir,' I said. 'I haven't completed my education yet. I'm sure you wouldn't want me to leave before then.'

'Going on to university are you?' he said sarcastically.

'I hope to, sir,' I replied earnestly. 'Magdalen, I thought. Or maybe Trinity?'

Barely controlling his anger, he busied himself by tidying his already tidy desk. I took this as my cue to leave and went to get my coat and satchel.

We slouched down the long school drive, conscious that most of the school were watching us through the class-room windows, consumed, we presumed, with admiration tempered with worship. We began to sing quietly to ourselves:

Give me some men who are stout-hearted men,
Who will fight for the right to be free...

a gathering of eagles

We stood at the bus-stop outside the school gates and waited for the next bus to town.

'I don't fancy going home,' said Geoff.

'Neither do I.' I said.

'Nor me,' said Mike.

'Let's go to my place,' said Hugo. 'My parents are out at work. We can play some records.'

We spent an idyllic day in Hugo's, listening to every record Elvis ever made. At lunch-time Mike went out for chips and at tea-time we knocked off and went home. See ya later, procrastinator!

'I'm not looking forward to this,' said Geoff.

'Neither am I,' I said.

'Nor me,' said Mike.

'I'm not going to tell my parents,' said Hugo. 'I'm going to pretend to go to school every day as usual. I'll wait till they've gone out to work then slip back in and play records all day.

'What about the note from the headmaster requesting their presence at the school?' I said.

'One thing at a time,' said Hugo. 'One thing at a time.'

This was the last straw for my mother. She exploded. My father immediately made a run for the garage, remembering some ultra-urgent work he had to do on the car, this minute, if imminent vehicular disaster were to be averted. My mother let rip. I had brought public disgrace on the family. I wasn't her son. There had been a terrible mix-up at the hospital the night I was born and she had been given the baby of a Nazi war criminal by mistake. I was forbidden on pain of slaughter to leave the house on any pretext for the duration of my suspension, even if the house was on fire.

'And don't think you're going to lay in bed all day,' she added ominously. 'I've got a few jobs I want you to do around the house.'

First thing the following morning my mother, dragging my father behind her, went to see the headmaster. He told her he couldn't understand it. I seemed to be a reasonably intelligent boy but my attitude was deplorable and well below the high standards expected of a grammar school boy. I was lazy and disruptive and if I didn't pull my socks up I would end up on the occupational scrap-heap. Were there, he wondered, any problems at home?

'No,' said my mother, her voice dropping to a lethal whisper. 'There – are – not!'

Dad told me later that it was a miracle that Mum didn't go for his throat, right then and there.

'Stan Rees is very lucky to be alive,' he said.

As soon as they got back home my mother laid into me again.

'You've been suspended for two weeks,' she said, 'which is just enough time for you to paint the house, top to bottom, inside and out. The paint's in the cellar.' She stomped into the kitchen. I went out to the garage to see Dad. He was pretending to work on the car. He was in reflective mood.

'What's the matter with you, boy?' he said. 'You're living on the wind.'

'That's where I like it, Dad,' I said.

He didn't say anything. He just carried on pretending to tinker with the engine, shaking his head.

Painting the house gave me time to think about a stage-name. I ran through the names of the characters Elvis had played in his films. Clint? – a bit 'git along little doggies' for me. Deke? – not bad. Vince? – not explosive enough. Danny? – too ordinary; every Tom, Dick and Harry was called Danny. I settled on Deke. I tried it out loud on top of the ladder.

'Ladies and gentlemen, the greatest rock'n'roll singer in the history of the performing arts – Clint Leonard!'

No, it had to be Deke.

Two weeks later, knackered and smelling of turps, I emerged from purdah and rejoined the human race. Mike met me at the school gates.

'How did it go?' he asked.

'Don't ask,' I said. 'I had to paint the whole house, top to bottom, inside and out. How about you?'

'Not bad,' he said. 'All I had to do was stay in my bedroom and study.' He sniffed the air. 'What's that smell?'

'Turps,' I said, stomping off up the drive. After only a few paces I turned on my heel. 'By the way,' I said, 'I've changed my name to Deke.'

'OK,' he said.

We were greeted by our fellow students as conquering heroes freshly returned from the front.

5
be-bop-a-lula

We couldn't wait for the weekend to roll around. Friday nights at the Ritz were for star names: Johnny Kidd and the Pirates, Freddie and the Dreamers, The Big Three, Gerry and the Pacemakers, Nero and the Gladiators, Screaming Lord Sutch and the Savages, and The Undertakers. Saturday nights were for local bands because Saturday nights would be full if my mother was the headline act. There were only four local bands anyway – the Blackjacks. the Fireflies, the Fleetwoods and the Meteorites – and they played on a rota system. My cousin, Roland, was the lead guitarist with the Meteorites. I hadn't met him but if he could do it then why couldn't I?

One day, Mike arrived at school looking pale and drawn.

'I haven't slept all night,' he said.

'What's the matter?' I said. 'You look terrible.'

'Gene Vincent's coming to the Ritz,' he said.

'Brilliant!' I shouted, giving him a bear-hug.

'He isn't here yet,' said Mike sombrely. 'Remember the last time he was supposed to come?'

The last time he was supposed to come to Llanelly, he and Eddie Cochran were booked to play at the Odeon Cinema. Mike and I had been the first two in the queue to buy tickets. We were in teenage heaven. Then a week before the gig was due to take place came the awful car crash. It killed Eddie and crippled Gene, who was already disabled from a Navy accident when he, according to legend, had fallen down the hold of a ship. The gig was cancelled and Mike and I went into mourning. The following day we bought all the newspapers and read every report of the crash, trying to find some meaning in a senseless event. But meaning there was none. It was rumoured that Eddie's last act had been to crawl across the oil-drenched road, stretching out his hand toward his guitar which, having been thrown clear of the crash, now lay just out of reach on the other side of the road. To us this impossibly romantic gesture seemed to confirm our belief that rock'n'roll was more than music. It was a spirit that shone, like the light at the end of the world, into the hearts and souls of the chosen. We were in good company. We were walking with giants.

For about a month before the gig Mike was almost catatonic. On the big night I had to lead him, in a trance-like state, to the Ritz which was packed and sweaty. It was billed as Gene Vincent and the Bluecaps but it couldn't be them, could it? When they walked on, we scanned the stage for a first glimpse of 'Galloping' Cliff Gallup, the Bluecaps' legendary guitarist. He wasn't there. None of the Bluecaps were. We later discovered they were a British pick-up band called the Jokers. They opened up with an instrumental. They weren't the Bluecaps, but they weren't bad. Then the guitarist walked up to a microphone.

'Ladies and Gentlemen,' he shouted, 'The King of Rock'n'Roll – Gene Vincent.'

A trifle inaccurate I thought. Elvis was the King of Rock'n'Roll. Gene Vincent was a prince, to be sure, but not the king.

Then Gene exploded on to the stage and I forgot my name, address and religion. He flew from one end to the stage to the other, dragging his gammy leg behind him, eyes fixed on a point somewhere high up in the roof. He sang, in that high soulful whisper, everything we wanted to hear and we entered a state of bliss. He took us to the outer limits of ecstasy. But even in our ecstatic condition we couldn't help noticing the dirty looks he shot at the band who seemed to us, and the rest of the audience, to be doing a fabulous job. The place went wild. Two encores and he was gone. Mike and I were drained, but not too drained to try and get backstage to meet him. We had to. It was a moral imperative.

Jinks had the same idea. We had just met him. He had an angelic face topped with a blue flat-cap (de rigueur for serious Gene Vincent obsessives), and he was in the same state as we were; glassy-eyed, distant, and imbued with a sublime otherness. He had come down from Pontyberym with his mates, fifteen slouchers all wearing blue caps.

'We've got to get backstage,' said Jinks. 'We've got to.'

So we scrambled over the stage and into the wings. There was only one door in sight so we knocked on it. There was no answer so we went in. Two big men dressed in neat, dark suits, obviously Gene's bodyguards, stood up and blocked out the light.

'Can we see Gene, please?' said Mike,

One of the men looked over his shoulder.

'It's OK,' said an American voice from behind the wall of muscle. The bodyguards stood apart and there was the great man. I was excited but Mike and Jinks were dancing in the ripples at the edge of the universe. Gene, now dressed in a black and white, chequered overcoat, sat on a wicker chair in a corner of the dressing room. We rushed toward him and Mike and Jinks knelt at his feet while I stood to his right. We asked him a lifetime's worth of questions and he answered them all. He seemed to know how important it was to us. We got one of the bodyguards to take some photographs. Standing at the great man's shoulder, I was afraid I wouldn't be in the frame so I leant in closer. Too far, I'm afraid. The resulting photograph shows me, like a priest reading the last rites, peering into Gene's right ear while he recoils, wondering what the hell I was doing just out of his eye-line. I didn't care. At least I was in the photo.

The guitarist of the Jokers came into the dressing room. Gene looked at him coldly. The guitarist started to talk business but Gene held up a hand and stopped him.

'You're fired,' he said with barely-concealed contempt. 'The whole band's fucking useless, man. I never want to see you again.'

be-bop-a-lula

The guitarist protested but Gene's mind was made up. Things turned ugly. The room went cold and there was a whiff of sulphur on the air. The guitarist moved threateningly toward Gene. Before anybody could blink, the two bodyguards snapped into action, grabbing the guitarist by the arms. He began to struggle and a scuffle broke out. It was short-lived and he was frog-marched out of the room. A couple of minutes later the bodyguards returned, shaking their heads and shrugging their shoulders, but obviously pleased with themselves. They'd enjoyed that. Throughout the affair Gene just sat there. not moving a muscle.

'Get me a new band,' he said matter-of-factly.

'OK,' said one of the bodyguards and left the room, as if he was just nipping down the corner-shop to buy one ('Give me twenty Woodbine and a bottle of sherry-from-the-wood, luv. Oh, and while you're there, give me a four-piece band with a drummer who knows what a back-beat is.').

We were embarrassed but impressed. We felt privy to some mythical secret. We had been granted a glimpse of the dark wheels that turn beneath the assiduously-polished, glossy machine. We felt we ought to leave so we got up and said goodbye. Gene seemed surprised.

'Don't let that upset you,' he said, laughing. 'It happens all the time.'

So we hung around a bit longer. We got him to sign autographs. I still have mine. Two, in fact. The first is a general 'regards' autograph, the second a personal dedication. I told him my name was Deke and he, frowning, wrote 'To DleR'. Close enough. We left, walking on air.

'He didn't look too well, did he?' I said. 'He was a bit pasty-faced.'

'Well, he'd just come off stage.' said Mike. 'He must have been knackered.'

'He looked great to me,' said Jinks.

Singing 'Be-Bop-A-Lula' we walked Jinks to the bus-stop to catch the last bus to Pontyberym. We exchanged addresses and swore blood-oaths that tonight would be the start of a life-long friendship. A friendship forged in the white heat of teenage euphoria. We waved him away into the distance. Naturally we never saw him again.

We walked home up the Black Path, across Maes-Ar-Dafen fields and along the banks of the Lliedi, talking, usually at the same time, about Gene Vincent. Now, we knew there really was a Rock'n'Roll Heaven. We knew because we were in it.

Be-Bop-A-Lula!

6
the problems of being too sexy

We became righteous, holier than thou, the keepers of the secret. We dismissed our peer group as people of no account. They were all vulgarians leading blinkered lives who couldn't tell the difference between Jerry Lee Lewis and Jerry Lewis. We, on the other hand, were the coolest people in Llanelly, if not the planet. But we were still spectators. We were still part of the audience. We wanted to be on the stage. Our golden opportunity came by chance, literally through the back door.

It was Mike's 18th birthday and I went up his house to help him celebrate the occasion. We were sitting in the kitchen singing every song we knew when, in the middle of 'Tutti Frutti', there was a knock on the back door. It was the next-door neighbour. He was, he said, the head of the entertainments committee at the Car Bay Club, He'd heard us through the adjoining wall, liked what he'd heard, and wanted to book us for his club. Were we free this Saturday? Yes, we bloody-well were. We shook hands on it.

At last, the first gig. It was a big club but we weren't nervous. What was there to be nervous about? Excited perhaps, but nervous? – not on your life. I'd suggested changing the name of the band. 'The Corncrackers', it seemed to me, was a bit tame. It needed sharpening-up. So we enlisted the help of the Devil. We agreed it should now be 'Lucifer and the Corncrackers'. Nobody would actually be Lucifer. He wouldn't exist. Well, there's no such thing as the Devil, is there? If there's no God, how can there be a Devil?

The next day at school we went to find Geoff and Hugo. Geoff was as excited as we were but Hugo shit himself.

'We're not ready,' he said. 'We haven't had any proper rehearsals. I've got a bad finger. There's an 'r' in the month.'

'OK,' we said. 'We'll do it without you.'

Conduct unbecoming. Desertion of post and cowardice in the face of the enemy. Hugo was as guilty as hell. I'm told that during the Indian Wars, Sioux warriors in pursuit of the US cavalry considered it beneath their dignity to kill troopers who, having no stomach for the fight, had surrendered and were begging for mercy. They rode past these whimpering blue-bellies without a second glance, leaving their fate in the hands of the squaws and children who followed closely behind. We thought that Hugo's fate should lie in the hands of squaws and children.

As for me, I was paralysed with fear. There weren't enough wild horses in the world to drag me on to that stage. No way, Nez Percé.

On the afternoon of the gig Mike came over to get me. My mother answered the door.

the problems of being too sexy

'Hullo, Auntie Ella,' he said. 'Is Roger coming out to play?'

'He's still in bed,' she said. 'He won't get up. He doesn't want to play tonight. I've tried reasoning with him but he's got an answer for everything. You'd better go up and see him.'

Mike came up to my bedroom and sat on the bed.

'Come on,' he said, 'we've got a gig to do.'

'Get lost,' I said, pulling the blankets over my head. 'I'm not doing it. We're not ready. We haven't had any proper rehearsals. I've got a bad finger. There's an 'r' in the month.'

Mike dragged me out of bed, stood over me while I put my clothes on, and marched me downstairs to the kitchen. While Mum made us breakfast Mike gave me a pep talk. Eventually he wore me down and I sulked off to get my guitar. Holding me by the sleeve, in case I made a run for it, he led me off to pick up Geoff. My mother waved us off.

'I'm going to regret this,' I said to Mike.

'No, you're not,' he said.

And I didn't, although now and again, sitting in a freezing cold, broken-down van on some god-forsaken motorway at three o'clock in the morning, I sometimes ask myself – maybe I should've stayed in bed?

And so we did our first gig which, you will recall from the opening chapter, was a roaring success. Over the next few days it was subjected to a severe post-mortem examination; the first of many. We could only find one fault – me; or, rather, the lack of me. It was universally agreed that I needed an amplifier.

The following day I went to Falcon Music and bought a Selmer 15 watt amplifier and a De Armond pick-up on the never-never. My mother signed the agreement. At first she refused but I was ready for her.

'Of course, it's up to you,' I said. 'You must know how much I've always admired your common sense in monetary matters, and I know that, to you, this might appear to be a waste of money but, if successful, the group will keep me off the streets. I'll be too busy playing the guitar to have time for drinking and fighting.'

Game, set and match!

I fixed the pick-up on the guitar and plugged it in. It was marvellous. It was too loud to turn up full. My mother went apeshit.

'Look on the bright side,' I said to her, 'I could be lying in a gutter in a pool of blood.'

Hugo seemed to be avoiding us, so we went to his house. We told him how great the gig had been. He was crestfallen. He'd let us down. If there was only some way he could atone for his sins, some way in which he could redeem himself. If only he could turn the clock back. If only there was another gig.

'There is,' we said. Fear flashed across his eyes.

'Oh, good,' he said, now on the back foot. 'Where?'

'At the Electricity Club.'

'When?'

'This Saturday. Think you'll be able to make it?'

'I'll be there,' he said unconvincingly.

The Electricity Club was the watering-hole for those who worked at the Electricity Board. As chance would have it, a member of the Electricity Club committee had been at the Car Bay Club. He'd seen us, liked us, and booked us. We were on our way.

We arrived at the Electricity Club and I set up my new amp. The committee didn't like it. They'd never seen one before but they didn't like it. They clustered around it making snuffling noises, like a group of chimpanzees discovering a crashed UFO in the jungle. I set the volume knob on one and played a few quiet chords to reassure them. They backed off suspiciously, talking amongst themselves. Finally they agreed to let me use it, When they'd gone I turned the volume knob up to eight, ready for the show.

Hugo turned up. He was as white as a sheet and jumped nervously when spoken to.

The list of acts was exactly the same as at the Car Bay Club with the exception, we were relieved to hear, of the old woman with the drinks tray. Nobody knew where she was, but the consensus of opinion was that she had either gone on to better things with her new agent or she was in hospital suffering from a cerebral haemorrhage. Once again we went on after the semi-famous rugby player who once again sang 'Do Not Forsake Me, Oh My Darling' in the now-familiar, slightly-sharp, tremulous baritone voice. Once again he gained polite, indulgent applause.

And once again, thanks to Mike, we went down a storm, Hugo didn't play much of a part in the proceedings, preferring to lurk at the back of the stage playing his unamplified acoustic guitar, so you couldn't see him and you couldn't hear him.

When we walked offstage the committee were waiting for us. They were clearly agitated. They complained about my guitar, which was 'too bloody loud', and they complained about Mike's gyrations, which were deemed 'too sexy'. The committee told us that if we wanted to play the Electricity Club again we would have to 'tone it down'. We refused on purely artistic grounds. We were artistes, we said, and if we chose to wriggle and shake during a performance then we would bloody-well wriggle and shake. In that case, they said, we were banned.

Seeing as our pay amounted to two drinks-vouchers each, worth two shillings, we weren't too fussed about playing the Electricity Club again, thank you very much. Anyway, we didn't care. The following Saturday we had a return booking at the Car Bay Club.

We arranged a rehearsal at Geoff's house to learn some new numbers but Hugo wasn't interested.

'I've had enough,' he said. 'I don't enjoy it. I'm hanging up my guitar.'

We wouldn't miss him musically or visually, but he was awfully good company.

Our return to the Car Bay Club was less than triumphant. Once again we went on after the semi-famous rugby player but this time we couldn't help but notice that most of the audience spent the entire set with their hands held over their ears. The committee were furious.

the problems of being too sexy

'We've had hundreds of complaints,' they said. They singled me out. 'You can hear that bloody guitar of yours in Aberystwyth, and you,' they turned to Mike, 'are a bloody pervert.'

'Thank you very much,' said Mike. 'I suppose a return booking is out of the question?'

'It is,' they said, 'and what's more you are now officially banned from the Car Bay Club.'

We didn't mind at all. Being seen as 'too sexy' was hardly an obstacle to an aspiring rock'n'roller. It had echoes of Elvis to it. I'd made things worse, or better in our opinion, by joining in on the more outlandish bumps and grinds. The highlight of our act was breathtaking. At a particularly apt moment Mike and I, still playing furiously, hurled ourselves down on our knees and lay back till our heads touched the stage, We thought it was a great moment in rock'n'roll but the Car Bay Club committee thought it was a disgusting example of the decline of morality in society. Somebody had to take a stand against this simulated fornication, and if it had to be the Car Bay Club committee then so be it.

So now we had done two gigs and been banned from both. We decided it was time to spread our wings. We decided to get a manager. We picked Quasimodo, a friend who'd been hanging around on the fringes for some time. He had the gift of the gab, which we assumed made him ideal managerial material. He was called Quasimodo, to his face, because he appeared to be a hunchback. He wasn't a hunchback, he just looked like one. His first managerial act was to get us a gig at the British Legion Club.

Our reputation preceded us. Upon arrival we were ordered to behave ourselves. 'No antics,' we were told. We did our normal show and were promptly banned. We were running out of gigs. But Quasimodo came to our rescue. He got us a Saturday night gig in the RAF Club in two weeks time. A week before the gig we decided we needed a bass-player. Quasimodo offered his services.

'But you can't play bass,' I said.

'I've got a week to learn,' he said. 'It can't be that hard. You only play one note at a time. I'll buy a bass tomorrow.'

The next day he bought a Framus violin bass just like Paul McCartney's and suggested a rehearsal before the gig.

'Give me a week,' he said.

We didn't know what to expect. By rehearsal time he'd had a few days to get to grips with the thing. Maybe he was a natural?

He wasn't. He was excruciating. He had no musical talent whatsoever and he couldn't feel the chord changes so he had to count everything.

'A-2-3-4, A-2-3-4, A-2-3-4, A-2-3-4, B-2-3-4, B-2-3-4...' and so on. And he couldn't do it without moving his lips. When you're standing at the microphone, legs apart and shakin', giving it all you've got, the last thing you want to see out of the corner of your eye is the bass-player mouthing the beats to the bar. But we didn't like to say no, so we arrived at the RAF Club full of trepidation.

We set the gear up and had a quick run-through. Quasimodo hadn't improved and Mike, Geoff and I exchanged rueful glances. We ran through a few songs but it was too painful, Quasimodo thought it sounded great. He strolled off toward the bar with a spring in his step. I stayed on the stage and twiddled half-heartedly to myself on the guitar. That's when Wes stepped into the picture. Wes was Quasimodo's mate and sort of road manager. Until then he hadn't said much. He ambled onstage and checked Quasimodo's gear; a valve-driven radio linked to a small speaker that lay cabinetless on the floor, pointing at the ceiling. I was playing 'Baby, I Don't Care'. Wes picked up Quasimodo's bass and joined in. He was terrific, he was bouncy, he was accurate, and he didn't count the beats to the bar. Without realising it, he had passed the audition.

But we still had to do the gig with Quasimodo. It was terrible but Mike got us out of trouble by being particularly lewd. At the end of the night everybody was happy. We were paid off and banned. I sacked Quasimodo and offered Wes his job. Wes accepted. Quasimodo got the huff and amid much acrimony disappeared from the scene. But only for a while. Within a fortnight he was back managing the band as if nothing had happened. During his absence he'd slashed his wrists but, he said, that was because his girlfriend had left him. It had nothing to do with the band sacking him. He showed us the scars. They seemed rather perfunctory. Just enough to impress a girlfriend but not enough to convince a rock'n'roll band.

We were booked by the Melbourne Jazz Club. They couldn't ignore us, no matter how hard they tried. The club was run by Wyn Lodwig, a local clarinet-player, for the benefit of people with beards and long pullovers. He rented the back room of the Melbourne Hotel every Saturday night and the main attraction was the Wyn Lodwig Traditional Jazz Band, but when a better-paying gig cropped up he would book a replacement band, always of similar ilk. Everybody was telling him to book the Corncrackers but he flatly refused. He loathed us. He saw rock'n'roll as part of Mankind's headlong plunge back into barbarism; part of the unstoppable tide of vulgarity that was engulfing the civilised world. But our notoriety was such that it became impossible to ignore and he reluctantly booked us.

Much to his disgust, we sold the place out. Much to his delight, he made a small fortune. We were paid £1-14s; our biggest purse yet. Although it stuck in his craw he was forced by popular demand to swallow his prejudices and re-book us for the following Saturday, which was also free.

The following Saturday rolled around and I threw a tantrum. It was all because of Wes's father. His nickname was 'Ychan' (a contraction of 'bachgen', the Welsh for 'boy', and pronounced as if you were trying to dislodge a particularly stubborn gob of phlegm from the back of your throat). He earned this sobriquet because he said 'ychan' at the end of every sentence he spoke. He didn't like me. Well, he didn't like anybody. He'd been coming to our gigs, no doubt convinced that we needed keeping an eye on. I banned him, as I had banned my own parents, because we were a rock'n'roll band, and it is one of the immutable laws of Nature that rock'n'roll bands do not have their mums and dads coming to gigs. Wes's father reluctantly agreed not to attend but continued to do so on the sly. I'd always

the problems of being too sexy

catch a glimpse of him peering around a door at the back of the hall. It all came to a head at the Jazz Club. As we were setting the gear up I saw him lurking around the foyer. I confronted him. We had words.

'It's your father or me, Wes,' I said, 'Take your pick.'

I stormed out, without any idea of where I was going. I went into town. I passed the Odeon Cinema. They'll never find me in a cinema, I thought. The film was 'Billy Budd', the Herman Melville novelette, starring Terence Stamp. I thought I'd got away with it until, halfway through the film, a shadowy figure appeared at my shoulder. It was Wes. He tried to persuade me to come back to the Jazz Club and I allowed myself to be persuaded. When I got back there, Wes's father had gone. The boys had done the first set without me, and without a PA system. Wyn Lodwig, the ulcerous little shite, had taken his PA out, just to fuck us up. So the boys just sung the songs as normal but without a microphone. To the audience it must have appeared as if the band were playing instrumentals and making faces at them. Things had got so desperate that Ken Marks had come up and sung three songs. Ken, a school friend, only knew one song, 'Peggy Sue', so he sang it three times. But now I was back and things were going to change. However, the only thing that changed was that someone new was making faces at the audience. Astonishingly, we went down a storm.

The next gig that flooded in was at the Railwaymen's Club. It was a ghastly place that hadn't seen a dob of paint this century. The house microphone, circa 1650, hung from the ceiling above centre-stage. It was lowered on a long cable, by means of a winch, to the required height of the vocalist's mouth. The audience were mainly old railwaymen supping their pints. They looked at us with bewilderment and the only crowd reaction we got was a belly-laugh when, in the middle of one of my vocals, the microphone was accidentally winched back up into the ceiling. Maybe it was an accident or maybe they did it to everybody. Who can fathom the mindset of the retired transport functionary?

As we were leaving, Providence dealt me a cruel blow. We were getting the gear out and I leant my guitar against the gatepost outside the club; naturally, I didn't have a guitar case. Wes came breezing past carrying an amplifier. He caught my guitar with his foot and it crashed on to the pavement, making a horrible twanging sound and splintering into bits. There was a brief silence. Then Wes began to apologise. I brushed his apologies aside.

'It's OK,' I said, 'It's about time I got a new guitar.' But I felt sick.

The next day I got a guitar catalogue from the Falcon and ordered a new guitar – a cherry-red Hofner Verithin with a Bigsby tremelo arm. Eddie Cochran had used a Bigsby, and it was worth more than the guitar. The whole thing cost me thirty-five quid on the never-never. Mum, with an air of resignation, signed the agreement and a couple of weeks later it arrived. It was beautiful.

As we started to earn some money we decided that, rather than take any for ourselves, we would plough it all back into the band, paying for new gear and sorting out some transport. Geoff balked at the idea. Why should he, a drummer who already had a drumkit, pay for amplifiers for Mike, Wes and me? We pointed

maybe i should've stayed in bed?

out that his drumkit was somewhat ancient and would, if carbon-dated, probably turn out to be of Greco-Roman provenance; didn't he think that it could just possibly be due for renewal? And if he did, didn't he know that we, his brothers in music, would be only too happy to contribute to that renewal, even though there would no direct benefit to us. Faced with our impeccable generosity of spirit he had no choice but to concur, but he wanted independent financial arrangements. So we agreed to split the money on condition that Geoff promised to spend his share on a new set of drums. We were going to buy new amplifiers on the never-never and suggested he do the same, percussion-wise.

Within three weeks we had our new amps but Geoff still had the same prehistoric drum-kit. When challenged, he admitted he hadn't been diligently saving his gig money as promised, he'd been squandering it on girls, alcohol and – this really hurt – a box of new tennis balls. We were supposed to be dedicated musicians and here was Geoff, apparently without remorse, brazenly admitting to frittering away our hard-earned bunce on La Dolce fucking-Vita. And tennis balls? How could he think that tennis, a mere peccadillo for the idle middle classes, was more important than rock'n'roll. The fact that he was Welsh Junior Tennis Champion, and regarded as a real prospect by those who understand such things, didn't seem to come into it. We were mortified and we said so. He told us in no uncertain terms that he had no intention of changing. We could take him or leave him. Fair enough, we said, we'd get a new drummer. A drummer who wouldn't mind spending his cash for the sake of his art. A reliable drummer. One who didn't have a 28 inch bass drum. And one who didn't play fucking tennis. He packed his kit and left.

'Well, boys,' I said, 'know any good drummers?'

'Not off the top of my head,' said Wes, miles away, 'but I've been thinking.'

'Fire away,' I said.

'Well,' he said, 'Wyn Lodwig rents the back room of the Melbourne and runs the Jazz Club himself. So he gets a regular gig for his band and he gets all the profits from the door on top. We could do that.'

'Great,' I said. 'Got anywhere in mind?'

'The Mansel Hotel has got a big room upstairs. I'll go and see them.'

'Fine,' I said. 'Now, all we need is a drummer.'

'And a singer,' said Mike. 'I'm leaving the band.'

We'd seen this one coming. Mike had left school and was now working as a metallurgist at Trostre. Sponsored by the company, he was due to start a degree course in Swansea University in a couple of weeks time. I knew it would come down to the degree or the band. Mike chose the degree. He would, he said, do the next few gigs to give us time to find a replacement.

7
the years of bondage

By now we'd all left school and entered the job market. Wes went to work in his father's barber shop and I got a job as a management trainee at EM Turner & Sons. a firm of builders based on Walter Road, Swansea. Every day I commuted to Swansea, twelve miles there and twelve miles back. Sometimes I'd get a lift from the Llanelly-based manager of the Swansea branch of Lipton's Tea, a friend of my Dad, but mostly I took the bus. Of course, on bus days I missed the glamour of arriving at work in a Lipton's Tea van, but you can't have everything, can you?

I was indentured for five years. The theory was that you spent those five years learning the building trade from top to bottom. During that time you were expected to amass all the qualifications necessary to scale the dizzy heights of the boardroom and of course, with a trade behind you, you'd have a job for life. The reality was that you worked like a slave for a pittance. My monthly salary was a fiver. Never mind, I was told, once I'd qualified I could work anywhere and earn, if not a fortune, then a very good living. I might even, they hinted, get a job with Thyssen, the German road-building empire who'd just moved into the area.

Thyssen, most famous for bankrolling Hitler, had opened a huge, shiny, ultra-modern, office block on Bynea Flats, just outside Llanelly. I passed it every day on the bus. The building was a statement of sorts. It said: 'We are the biggest. We are the best. And we have enormous amounts of capital.' I still pass it occasionally. Now its glossy, glass frontage is layered with grime and the office staff, visible through the yellowing windows, seem to be as shabby as the building.

I settled in at Turners and soon adopted the uniform; a subtly-checked jacket with leather elbow patches, cavalry twill trousers and hush puppies. I put them on and aged ten years. My route through the company was much travelled. Five yearly stints in five different departments. I started out, as everybody did, in Costing. We measured everything the firm built, wrote it all down and sent it to Accounts, who then worked out what it all cost. Worthwhile stuff I'm sure, but not guaranteed to set the pulse racing. It was also a pain in the neck. Mainly because it is in the nature of the building trade that it occurs outside, in the fresh air, exposed to the elements. My enduring memory is of wallowing in mud during torrential rain, measuring a trench dug in yesterday's fine weather by a workie (as we called a member of the proletariat), while he and my boss shared a cup of tea and a cigarette in the warmth of the site hut.

Life in the Costing Department was a leisurely affair. John Ace, my boss, was affable but aloof in a boss-like way. If he ever had cause to admonish me, which he did on a daily basis, he would do so with a heavy heart, sighing and shaking his head slowly. Then he would dismiss me with a remark that sounded as if it was meant to reassure me that, in spite of my defects, I would one day join the ranks of qualified surveyors, and it heartened him to think that Britain's architectural continuity would be safe in the hands of people like me. I would go away resolving to do better in future. After all, I was destined to play a crucial part in making this land of ours a more beautiful place in which to live. Half-an-hour later I'd realise he was being deeply ironic.

Harold, his second-in-command, was a force of nature. He would sweep through the office, his rather foppish blonde hair blowing back off strong features, throwing his tape-measure and paperwork in the general direction of his desk, while barking orders to us, his minions. The orders thrown in my direction were depressingly predictable and always involved coffee and buns. As office junior I was required to fetch refreshments for the whole building, once in mid-morning and once in mid-afternoon. This took an hour and required reams of paperwork. The men usually had ham rolls, a doughnut, and two sugars in their coffee. The typing pool usually had cottage cheese, yoghurt and Sweetex in their coffee. It was the first time I had ever been exposed to cottage cheese and yoghurt; they both tasted off to me. Harold didn't recognise official bun-run times and if he wanted a bloody coffee, he had a bloody coffee. And I had to fetch it. He was a bit of an individual and when he went out on a job we were glad to see the back of him. Unless of course he picked you to go with him. Then you felt like one of Dr Who's assistants.

It was rumoured that Harold was having some sort of tryst with the head of the typing pool, a strong-limbed, pain-in-the-neck called Anita. Whenever Harold emerged from the typing pool he always had a half-smile on his face. This was regarded, by the office inquisition, as conclusive proof of wrong-doing. I say wrong-doing because Anita was married to Dennis, the head of Accounts. Harold was put under round-the-clock surveillance by the office detective agency; well, me and Gerald Weekes actually. Nothing was ever proved. Not through want of trying.

Then Les Girling arrived and I was no longer the office junior. I was immediately relieved of bun-run duties. He was a bluff, self-effacing lad who liked cars – that doesn't cover it. He was obsessed with cars? – no, that's not enough. He lived and breathed cars? – I'm sorry, it still doesn't capture it. One incident illustrates the depth of Les's compulsion.

Walter Road is a wide boulevard with offices on both sides. Many firms had more than one office and there was much inter-office traffic. Pin-striped mandarins, brows furrowed with fiscal purpose, taking the Jag for an early lunch, and three hours later the same Captains of Commerce, now slew-eyed and pink-cheeked after a vat or two of gin & tonic, tumbling out of cabs just in time to go home; hordes of office juniors bun-running for all they were worth; and squadrons of secretaries, clutching at wayward paperwork, nipping in and out of the traffic. One of these secretaries, from the office directly opposite, became an icon to us. Raven-haired and languid with an hour-glass figure, she moved with panther-like

the years of bondage

grace. Her every appearance was greeted by a joyful shout from the duty sentinel. There would be a mad rush to the window, followed by collective declarations of undying love from the assembled company. One day Harold caught us at it.

'What's going on here?' he said sternly.

'Come and look at this, Harold,' we said, 'then you'll understand.' Harold craned his head toward the window.

'Hmmm,' he said. Testament indeed. I think he understood how important she was to us. He could see that we were no longer in control of ourselves. Our hormones were now in complete command. We didn't even know her name but we were all head-over-theodolite in love with her. None more than Les, who came over all poetic whenever she glided into view. One day, while the management were out on a job, we were having one of our philosophical discourses. The talk turned, as it so often did, to our favourite secretary. But Les kept interrupting with irrelevancies.

'Have you seen the new Maserati?'

'What?'

'The new Maserati. The MX 5000XE – Series Two. Haven't you seen it? It's beautiful.'

'Sometimes I worry about you, Les,' I said. 'I don't know which you prefer – girls or cars?'

Les frowned. Then he frowned again. I'd hit a dark spot. We could see he was wrestling with his mortal soul.

'Well?' we chorused, now riveted.

'I don't know,' he said, finally.

'Let me put some meat on the question,' I said helpfully. 'They drop the bomb and you've got four minutes to live. Outside this office you will find two things – our favourite secretary, naked and hot to trot, and a high-performance sports car with the keys in the ignition. Which would you choose for your last ride, Les?'

Les rubbed his chin. Then he shook his head. Then he rubbed his chin again.

'Depends,' he said.

'Depends on what, for Christ's sake?' I yelled.

'Depends on what kind of car it is.'

At the time, we thought he was mad but now I'm not so sure. I think he may have been showing a maturity way beyond his years.

After a year I was moved from Costing to Quantity Surveying. This meant moving from the main office to a Portakabin in the middle of the firm's building yard down in the dock area. It also meant I was on my own for most of the day. It was awful. No office intrigue, no dialectic discourses, no secretaries to ogle at. I even missed the bun-run. My new job was to co-ordinate the arrival of building materials on-site at the exact moment they were needed. It would be pointless, for instance, for roof slates to arrive on-site when the foundations were being laid. The whole system depended upon the 'Kalamazoo'.

The Kalamazoo was a large diary into which were entered the schedule of works of each job the company had undertaken. Pink slips denoted the delivery date of the building materials on each site and yellow slips were entered three weeks before as an early warning system. Every day I had to check the yellow slips and send out reminders to building suppliers that they were due to deliver whatever they were supposed to deliver on such-and-such a date. It was an extremely tedious job involving much paperwork. I had to list details of the relevant materials, which sometimes required two or three pages of building jargon. My life appeared pointless. What I didn't realise, sitting there in an isolated portacabin singing Elvis songs to myself, was that the smooth running of the company depended entirely on me.

I began to let things slip. One day I didn't send out the reminders. I told myself I would do it tomorrow. When tomorrow arrived I told myself I would do it the next day. Nothing happened. Mr North from Head Office didn't ring up demanding to know what the hell was going on. The sun still came up in the morning and the moon still came out at night. I continued to let things slip. After a while I didn't even bother putting the pink and yellow slips into the Kalamazoo. No one ever looked at the bloody thing anyway.

Now, the beauty of the system was that, for a while, it sustained itself, and, for a while, life pursued its usual course with a monotonous languor. Then, after three weeks, all hell broke loose. All the building sites began ringing up Head Office, demanding to know how the hell they were supposed to build whatever it was they were supposed to build without concrete or bricks or the damp-proofing they needed. Head Office rang me up with murder on their minds. Luckily I was off sick at the time. Well, I wasn't really sick, unless you consider boredom a sickness.

When I returned to work some three days later I was summoned to Mr North's office. Mr North was the chief executive. He gave me a huge bollocking.

'Well done!' he said. 'Oh, well done! You've brought this company to its bloody knees.' He said I had done untold damage to the company reputation and lost the firm tens of thousands of pounds. Then he paused, waiting, no doubt, for an explanation. I said nothing. Furthermore, he said, his daughter had gone to Skewen Ritz on the weekend and had a very entertaining evening dancing to the music of a band called the Corncrackers.

'Isn't that the name of your pop group?' he asked. I nodded. 'Well, you can't have been very ill then, can you?' he said, sitting back and folding his arms in triumph.

The game was up.

'I'd like to hand in my notice,' I said. 'I'm not cut out for this job. It's about time I became a professional musician.'

Mr North seemed relieved.

'I agree,' he said. 'I think it's high time you became a professional musician too. I don't know how good you are as a musician but you can't be as bad at it as you are at this job. Good luck in your new career.'

'Thank you,' I said. We shook hands and I left.

I went straight to see Wes at the hairdressers. He'd just finished giving someone a haircut.

the years of bondage

'I've turned professional,' I announced grandly.
'You've had the sack,' he said.
'No, no, no,' I said, hurt. 'I resigned.'
'You've had the sack.'
'No, really,' I said, 'I resigned. Well, if I hadn't resigned they'd have sacked me but, technically, I resigned. How about you?'
'What about me?' he said, frowning.
'Why don't you turn professional? Why don't you jack your job in?'
'Because it's a family business,' he said. 'How can I jack it in?'
'Easy,' I said. 'You just tell your father that although he has spent years training you as a hairdresser, he has been wasting his time. You can tell him that any fool can spend a lifetime cutting hair but you have been blessed with a sublime talent and to waste it would be a crime against Art, comparable to the burning of the library at Alexandria. You can finish by telling him that there comes a moment in every man's life when he must leave the nest and strike out alone, but you know that, as your father, he will be the first to shake your hand and wish you well on this most momentous of journeys.'
'Oh, yeah,' he said, beckoning the next customer into the chair.
Now, all I had to do was tell my parents. They'd understand. They'd understand that their son had the soul of an artiste. And not your common-or-garden artiste either, but one destined to become the brightest star in the rock'n'roll firmament. They'd understand that the building trade was no place for a delicate hothouse orchid like me and that I couldn't possibly spend the rest of my life wearing cavalry twills and hush puppies. They'd understand that this wasn't just a phase I was going through, this was the real thing. They'd understand that I was on the brink of a great adventure. They'd understand. I knew they would.
They didn't understand. They went apeshit. Well, my mother did. Dad, who if the truth were told was just as scared as I was, just sat in his chair, shaking his head and tut-tutting. He knew there was no point in trying to get a word in edgeways while my mother had something to say. And did she have something to say? I weathered the initial storm but it worked against me. Heartened by my survival, I got cocky and stupidly strayed out where the ice was thinnest. I explained to her that the deed was done, that there was no turning back, and that, to be frank, I'd expected, rather foolishly as it turned out, some parental support in the matter. Some sympathy for an artistic soul in torment? After all, I added, they had conceived me, nurtured me, fed me, clothed me and educated me, but for what? To be a robot stuck in a nine-to-five, dead-end job?
'It's good enough for your father,' she said.
Undeterred, I ploughed on. Thanks entirely to them, I said, I was superbly equipped to face the world and its tribulations, so to falter on the brink of this great adventure would be a betrayal of their tireless parental struggles. And if they didn't think music was a noble calling, why had they given me piano lessons?
Dad froze and Mum went for the cutlery drawer. Then she came at me with a kitchen knife. After a brief but vicious struggle we disarmed her and, after an hour

or two, she calmed down. She must have decided that murder was a little extreme, even in these circumstances. Instead she embarked upon a war of attrition that persists to this day. She still thinks now, as she did then, that this rock'n'roll thing is merely a phase I'm going through and that one day I'll grow up and get a proper job.

The next day was my first as a professional musician. I celebrated by staying in bed until the early afternoon. When I finally came downstairs Mum was sitting at the kitchen table, shelling peas and glowering. I noticed the room was cold. I put it down to my imagination.

'Any chance of a bit of breakfast, Mum?' I asked cheerfully.

'Is this what it's going to be like from now on?' she said, her deep voice resonating around the kitchen. The lace curtains billowed, even though the window was shut, and a potted plant on the sill withered and died. 'Are you going to spend the rest of your life in bed?'

'Well, I don't have to get up until gig-time now.'

'Hmm,' she said, her eyes narrowing. 'Well, if you think that you can lay in bed all day…' And she was off again. I listened morosely. I was beginning to yearn for the peace and quiet of a builders' yard. I tried pointing out that with the Corncrackers I was already earning twenty times my Turner's pittance.

'And how long is that going to last?' she said.

I assumed it was a rhetorical question and went out. I called in to see Wes but the shop was full and he was too busy to talk. I hung around Rabiotti's café for an hour or so, then I went down the beach. I used to go down there when I was mitching school. It seemed only natural to go there again.

8
the L-club

Wes's negotiations with the Mansel Hotel had been successful. The landlord was only too pleased to rent us his little-used, upstairs room every Friday night. We had decided to call it the Hell Club. Lucifer, even if he didn't exist, needed a home. Naturally, the landlord didn't like it.

'It'll attract all the nutters,' he said.

So we shortened it to the L-Club.

'When do you want to start?' he said.

'Week Friday,' said Wes. 'We'll need some time to advertise.'

Back in Wes's hairdressers, we started to map out our advertising strategy but Mike stopped us.

'The Mansel will be my last gig,' he said 'so I'll leave you to it.'

'OK,' we said, and he left.

'And then there were two,' I said. 'Now all we need is a drummer.'

'What about Keith Hodge,' said Wes.

'Who?' I said.

'Keith Hodge. That mouthy kid who's always pestering us for an audition.'

'He's only about twelve,' I said, appalled.

'No, he isn't,' said Wes, 'He's about fifteen.'

'Are you sure?' I asked. 'The last time I saw him he was wearing short trousers.'

'No, he wasn't,' said Wes. 'That's just wishful thinking on your part. We might as well give him a go. There isn't anybody else around. Besides, he might be as good as he says he is.'

'Nobody's that good,' I said.

Keith wasn't much younger than us, but at that age it seemed like centuries. He'd been in the Grammar School the same time as me but because he was three years behind, I didn't know him. He was still in school and lived in a cycle shop kept by his parents. He was a twenty-four carat pain in the neck. If I saw him coming down the street I'd hide in a doorway, but he always saw me. He didn't miss a thing. I think he might have been fitted with radar. He'd come bouncing up.

'Hi, Deke,' he'd say, bubbling with the sheer joy of life. 'When are you going to audition me? I'm a much better drummer than Geoff Griffiths. The sooner you give me an audition, the sooner you'll see how good I am.'

'No,' I'd say, 'no, no, no.' I'd walk away but he'd follow me down the street, still pumping his gums.

'You might as well audition me. One day I'll be in the band. It's only a matter of time.'

'Bog off,' I'd say, but there was no stopping him. He was relentless. And now we had to tell him his dreams had come true. It seemed a shame to make him even happier than he already was, but we had no choice. We found him in the cycle shop.

'I knew you'd come around in the end,' he said. 'When's the first gig?'

'You haven't passed the audition yet,' I said.

'It's only a formality,' he said.

We auditioned him that evening in the Mansel. He wasn't as good as he said he was, but he wasn't far off it. After two or three numbers he asked for a microphone. I gave him mine. He set it up next to his hi-hat and sang a song. Not bad. Then he sang another one. Then another one. We couldn't stop him so Wes switched his microphone off.

'I think we've heard enough,' said Wes. He turned to me and raised an eyebrow. I steeled myself. Nothing ill-becomes a man more than the futile attempt to avoid the inevitable. I nodded assent.

'You're in,' said Wes.

'Of course I am,' said Keith. 'Shall we start rehearsing now?'

'We'd better,' I said. 'The first gig is only ten days away. That's when the L-Club opens.'

'I can't do it,' said Keith.

'What?' we said.

He couldn't, he said, join the band for a fortnight because of a prior commitment to the National Youth Orchestra of Wales.

'Fuck the National Youth Orchestra of Wales,' I said.

'I can't,' he said. 'It's the National Youth Orchestra of Wales, for Christ's sake.'

'I don't think you heard me properly,' I said. 'I said "Fuck the National Youth Orchestra of Wales." The L-Club has to open on time.'

'Get a stand-in for the first gig,' said Keith.

'Like who?' said Wes. 'You were our last resort. If we knew another drummer, we wouldn't have auditioned you.'

The slight just bounced off Keith. Everything seemed to bounce off him.

'How about David Cadwallader?' he said.

We blanched. David Cadwallader was a local superstar. He was a professional jazz drummer who played with the National Jazz Orchestra of Wales and did regular sessions for the BBC. He had appeared on several records. He was about ten years older than us and he looked like Anthony Perkins. He was spoken of in hushed tones.

'He's a bloody jazzer,' I said.

'He's a bloody great drummer,' said Keith. 'He's been giving me lessons. He doesn't sing, but you can't have everything.'

'It's only for a fortnight,' said Wes. 'It'll be all right.'

We had no choice. We rang him up and offered him the gig. He accepted. We arranged a rehearsal in the Mansel. I wasn't looking forward to it. I was expecting some cynical jazz bore who wouldn't know a backbeat if he fell over one, but what I got was an enthusiastic, genial professional who rolled up his sleeves and got down with the boys. And his backbeat was immaculate.

the L-club

'See,' I said to Wes, 'I told you it'd be all right.'

We plastered the town with handbills and, at great expense, put an advert in the Llanelly Star. Now all we had to do was sit back and wait, And of course rehearse, although we didn't need much rehearsal with Cadwallader; one run-through and it was in his head forever.

The opening of the L-Club was a triumph beyond our wildest expectations. I thought we'd start slowly with the place about half-full and build from there, but an hour before we were due to play there were queues all around the Mansel and halfway around the Parish Church next door. We charged 2/6d admission and turned away about two hundred people. The gig was a stormer and Cadwallader was as excited as we were. Mike came up for a few songs and really turned it on. He didn't sing like a metallurgist. Ah well, Science's gain is Art's loss.

There was one unforeseen circumstance. When everybody started dancing the floor bounced up and down alarmingly, catapulting the dancers into positions of balletic surprise, and a new dance was born. It wasn't destined to sweep the nation because you couldn't do it without the sprung Mansel floor, however, with the passage of time, I have seen many of the moves transfer successfully over to Olympic Trampolining. So they did not dance in vain.

'How did we do?' I asked Wes, after it was all over.

'We made thirty-five quid,' he said casually.

'You're joking?' I said.

A good gig was five guineas. A very good gig. Suddenly, we had untold riches. Suddenly, we had the map that showed the exact location of El Dorado. We were on our way to the fleshpots of Egypt. It was as if God had leaned over, opened his wallet and said, 'Help yourself, boys'. But I resolved then and there that unimaginable wealth wouldn't change me. I came from sensible, down-to-earth, Welsh, working-class stock and my feet were firmly planted on the ground. There would be no fiscal fripperies, no burning the economic candle at both ends, and no unnecessary extravagances.

'How much does an Aston Martin DB5 cost?' I asked Wes. 'One with tinted windows.'

But now there was a more important item on the agenda – Gene Vincent was back in town. He was playing at the Ritz, backed by Sounds Incorporated. We towelled off and headed straight there. He was sublime. He looked healthy and happy. He obviously liked Sounds Incorporated more than the Jokers and there was a whole lot of inter-band grinning going on; always a good sign. We didn't try to get backstage to see him, we just cheered our hearts out and went home. Mike and I walked some of the way together. We were going our separate ways and it seemed fitting that the knot should be untied at a Gene Vincent gig. For the last time we walked home along the Black Path and, at Maes-ar-Dafen fields, on the banks of the Lliedi, we shook hands, wished each other luck, and said goodbye.

Two weeks later Keith was back, his patriotic duty now discharged.

'How did it go?' he asked.

'All right,' we said. 'Cadwallader was a bit sharp.'

maybe i should've stayed in bed?

'Was he?' said Keith, warily. Did we see a brief look of uncertainty pass across his face? No, we didn't. 'How was his singing?' he asked innocently. I was beginning to hate him.

The following Friday seemed to confirm that we were on the brink of vast funds. We made another thirty-five quid and turned another two hundred people away. We'd expected some rumblings of dissent from the Ritz because our Friday nights were a direct threat to their monopoly but nothing was said. When we talked to Dave Scott, the owner of the Ritz, he seemed unconcerned and brushed the subject aside. We persisted, reasoning that we were an early gig finishing at 10.30 whereas the Ritz didn't get going till the pubs shut.

'You're probably right,' he said.

And we were right. People came to the L-Club first, then, all tanked-up and raring to go, went on to the Ritz, there to brawl and vomit to their hearts' content. In fact, if you were a thug-about-town, Friday night wouldn't be Friday night unless you danced to the Corncrackers in the L-Club and beat up some mongoloid from Five Roads in the Ritz.

Dave Scott's solution to any conflict of interest was masterful. He simply booked us for a Friday residency at the Ritz as support for the big name acts, so anyone who couldn't get in to see us at the L-Club could see us at the Ritz. It was a little hectic for us. After we finished at the L-Club we'd bundle the gear into the van and drive across town to the Ritz to play to exactly the same audience we'd played to an hour before. We didn't mind and neither did they. We only got four quid for it but after the L-Club we usually went to the Ritz anyway, so now at least we'd get in free.

Then we got to thinking. If the Mansel worked on a Friday, why shouldn't it work on a Saturday? The landlord, boasting astronomical bar-takings, loved the idea. We tried it out. Same story. Queuing around the block and another 35 quid in the kitty. And, we reasoned, Dave Scott couldn't complain, because the same arguments that applied to Friday applied equally to Saturday. And Dave Scott didn't complain. He just booked us for a Saturday residency too. There was a touch of overkill involved. Even a casual carouser couldn't get through a Llanelly weekend without seeing the Corncrackers at least four times.

If we did have a problem, it was the two hundred people we had to turn away from the L-Club every night. Rather than bugger off they chose to stand outside and listen to us. Then – seduced, no doubt, by our irresistible rhythms – they took to dancing in the street, causing dreadful traffic congestion and frightening the life out of innocent passers-by. The police started complaining to the landlord and he passed the complaints on to us.

'You've got to find a way to limit the audience,' he said.

This seemed like sacrilege to me.

'Do you want us to play badly to put some of them off?' I said.

'How about membership cards?' said Keith. 'Only members would get in, and we could control their number by the amount of membership cards we decided to issue.'

the L-club

The landlord liked that.

So we had L-Club membership cards printed and sold them for five bob each at the next gig. They sold out immediately and we still had two hundred people outside. The landlord went out and explained to them that there was now a members-only policy at the L-Club, but unfortunately all the membership cards had gone, so the only way to get one was to put their names on a waiting list, in the hope that someone might die or relinquish their membership; death seemed to offer the best chance. The two hundred people rushed upstairs to the L-Club to put their names on the waiting list. We hadn't seen this one coming and our doormen recorded their names on a piece of cardboard box with a pencil stub. At the end of the night we had a waiting list of two hundred disgruntled people. The potential for civil unrest was enormous.

Fortunately, the membership cards we issued were simplicity itself; just a card with a name on it. They could be borrowed, stolen, or sold-on, and a huge black-market developed in their exchange. Also our admission policy was flexible to the point of indifference. If somebody produced a card they got in, no matter what the name on it. On several occasions a famous Llanelly rugby player was granted admission using Marlene Davies's card.

'Evening, Marlene,' we'd say

'Evening, girls,' he'd say.

Then one day I had a letter. It was the kind of letter I'd dreamed of getting ever since I'd become a musician. It was from the head of the local branch of the musicians' union. His daughter, he wrote, had applied for membership of the L-Club but there was a long waiting list. Bearing in mind that she was his daughter, he was sure I could facilitate her entry. He thanked me for my time and trouble.

I could picture the scene.

'Da-ad,' the daughter'd say, 'I tried to join the L-Club but they say it's full and I've got to go on the waiting list.'

'What's the L-Club, my dear?' he'd say, looking up from his dinner but continuing to chew.

'It's the coolest place in town, Dad,' she'd say. 'If you're not a member, you're nobody. Squaresville. A social outcast.'

'Don't worry, my precious,' he'd say, wiping chicken grease off his chin with his tie. 'I'll get you in. Don't forget I am the head of the Gorseinon Branch of the Musicians' Union and that makes me one of the most powerful men in the land. When I raise my hand the world trembles. Leave it to me. I'll write them a letter,'

I wrote back saying that he could be sure that as soon as his daughter's name came to the top of the waiting list her membership would be guaranteed. Until then, of course, my hands were tied. To interfere with due process would not only be extremely unfair to those above her on the list but, and I was sure he would appreciate this, morally repugnant and a breach of public trust. I thanked him for his time and trouble.

I could picture the scene.

'Well?' his daughter'd ask. 'Am I in?'

maybe i should've stayed in bed?

'Er...no,' he'd reply, trying to get a soup stain off the front of his shirt, 'I failed. It appears that Deke Leonard is one of the few people on this earth who are incorruptible, public-spirited, and selflessly dedicated to making the world a better place in which to bring up our children. There have been others of equal stature – Gandhi, maybe; St Thomas Aquinas, possibly – but not many. I consider myself fortunate to have been born in his time, I am going to renounce all my worldly goods and serve soup to down-and-outs under Westminster Bridge.'

I'd like to think that his daughter disowned him, left home and married a drummer.

The phone started ringing. Our reputation, enhanced by extensive local press coverage, was blossoming. Everyone, from one end of South Wales to the other, wanted to book us. But they were only offering the going rate which, with the financial base of the L-Club behind us, was not enough. The going rate at the time, pretty standard across South Wales, was seven guineas for a weekend gig and five for a weekday. Now we could afford to be choosy.

The De Valence Pavilion in Tenby rang up, offering seven guineas for a Saturday night.

'Sorry,' said Wes, 'it's not enough money. It's a long run and it won't be worth our while doing it.'

'How much to you want?' said the De Valence. Wes, who hadn't given the matter a moment's thought, said the first figure that came into his head.

'Twenty-five guineas.'

The De Valence gulped. It was an awful lot of money.

'That's an awful lot of money,' they said.

'Sorry,' said Wes. 'We can't do it for less.'

'OK,' said the De Valence, audibly swallowing. 'The 23rd of August all right?'

That became Wes's standard technique. Quote an astronomical figure then, when they'd got their breath back, work down from that. But every ointment has its fly. The best offers came in for Friday and Saturday nights, when we were committed to the L-Club.

'We could do a Wyn Lodwig,' said Wes. 'We could do the gigs and book a stand-in band at the L-Club.'

'Good idea,' I said. 'How much shall we pay them?'

'Seven guineas?' said Wes. Altruism was never Wes's strong point. 'We'd have the gig money plus the thirty-five quid from the L-Club, less seven guineas. We could be making fifty quid a night.' At the time, you could get pissed, go to the Ritz, buy a packet of fags and still have change from ten bob.

We set about booking bands. We were really picky. We felt an obligation to our audience. If they couldn't have the Corncrackers, they'd have the next best thing. We'd only book bands we'd seen, or bands that were recommended by someone whose judgement we trusted. We conducted interviews over the phone. You can tell whether a band is any good just by talking to them. A set list is a dead give-away. Any band that included any Cliff Richard and the Shadows numbers need not apply.

the L-club

The first band we booked was Tommy Scott & the Senators from Pontypridd. We hadn't seen them because Pontypridd was so far away it seemed like the other side of the world. In pre-motorway days it took about four hours to get there. Abercrave, only twenty-five miles away from Llanelly, was deemed sufficiently distant to warrant taking sandwiches and a flask of tea, and Dad even got the AA to work out an advance route for us; they did that kind of thing in those days. Anyway, Tommy Scott & the Senators were supposed to be halfway-tidy, and, because they'd have to travel so far, we paid them eight guineas.

The following day, we rang around our associates for a critique. The consensus was that they weren't bad, and they'd gone down well. The singer. in fact, had been rather good. Of course, it didn't have the magic of a Corncrackers gig, but the audience had enjoyed themselves.

'They weren't a patch on the Corncrackers,' said Lewie, who we'd left in charge. 'Different class.'

Just after the L-Club gig, Tommy Scott changed his name to Tom Jones.

Sometimes a band would call in at the L-Club on gig night to discuss a booking in person. One night, the Jets phoned up and said they were coming down. We'd never seen them but they had a fearsome reputation. They were one of the hottest bands on the circuit.

They arrived halfway through our set and stood together in the semi-darkness, just to the left of the stage. They were all dressed in long, black leather coats, black polo-necks, and black Annello & David, Cuban-heeled boots. Their hair was long and shaggy, except for the tallest, whose hair was pulled back into a PJ Proby velvet bow. They stood out from the crowd like exotic creatures from another dimension. We knew they were the Jets. Who else could they possibly be?

I looked at Wes and we both looked at Keith. It was time to turn it on. Wes and I put our shoulders to the wheel and Keith, not the most shrinking of violets at the best of times, got more flamboyant by the second and at the climax of the set kicked his drums into the audience. We jumped off the stage, walked over to them, and introduced ourselves. The one with the PJ Proby bow came over to me.

'Brilliant, mush,' he said, rubbing his hands together. 'Fucking brilliant!' He stuck out his hand. 'I'm Martin Ace.'

There should be a bell that tolls, or a fanfare of trumpets, to signal the momentous moments in a human life, but there isn't. These moments pass, like all the lesser moments, in the general whirl of existence. It is only with hindsight we see watersheds, crossroads, points of no return, and the ebb and flow of circumstance. I didn't realise it at the time, but I had just met Martin Ace.

'Deke Leonard,' I said, shaking his hand, thinking I had just met another human being.

As the crowd thinned, the Jets and the Corncrackers went into stately conclave. We immediately offered them a gig. You could tell they were good just by looking at them. Tony 'Plum' Hollis, the singer, and Martin, who turned out to be the bass-player, held court with the assurance of a seasoned double-act. They were irreverent, cynical, and seemed to have a vocabulary of their own. The other two Jets, guitar-player John Phillips and drummer Billy 'Doc' Evans, said very little, preferring to sit back and enjoy the show. They stayed for an hour and when they left my cheeks were aching with laughter.

A month later they played the L-Club. We were playing down west at Narberth Town Hall, where they had turned vomiting into an art form. We didn't want to be there. We wanted to be at the L-Club, watching the Jets. The following day we went in search of Drew, who we'd left in charge. How did it go, we wanted to know?

'They tore the place apart,' he said. 'They were really fantastic. We had a full house and they had a great time.

'We'll have to re-book them,' said Wes.

'I already have,' said Drew.

The Jets became regulars at the L-Club, as did the Mustangs. The Mustangs were the Kings of Neath. We met them when we played a Saturday gig at Skewen Ritz and they, local darlings, were the support band. They were terrific. At the end of the night we asked them how much they charged.

'Seven guineas for a weekend gig, five during the week,' they said. We booked them straight away. 'By the way,' they asked, 'how much did you get tonight?'

'Fifteen guineas,' we said. They erupted into animated discussion.

'We normally top the bill here on a Saturday,' they said, 'and we only get seven guineas. Verney said he never pays anybody more than seven guineas.'

Verney was the boss of the Skewen Ritz.

'We never work for less than fifteen on a weekend,' we said. 'You should bump up your price.'

'We fucking will,' they said and, mob-handed, went looking for Verney. As we left, we saw them standing by the bar having a heated argument with him. He was shaking his head and shrugging his shoulders. I do like to see the managerial classes squirming.

9
swashbuckling

A seminal moment in my life loomed. We were booked to play support for Johnny Kidd and the Pirates at the Ritz. Johnny Kidd was one of the brightest stars in the rock'n'roll firmament. He was the only British singer who was the equal of his American counterparts. He was right up there with Chuck Berry, Jerry Lee Lewis, Gene Vincent and Bo Diddley. More than that, he was a great songwriter. I'd have given my left bollock to have written 'Shakin' All Over'. His backing band, the Pirates, were quite simply the best band in the world. I'd seen them twice before; once at the Regal Cinema in Llanelly, supported by Vince Eager and Wee Willie Harris, and once again, about a year later, at the Ritz. But this was different. Until now I'd only been a member of the audience at a Pirates' gig, but this time I'd be sharing a stage with them. I'd get to meet them. I'd get to talk to them. I was ever-so-slightly straining at the leash.

The big night rolled around, but we had to play the L-Club first. The moment the last chord died away we started packing the gear. We slung it in the van and raced over to the Ritz. The Pirates' gear was already set up. Like us, they were a three-piece. On a centre-stage rostrum was an industrial-size drum-kit and, on either side, matching cream Fender Showman Amps tipped back on their stands, aimed at the balcony. Just looking at the stage sent a shiver down my spine. I got the same feeling, years later, when I stood in front of the temple of Rameses II at Abu Simbel in Upper Egypt.

We found them in the dressing room and, starry-eyed, shook hands with them. They were friendly but self-contained, keeping a humorous distance. Johnny wasn't wearing his eye-patch.

The eye-patch was source of much controversy. The music press was agog with curiosity. Did he really have something wrong with his eye? Or was it just a sick gimmick? Johnny told reporters that he had been changing a string on his guitar just before going onstage and it had snapped and hit him in the eye. He'd borrowed an eye-patch – there's always someone around with a spare eye-patch, isn't there? – and because it went down well with the audience he'd continued to wear it. If it offended anybody, he said, he would stop wearing it, adding pricelessly that he'd probably have his leg off and wear a peg-leg instead.

'I only wear it when I want to be recognised.' he told me. 'When I take it off, nobody recognises me.'

'I would,' I said.

We went on and played out of our skins. The highlight came when Johnny Kidd stood in the wings and watched us for a couple of numbers. Then it was their turn. As Micky Green, the Pirates' guitarist, walked past me on his way to the stage he held up his guitar for me to see. It was the most beautiful guitar I'd ever seen. It was beautiful, like a bulldog is beautiful.

'It's a Fender Telecaster,' he shouted over the back-stage noise. 'It's the same guitar that James Burton uses.'

Earlier in the dressing room we had declared our mutual love of James Burton, Ricky Nelson's legendary guitar-player. It was no surprise to me that James Burton was one of his influences. You could hear it in his playing. Green was probably the most startlingly original guitar-player in the world, but in there somewhere you could hear James Burton. If you want to hear Green at his most sublime then listen to his solo, done in the style of Burton, on 'Ecstasy', itself a beautiful song. Burton must be turning in his grave. If he was dead. Which he isn't.

I stood in the wings and listened to the best band in the world. The Telecaster was a revelation, sounding fat and percussive. Now, I'm quite prepared to admit that this may have had something to do with Green's monstrous talent, but even so there was no disguising the sound of the guitar.

'I'm gonna get one of those,' I said to him after the gig.

The following day I dispatched Quasimodo to London to buy me one. I didn't know how much it would cost so I gave him £200. Three days later he came back with a Telecaster – £127, plus case. It was a sun-burst, Custom Telecaster. The only difference from a regular Telecaster was white piping around the bodywork which, to the uneducated eye, gave it the appearance of a semi-acoustic. I tried it out and it was magnificent.

'It was the only one in London,' said Quasimodo. 'I got it in Ivor Mairants' shop. They said they'd had it in the back of the shop for about two years and I was the first person to ever ask for one. At first they thought I was joking. They asked me what gear you used and I said an AC 30 amp. They asked me what echo-unit you used. I said you didn't use one. Just the AC 30. They didn't believe me. They said everybody uses an echo-chamber.'

These were the days when ninety-nine per cent of guitarists were Hank B. Marvin clones. Marvin, the pedestrian lead-guitarist with Cliff Richard's backing band, the Shadows, played ghastly, wooden riffs, drenched in echo. It proved to be a seductive style because it required very little skill to execute, thereby putting it within the reach of the most average of guitar-players. Eventually it went the way of most fads, dying from lack of substance, and a thousand useless guitar-players hung up their guitars and became accountants – which is what they should have been in the first place. They were part of the past and I was part of the future. Who says London is ahead of the game?

As chance would have it, we supported Johnny Kidd again at the Ritz a couple of months later. This time we booked another band in at the L-Club and got to the Ritz early. We set the gear up in the darkened hall and ran through a few numbers, among them 'My Babe', a Pirates tour-de-force. Halfway through the song the swing doors at the back of the hall burst open and a bass-drum case slid across the polished dance floor, followed by a guitar-case. Then Johnny Kidd and the Pirates *swashbuckling*

walked in. They stood at the back of the hall and listened to us. At first we felt a bit sheepish but then we saw the smiles on their faces so we turned it on. Suddenly Johnny Kidd, dressed in a black, thigh-length, leather coat, ran towards us. He leapt onto the stage, grabbed the nearest microphone and began to sing.

The beauty of rock'n'roll dreams is that, occasionally, they come true. We kept 'My Babe' going for far longer than necessary. When it was time for my solo Johnny Kidd pointed at my Telecaster and grinned.

When we finally finished, the rest of the Pirates jumped up onto the stage and clustered around my Telecaster. I handed it to Micky Green. He looked it over, then played a few searing, chopping licks.

'It's great,' he said. 'It's a Custom. I've never seen one before.'

Then Johnny Kidd had a go. He liked it too. Then Johnny Spence, the bass-player, had a go. Even Frank Farley, the drummer, played a chord or two. We talked guitars for a while and then they began to wander off. As Johnny Kidd left, he took me by the arm.

'If you're ever looking for a singer,' he said, 'give me a call. Who knows? – the Pirates might sack me one day.'

'The job's yours,' I said.

As if I wasn't happy enough, Micky Green stood in the wings and watched our whole set. Occasionally we caught each others' eye and exchanged knowing smiles. My life has been downhill ever since. Of course he could have been bored. I know how tedious all that hanging about can be, killing time until the show starts. But he could have gone for a drink in the bar, couldn't he? And he didn't, did he?

Then Johnny Kidd and the Pirates went on. I stood in the wings and for the last time watched the best band in the world. Occasionally I caught Micky Green's eye and we exchanged knowing smiles. At the end of the night we said goodbye, wished them luck, and waved them off. We never played together again because two years later, in October '66, Johnny Kidd was killed in a car crash.

Why do they always take the good ones? Why didn't they take Hank B-bloody Marvin instead?

The Telecaster, being such a rarity, proved to be a major fascination for visiting star bands. Whoever we supported at the Ritz would first enquire what it was, then ask if they could try it. The Hollies came to town and after the sound-check Allan Clarke, their singer, took one look at it and commandeered it. He sat on the drum rostrum and started to play. I waited politely, hoping he'd get fed up, but he didn't.

'Can I have my guitar back?' I said finally. 'I've got to shoot off,'

'Oh, hang on a minute,' he said, playing an A chord and letting it ring. 'This is great.'

I couldn't get it off him. Just then Graham Nash wandered across the stage, obviously bored.

'It's an Esquire, isn't it?' he said, after a cursory glance at the guitar. 'They're a bit limited.'

'It's not an Esquire,' I said frostily, 'it's a Telecaster.'.

maybe i should've stayed in bed?

'It's great,' said Clarke.

I had to go over to the L-Club so I told him to leave it in the dressing room when he was finished. And off I went. When I came back, about an hour later, he was still sitting on the drum rostrum playing the Tele. We had to go on so I wrenched it off him.

'I'm going to get one of those,' he said.

I have to say that the Hollies were a bit sharp. They didn't seem to count numbers in. They just started together. I tried to spot somebody counting-in on the sly but I couldn't see anything. 'Just One Look' and they were off. But I did notice that Graham Nash, who played a black, acoustic guitar, was plugged in but not switched on. Now what do you make of that?

One Saturday night after the gig in the L-Club we rushed across town to close the show at the Ritz. There was a band already playing when we arrived but we didn't pay much attention to them as we slung our gear into the backstage area. But then we stopped to listen. They were a bit good. They were a band from Merthyr called the Bystanders. They had quite a reputation and Dave Scott had been trying to book them for some time. They were playing the Shirelles' song, 'Baby, It's You'. From behind the curtain they appeared to have about twenty-five singers; four-part harmonies soared into the ether and someone out there had a majestic falsetto voice. We walked around to the wings to see what they looked like. There were five of them and, inexplicably, they were all wearing fancy dress. The falsetto voice came from the lead guitarist, a diminutive figure enveloped in a huge Bud Flanagan fur coat. We met during the changeover. While he took his amp down I set mine up.

'How's it going, buttie?' he said, offering his hand. 'My name's Micky Jones.'

I could have turned and walked away. I could have saved myself a lot of trouble. But I didn't. I took his hand and shook it.

'Deke Leonard,' I said, not realising that, when the history of the world is finally written, this meeting would take its place in the pantheon of memorable encounters alongside Livingstone and Stanley; or Roosevelt and Stalin; or Noddy and Big Ears.

I later discovered that the Bystanders liked dressing up. I'd see them many times in the years to come and they'd usually wear snazzy, blue suits with collar and tie but, suddenly and for no apparent reason, they would adopt fancy dress. I assumed they were filling some gaping chasm in their collective psyches but I didn't dare delve too deeply. Some things are best left locked up.

10
call an ambulance

Now that we spent so much time travelling, we decided to invest in some de luxe transport. Until now, we had been relying on the kindness of the Bevan boys – Ron and John, friends since the Grammar School days. Their parents ran an hotel and bakery in Station Road and they had unfettered access to the family bread van, which they placed at our disposal. It had its drawbacks. It had no accelerator pedal to speak of. If acceleration were required then the driver, or passenger, pulled vigorously on a piece of string that hung through a hole in the dashboard. The headlights, fairly crucial on the long drives home, were slightly biased towards the left, illuminating none of the road ahead but giving a marvellous spotlit view of the passing countryside. On full beam, they sent twin searchlights probing into the night sky, as if searching for lone Heinkel 111s; on dip, they were twice as bright and provided fleeting visions of startled cows.

'Top of tree…', John would say, flicking the dip-switch, '…bottom of tree.'

However, the greatest drawback of the bread van was that the gear was permanently dusted with a thin layer of self-raising flour, but, we reasoned, if anything got stolen at least there would be no shortage of fingerprints. It was quite small so most of us had to travel in the back, sitting on the gear. Within five minutes we too were dusted with a thin layer of self-raising flour and, on arrival, we jumped out of the van looking like the Undead.

Ron drove a Hillman Minx at bowel-churning speeds. He could do Llanelly to Kidwelly – eight miles, town-centre to town-centre, at night – in six minutes and twenty seconds. We spent many happy nights trying to break the six-minute barrier. He was a keen photographer so our early career was well-documented and many of the photographs in this book are his work. Both he and John had an air of puzzlement about them, as if they couldn't quite believe how stupid their fellow human beings were. Llanelly was too small for them. They couldn't wait to get out of town, which they did as soon as circumstances permitted. In the meantime, we couldn't use the bread van for ever. We needed a van of our own. A big one.

We bought a second-hand ambulance. It was big enough to carry all the gear and leave enough space for the band and half-a-dozen hangers-on to stretch out in the back. It also had shaded windows that allowed us to do the most appalling things, invisible to passers-by, whilst parked in the middle of town. We kept it in its full NHS livery, which meant that traffic always gave way to us, assuming that we were on a mission of mercy, our good works to do. Best of all it had a siren, and a quick blast, we soon discovered, was enough to make every car within a fifty-mile radius pull over to the side of the road. On the first night we took it out, the police stopped Wes for dangerous driving. He was driving, siren blaring, down Station

Road, holding a bag of freshly-bought fish and chips at arm's length out of the window. A panda car, lights flashing, pulled us over.

'And what do you think you're doing?' said the copper.

'My chips were too hot,' said Wes. 'I was trying to cool them down.'

The copper closed his eyes and shook his head. He was, he said, about to escort us to Llanelly General Hospital, assuming a medical emergency, when he spotted the bag of chips. He started to give us a lecture about social responsibility and good citizenship but, realising the futility of such a speech, stopped in mid-sentence and let us off with a caution.

'And get that bloody siren disconnected,' he said, walking back to the panda. 'If I hear it again, I'll throw the lot of you in jail.'

Some people just don't have a sense of humour. It had been on the tip of my tongue to tell him to lighten up a bit, reminding him that life was too short for petty conflicts, too valuable to be thrown away in the vindictive pursuit of a fellow creature. After all, I should've said, we're all merely chips that pass in the night.

As fully paid-up members of the outlaw fraternity we didn't disconnect the siren, but it did make us a little more circumspect about its use.

Then Keith passed his driving test. He naturally assumed that he would now be able to drive the ambulance but Wes flatly refused, on the grounds that Keith, having only just passed his driving test, was not ready to handle such a large vehicle. He also believed that Keith, being Keith, would drive without due care and attention bordering on reckless abandon. But Keith, being Keith, persisted. And persisted. And persisted. Wes, worn down by the relentless drip-drip of the Hodge water torture, finally agreed to let him drive to the next out-of-town gig. When the big day arrived Keith, being Keith, was flamboyantly confident; he even had a pair of half-leather, half-knitted, driving gloves. Wes, being Wes, was a forest of nerve-endings. Predicting doom, he'd climbed into the back of the ambulance, explaining that he wanted to get as far away as humanly possible from the likely point of impact. And I, being me, didn't give a fuck. Thinking that a little cheer-leading was called for, I sat up front with Keith. Just outside Llanelly we arrived at an intersection.

'Any cars coming?' said Keith.

'No,' I said.

Keith pulled out and drove straight into a bus. There was a sickening crunch and the bus zig-zagged across the road, mounting the grass verge, before tipping over into a hedge.

'I thought you said there weren't any cars coming?' said Keith.

'You didn't say anything about buses,' I said.

The driver of the bus, ashen-faced and quivering, helped his passengers out onto the road. They sat on the grass verge, staring into space, The bus was a write-off but the ambulance, built like a tank, emerged without a scratch. We exchanged addresses with the bus driver and drove to the gig, this time with Wes at the wheel. He turned to Keith, now sitting in the passenger seat.

'I told you so,' he said.

call an ambulance

'It wasn't my fault,' said Keith. 'Deke said it was all clear.'

'No, I didn't,' I said. 'You asked me whether there were any cars coming. You didn't say anything about buses. It's not my fault if you asked the wrong question.'

Keith and I bickered all the way to the gig. We tried to involve Wes but he wouldn't be drawn. We continued to argue about it for the next six months, which was just about the time that elapsed before Keith was allowed to drive the ambulance again.

Inevitably, when the ambulance was parked outside a gig, fans wrote messages all over it, mainly in lipstick, But this wasn't enough. They took to bringing pots of paint to gigs and splashing their names all over it. We didn't really mind, but regretted the fact that every day it looked less and less like an ambulance.

We decided to go to London for a few days, just to see what was happening up there. Lewie came with us, mainly because he'd been to London before. Allan 'Lewie' Lewis was a policeman by trade. He spent most of his spare time, when not playing rugby, with the Corncrackers, doing everything but play in the group. But inside the policeman was a salesman, struggling to get out. Lewie could sell Satanist starter-kits to Billy Graham.

I'd been to London as a child. My Dad used to take me up there at least once a year. We'd stay for two weeks in an hotel in Russell Square and do the usual rounds of museums, cinemas, and the zoo. One morning at breakfast an American hotel guest told me he was Wyatt Earp, over in London for a US Marshals' conference. He kept winking at my father. I didn't believe him for a second. He was clean-shaven and Wyatt Earp had a moustache. Most nights we ate at the Silver Slipper in Leicester Square. I always had sausage, beans and chips with onion gravy. It was the first time I realised onions were edible.

We – the Corncrackers – booked into the Madison Hotel in Sussex Gardens which, we had been reliably informed, was a rock'n'roll hotel. We hit London right in the middle of the evening rush-hour. The traffic was daunting but Lewie threw the ambulance into the clamour with something approaching abandon.

'Look after the front end,' he'd say, gunning the ambulance toward a frighteningly narrow gap in the traffic, 'and the back end will take care of itself.'

It took us so long to find it, we took a break. We spotted a cafe in a busy street and Lewie pulled the ambulance over and parked down the road a-piece. We walked back to the cafe and ordered coffee. When, twenty minutes later, we returned to the ambulance it was surrounded by police vehicles. Six policemen milled about, some trying to peer through the shaded windows into the back, some writing in notebooks. They were clearly agitated.

'Maybe I shouldn't have parked there,' said Lewie.

The police saw us coming and, putting two and two together, came to meet us.

'What the hell is that?' said a copper, pointing at the ambulance.

'It's an ambulance,' said Lewie.

'I can see that,' said the copper angrily, 'and I suppose you're going to tell me you're a doctor?'

'No,' said Lewie, 'I'm a policeman.' He pulled out his warrant card and waved it in the air.

The copper was speechless for a couple of seconds, then he recovered.

'Do you know,' he said slowly, 'that impersonating a police officer is a very serious offence?'

'I'm a real policeman,' said Lewie, offering his warrant card for inspection.

There followed a heated discussion, during which Lewie, dressed in a white, polo-necked jumper and pink jeans, tried to convince the copper that he was a copper too. They didn't believe it and checked him out over the radio. Half-an-hour later, finally convinced, they handed Lewie his warrant card, gave him a little speech about the inadvisability of parking a suspicious vehicle in the middle of Oxford Street, and left in a huff.

'That's fucked it,' said Lewie. 'I didn't think they'd check me out. I'm supposed to be on the sick. They won't be too happy back home. I think I'd better resign and get a proper job.'

After driving around for another hour or so we eventually found the Madison. It must have been among the leading contenders for the seediest place on earth. Everywhere we looked we saw faded wallpaper and threadbare carpets. To save money, the four of us had decided to share one room. It was dormitory-sized with functional single beds. The only other furniture was a formica-topped table and a couple of chairs. There was a communal toilet on every floor. There was no evidence of a rock'n'roll aura so we went out for a curry. We found an Indian restaurant just opposite Paddington Station. To our collective amazement they didn't serve chips and they didn't have any tomato ketchup.

'A prawn vindaloo, two onion bhajis, half-and-half, and six popadoms, please,' said Keith.

'Half-and-half?' said the bemused waiter.

'Yes,' said Keith, with all the impatience of somebody who's just spent the last eight hours in an ambulance on the A40. 'Half rice and half chips.'

'I'm sorry, sir,' said the waiter, 'we don't serve chips.'

'You don't serve chips?' snorted Keith. 'Are you sure this is an Indian restaurant?'

'Yes, sir,' said the waiter, 'and we don't serve chips.'

'All the Indian restaurants in Wales serve chips.' said Keith.

'I'm sure they do, sir,' said the waiter, shrugging his shoulders, 'but not here in London. No Indian restaurants in London serve chips.'

'Don't be ridiculous,' said Keith. 'Don't you eat chips in India?'

'No, sir,' said the waiter.

We struggled to come to terms with this cultural earthquake. Coming from Llanelly, our only contact with the subcontinent had been our nightly visits to the Asian Grill, where they served chips. It didn't occur to us that the Asian Grill might be tailoring its cuisine to cater for our sophisticated Celtic palates. We naturally assumed chips formed part of the staple diet of India. Well, you live and learn, Grudgingly, we ordered rice. When the meal arrived I asked for some tomato ketchup.

'Tomato ketchup?' the waiter said, frowning.

call an ambulance

'Don't tell me you don't have tomato ketchup in India,' I said sarcastically.

'No, sir,' he said, 'we don't have any tomato ketchup in India.'

'Don't be ridiculous,' I said. 'Everybody eats tomato ketchup. Tomato ketchup is one of the building blocks of civilisation. You must have some.'

'I'm sorry, sir, but I'm afraid we don't.'

Another shattered illusion.

What was the world coming to? I'd assumed that India was a civilised country, bearing in mind they'd had about thirty years since independence to rectify the stifling confines of British rule. I further assumed that, in throwing off their shackles, they had become a confident, modern nation, re-born into the whirlpool globality of the 20th Century; standard-bearers for the emerging third world, technologically-sophisticated, governed by that most fearful of masters – the ballot box. The largest democracy in the world, head held high, forward-looking, but tempered by all-too-recent memories of a time when the boot of oppression, unthinking and arrogant, had been jammed on her throat, stripping her of her assets and rendering her docile. What price a nation governed by another? But, thanks in no small part to Attlee's enlightened Labour government, they had broken free. Now, I finally assumed, India stood on her own two feet, gaze fixed on the far horizon, ready for anything Destiny might throw at her. But I appeared to be wrong. How can a nation be civilised without tomato ketchup? Or chips?

Another assumption down the drain. Life is a series of assumptions based on skimpy half-knowledge, selective observation, misinterpretation of experience, and lack of evidence to the contrary. People's assumptions are based on other people's assumptions. Their assumptions are, in turn, based on other people's assumptions. And so it goes, cartwheeling around the world – I assume.

Over the next few days we took in the sights and walked about a bit. On Saturday we went to see the Yardbirds at the Marquee. The support was a new band from Birmingham called the Moody Blues. Denny Laine, their singer and guitarist, had a beautiful voice. They unveiled their latest single, 'Go Now', which, they said, they hoped would be a hit. I didn't realise it at the time but I was watching the worst band in the world. When, a while later, Laine left the band, it became startlingly obvious that none of the others had even the merest whiff of talent. Without Laine they were, and still are, a useless pile of shite.

The Yardbirds were right on the button and we were much impressed by the massive, pounding crescendos that dominated their set. After the gig I spoke to Eric Clapton.

'You don't do any trills,' I said.

'No, I don't suppose I do,' said Clapton.

Well, what do you expect from two guitar-players? Profundity?

On Sunday, the last night, we went out on the piss. Somewhere along the way we got separated from Lewie. We looked for him for a while but then gave up and went back to drinking. At the end of the evening we made our way back to the Madison. There was no sign of Lewie. All we had to drink at the hotel was a bottle of sherry. I have no idea why we had a bottle of sherry.

maybe i should've stayed in bed?

'I know,' said one of us, 'let's put all the sherry into a pint glass and tell Lewie we've brought him back a pint from the last pub we went to – sherry and beer are the same colour so he won't spot the difference. We'll tell him he's got to drink it down in one or he can't have it. Then he'll gulp it down, puke his guts up, and we'll have a good laugh.'

It seemed like a reasonable idea. We poured the sherry into a pint glass; we had just been on a pub crawl so, of course, we had a selection of glasses. We stood it on the window sill and waited for Lewie to arrive. Half an hour later he was back. Keith was in bed, fighting to stay awake for the big moment. Wes and I were sitting at the table.

'We brought you a pint back from the pub,' we said, gesturing toward the window sill and trying not to giggle, 'but there's one condition. You've got to drink it down in one or you can't have it.'

'OK,' he said and walked over to the window sill. He picked up the pint of sherry and drained it. 'Great,' he said, smacking his lips. Then he came over to the table, pulled up a chair and sat down. 'So,' he said, leaning back, 'where've you been tonight?'

'Just drinking,' we said, disappointed by his lack of reaction to our witty, little prank. Then we had one of those where-did-you-get-to? conversations. Keith slipped off into a drunken sleep and we talked into the night. After a while Lewie started looking a little green around the edges.

'Are you all right?' I said.

'Yes,' he said unconvincingly. He burped loudly. 'By the way,' he asked coldly, 'whose idea was the sherry?'

Wes and I looked at each other. This was a moment for solidarity. This was laying your life down for your friends. 'All for one, and one for all!' as Alexander Dumas would have us believe. It was a moment that called for, above all things, nobility of spirit.

'It was Keith,' we said, pointing at his bed.

'Right!' said Lewie. He got up and walked out of the room. Ten minutes later he was back, carrying the instruments of Keith's destruction.

'I've been to every toilet in the place to get these,' he said.

Common decency prevents me from revealing the nature of his revenge but it was swift and terrible. Keith, in a drunken stupor, didn't stir, but his first act upon waking was to rush to the nearest bathroom where he stayed for nigh-on three hours, removing at least three layers of skin. I'm told that, even now, he occasionally wakes in the middle of the night, dripping with sweat and screaming, re-living that terrible moment again and again.

11
what could be more pointless than playing a banjo?

When we got back to Llanelly things started to fall apart. The landlord of the Mansel, no doubt resenting the vast amounts of money we were taking on the door, decided to increase the rent by a substantial amount. We balked and threatened to take our business elsewhere. We tried to explain to him that people weren't coming to see the Mansel Hotel – they were coming to see the Corncrackers. But the landlord was adamant, so we pulled out. The Mansel wasn't the only pub in Llanelly.

We went to see the landlord of the Albion, another pub with a big backroom, who had always expressed an interest in poaching us from the Mansel. He was delighted and agreed immediately. We fly-posted the town, informing our audience of our change of address,

Our first and last night at the Albion was a disaster. The first signs were good. The house was full and we turned about two hundred people away – no change there, but I hoped they weren't the same two hundred we'd turned away from the Mansel. All went well until about halfway through the set. Then the complaints started coming in. The neighbours arrived in droves, whinging and moaning, We came off the stage to listen to their gripes. They couldn't hear their TVs. They couldn't hear each other talk. They couldn't even, they said, hear themselves think. I tried reasoning with them.

'I'm surprised that cultural imbeciles like yourselves would have any truck with thinking,' I said. 'Thinking is normally associated with the higher primates, which you are obviously not. If Elvis himself was playing here, backed by Beethoven, and supported by Ravel & his Boleros, you'd still complain. Whinge, whinge, whinge! You make me sick.'

Things went downhill from there. A scuffle broke out and the police were called.

'I don't think it's going to work,' said the landlord, sweeping up broken glass after the gig.

'You could be right,' said Keith. 'Never mind. We'll try somewhere else.'

But we didn't. We were overtaken by events. The Jets rang up Wes and asked him to join the band. Martin Ace was leaving to join the Brothers Grimm, who were the Vikings from Carmarthen with a new name and a new style. The wild R&B had been replaced by a more studied music, which included a complicated, harmony-laden version of Le Compagnion de la Chanson's 'Little Jimmy Brown'. I couldn't imagine Martin singing the bong-bong-bong-bongs with a straight face. But the clincher for Martin was that the Grimms had turned professional.

maybe i should've stayed in bed?

'I wanted to be a musician,' he explains. 'I wanted to play music for a living with like-minded people. The Jets all had jobs and they didn't want to give them up. If a gig came up in Germany, or London, or Torquay, I wanted to do it. I wanted to be a professional musician.'

Wes handed his notice into the Corncrackers and joined the Jets. Keith and I briefly discussed finding a new bass-player but we couldn't be bothered. Keith went back to betting on the horses (an area of life in which he can be said to approach genius) and I panicked.

I'd quickly got used to the life of a professional musician. Blessed is the artist who can devote twenty-four hours a day to perfecting his, or her, craft. Blessed is the artist who can spend twenty-four hours a day at the coal-face of creativity. Blessed is the artist who can spend twenty-four hours a day in bed. Blessed is the artist, full stop. But now I was alone, exposed to the chill winds of circumstance. What if I couldn't find another band? What if I had to get a proper job?

'Isn't it about time you got a job?' said my mother.

'I'm looking,' I said tetchily, preparing myself for the inevitable third-degree. 'I've had a few offers,' I lied, 'but most groups have already got guitar-players.'

'I mean a proper job. Wes works everyday in the hairdressers and plays in the night. Why can't you do that?'

'Because Wes works in the family business,' I said, explaining it for the millionth time. 'It's easy for him. He can take time off whenever he likes for out-of-town gigs. If I had a proper job they wouldn't let me take time off. I've got to be free to do gigs.'

'What gigs?' said my mother. 'I thought you didn't have any gigs.'

'Well, I don't at the moment,' I said, feeling like a drowning man, 'but I'm sure I will, in a minute.'

'You could ask Turners to take you back.'

'They wouldn't take me back. If I hadn't resigned they would have sacked me.'

'So you say.'

My mother has never believed me on this matter. She thinks I made up the story of my resignation because I was sacked for some heinous crime I won't admit to. She couldn't believe that Kalamazoo-neglect was a sacking offence. I tried to explain to her that I'd brought the firm to the brink of financial ruin, but she thought that was a just smokescreen I'd laid to prevent any further discussion of the subject. Some chance.

'You're an intelligent boy,' she said. 'You can't tell me that you were flummoxed by a filing system?'

'I wasn't flummoxed by it,' I said. 'I just couldn't be bothered. It seemed so pointless.'

'It may have been pointless, but they paid you to do it.'

'But we've only got one life, Mam. We shouldn't waste it doing pointless things.'

'And what could be more pointless than playing a banjo?' she said.

'It's not a banjo,' I said, almost giving up, 'it's a guitar. And it's not pointless.'

'So you don't want to do pointless things, do you?' she said, slowly and quietly.

what could be more pointless than playing a banjo?

Dark storm clouds moved in from the Atlantic and headed for 25 Frondeg Terrace. The Earth's core, no doubt belching molten lava, shuddered beneath my feet. The house lights, had they been on, would have flickered, I felt cold. And afraid.

'Right!' she said. 'The living room ceiling needs painting. Get cracking.'

Painting the living room ceiling was a task that even Hercules would have side-stepped.

'Sorry, Mrs L,' he'd have said. 'I can't do the ceiling today, I've got to clean out the Augean stables. I've been putting it off for ages.'

There was a shelf running around the living room, about a foot from the ceiling. On this shelf, at intervals of approximately a foot, were the collected ornaments of my parents' life. There was a full dinner set of Welsh crockery that had been in the family for centuries. It included three huge salvers (intended, no doubt, for boars' heads or shanks of venison), two gravy boats, hundreds of cups and saucers and a cake tray. There was a set of porcelain bulldogs, a League of Nations coffee pot with accompanying hot water jug, and a mysterious, black, oriental-looking vase embossed with gold dragons; mysterious because nobody, not even Grandpa, could remember where it had come from. Before the ceiling could be painted, these bloody heirlooms had to be carefully taken down – as if each item was the last brontosaurus egg – and washed. This alone took an hour. Then, and only then, could the ceiling be painted. When, hours later, it was finally done, the ornaments had to be replaced in exactly the same positions they had originally occupied. No matter how fastidious I was, I always ended up with something left over; usually one of the porcelain bulldogs. It was a pain in the neck and it took a whole day. A day I could have spent slaving over a hot guitar, crafting the music that would one day make the world dance. I tried to explain to my mother that she was robbing future generations of their musical heritage.

'The paint's in the cellar,' she said.

My mother has no poetry in her. I had to find another band. It was, much like atheism, a moral imperative..

12
more, roger, more!

Then the Jets phoned up. 'What're you up to?' asked Plum. 'Nothing much,' I said. 'Do you want to join the Jets?' he said. 'But you've already got a guitar-player,' I said. 'We want you to play piano. Wes says you're a good piano-player,' he said. Wes, bless him, thinks I can play the piano. 'I haven't got a piano,' I said. 'Buy one,' said Plum.

So I went down to Falcon Music and bought the only electric piano in the shop, a Hohner Pianet. It wasn't much to look at; it had screw-in legs and looked like a coffee table. That said, it wasn't a bad sound and, thus equipped, I faked my way through several rehearsals and did a few gigs. They were stormers. Plum suggested turning professional.

'I am professional,' I said.

'I know you are, Leonard,' said Plum, 'I'm talking about the rest of us.'

Everybody was in favour except Wes, who said he couldn't leave the family business. The ensuing discussion was heated but in the end we reached an agreement of sorts. Wes was allowed to continue working on condition he would take time off for out-of-town gigs.

'If he wants to cut hair in his spare time instead of lying in bed all day, that's up to him,' said Plum.

But way down deep it rankled. When a group of people decide to burn their respective boats and set out for uncharted seas, it is hardly surprising if *l'esprit de corps* suffers somewhat when a member of that company decides to keep one foot on the departing shore. (I know that burning your boats on the eve of a voyage into uncharted waters isn't the brightest course of action, but I am not famous for my common sense, although I am becoming increasingly well-known for my mangled metaphors.)

Once Martin heard that the Jets were turning professional he wanted to come back. He wasn't too happy with the Grimms, and the Grimms, it seemed, weren't too happy with him. He didn't like the music and relations with Mike Grimm, the singer, were becoming fractious. They suggested a straight swap – Ace for Wes. Wes agreed. He wasn't too happy with the Jets either. I think you could put it down to musical differences. The rot had begun to set in before I joined the group, during a Lionel Digby tour of the West Country. They got to one of the gigs early to learn a few new numbers. Wes, who has a penchant for big, romantic ballads, suggested doing 'The Wedding'. Billy Doc, the drummer, freaked.

'You must be fucking joking,' he said, throwing down his sticks and storming off to the dressing room. Plum followed him. Billy was outraged.

'I wouldn't be seen dead doing the fucking 'Wedding', he said, pacing up and down. 'There's something wrong with you boys.'

'Don't blame me,' said Plum. 'I didn't suggest doing the fucking song.'

more, roger, more!

I'd like to be able to tell you that we exchanged bass-players at night on the Lougher Bridge, with the Jets' van parked on the Swansea side and the Grimms' van parked on the Llanelly side, and that the two bass-players – in a perfect world, wearing fur hats – walked across the bridge, passing each other silently in the middle, before reaching the other end, to cheers and celebrations. But, I regret to say, there was no formal ceremony.

All it meant was that the Grimms didn't have to drive all the way to Swansea on gig nights to pick up and drop off Martin, and the Jets didn't have to drive all the way to Llanelly on gig nights to pick up and drop off Wes. Of course, they still had to drive all the way to Llanelly on gig nights to pick up and drop me off, but there seemed no way around that. Nevertheless, Plum assured me, he was working on it.

Keith, meanwhile, had joined Brian Breeze's group, the Casanovas – surely an ironic name.

The Jets were as busy as the Corncrackers had been, but the money wasn't as good. But it wasn't bad either. When I'd first met them, Plum and Martin both appeared to be forces of nature, although Plum had seemed the dominant, probably because he was the singer and therefore the front-man but, with the passage of time, it became apparent that Ace was the elemental force. Plum had his cut-off point but Ace didn't. There were occasions when Plum would say enough was enough, but Ace just kept on going. He was fearless. I was always delighted when Plum reached his cut-off point because it gave me an excuse for stopping too. Well, not stopping exactly, but the relief of not being the first to see sense was palpable. I felt, and still feel, duty-bound to follow Ace whenever he goes on one of his metaphysical jaunts. If you want an LBW decision, Don Quixote and Sancho Panza are pretty adjacent.

Ace can remember the exact moment he decided to become a musician. He was at a dance in the Pioneer Youth Club – 'a shed in Blackpill' – with his girlfriend, Jackie Williams. The band were terrible and Ace was slagging them off.

'Martin,' said Jackie, 'you're always moaning about the bands, If you think you can do better, buy a guitar.'

'OK,' said Martin, 'I will.' And he did.

John P, the Jets' guitarist, was quiet and handsome. He had his own personal following, exclusively girls, who would melt to nothing in his presence. In unguarded moments they would talk in hushed whispers about his magnificent bottom, and when he bent down to change the settings on his amp an audible, female sigh rippled across the audience.

Billy 'Doc' Evans, the band's drummer, was a rugged individualist amongst rugged individualists. He was called 'Doc' because he looked like an Oxford don – baleful eyes, looking out from behind owlish glasses, dominated a round face, framed in straggly hair. He had extremely strong views about the playing of rock'n'roll. These views were not subject to negotiation and most definitely did not include songs like 'The Wedding'.

'Billy didn't even want to do "Don't Think Twice, It's Alright",' recalls Martin. 'Anything with the slightest whiff of sentimentality was out the window.'

Billy had a standard drum-kit-of-the-day with two tom-toms, one rack and one floor. But he never touched the tom-toms. After a month or two I asked him why, if he didn't use them, he bothered to set them up?

'They came with the kit, mush,' he said

Billy's audition with the band had been a public affair. The Jets were playing at the Pioneer Club and Tony Court, their drummer, was on the verge of leaving because his wife didn't like him playing every night. Billy was in the audience. He was one of the Mumbles Boys, the local biker gang.

'He was one of the leather jackets,' says Martin. 'When they came in it was "Look out, there's gonna be a scrap." I always had Billy down for being a really hard bastard. Little did I know.'

During an inter-song chat with the audience, Plum happened to mention that the band were looking for a new drummer.

'Any drummers in the audience?' he asked, not expecting a response.

'Yeah,' shouted a voice.

Cheered on by the Mumbles Boys, Billy climbed on to the stage, walked up to Tony Court and held out his hand. Meekly, Tony handed over his sticks.

'Billy got on the drums and nobody would tell him to get off because he was with all his mates,' says Martin. 'He went "Boom-bang-boom-bang-boom-bang" in Billy's style. And he didn't alter it at all. He was exactly the same when he joined the band as when he left it, and he's probably exactly the same now.'

Martin's audition, at the Gwent Boxing Club, had been brief but effective. The Jets were looking for a bass-player but Martin was a guitarist. Plum wanted him in the band but John P wasn't too keen, on the reasonable grounds that Martin wasn't a bass-player and had no track record as such. Plum took Martin aside.

'Look,' he said, 'you learn "I'll Never Get Over You" on the bass and I'll suggest it at the audition.'

Martin learnt it off pat. At the audition, Plum got the ball rolling.

'Let's do something,' he said. He turned to Martin. '"I'll Never Get Over You". Have you heard that?'

'Go on then,' said Martin, and played it perfectly.

'All right,' said John P, impressed. 'We'll have him.'

'I'm glad he didn't suggest playing anything else,' said Plum, 'or Martin would have been out the door.'

The Jets gig circuit was quite small and concentrated around the Swansea area, with the occasional jaunt down west to the Black Lion in Cardigan – The Land That Time Forgot. We needed to widen our scope of operations. We decided to venture further afield. So we started to probe in the east, into the grimy, demonic hills and valleys of the Rhondda. Inevitably, this brought us into further contact with the Kings of Merthyr – the Bystanders. We found ourselves sharing a stage with them on a semi-regular basis. We got along like a venue on fire and took the piss out of each other mercilessly. It was a good night out for the punters; the lush precision of the Bystanders contrasting nicely with the raucous, no-nonsense anarchy of the Jets. We decided to learn some of the Bystanders' big numbers, just to show them

more, roger, more!

how it was done, We picked 'I Get Around' by the Beach Boys and 'Walk Like A Man' by the Four Seasons. We tried them out in rehearsal. It was a disaster. We were like boxers trying to be ballet dancers. But we persevered and licked them into some sort of shape.

The next time we played with the them, we opened up with 'I Get Around'. It was still pretty ropey and some of the audience had to be sedated but what we lacked in vocal dexterity we made up for in panache. The Bystanders watched open-mouthed, stunned, whether by our capricious daring or our matchless stupidity, it was hard to tell.

Then they went on and did our set, opening up with 'You Can't Judge A Book By Looking At The Cover.' This was a surprise. Freed from the strictures of classic American pop, they howled, and Micky Jones was particularly abstract on the guitar. They were, it seemed, ballet-dancers who packed a punch – a cross between Rudolf Nureyev and Roberto Duran; or, we preferred to think, Wayne Sleep and Joe Bugner.

I lasted about six months with the Jets. Then shards of darkness began to stab into the sun-drenched uplands of my artistic soul. I was becoming increasingly unhappy. The company was excellent but I was getting fed up with the piano. I'm not a proper piano-player, I'm a heavy-handed vamper. I can manage a chord or two but I require at least two weeks notice to do a solo. Sometimes Plum – who, at the best of times, teetered on the brink of chaos – would turn to me, when least expected, and order me to play a solo. I'd be fine for about half the sequence, when I would be overtaken by my lack of talent. In the grip of panic I'd thrash away at the keys, making the most awful racket. I'd reach the end of the solo at roughly the same time I'd reach the outer limits of my ability and be overwhelmed by a sense of relief. This rarely lasted. Plum would suddenly appear in front of me, pointing maniacally at the piano and yelling: 'MORE, ROGER. MORE!' The next solo would be the same as the last one, only this time stripped of all coherence. Plum would sometimes demand a third solo. This wasn't even music. I developed a siege mentality and, under the guise of minimalism, played purposefully repetitive solos, sometimes spinning the same riff out from beginning to end.

'I hate those flowery keyboard players,' I'd say, if asked. 'They're so obvious.'

But, inside, I felt like I was wearing someone else's shoes. I'm a guitar-player. I don't have to think when I'm playing guitar.

I still saw Wes regularly. He wasn't happy with the Grimms either. They were, it seemed, on the brink of extinction. When the talk turned to money we discovered that we were earning about half of what we used to make with the Corncrackers. Wes mentioned that he still had phonecalls, three or four a week, from promoters trying to book the band. We went to see Keith. He wasn't too happy with the Casanovas. I'm sure that there must have been some excellent reasons for us not to reform but we couldn't, off the top of our heads, think of any. So I handed my notice in to the Jets, Wes finished with the Grimms and Keith jacked in the Casanovas.

The Corncrackers were back on the road.

13
the committee-man cometh

I do enjoy a good seismic shake-up, but it has its ups and downs. It's not the easiest thing in the world to leave a band you love – I know, I've done it hundreds of times. Cutting your fingers off to spite your technique, so to speak. If I had a technique. But then, on the upside, there is all the rushing about. The Keystone Cops-like transference of amplifiers and drums from one van to another. Or, in this case, three vans. And the concentrated rehearsals. There's nothing quite so invigorating as playing the guitar for eighteen hours a day, six days a week. It is an immutable Law of Nature that no matter how much rehearsal time you decide on, it is never quite enough. You could always do with another day or two. This time we could have done with another year or two.

We'd decided to change our style completely. Out went the wild rock'n'roll and in came close-harmony pop, inspired, no doubt, by the Bystanders. Out went Mississippi and in came California. This meant learning an entirely new set, complete with intricate vocal harmonies. With only three voices, the four-part constructions, like the Beach Boys' 'Good Vibrations', were a little tricky. Wes might sing the 5th harmony on the first part of a sequence, then change to the lead on the next section, and then swoop down to the bass part for the last two notes. Keith might sing the 3rd harmony on the first part of a sequence, drop down to the bass-part on the central section and then finish off with a high falsetto. And I, going up and down the register like a howler monkey with hiccups, might act as a sweeper, blocking any holes I spotted along the way. Individually, we sounded ridiculous. Together, we sounded magnificent. There was no time for breathing, of course, but there's a lot of nonsense talked about breathing technique for singers. I'm told that Frank Sinatra's technique was so advanced he could breathe in whilst singing a note. I've tried it myself. I can do it in theory but the best sound I can produce is a wheezing honk. We used the tried and trusted Welsh method – take a huge gulp of air at the beginning of the verse and hope it lasts until the end. Now and again an eye would pop out of its socket, but that's an occupational hazard, isn't it?

And then there's the long, convoluted discussions, well into the night, about the bloody set list. You have to open the show with a bang then, while they're recovering, you slip in all the dodgy numbers; the ones that don't quite yet gel. During these songs it is advisable to jump around as much as possible, in the hope of distracting the discerning listener from the essential crappiness of the music and its execution. Then, at the precise moment that the audience's restlessness turns into ugly revolt, you start to build to a spectacular finale, bunching all the show-stoppers back-to-back, uninterrupted by announcements and introductions, until

the committee-man cometh

the band and audience, now a single, elemental force, enter into a state of rock'n'roll bliss. This is a state wherein anything is possible, including the possibility that some things are impossible. A state wherein time becomes just one damn thing after another. Here is deliverance from mundanity. Here is elevation to the firmament. Got catharsis if you want it?

Well, that's the theory. Unless you're playing at the Regal, Ammanford, where their idea of bliss is to kick seven kinds of shit out of some farmer from Llannon. This is a state where anything is possible, including the possibility that an innocent guitarist can be rendered senseless by a well-aimed beer bottle. Although the punters were obliged to check in their weapons at the door, this could not be relied upon. Their native cunning always meant that some Strongbow-addled neanderthal would manage to smuggle in a kitchen knife, usually in his sock. A favourite weapon, especially for girls, was a sugar-cube. During a melee, a slash across the face with the serrated edge of a sugar-cube caused a jagged cut that would bleed forever. Then they could eat the offensive weapon. No weapon, no crime. Every time there was a gig at the Regal, Tate & Lyle shares went through the roof.

None of the bands that played the Regal went unarmed. We all had our favoured weapons, mine being a substantial hammer which I kept on top of my amp, just in case. Pugwash, the drummer with the Vikings, had a meat-hook which he hung, out of the audience's sight, on the back of his floor tom-tom. Any members of the audience stupid enough to venture on to the stage – and the candidates were legion – were greeted by a snarling Pugwash, waving a meat-hook, shouting, 'Die, Fuckdog! Die!' No matter how profound the depth of their stupidity, even the most belligerent Ammanforder would meekly return to the audience, there to stand, looking sheepish, until his eyes, once again, lost their focus and he headed, once again, for the bar.

It has always surprised me that the music industry – usually so adept at wringing the last drop of financial blood from the most bankrupted stone – hasn't moved into weaponry specifically designed for the jobbing musician. The Fender claw-hammer, the Marshall knuckle-duster, the Vox gas-gun, the Gretsch battery-operated castrator. Come on, boys, there's a fortune to be made here. But what can you expect from an industry that considers Cliff Richard a serious artist?

My favourite Pugwash incident happened at a Cops'n'Robbers' gig at the Tivoli Ballroom in Mumbles. Cops'n'Robbers, a London band, were a sort of second-hand Downliners Sect, who themselves were a sort of second-hand Pretty Things. I was watching them from the foyer door at the back of the hall. Just in front of me, also watching, stood Pugwash and a local girl, holding hands. Pugwash, eyes fixed on the stage, was nodding in time with the music, but the girl, obviously pissed, was swaying alarmingly. Suddenly, her knees buckled and she collapsed in a heap. Pugwash, engrossed in the band, didn't notice and continued to hold her hand. I waited for him to notice but he was miles away. I sauntered over.

'Aren't you going to introduce me?' I shouted in his ear.

'Oh, yes,' he said, 'this is…' He turned to the girl but she wasn't there. You could see his brain struggling to rationalise the conflicting messages – she should be there because he was still holding her hand, but all the visual indications were that she'd gone. I pointed down at her. Pugwash, frowning, followed my finger.

'Jesus Christ!' he said. He bent to pick her up but she was dead-weight. I helped and we carried her into the foyer. The fresh air soon brought her round. She was a very strange colour, but I assume no lasting damage was done because, ten minutes later, they were back in the hall, dancing furiously.

I have an enduring memory of the Regal Ammanford which keeps me warm in the long, cold watches of the night. While we were playing, the foyer door burst open and a local luminary swaggered in. He was wearing a small, black, cardboard, cowboy hat; the kind you might buy at the seaside. On the front of the hat, in silver letters, was written: 007 – SECRET AGENT. He stood there, hands on hips, scrutinising the crowd, like a hungry wolf sizing up a herd of passing elk, looking for the weak, the infirm, the helplessly drunk. He stood there for about three seconds – the King of Ammanford – until a haymaker, thrown by an enormous farmer wearing a suit at least three sizes too small, caught him squarely on the jaw, catapulting him back through the foyer door. The door swung shut behind him and the crowd carried on dancing as if nothing had happened. Well, I say dancing, but it was more like moving your arms and legs around in no particular direction and bumping into each other. In Ammanford, dancing was a contact sport.

But thankfully Ammanford wasn't on the up-coming gig sheet. We had other things to worry about. Not least stage clothes. We scanned the Lewis Leathers catalogue for inspiration and sent away for three matching, sleeveless, black leather coalman-jackets. Worn with white, polo-neck jumpers, dove-grey, slimline trousers, and set off by white, Cuban-heeled boots ordered from Annello & Davide, we would look like rock'n'roll gods. Or, depending on your angle of vision, distressed penguins.

You drive to the first gig. A general exuberance is evident, broken only by long periods of silence when everybody's running through possible pitfalls ahead. Little grey areas in the set. That tricky little guitar part that you fucked up every time you played it in rehearsal. The tortuous harmony that sounded brilliant the one and only time you got it right, despite the fact that you tried it a hundred times. The mountain of new lyrics to learn. You've got the first two verses down pat, but how the hell does the third verse start? Oh well, sing the first verse again. Nobody'll notice.

The first gig is always chaos. With so much to think about, time passes quickly and you're back in the dressing room, dripping with sweat, before you know it. How long did we play? An hour? Are you sure? It seemed like ten minutes.

Once again, the work flooded in. I'd like to think that it was something to do with our new style but it was more to do with our reputation amongst promoters that our appearance would guarantee them a full house. This is an observation not a complaint. We still had full houses, we still went down a storm, we always got rebooked, and we still earned more money than any other local band, so we had nothing to moan about. But musicians love a good moan. We're never satisfied. We want to be appreciated for our creative daring, not for our incidental appeal to a fickle public. Popularity, we maintain, is no barometer of worth. Terrible bands, who

the committee-man cometh

have a string of hits, long for critical acclaim, and terrific bands, who have the critics rolling over in ecstasy but make no impact on the charts, yearn for a Rolls Royce or two. It is in the nature of things.

We were booked to do a Christmas gig at Cwmllynfell Workingmen's Club. Cwmllynfell is an arrondissement of Upper Cwmtwrch, a place I thought was a fictional town invented by Welsh comics to symbolise the outer limits of civilisation but, apparently, it was real. It was new territory for us so our agency, Verney Ley Enterprises, had agreed on an introductory fee of £14. Verney would take his ten per cent, leaving us with £12.10s. Hardly a fortune but not bad for a Thursday gig.

We were welcomed by a committee-man. Every Welsh workingman's club is run by a committee. Apart from monthly committee meetings the members are never seen together, thereby making it nigh-on impossible to determine how many there are at any given time. During the course of the evening you will have to deal with at least four of them, all, apparently, in supreme command. They are always men and they are always elderly. They are secretive by nature and defensive by habit, and usually subscribe to the view that the general public are a necessary evil. They didn't understand this new-fangled, rock'n'roll razzmatazz but their younger patrons demanded it, so they had to provide it, but that didn't mean they had to like it. They regarded all bands as the spawn of Satan, somewhere, on the social scale, between arsonists and child-molesters. We were barbarians at the gates, and they treated us with an almost paranormal caution. This one was typical of the breed.

'You're not going to play too loud, are you?' he said welcomingly.

'No,' said Wes. 'Some clubs complain because we're too quiet.'

'That's all right, then,' said the committee-man, confirming that irony had yet to reach this far up the valleys. 'There's the stage,' he added, pointing at a minuscule platform, a foot-high, dominated by a large Christmas tree, covered in lights and topped-off with a fairy. 'You haven't got lots of equipment, have you?'

'No,' said Wes. 'We won't be using our amps tonight, we'll only use one drum, and we'll whisper the vocals. OK?'

'Good,' said the committee-man, obviously relieved. Maybe we weren't as bad as he'd expected. Maybe it was time to be magnanimous? 'Do you want me to move the Christmas tree over to give you a bit more room?' He smiled for the first time.

'That'd be nice,' said Wes. 'By the way, have you got any daughters?'

'Yes,' said the committee-man. 'One.'

'Is she coming tonight?'

'Yes,' said the committee-man. 'Why?'

'No reason,' said Wes, rubbing his hands together and giving a leer that Bluebeard would have been proud of.

The committee-man, eyeing Wes suspiciously, moved the Christmas tree over to the side of the stage and hurriedly left the room.

'I'm just going to make a phonecall,' he said as he left.

'I bet he's going to warn off his daughter,' said Wes.

When the gear was set up, Wes plugged in and tested his amp. The committee-

maybe i should've stayed in bed?

man returned and stood watching us.

'Those Christmas tree lights won't sap your power, will they?' he said.

'I think it'll be all right,' said Wes, 'but we'd better test them. Switch them on for a minute.'

The committee-man stepped on to the stage and stood next to the power point. He switched the lights on. Wes played a few notes.

'Right,' he said, 'switch them off.' The committee-man switched them off. Wes played a few more notes, bending down and listening to his speakers. 'Now, switch them on again.'

The committee-man did as he was told. Wes played a few more notes.

'I think it'll be all right,' said Wes, 'but when we play you'd better stand by the plug, just in case.'

The committee-man began to lose his temper. 'I can't stand here all night,' he said, 'I've got things to do.'

'OK,' said Wes, shaking his head, 'Be it on your own head.'

'Look,' said the committee-man, 'I'll just switch them off now and leave them off. It'll save a lot of trouble.'

'Won't the punters complain if the lights aren't on?' said Wes.

'Well, they will,' said the committee-man, torn between art and commerce, 'but I'll explain to them that it was sapping your power.' He left the room, shaking his head.

'You almost feel sorry for 'em, don't you?' said Wes.

'Almost,' said Keith,

Once the gear was set up, we sat around the empty club and waited for the punters to arrive. For a while we watched the barman – an eighteen-stone, pinch-eyed creature who would have given Darwin pause for thought – trying to work out how to open the till. We took bets on how long it would take him. Keith, who has a knack for these things, won with a time of eight minutes.

To help pass the time, Wes told us a story about Sherlock, a some-time road manager, who had been banned from driving for two years.

'He was nine times over the legal limit.' he said.

'Sherlock was five times over the legal limit when he was born,' I said, unaware that one day Sherlock would try to murder me.

Then Keith, who is easily bored, picked up a beer-mat off a nearby table and lobbed it at me. I, just as easily bored, threw one back. Wes, who doesn't like to be left out of things, picked up two or three and frisbeed them in our general direction. Then we picked them up and put them back on the tables. It killed a minute or two.

The gig went well and the punters, unlike the committee, certainly knew the score. Occasionally the committee-man would appear at the front of the stage and asked Wes if he could switch the Christmas tree lights on for a while. The answer was always the same.

'Better not,' said Wes. 'Just in case.'

While we were loading the gear into the van, the committee-man appeared again.

'I've had a complaint about you,' he said solemnly.

the committee-man cometh

'Too loud, were we?' said Keith, ostentatiously dropping his bass-drum case.

'No,' said the committee man. 'Well, yes, you were too loud, but that's not the complaint.'

We waited for the Upper Cwmtwrch Inquisition to get to the point.

'I've had a complaint that before you played you were throwing beer-mats around. Is that right?'

We looked at the barman, who was pretending to wash beer glasses.

'Oh, God,' said Wes, putting his head in his hands. 'You've caught us bang to rights, guv'nor. We'll come quietly.' He thrust his hands forward to be cuffed.

'There's no need for that,' said the committee-man, 'but don't do it again.'

'Again?' said Wes. 'Does that mean you want to re-book us?'

'Yes,' said the committee-man. 'We had a good night. Apart from the beer-mat throwing incident, of course. But there's just one thing.'

'I know,' I said. 'You want us to bring our own beer-mats?'

'No,' said the committee-man, 'it's about the money.'

'What about the money?' said Wes, eyes narrowing.

'Well,' said the committee-man, 'you're getting £14 for tonight but you've got to pay Verney Ley his ten per cent, which means you're really getting £12.10s, aren't you?'

'Ye-es.' said Wes.

'Well, what if we booked you direct for £13. We'd get you a pound cheaper and you'd make ten shillings more. Cut out the middle man, see?' His eyes glinted with duplicity.

'Hang on,' said Wes. 'Let me work this out. We'd get ten shillings more. Split three ways that would mean we'd get three shillings and thruppence each, given a farthing or two.' He looked at Keith and I. 'How about it, boys? What do you think?'

'It's a tempting offer,' said Keith.

'If we pooled the money we could save it up and buy a new PA system,' I said. 'It would only take us, ooh, fifty years or so?'

'We'll have to have a band meeting about this,' said Wes, putting a friendly hand on the committee-man's shoulder. 'We'll have to get back to you, OK?'

'OK,' said the committee-man, delighted. 'We'll cut out the middle man, see?'

The committee-man counted out 14 pound notes into Wes's hand, winking conspiratorially. We finished loading the gear into the van. Just before we drove off, the committee-man appeared at the driver's window.

'Think about what I've said now, boys, and we'll forget about the beer-mat throwing incident, OK?' He put his thumbs up and gave us a huge wink. We put our thumbs up, winked back, and drove off.

'I've a suggestion,' I said, as we headed for civilisation. 'Let's not play in Upper Cwmtwrch again.'

'Not on your life,' said Wes. 'It's a gig.'

' Yeah, and that three and thruppence might come in handy one day,' said Keith.

How right he was.

14
a perfect right-hook

We played up-country in Lampeter. I'd never been there before. I was looking forward to it because it was the remotest outpost of the Leonard family. I had three cousins living there. They were all housemasters at Lampeter College so, in my mind's eye, I envisaged a town of stately academic halls and wide boulevards decked in autumn leaves, down which strolled people with large brains contemplating the great conundrums of existence. The town straddles the Teifi river so I imagined boatloads of scholars, with eager faces yet unsullied by the cynicism that comes with experience, punting up and down the river. The only sounds would be the gurgling of the river, the cackling of water-fowl, and the occasional gentle laughter of erudite souls.

Our ambulance was in for a service so Ron, Keith's father, agreed to take us in his new Bedford Caravanette. This was an opportunity for Mary, Keith's sister, and Beth, Wes's sister, both nudging adolescence, to come to their first gig. If Ron, a responsible adult and a father to boot, was present then, the girls reasoned, what could go wrong?

'No,' said Wes to Beth, 'you're not bloody coming. You're too young.'

'But Mary's going,' said Beth. 'She asked Keith and he said yes.'

Wes, trapped, had to agree.

'No,' said Keith to Mary, 'you're not bloody coming. You're too young.'

'But Beth's going,' said Mary. 'She asked Wes and he said yes.'

Keith, trapped, had to agree.

I, mercifully sisterless, watched all this with some suspicion. This could set a precedent. This could be the thin end of the wedge. We were a professional band doing a job, but if this situation were allowed to develop our gigs would soon become family outings. On principle, I didn't believe that relatives should be allowed on gigs. If they got there under their own steam and paid to get in then fair enough, but take them with us? But I had no choice in the matter. The girls had staged a *fait accompli*.

'Well,' said Keith, 'if Mary and Beth are coming, then I might as well bring Andrea.' Andrea was Keith's girlfriend.

See what I mean? These things escalate. Taken to its logical conclusion this could result in my mother demanding to come along.

'Well,' she would say, 'if Keith and Wes are taking their sisters and girlfriends along, I don't see why you can't take your mother.'

All right, this is a worst-case scenario but, I think you will agree, it doesn't bear thinking about.

a perfect right-hook

So we set off for Lampeter. I was in a grumpy mood. How was I, a serious musician, supposed to concentrate on preparing myself for my upcoming performance with all this chatter and giggling going on. The girls, to be fair, weren't too bad but Keith, with a girlfriend to impress, was in coquettish overdrive. I drew heavily on my inner strength and pretended I was somewhere else.

Lampeter was not the dreaming spires of my imagination. It was just another pretty, little market town. We found the gig, which was in the town hall, and started offloading the gear. We were met by the promoter who said there wouldn't be many people in at the start but once the pubs shut the place would be jumping. The first punters filed in. I was filled with foreboding. They were not the capped and gowned scholars of my fancy – they were ruddy-faced young farmers, already the worse for drink, who jostled and shoved each other around the empty hall, shouting in guttural Welsh.

There were only about thirty in when we started, but at least twenty-nine of them were looking for trouble, The girls were worse than the boys. Farmers' daughters were terrifying creatures. Strong-limbed and disgustingly healthy, they were more than a match for a soft towny like me and even a friendly pat on the shoulder from one of them could result in serious muscular damage. And if you fucked one, her cries of ecstasy were in Welsh.

Almost as soon as we started, a bunch of blokes gathered in front of me, making threatening gestures and inviting me, with elaborate boxing mimes, to come down off the stage and fight them. At first I ignored them but they persisted and by the end of the set they were beginning to get on my nerves. I stomped back to the dressing-room in a foul mood.

'I've had enough of this,' I said to Wes. 'Let's go and sort them out.'

They were still standing in a huddle by the stage and we walked over to them. When they saw us coming they fanned out like gunfighters. I walked up to the ringleader.

'What's your problem, pal?' I said.

He didn't answer. Maybe he didn't speak English? He did look surprised. He inclined his head away from me, fearing, no doubt, a head-butt, and muttered something in Welsh. Then he threw a punch.

I ducked but it caught me on the left ear. The red mist came down. I caught him with a perfect right-hook which spun him 360 degrees. As he came around to face me again, I hit him with another right and he dropped like a stone. There was total silence. Then a girl's voice.

'What a punch,' it said.

I stood over the unconscious cro-magnon, fists cocked. I looked at his mates who didn't move a muscle.

'Anybody else?' I enquired.

They shook their heads. Our work completed, Wes and I retired to the dressing room, feeling like John ap Wayne and Kirk ap Douglas.

By eleven o'clock the place was indeed jumping. It was like Tombstone on a Saturday night. When they weren't fighting, they were vomiting. While we were

maybe i should've stayed in bed?

playing, Mary, Beth and Andrea sat huddled together on a row of chairs running down the left-hand side of the hall. We had advised them to stay in the dressing room but – women being more intelligent than men – they had dismissed our advice and entered the lions' den. They weren't bothered for a while but then the locals began to sniff the air. Clearly agitated, they pawed the ground. Then one of them spotted the girls. Warily, he approached. He nervously scuttled back a couple of yards when Andrea made a sudden movement toward her handbag, but he soon plucked up courage again and continued his advance. When he was within hearing distance he shouted an invitation to dance in the general direction of the girls. Andrea, assuming it was directed at her, politely declined. He stood there, frowning. Then he started shouting again. Andrea continued shaking her head but he wouldn't take no for an answer. Keith, watching like a hawk from his drumstool, leaned into his microphone.

'Oi, shithead,' he shouted, 'Leave my girlfriend alone!'

Things went downhill from there. The citizens of Lampeter, united by a common enemy – namely, a mouthy, out-of-town drummer – gathered at the front of the stage and bayed for his blood.

'We're really in trouble here,' shouted Keith above the din.

'What do you mean "we"?' shouted Wes.

'I think he means him and his mouth,' I yelled.

But, apart from dodging the odd beer bottle, we finished the night without further incident. We didn't go down too well, but we sort of expected that. Ron, who'd hustled the girls into the dressing room with orders to stay put, was straining at the leash at the side of the stage, ready to get the gear out as fast as possible. The house lights went up but the mob didn't move, preferring to hurl abuse at Ron packing up the gear. We changed quickly and returned to the stage. Things had calmed down a little. The mob had begun to drift away, throwing the occasional shouted obscenity over their shoulders as they left. Relieved it was all over, we packed the gear in some humour. Then the promoter appeared, looking a little grey.

'They're all waiting outside for you,' he said. 'I wouldn't take your equipment out for a bit, if I were you.'

'They'll soon get fed up,' I said.

'You don't know young farmers,' he said. 'They won't leave until milking time, and that's about five o'clock. You can stay here for the night, if you like?'

'No thanks,' I said, 'but we'll leave it for a while.'

We waited half-an-hour but they didn't move. We risked a glance through the glass front doors. but they saw us and started howling.

'Right!' said Ron, a World War Two veteran, 'Bugger this.'

He immediately went into NCO mode. He ordered us to bring all the gear into the foyer and get ready to load the van. He would create a diversion by opening the side door of the hall and making a lot of noise, thereby drawing the Germans – sorry, the young farmers – away from the front door, allowing us to get the gear and the girls into the caravanette. We stacked the gear in the corner of the foyer,

a perfect right-hook

just out of the mob's eye-line and waited. Ron opened the side door and found himself in an alley where, to his delight, he found some dustbins. He started banging two dustbin lids together and shouting. We, watching the mob through the glass doors, saw the mob, as one, turn their heads toward the sound. They were like the crowd at a very short tennis match in Purgatory. Then, on a shout, they rushed off to find the source of the sound and kill it.

The promoter unlocked the front doors and Wes made a run for the Bedford, parked across the road. He pulled the caravanette around in front of the foyer. The girls went in first, then we started throwing the gear in the back. The diversion worked, but not for long. As soon as the mob reached the side door, Ron nipped back inside, locked the door and ran to the foyer. The mob, realising they had been duped, turned around and ran back to the front of the building. We only had half the gear in the van. All looked lost. Suddenly Ron appeared and – using crowd-control techniques perfected, no doubt, during the Italian campaign – kept the mob back while we finished getting the gear in the van.

I picked up the last amp in the foyer and headed for the glass doors. One of the mob, a crumpled meat-head grinning from ear to ear, stood outside. He opened one of the doors and gestured me through. Ah, I thought, a globule of cool water in an unforgiving desert. A man with sensibilities. Disgusted by the behaviour of his peer group, this man had decided that enough was enough. This good Samaritan come down to Lampeter had decided to reach out a helping hand to a fellow human being in his time of vexation. I grinned back and stepped through. As I did so, he slammed the door shut. The glass shattered and I dropped the amp. For a moment I stood there at the epicentre of a whirlwind of flying glass. Then I felt a pain in my left hand. I looked down. My hand, which had caught the full impact of the door, was porcupined with shards of glass and bleeding alarmingly. Very gingerly, I started to pull them out. Then Ron, with that coolness under fire which is the hallmark of the professional warrior, appeared carrying a towel. I have no idea where he got it from. He dispatched the meat-head with a right jab that didn't travel more than three inches, wrapped my hand in the towel, and escorted me to the van, where Wes was fighting a rearguard action using a microphone stand. Ron went back for the amp. He threw it in the back of the van.

'That's it!' he shouted. 'Everybody into the van!'

Now all that remained was getting Keith out of the toilet, where he'd been hiding since the end of the set. Ron disappeared into the building and the mob surrounded the van and started rocking it. Five minutes later Ron returned with Keith, still dressed in his stage clothes, and the mob, recognising the root cause of the trouble, closed in for the kill. Ron, dragging his bloody son behind him, fought his way through to the van. He bundled Keith into the back and barged his way around to the driver's door. He climbed in and started the engine. But he couldn't move. The mob were packed in close to the van, rocking it and yelling. To drive off might cause serious injury. The mob started rhythmically banging the van and chanting in Welsh.

'Sod this for a game of soldiers,' said Ron, putting the van into gear. He jammed

maybe i should've stayed in bed?

his foot down on the accelerator pedal and the caravanette shot forward. Bodies flew everywhere and we seemed to be driving over railway sleepers. Ignoring the screams of agony, we were soon clear and on the road to Llanelly. Keith wasn't quite as coquettish as he had been on the outward journey, preferring to sit quietly with his head resting on Andrea's shoulder.

I didn't say much either. The bleeding had stopped and I spent most of the journey picking the remaining bits of glass out of my hand. I expected some sympathy.

'Will you still be able to play?' said Wes. 'We've got a gig tomorrow night.'

Dear old Wes. Always has my welfare at heart, does Wes.

'Yes, I'll be able to play,' I said. 'I'll drag my shattered, blood-stained body onstage tomorrow night and, even though I'll be writhing in agony, I'll deliver the goods.'

'That's all right then,' said Wes.

And I didn't miss a gig, because all the injuries were to the back of my hand. I found I could still bend my fingers, albeit somewhat painfully. So, the next night, I dragged my shattered, blood-stained body onstage and, even though I was writhing in agony, I delivered the goods. What a professional. Well, any musician worth their salt would do the same. wouldn't they?

15
i am forced to write a song

We went to Cardiff to do an audition for 'Ready, Steady, Win', a TV talent show. The TV people didn't like us and we were fobbed off but while we were there I was approached by a chap who said he worked for Keith Prowse, the music publisher. He'd liked an original song we'd played called 'You Don't Know' and wanted to know who'd written it. I told him I'd written it. He said I should put it on tape and send it to his head office. He gave me the address and said if I had any more songs I should send them too. I told him I had hundreds of songs. He said four would do.

I'd been writing songs for years but none of them sounded like real songs to me. The trouble was that they all sounded as if I'd written them and I wanted to write songs that sounded as if somebody else had written them. I'd never suggested doing any of them but I'd reluctantly agreed to do one for the TV audition, because majority opinion seemed to suggest that it would give us an edge. It didn't, but it did excite some interest from a big London publisher. I experienced qualified euphoria.

I selected three of my least embarrassing songs to go with 'You Don't Know' and played them to Keith and Wes. I found it an excruciatingly uncomfortable experience. To my utter astonishment they liked them. So now all we had to do was record them. Easier said than done. We didn't know anyone who had a tape-recorder. Then Joss came to the rescue.

Joss was a Llanelly sax-player. And not just any old sax-player. Joss had once played with the Joe Loss Orchestra but had been forced into early retirement by severe arthritis. He returned home and got a job in the Falcon music shop. He had a reel-to-reel tape-recorder. He offered to tape us and suggested we use our regular rehearsal room as the location. Our regular rehearsal room was the Hodge Bicycle and Model Shop.

They were not tranquil occasions. Ron just about tolerated our existence. cursing us to high heaven and never missing a chance to remind us that we were useless creatures incapable of performing the most simple of tasks. He repeatedly disowned us but we took this with a pinch of salt because the word seldom suited the action, and when the van broke down on the way home from a gig, as it often did, he was always the one who would come and rescue us, whatever the time or distance involved, still cursing us to high heaven. Min, Keith's mother, would be actively involved in our rehearsals, pointing out mistakes, arbitrating during disagreements, and providing an endless supply of tea and biscuits, while sister Mary and her teenage friends, decked out in the latest Biba fashions, provided instant feedback, signalling their approval by dancing and their disapproval by derisive laughter.

The recording went without a hitch, although Min had to be ejected at an early stage for criticising, at some length, my diction.

'I can't understand the words,' she said. 'What's the point in having lyrics if you can't hear them properly?'

'I'm slurring for effect,' I said.

'Well, it's not a very good effect,' she said. 'Sing them properly.'

So we locked her in the back room of the shop. In between takes we could hear her muffled cries, still complaining she couldn't understand the words.

'Bloody women,' said Ron.

I sent the completed tape to Keith Prowse Music Publishing Co. Ltd. and allowed myself a little cautious optimism. Two weeks later they sent it back, with an accompanying letter. They thanked me for sending the tape. They had, they said, played it to several recording managers but, they were sorry to report, it didn't suit their requirements. They further thanked me for my prompt reply to their correspondence.

I was gutted. In my heart of hearts I knew this was going to happen. I shouldn't have allowed myself a shred of optimism. Optimism is one of the banes of humanity – it is better to be a delighted pessimist rather than a disappointed optimist. Believe it after it's happened, but assume it won't. I blotted out all thoughts of fame and fortune and resigned myself to being a big fish in a little pond.

But there was plenty to do to distract from my essential worthlessness. Our gig sheet was brimming with work and were always re-booked, although we were starting to get complaints. And it was always the same complaint – there were only three of us. It was a common prejudice among promoters that the minimum number of people required for the production of rock'n'roll music was four. We were a three-piece, therefore, ipso facto, deficient. We sounded good and we looked good but, they said, something wasn't right. This was a smokescreen. The truth was they felt cheated. They were paying for four people but they were only getting three. At first we bloody-mindedly stuck to our guns but the constant drip-drip of criticism finally wore us down. We decided to get another musician in just to shut them up. We decided to get another guitarist. We decided to get Brian Breeze.

I hadn't heard him play guitar but apparently he was something of a virtuoso. I'm always suspicious of virtuosos – or should it be virtuosi? – because they are usually so intoxicated by their own ability that they often forget the big picture. I'd been at school with Brian but because he was three years behind me and, as such, a junior, we didn't mix socially. I may have given him the odd clip around the back of the head when passing him in the corridor, but who knows? What is one clip amongst many? The word around school was that he was good. Even as good as me, some said. No chance, I thought. I held the belief, then, that age had a direct bearing on talent, so I dismissed reports of his prowess with disdain because he was younger than me and therefore inferior. But, as Plato rightly maintained, the

i am forced to write a song

seeds of Mankind's downfall lie in the gulf between belief and knowledge, and life soon put me right. Age is only important to the young.

Incidentally, Samuel Johnson's excellent dictionary defines a breeze as a gentle gale, which, if applied to Brian, amounts to a character reference. We invited him to join the Corncrackers and he accepted. We went into intensive rehearsals but before we could do a gig I had a phonecall. It was the Blackjacks.

16
the blackjacks

The Blackjacks offered me a job as bass-player. 'I'm not a bass-player,' I said. 'If you can play guitar, you can play bass,' they said. Not strictly true. In theory perhaps, but certainly not in practice. Bass-playing is too much like hard work for your common-or-garden guitarist, who is a delicate hothouse flower in need of constant attention. Guitarists regard bass-players as rather coarse fellows, somewhat akin to bodybuilders. I didn't want to be a bass-player, thank you very much, and I couldn't, for the life of me, imagine why anyone else would want to be.

For that reason I was about to turn them down when I hesitated. I hesitated because I was intrigued. The Blackjacks had once been the top dogs of the Welsh gig circuit, earning fabulous money; twenty-five quid a gig, it was whispered. But fashion had passed them by – they still did the occasional Shadows number, a true sign of musical redundancy – and they had almost disappeared from the local gig circuit, preferring to tour American bases around Europe. They were also the first Welsh band to have released a single – an instrumental version of Sospan Fach, the Llanelly anthem guaranteed to instil fear into the hearts of any rugby team visiting Stradey Park. Well, it used to.

Don Callard, their guitarist, who had once inspired us all with his chiming, pink Stratocaster, now sounded staid and wooden. He was still trying to sound like Hank B Marvin, while we were trying to sound like Buddy Guy. Pete James, the drummer, was still immaculate but there wasn't much scope in the Blackjacks for him to let his hair down. Christine Corvette, the singer, had a big voice with a break in it that Connie Francis would have sold her soul to possess (you had to have a girl singer if you wanted to play the American bases; something for homesick GIs to letch over). Vic Oakley, the bass-player whose job I was being offered, was a class act: a beautiful bass-player and a singer who could break your heart. He was leaving, for reasons unspecified. Hearing my hesitation, the Blackjacks jumped in.

'We've got three months work doing American bases in France. A month in Orleans, a month in Paris and a month in Bar-le-Duc, in eastern France.'

'Abroad?' I said. I'd never been abroad.

'Yes,' said the Blackjacks. 'You've got to go abroad if you want to get to France. There's no other way of doing it.'

'Yes, I suppose so,' I said, miles away.

Three months in France! Orleans! Paris! I pictured myself sitting at a table outside the Dome cafe, drinking cognac and looking tortured, while all the Left Bank intelligencia circled me, whispering to each other, wondering who this

the blackjacks

mysterious stranger could be. I would take a dogeared note-book out of my coat pocket and begin writing furiously. '*Zut alors!*' they would whisper, 'a driven man.'

On the other hand, there was a catch. I would have to join a band that most of my peers regarded as an anachronism. I would have to endure, if you want a euphemism, a certain amount of good-natured ribbing, I would also have to play the occasional Shadows number. I shuddered.

'It's twenty-five quid a week,' said the Blackjacks.

'I'll take it,' I said. My artistic soul winced.

I say it was the Blackjacks on the phone, but it was Lyn Callard, Don's wife and the band's manager. It was rumoured that she ran the band, and Don, with an iron hand. I'd met her a couple of times and she'd seemed quite nice. I enquired about rehearsals.

'No time for rehearsals,' she said. 'I'll send you a set list. You probably know most of them.'

'OK,' I said. 'Any Shadows numbers?'

'One or two,' she said.

My artistic soul grabbed me by the lapels and head-butted me. Well at least all this would take place in a distant land, far, far away from the eyes and ears of my peer group.

'When do we leave?' I asked, hoping she would say, 'Tomorrow, at first light.' Then I could then slink away in semi-darkness.

'Week Monday,' she said. 'But first we've got a gig on Saturday at the Ritz in Skewen.'

'THE RITZ IN SKEWEN?' I yelled. Everybody would be there. I'd have to be seen playing 'Flingel Bunt' in full view. My artistic soul sniggered.

'Any problem with that?' she enquired.

'No.' I said. 'Everything's fine.'

My artistic soul walked out of my life, slamming the door behind it.

I resigned from the Corncrackers at our next rehearsal, which now took place in the relative quiet of Llanelly's Moose Hall.

'I'm sorry,' I said, 'I'm leaving. I'm joining the Blackjacks.'

Silence.

'The Blackjacks?' said Keith.

'Yes,' I replied.

More silence.

'What? THE Blackjacks?' said Wes.

'Yes,' I said, warily.

A bit more silence.

'What? THE Blackjacks from Carmarthen?' said Breezy.

'Yes, yes, yes,' I said tetchily.

They began to giggle. In no time at all they were hysterical. I tried to give them my reasons but they'd lost interest, so I gave up. I said goodbye and left. As I walked down the street I heard Breezy play the intro to 'Flingel Bunt,' to renewed gales of laughter.

maybe i should've stayed in bed?   94

The following day the Blackjacks set list arrived in the post. There were about a hundred and twenty songs, most of which I hadn't heard of. I suspected they might be obscure Shadows songs. I rang up Lyn.

'I haven't heard of half of these,' I said, and ran a few titles past her.

'Oh, they're old Shadows songs.' she said. 'We don't do them very often but now and again Don will slip one in if the mood takes him. If you don't know a song, just busk it. You're supposed to be a musician, aren't you?'

Saturday arrived and they picked me up in a Bedford Dormobile. They'd had it for years and made it a second home. There were flip-top tables, reading-lights, drink-holders, and curtains with a rather attractive floral motif. I slid the front door shut behind me, put my collar up and hoped that none of the neighbours would see me. When we got to Skewen they gave me Vic's old bass, a Fender Jazz with his name painted on it.

'I've never played bass in my life,' I said, strapping it on.

'You'll soon get the hang of it,' said Don. 'I'll call out the songs, give you the key, and see you at the end.'

The Ritz was packed and I hid in the dressing room until showtime. The show went rather well in an unfashionable sort of way. Don put some elbow into it, Christine bubbled with enthusiasm, and Pete sparkled with power and precision. 'Flingel Bunt' came and went, leaving me scarred for life. I sang some songs then retired to the back of the stage, keeping my head down. We went down well. Lyn was ecstatic and I grudgingly admitted we'd had our moments. I began to feel better about things. I decided to venture out into the hall and face my public. I passed Spiv, a local personality, on the dressing room steps.

'What the fuck are you doing, Leonard?' he said.

As I got to the bar, a punter stopped me, placing a hand on my chest.

'What the fuck are you doing, Deke?' he said.

Deflated, I returned to the safety of the dressing room, passing a bouncer on the way.

'Great, Deke,' he said. 'When are you starting the Old Tyme Dancing?'

I'd worked myself into a fugue by the time they dropped me off at my house. They said they'd pick me up at 6.30, Monday morning.

'Bring your guitar,' said Don. 'You can do a few numbers and I'll play bass.'

The van was already full when they picked me up. Don was driving and Lyn was navigating. Don always drove and Lyn always sat in the passenger seat with a map on her lap. Pete had brought along his wife, Gwyneth and their two-year old son, Anthony, so they, Christine and I crammed into the back. The first gig was at Orleans, but on the way we had to stop off in Paris, where we had to call in at the French agency who had booked the tour, to pick up an advance to see us through until the first paycheque, due after the first week. The weather was glorious and we drove down through France with all the windows open. In the back of the van the mood was one of contentment tinged with anticipation, but up front, from departure to arrival, Don and Lyn bickered. With immaculate timing, we arrived at the agency on the Boulevard de Rochechouart at midnight. All the money we

the blackjacks

had was earmarked for petrol so a hotel was out of the question.

'We'll have to sleep in the van,' said Lyn.

The long drive and the Paris traffic had frazzled Don and he fell asleep as soon as he turned the engine off. Lyn bickered away to nobody in particular for ten minutes or so, until she too nodded off. Pete leaned over to me conspiratorially.

'Welcome to the Blackjacks,' he whispered, rolling his eyes upward.

Sleep was impossible because at midnight the Boulevard de Rochechouart is buzzing. An endless procession of Gallic carousers streamed past and most of them tapped on the windows of the van and shouted what I assumed were humorous remarks. I decided to go for a walk. This might be my only chance to see Paris and I wasn't going to miss it. I wandered down to the Rue de Pigalle and, for a couple of hours, sat at a pavement table outside a cafe, drinking a coffee. I strolled past the Moulin Rouge, stopping outside to tie my shoelaces, while sneaking a look at pictures of the impossibly sultry, scantily-clad showgirls in the display cabinets – they've got nothing like this in Llanelly, I remember thinking. I stopped and watched two motorists, who had arrived at the same parking-space at the same time, try to out-gesticulate each other. What I liked most about Paris was that you could walk around looking mysterious and nobody gave a toss, because they were all walking around looking mysterious too. This was the life. I was overwhelmed by a feeling of well-being. I felt so cosmopolitan, so worldly. Then I went back to the van and tried to get my head down.

At a quarter-to-nine I was awoken by the sound of bickering as Don and Lyn sorted out their paperwork in preparation for the opening of the agency. Nine o'clock rolled around but no-one arrived. A quarter-past. Half-past. Nothing.

'Maybe they don't start business in France till ten?' I said.

'Maybe,' everybody chorused optimistically. A chink of light, perhaps?

Ten o'clock rolled around. A quarter-past. Half-past. Nothing.

'Maybe they don't start business in France till eleven,' I said.

Silence.

We waited until two in the afternoon, just in case they only worked afternoons in France, then we gave up. We had just enough petrol money to get to Orleans, but eating was out of the question. I had ten francs but that was neither here nor there.

Getting out of Paris in mid-afternoon meant hours of sitting in grid-locked traffic with only exhaust fumes for company. The broiling sun beat relentlessly down on the Bedford and, even with all the windows open, it was stifling inside. Driving must have been an exhilarating experience for Don. He edged forward, he stopped, he edged forward, he stopped, he edged forward…then, as if the gods of motoring had decided to take a tea-break, the traffic ground to a complete halt. Drivers got out of their vehicles to stretch their legs, peering on tip-toe with shaded eye into the muggy distance for some hopeful sign of movement ahead. Conclaves of motorists, yawning, shrugging their shoulders, passed the time of day. All this to the accompaniment of the non-stop, ever-present, deafening blare of car horns. You could hardly hear Don and Lyn bickering.

We only had half a bottle of warm lemonade between us so dying of thirst became a palpable threat. Very occasionally, we allowed ourselves a tiny sip but the bulk had to be kept for little Anthony, who was no trouble at all. He didn't whinge, he didn't cry, he didn't raise his voice, and every time he caught your eye he gave you a big grin. No trouble at all.

The Peripherique is the ring-road system of Paris. It is a nightmare by anybody's definition – four lanes of mad Frenchmen driving around in circles at enormous speed? If you miss your exit there is no option but to go around again. Don went around a few times while Lyn screamed in his ear. By the time he found the right exit he was almost catatonic, staring, with glazed eyes, at some point just beyond the horizon.

The camp was ten kilometres south of Orleans, way out in the countryside, but we found it easily. There were enough signposts. There were signposts pointing to other signposts. It was early evening when we arrived and the oncoming night was just beginning to take the edge off the heat of the day. The sentry at the gate was dozing peacefully in his cubicle. Lyn tapped on the glass. He roused himself, checked our papers with bleary eyes, directed us to the club, and went back to dozing. The camp, as we drove through it, appeared to be deserted. So did the club, if you could call it a club. It was just a canteen, filled with trestle tables and tubular chairs. The stage, if you could call it a stage, was a foot-high platform, illuminated by two tiny spot-lamps. In the absence of evidence to the contrary. we assumed this was the venue and, with peerless optimism for the certainty of outcome, set up the gear.

When this was done, we started trying doors and shouting hellos but nothing stirred. We found a door with MASTER SERGEANT written on it. We assumed it doubled as a generator room because it hummed from within. We knocked. No answer. We tried the door. It was open. We went in. The rush of air took our breath away. There was a gale blowing in the master sergeant's office. It whipped our hair and ruffled our collars. The din was deafening.

The room was filled with fans – small, table fans; sturdy, office fans; and, the cause of most of the din, a huge industrial fan. There were two desks in the room. One was piled high with paperwork, weighted down with whatever had come to hand, in one case an army boot, and at the other sat the sergeant. A tall, blonde man with a toothbrush moustache, he was sitting on a swivel-chair, leaning precariously backwards, with his stockinged feet crossed on the desk, head thrown back, mouth wide open, snoring loudly. You could even hear it above the gale.

Lyn shook him by the shoulder and he jerked awake, nearly tipping over backwards. He caught himself and stood at semi-attention, adjusting his uniform. His lips began to move. We listened politely but we couldn't hear a word. Suddenly he twigged and rushed around the room turning off all the fans. The industrial fan whirred to a stop and there was silence. Then he turned to us and snapped to attention.

'Well now, ladies and gentlemen,' he said in a courtly manner, 'what can I do for y'all.'

the blackjacks

'We're the band,' said Lyn.

'Well, welcome,' he said. 'Let me show you where to set up.'

'We've set up.'

'Well then, let me buy you a drink.'

We almost sank down on our knees and kissed his feet. We followed him to the bar, My mouth was full of grit and it was becoming hard to swallow because my saliva glands had all but packed in. I had an ice-cold coke. It was one of the great Coca-Colas of all time. Giants refreshed, so to speak, we were ready for life's next hammer blow. It wasn't long in coming.

'I'd better take you to the hotel,' said the sergeant. 'You don't have much time. You start playing at seven.'

We gulped and looked at our watches. It was five-thirty.

'I thought we didn't start until tomorrow,' said Lyn.

'No,' said the sergeant, with a Pontius Pilate gesture, 'I'm afraid it's tonight.'

Lyn flapped around in her contracts. She found what she was looking for.

'There!' she said, triumphantly. She showed the sergeant the relevant passage. 'Not till tomorrow.'

He took the contract and shook his head.

'It's the agency in Paris,' he said. 'They're always doing this. I'm sorry, you'll have to play tonight. I'd better take you to your hotel. It's in Ardon. It's only ten minutes from here.'

He took us to the hotel; he, in a jeep, driving like a lunatic, us, in the Bedford, chugging along behind. The hotel was a rustic affair with a wooden balcony running along one side. It was set in a cluster of houses that might just have qualified as a village. It was deserted. The front door was open and we went in. Inside it was cool and gloomy. The sergeant rang the reception bell and we waited. He rang it again. Again we waited. After ten minutes a little old woman dressed in black shuffled out from the back, gave us our room keys, and shuffled off again. The sergeant, having discharged his duty, said goodbye.

'See you later,' we said.

'As sure as a bear shits in the woods,' he said, and left.

All our rooms were along the balcony and we had two minutes gazing at the rolling countryside before showering and shaving, and getting the least-creased item of stage clothes into some presentable form.

The club was already packed when we arrived. There was a very strange atmosphere. There were two separate audiences. On one side of the central aisle were the black GIs and on the other were the whites. The two sides completely ignored each other. We started at seven o'clock and played forty-five minutes on and fifteen off until midnight, by which time we were nearly asleep but still functioning. We'd had a rapturous reception, although song selection was a minefield. Every time we played white music – 'Wipeout', 'Who's Sorry Now?' or 'Downtown' – the white GIs leapt from their seats, cheering and clapping and giving each other high-fives, while the black GIs sat stock-still, scowling. When we played black music – 'Shout', 'Shotgun' or 'Can I Get A Witness?' – the black GIs leapt from their seats, cheering and clapping and giving each other high-fives, while the white GIs sat stock-still, scowling. We quickly discovered that the best way to keep everybody happy, and upon that seemed to depend our survival, was to alternate black and white songs. This uneasy truce lasted all night but much to our relief the final ovation was a multi-racial event.

We still hadn't eaten. There was a kitchen and they were serving hot food but we had no money. Everybody wanted to buy the band a drink but nobody offered us a meal. The sergeant insisted on buying us a final drink and we sat talking while the club emptied.

As we left, a dozen or so GIs were waiting for us, gathered around the van, They were hoping to have a word with Christine. During the evening they had fallen hopelessly in love with her, and they milled around her and chattered excitedly while she flirted their hearts away, her twinkling laughter echoing around the deserted camp. As we drove off they huddled in a group, shadows under a streetlight, waving forlornly at the departing Bedford, before going back to barracks and dreaming of Christine, who thought they were all sweethearts. Two or three had even proposed marriage.

By the end of the first week we'd all lost about two stone. I was better off than most because, with my ten francs, I selfishly bought a packet of Laughing Cow cheese and rationed myself to one cheeselet a day. When payday arrived, we lined up outside the sergeant's office, a little peckish to say the least. The sergeant paid Lyn, she divvied the money up, and we all ran to the kitchen. I ordered a club-steak sandwich, about the size of a Harold Robbins paperback, two portions of French fries and a large cardboard plate of baked beans. After the banquet, we all sat back, let our belts out a notch or two, and smiled. Contentment reigned. Even Don and Lyn stopped bickering.

The sergeant watched our feeding frenzy with puzzlement.

'You guys were kinda hungry,' he said.

'Well, we haven't had any money for a week,' said Lyn. 'We were supposed to pick up some money from the agency in Paris but they were closed.'

'You should have told me,' he said, shaking his head. 'I could have given you an advance.'

'It's all right,' I said. 'We're artistes. We're supposed to starve.'

The sergeant, it emerged, hailed from Tennessee.

'Memphis?' I asked, hoping for a little Elvis background.

'Frogjump,' he said.

'Frogjump?' I queried.

'Yup,' he said. 'Frogjump, Tennessee. Well, somebody's got to live there.'

For the rest of the month things went smoothly. We played softball every day with a bunch of Christine's suitors, who stuck to us like glue, assuming, correctly, that everywhere the Blackjacks went, Christine was sure to follow. Every time she spoke to them they fell to pieces.

We took in the sights. We went boating on the Loire. We visited a frog farm, which was the only time in my life when I felt the need of earplugs. We paid the occasional visit to Orleans, where I bought a postcard of Joan Of Arc, sitting on a motorcycle, holding an American flag. I think the world would be a better place if

the blackjacks

we made an effort to understand each others' cultures.

Don was as good as his word. Each night, at his suggestion, I played more and more guitar.

'Whatever's best for the band,' he said, unselfishly.

Then, suddenly, it was the end of the month. The last time I saw the sergeant he was pinning an official-looking notice on the club's bulletin board. As he stood back to admire his handiwork he caught sight of me out of the corner of his eye and beckoned me over. He gestured toward the notice. I read it. It warned GIs that there was a thief in the camp. There had, it said, been mounting reports that items of an air-conditioning nature, mainly fans, had gone missing. This, it further said, was a particularly heinous crime, given the current abnormally hot weather. This callous thief must be brought to justice. Special alertness was required from all.

'Some people just have no feeling for their fellow man,' said the sergeant wistfully. 'What a world we live in.'

'Think this heinous criminal will get away with it?' I said.

'As sure as a bear shits in the woods,' he said.

On the last night the whole camp turned out. This was way beyond the club's capacity so a system of relays had to be instituted in order that everybody could see us for at least one set. There were about twenty GIs milling around the van as we prepared to leave, most of them carrying bunches of flowers which they presented to Christine. They were all crying. Christine was crying. We all got into the Bedford, which now looked like a delivery van for Interflora, and drove off, Christine hung out of the window, waving and crying. The GIs, en masse, ran alongside. One by one they fell away, dropping to their knees, gasping for breath, broken-hearted and knackered.

The next gig was in St Germain, just west of Paris, at one of the army bases that form a security buffer around SHAPE Headquarters. SHAPE is the acronym for Supreme Headquarters Allied Powers Europe, and it was the place to be if you wanted to be at the heart of the military action. We drove past endless rows of greystone buildings, set back from the road, surrounded by high-wire fences, patrolled by sentries with dogs. The military traffic was heavy and relentless and, while Don had a small nervous breakdown, the Bedford chugged alongside the most sophisticated weaponry in the world. The camp, when we found it, was huge and the guardhouse was bigger than the club in Orleans. There were about ten MPs on duty at the gate, immaculately turned-out, all spit and polish and blanco. They were serious but polite. No-one was dozing.

When our papers were cleared, we were asked to follow a jeep which would take us to the club. As we drove through the camp we passed squads of soldiers, all moving at the double, seemingly impervious to the blistering sun. Even the officers moved with purpose. The club was exactly the same as the club in Orleans but five times bigger. Once inside, the jeep-driver pointed at a sergeant playing a one-arm bandit near the bar.

'That's the sarge,' he said. 'Report to him and he'll show you the ropes.' He saluted us as we filed past. When Christine walked past, he seemed to stagger. He flushed and his eyes went vacant. Another victim of capricious love.

maybe i should've stayed in bed?

As Lyn approached the sergeant he stepped back from the one-arm bandit and kicked it viciously. It tipped back against the wall then rocked back into place.

'You miserable son of a bitch,' he growled. He kicked it once more. Then he noticed Lyn. 'Excuse me, Ma'am,' he said politely. He walked purposefully behind the bar, pinged the till open and took out a packet of quarters. He stomped back to the one-arm bandit and began to feed the them into the slot, cursing every time he jerked the arm. When they were all used up, he stepped back again.

'You fucking fuck,' he said quietly. He kicked the machine three times, but made little impression because one-arm bandits are built to withstand a certain amount of casual violence, so he searched for a weapon. The club was full of them – tubular chairs. He picked up the nearest one and ran at the fruit machine. The glass splintered with the first blow, which seemed to cheer him up no end. He set about his task with renewed relish but, apart from a few dents, made no headway. The machine remained stubbornly intact. He tossed the chair, now bent out of shape, over his shoulder and stopped to catch his breath.

'This fucking machine's a damn communist,' he spat, and yanked the plug out of the wall. Suddenly, he turned toward Lyn. 'And what can I do for you, Ma'am?' he said, brushing himself down.

'We're the band,' she said, warily.

'Hey, the band!' he said, beaming. 'Welcome to gay Paree, folks. What are you drinking?'

We sat at the bar while he gave us the low-down. There were, he said, two master sergeants running the club, he and Sergeant Washington, who we'd meet later. If we had any problems either he or Sergeant Washington would sort them out. And if there was a race riot we were to put our instruments down and lock ourselves in the dressing room until it was over.

'Pardon?' I said.

'I ain't joking, son,' he said. 'This place has been closed since the last race riot two months ago. It took that long to fix the place up. Tonight's the grand re-opening and you,' he pointed at us, 'are the star attraction.'

After we'd set the gear up, we drove into gay Paree to check into the hotel – the Stevens Hotel, on Rue Alfred Stevens, which runs parallel to the Boulevard Le Rochechouart, the main drag through Pigalle. And yes, it was as glamorous as it sounded. I lugged my case up four flights of dingy, narrow stairs and found *ma chambre*.

Around about the time of the French Revolution somebody had painted everything in the room brown. Just before the First World War somebody had laid down some magnificent brown lino. Just before the Second World War somebody had installed a sink and a toilet, which must originally have been white but was now gradually succumbing to the universal brownness. The only window overlooked a courtyard. Within this courtyard was all human life – clothes hanging out to dry on improvised washing-lines strung from window to window, delicious cooking smells wafting up, and, somewhere far down below, a lone saxophonist running through a few scales. I lay on the bed and read the first

the blackjacks

chapter of Henry Miller's 'Quiet Days In Clichy', which I had brought with me specifically for this moment. Cometh the hour, cometh the book.

We rendezvoused in the lobby at six and drove to the base. The club was almost full and our arrival was greeted with a rousing cheer which died away when Christine came into view. After a brief silence, there were whispered conversations and a few low whistles. Then a voice from the back spoke up.

'Excuse me, ma'am,' it said, 'my name is PFC Dwight Hackenabush from New Orleans, Louisiana. Will you marry me? Please?'

The place erupted with laughter and all the GIs started slapping each other on the back and giving each other high fives. For one awful moment I thought they were going to start singing 'There Ain't Nothing Like A Dame'.

I got on the stage, plugged in, and, with my back to the audience, fiddled with the tone controls of my amplifier. I was interrupted by a deep voice coming from behind me.

'Hey, boy,' it said. I turned around to see a large black man, nudging six-foot six, dressed in a dark lounge suit, spotless white shirt and black tie, standing at the front of the stage, looking at me with expressionless eyes. He beckoned me forward.

'Yes?' I said, smiling furiously.

'Are you an accomplished guitar-player?' he drawled, moving a toothpick around his mouth with his tongue.

'I like to think so,' I said, modestly.

'You'd better be,' he said. 'The last guy was shit.'

He walked away with a shambling gait. Those GIs who were standing in his path stepped out of his way. He stood by the foyer door and stared impassively at the stage. Just what I needed – militant criticism.

Once again the audience, like Orleans, had adopted a policy of voluntary segregation, split by the central aisle. Each side totally ignored the other. Each side was invisible to the other. But we went down a storm. Everything Christine did was greeted with ecstatic applause, by both black and white. In between her batches of songs – they usually came in threes – I did one or two. One song was 'The First Time I Met The Blues.' I was trying very hard to be Buddy Guy at the time. I could still see the large black man standing at the back so I threw everything I had into it. Half the audience loved it but the large black man showed no reaction. When the set was over I wandered over to the bar. The large black man walked over and stood right in front of me, looking down. I looked up.

'You,' he said, prodding me in the chest with a forefinger the size of a telegraph pole, 'are an accomplished guitar-player.'

My knees buckled with relief.

'My name is Master Sergeant Washington,' he said. 'You can call me Sarge. I run this club on Thursdays, Fridays and Saturdays. Let me buy you a drink, son.'

We talked about guitar-players, of which he was highly knowledgeable. I ranted on about Buddy Guy but he curled his lip.

'I don't like these new guys so much,' he said. 'Now, T-Bone Walker, that's my man. I've seen him play many times and he is so smooooth and so-phis-ti-ca-ted.' He rattled off the last syllables like a drum-fill.

The only time I'd seen T-Bone Walker was on a BBC-TV arts programme. In what must have been extremely rare concert footage, it showed the great man walking onstage, carrying his amplifier in his right hand, and playing guitar with his left, using hammer-ons and pull-offs (Whoops! Jargon alert! Klaxon! Klaxon!). He played a set of breathtaking eloquence then, when it was over, he picked up his amp and walked off, still playing. I mentioned this.

'Yup,' said the Sarge, smiling, 'that's one of his bits of business.'

I made a note to try to get some breathtaking eloquence into the next set. I resolved to try but I knew it would be beyond me. Breathtaking eloquence is not my forte. But if you want some random thrashing, then I'm your man.

As I walked back to the stage, a couple of white GIs stopped me.

'Hey, the Sarge likes you,' they said, grinning from epaulet to epaulet. 'Now you're gonna have some fun.'

At the end of the evening, while I was putting my guitar away, the Sarge shuffled up to me.

'Deke, m'boy,' he said, 'would you be so kind as to join me for breakfast in the sergeants' mess?'

'Breakfast?' I said, blanching at the thought of getting up early in the morning.

'Yes, breakfast,' he said. 'All the duty sergeants have breakfast after the show.'

'I'd love to,' I said, 'but I've got to get back to Paris tonight. That's where we're staying.'

'I know where you're staying,' he said, with exaggerated patience, 'I booked the damn hotel. You can go back to Paris on the shuttle.'

'OK,' I said, without having the faintest idea what the shuttle was.

The sergeant's mess was like a nightclub, discreetly lit by table-lamps and wall-lights, There were about thirty tables, each with a heavy, white, linen table-cloth and silver cutlery, monogrammed with the regimental crest, and a deep-piled carpet that ensured the waiter's approach was silent. About half the tables were occupied, two or three to a table, by burly, middle-aged men, some in uniform, some in civvies; those in uniform had a chestful of campaign medals. These were career soldiers. The conversation was subdued, but broken by occasional raucous laughter. As we picked our way through the tables, the Sarge stopped now and again to exchange small-talk and banter. They all spoke with that languid self-assurance that only comes from knowing that when you say 'frog', this man's army jumps. To me, they all sounded as if they were doing John Wayne impersonations.

We sat down at an alcove table and ordered. The Sarge ordered a T-Bone steak, three fried eggs, streaky bacon and hash browns, followed by blueberry pie with cream, and coffee. I had the same.

'So,' said the Sarge, 'tell me, what do you think of Robert Johnson?'

'Who?' I said.

the blackjacks

'GOD IN HELL, BOY,' boomed the Sarge, 'WHERE THE HELL YOU BEEN LIVING? MARS?' He sat back and shook his head. 'Robert Johnson,' he said slowly, 'was the King Of The Delta Blues.'

'Sorry,' I said, rather feebly, 'I've never heard of him.'

'Have you heard of Mu-ddy Wa-terrrs?'

'Yes,' I said, meekly.

'PRAISE THE LORD!' he said, and clapped his hands.

The food arrived. It was fairly perfect. While we ate, the Sarge gave me a lecture on the blues, breaking off, now and again, to lament my ignorance.

'OK,' he said after coffee, 'I gotta get back on duty. I'll take you to the shuttle.'

The shuttle was an army lorry that spent the night going back and forth between the camp and Paris, taking sober soldiers out on the town and bringing drunken ones back. Every GI knew that it left for the camp, every hour, on the hour, from the end of the Rue de Pigalle. I thanked the Sarge for breakfast and climbed in the back. As we drove off, the Sarge shouted after me.

'And for god's sake, boy, buy yourself a gaddamn Robert Johnson record.'

Every time the Sarge was on duty we went for breakfast at the sergeant's mess. Halfway through the month, Pete's wife and son went home. I can't remember why but I think little Anthony was poorly. The Sarge immediately roped Pete in for breakfast and beyond. Sometimes, when the fancy took him, the Sarge took us into Paris for a night out.

'OK, gentlemen,' he would say, 'let's go chase some foxes.'

One Saturday night after breakfast we went into Paris on the shuttle. We walked down the Rue de Pigalle to the Canada Bar, a GI hang-out, across the road from the Nebraska Bar, another GI hang-out. While we were in the Canada Bar, news came through that somebody had been shot in the Nebraska Bar. The Sarge went to investigate, and Pete and I followed. The French police were there in force and everybody was gesticulating furiously. A semi-circle of Gendarmes stood around a body lying, in a pool of blood, next to the bar, The Sarge approached them, showed his identification, and spoke briefly to them. There was much nodding of heads, then the Sarge came back to us.

'It's OK,' he said, 'It's only a Frenchman. Let's go.'

We returned to the relative peace of the Canada Bar, but not for long. The Sarge was restless.

'Let's go, boys,' he said. 'I know a great club down in the Latin Quartier.'

The club was a huge warehouse, the music was blues, and everybody in there was black, except for me and Pete and a couple of hundred French mesdemoiselles. The Sarge immediately started dancing. Pete and I had some hassle from a couple of GIs but the Sarge appeared and explained to them that we were 'hon-o-ra-ry ne-groes' and they disappeared, apologising.

When we got fed up of dancing, we went outside and hung around the main entrance, which was in a narrow lane, barely wide enough for two cars to pass. There were about twenty of us, ne'er-do-wells to a man. While we ribbed each other, a French black in a Renault Dauphine drove up and parked directly outside

maybe i should've stayed in bed?

the club entrance, blocking the lane. As he got out, several of our company had words with him about the inadvisability of his chosen parking space. He dismissed our appeals with a disdainful wave of the hand, said something obviously insulting in French, and went into the club.

'I don't think I like his attitude,' said the Sarge.

Almost immediately a Chevrolet pulled into the lane and the driver, a black GI who was known to us, asked us, in no uncertain terms, to move the fucking Renault. I started to work out the logistics. One of us would have to go into the club, find the driver and explain to him – in a foreign language and in direct competition with 'Shotgun' by Junior Walker and the All Stars – that his car was blocking the lane outside, and if he would be kind enough to move it, so that this chap we know could get past, we would be really grateful.

'Let's bounce it over to the wall,' said the Sarge.

The wall in question was opposite the club entrance. We lined up along one side of the Renault and started to rock it. A rhythm established, we started to bounce it toward the wall. When it reached the wall, I straightened up but everybody else kept on bouncing. Time and again the Renault crashed into the wall until its side was mangled and torn. Then they stopped. The Sarge turned to the driver of the Chevrolet.

'Can you get past now?' he said.

'I think I might just make it,' replied the driver, grinning from indicator to indicator.

We waited for a while to see if the Renault driver would come back but he didn't, so we went back to the Canada Bar and got down to some serious drinking. We were interrupted by two fresh-faced, white GIs. They had a problem. They cornered the Sarge and outlined their plight. They had been posted to Vietnam and, as the Sarge knew, they were thus entitled to two weeks home-leave, however, they had to report back to the camp by six o'clock or they would lose that entitlement and be shipped straight off to Vietnam. It was now five-past five and they had missed the five o'clock shuttle. Could the Sarge please phone the camp and inform the duty desk that they were in his custody, that he would put them on the six o'clock shuttle, and they would turn themselves in when they got to the guardhouse. They finished their spiel and waited.

'Pass me the phone,' said the Sarge, beckoning to the bartender.

'No telephone,' said the bartender. 'The telephone, eet ees, how you say, fucked?'

'Shit,' said the Sarge, getting up. 'Let's go find a phone.'

We spilled out on to the road. There was the Sarge, me and Pete, and the two GIs. It was just getting light. The Sarge looked up and down the road. A couple of doors away was the Hotel Algeria.

'They'll have a phone,' he said, and loped toward the hotel. As we neared the front door, we passed a black GI standing in the next doorway. His shirt was shredded and soaked in blood.

'Hi, Sarge,' he said, casually.

the blackjacks

'Hi,' said the Sarge. 'What happened to you?'

'A Frenchie started tearing at my shirt,' he drawled, 'so I started tearing at his head.' He pointed to his shirt. 'This ain't American blood.'

The Sarge headed for the Hotel Algeria and we followed. So did the guy with the bloody shirt. The lobby was dark and dingy and we followed the Sarge to the reception desk in single file. We must have looked like an hotelier's worst nightmare; the guy with the bloody shirt was the icing on the cake. A woman about forty and a boy about twelve stood behind the reception desk – mother and son? As we approached, the boy edged toward her for safety. The Sarge leaned on the desk and pointed at the phone.

'Excuse me, ma'am,' he said, 'I have to make a very important phone call. Can I use your phone?'

She shook her head and babbled in what I assumed was Arabic.

'Excuse me, ma'am,' said the Sarge, patiently. 'I just need to make one phone call. That's all.'

She shook her head again and continued babbling. Suddenly, the Sarge banged his fist on the desk.

'JUST ONE PHONECALL, FOR CHRISSAKES!' he bellowed.

Just then, from our right, came a sound like a baby's rattle. Instinctively, our heads turned toward it. Through a bamboo curtain, masking a door next to the reception desk, emerged a huge Algerian, as big as the Sarge, dressed in a shiny grey suit. The handle of a machete poked out threateningly from inside his jacket. He said something low and menacing in Arabic, which we took to mean, 'What the fuck's going on here, then?'

The woman behind the desk answered him with more babbling, more pointing at the phone, and more shaking of the head. The Sarge narrowed his eyes and raised himself onto the balls of his feet. We tensed ourselves, preparing for action. It wasn't long in coming.

The big Algerian went for his machete but, as he did so, it caught in the folds of his jacket and he dropped it. It clanged on the flagstone floor. The Sarge leapt forward and, grabbing him by the lapels, slammed him against the door-jamb. He slid down and ended up in a crumpled heap on the floor.

In all the excitement, nobody had noticed the young boy slip away but everybody saw him come back. He was screaming, frothing at the mouth and waving a revolver in the air. Everybody froze. My sphincter packed its bags and left for a two-week holiday in Morecambe. The boy waved the revolver in our general direction and, as one, we instinctively ducked. His eyes had glazed over and he was shouting in a mixture of Arabic and French. The boy's mother, the first to come to her senses, started talking to him in soothing maternal tones. The big Algerian got to his feet and, with panic in his eyes, purred reassurance to the boy. By their reaction we could tell the gun was loaded. The boy ignored them. Spittle flecked from his mouth. He continued to sweep the lobby with the revolver and we continued to duck. Then the gun went off. It was the loudest sound I'd ever heard, made worse, no doubt, by the confines of the lobby. The bullet smacked into the

maybe i should've stayed in bed?

ceiling above us, sending down a shower of plaster and covering us in a thin film of dust.

Silence.

Suddenly, the boy burst into tears and threw the gun down. It clattered across the floor and spun to a halt at the big Algerian's feet. He picked it up and gingerly put it on the desk. The boy rushed into his mother's arms, sobbing uncontrollably. She ran her fingers through his hair and whispered in his ear. He started to calm down and his sobs turned into whimpers. We started breathing again in great gulps. The big Algerian put his head in his hands and sagged, and the Americans started making phew-that-was-a-close-shave whistles. Pete and I had a moment of quiet reflection, and the Sarge rolled a toothpick around his mouth. The big Algerian straightened up and took a deep breath.

'Effreybody drink.' he ordered. He leant over the desk and produced a bottle of Algerian schnapps. It looked like urine and it tasted like urine. We drained it in one. We slapped each other on the back and said how brave we were, how we had exhibited grace under fire, and how it was only when looking down the barrel of a gun that a man could judge his true mettle. That moment of truth that cuts, like a knife through butter, into a life, rearranging its priorities, bringing the slings and arrows of outrageous fortune into sharp focus, and testing the efficiency and fortitude of the lower intestines.

Now that the danger had passed, we exchanged pleasantries with our foes, discussing the recent events in broken English.

'Now,' said the Sarge, eventually, 'can we make that fucking phonecall.'

The big Algerian shook his head, gesturing at the phone.

'Domestique,' he said. 'Domestique.'

'Sarge,' I said 'I think he means that it's an internal phone.'

'Oh, no,' said the Sarge, sighing deeply. 'All this fuck-up about fuck all. C'mon, gentlemen, let's go find a real phone.'

We said goodbye to the Algerians, now our bosom buddies, and headed for next hotel, where we found a phone. The Sarge phoned the base and then arrested the two GIs. We went to put them on the six o'clock shuttle. They made it with a minute to spare.

'Now,' said the Sarge, 'where were we?'

The Sarge finally called a halt around about midday, and Pete and I were in bed by half past. That night at the club our arrival was cheered to the echo.

'Hey boys, I hear you nearly got your hair cut last night,' accompanied by a wink of admiration, was a fairly common reaction.

The third Saturday of every month was 'Cabaret Nite!' Celebrity acts were shipped in at enormous expense to boost morale, so vital in a large, standing, peace-time army.

'Celebrities, my ass,' huffed the Sarge. 'Never heard of any of 'em.'

'Who's coming this month?' I asked.

'Some funnyman from the States and a English pop group called…' He shuffled through some papers on his desk and found the contract. '…the Dallas Boys.'

the blackjacks

'The Dallas Boys!' I yelled. 'They're great, Sarge.'

Years before, the Dallas Boys had been the resident vocal group on 'Oh Boy', the trail-blazing British TV rock show. When the show folded they had disappeared into the murky world of pantomime, surely the last resort of the desperate. I was surprised they were still going. I was surprised they were still alive.

'I hope, for your sake, that they are as good as you say,' said the Sarge, his toothpick disappearing into the left side of his mouth and reappearing on the right, 'because you will be backing them.'

My stomach turned over. I could picture it. The Dallas Boys would arrive, hand me sheaves of music manuscript, and tell me to get on with it. I, for whom written music might as well be Chinese pictograms, would have to fake it.

The Dallas Boys arrived on the afternoon of the big day. They were all about nine-foot tall with good upper-body development. After talking to them for five minutes my neck started to ache. The expected sheaves of music manuscript did not materialise. I couldn't stand the suspense.

'Do you want us to back you?' I said, dreading the worst.

'No,' said a Dallas Boy. 'We use backing tapes.'

My heart soared. The shackles fell from my legs, the manacles dropped from my wrists, and Freedom's dervishes whirled around my soul. I was off the hook.

'I need a drummer and a bass-player,' said a nasal American voice. 'I gotta piano-player but I need a drummer and bass-player too.'

I turned toward the voice. He was a short stocky man with a shock of frizzy red hair combed strategically over a bald head. He was obviously 'the Comic'. Behind him stood a tall, gangly man carrying sheaves of music manuscript. My heart sank.

'Are you the bass-player?' said the Comic, looking accusingly at me.

'Yes,' I said.

'Who's the drummer?'

'I am,' said Pete.

'I do a lot of tricky stuff in my show,' he said. 'Make sure you get it right.' Pete and I bristled. 'This is Merv,' he continued, jerking his thumb in the direction of the tall man. 'He's my musical director. He'll run you through the show. Now, where's the nearest bar?'

When he had left, Merv walked over and handed me sheaves of manuscript, as if serving a summons.

'It's all straightforward stuff,' he said, mournfully, in a soft Boston accent. 'It's mostly Sinatra. You can do it in your sleep. I do.' He walked over to the drums and handed Pete more sheaves of manuscript. 'It's all straightforward stuff,' he said. 'Mostly Sinatra. You can do it in your sleep. I do.'

I was beginning to like Merv. But he wasn't finished.

'There's a joke you have to emphasise.' he said, turning to Pete.

'The tricky stuff?' said Pete.

Merv nodded and ran Pete through the joke. It involved lots of knocking on doors. Every time the Comic would mime knocking on a door, Pete had to play a rat-tat-tat-tat-tat on the snare-drum.

maybe i should've stayed in bed?

The club was packed, but it always was on a Saturday night. We were handed a written schedule. We would go on first, then the Comic, then the Dallas Boys, and then we'd return to close the show. When we finished our first set, Pete and I waited on stage for the Comic. Merv arrived and took his seat at the piano.

'Fly Me To The Moon', he said.

'What key?' I asked.

'It's there on the music,' he said, frowning.

'I can't actually read music,' I said.

'It's in E Flat,' he said, shaking his head. 'Just fake it.'

'I intend to,' I said.

The Comic introduced himself from the wings, using a disguised voice. He painted a very rosy picture of himself, elevating his position in the comedic firmament to stratospheric heights. Merv played the intro, Pete and I joined in, and the Comic bounced on stage and started to sing. He was ghastly. He had all Sinatra's vocal mannerisms but none of his voice. I played a walking bass-run that contained the occasional E Flat, usually in the wrong place but nobody, apart from Merv, seemed to notice. Not even the Comic. When he had wrung the last drop of life out of the song, he started on the jokes. The audience took an instant dislike to him and he got virtually no reaction. The jokes got bluer. Enduring silence. Then he got to the joke that required Pete's participation. He gave Pete the nod and started the joke. When it came to the first knock on the door, the Comic mimed the action, but Pete was a smidgin late. The audience giggled. The Comic gave Pete a filthy look and made a little speed-up sign. On the second knock Pete didn't start until the Comic had finished. The audience roared with laughter. The Comic dropped his shoulders and closed his eyes. He knew he was on his own. In a flat voice he continued the joke. He did the last knocking mime, expecting nothing, and nothing is what he got. Pete just sat there, arms folded, smiling. The Comic thought for a second, then slowly delivered the punchline. Total silence. Then Pete did the last rat-tat-tat-tat-tat. The audience erupted. They cheered for about two minutes. The Comic stood and waited. Then, as the din died down, he jerked his thumb toward me.

'It's the first time I've played with a girl bass-player,' he said. 'Even my wife's hair ain't that long.'

Anger rumbled across the audience. The Comic didn't know this was an unwarranted attack on a house legend; the recent hero of a Paris gun battle. I was stunned. I suppose my hair was long compared to the GI regulation hair cut, but it wasn't worth making a fuss about. But he did. He minced up and down the stage, pursing his lips, and fluffing up imaginary hair. The audience bristled. To be fair to him, he didn't back down. He swaggered down the central aisle, making amusing comments about members of the audience. He stopped at a GI whose legs poked out into the aisle. He pointed at the soldier's shoes.

'Nice shoes, buddy,' he said, 'Whaddya step in?'

There was an exquisite silence, then...

'Your face,' came the murderous reply.

the blackjacks

There was a huge cheer and the Comic retreated to the stage, cat-called all the way. He told a few perfunctory jokes then headed for the exit, jostling his way through jeering GIs who, once again, looked like the cast of *South Pacific*.

It was a good twenty minutes before order was restored and the Dallas Boys Boys bounced onto the stage. Great singing, loads of funny business, all delivered with a frightening professionalism – they tore the place apart. When we returned to the stage to close the show we were greeted with a standing ovation. And it all went uphill from there.

When it was over we headed for the kitchen. We thought the evening worthy of an *apres-gig soiree*, so we sat at a trestle table and ate off the fat of the land. Most of the talk was about the Comic.

'I wonder where he is now?' I said.

Merv looked up from his steak sandwich, drained his 'Honolulu Lulu' cocktail, and smiled.

'He's out celebrating,' he said, sitting back and lighting a cheroot. 'For him, that was a good gig.'

As the end of the month rolled around, I started to work out how to say goodbye to the Sarge. I started rehearsing little speeches, little eulogies, that would sum up my admiration for the man. One of them was rather good in a Shakespearean sort of mode, but it just wouldn't do. It just didn't summon up the essence of the Sarge. The search went on.

The last night arrived. I spent that afternoon polishing the final draft of my farewell speech. It was a magnificent opus, discussing the ins and outs of heroism, providing an A to Z of integrity, and, for the first time I think, proposing a cast-iron method, illustrated by a wall-chart and coloured pins, of measuring the actual worth of a man. I arrived at the club at six o'clock, ready to orate.

The Sarge wasn't there. But that was OK. He was often late. But when we came off-stage after the first set, he still hadn't arrived. I checked at the foyer.

'The Sarge won't be in tonight,' said the desk orderly. 'He's phoned in sick.'

I was gutted. I knew I'd seen the last of him. The rest of the evening was rather flat. As the last vestiges of applause echoed into the military night, I felt somewhat detached. Switching to automatic pilot, I packed my gear. Around me, the last night rites were enacted. There was the usual phalanx of GIs around the van, most of them on their knees, proposing, tearfully, to Christine. There were the fond goodbyes to friends we'd never see again. And there were Don and Lyn, bickering gently about what time we would leave in the morning. As we drove off I thought of the Sarge; his wisdom, his certainty of foot, his heroic belief in the unreliability of Providence. And he never let me deliver my farewell speech which he must have known was coming. A wise man, indeed.

The next day we drove to Bar-le-Duc, near Metz in eastern France, close to the German border. Like Orleans, it was another sleepy outpost of American colonialism. The two duty MPs at the gate didn't even ask to see our papers and just waved us through. The club was just like the one in Orleans – a small, functional place to get drunk. We'd finished setting up the gear by mid-afternoon

maybe i should've stayed in bed?   110

so we drove to the hotel, hoping to get our heads down for an hour or two. It was identical to the one in Orleans. It even had a balcony running down the side. We checked in. The concierge was a little old woman dressed in black, who shuffled out from the back, gave us our room-keys, and shuffled off again. Just like Orleans. Small wonder the French came up with the concept of *déjà vu*.

All our rooms were along the balcony. We lugged our suitcases up the outside stairs. Pete and I, who were sharing, flung ourselves on our beds. Bliss! I immediately succumbed to the embrace of Morpheus.

We were due back in the club at six. Somebody must have had an alarm clock because we were outside the main gates at five-to. As we drove through the camp I was surprised to see military police everywhere. As the audience wandered in I was further surprised to note that they too were military police. After a few discreet enquiries, we established that Bar-le-Duc was a training camp for MPs – I expect they practised arresting each other. Then I started twitching. I was about to spend the next month in a confined space with a thousand policemen. This was right up there with four lanes of neurotic Frenchmen driving around in circles at enormous speeds. But they proved to be no different from regular GIs – a bit rowdier, it's true, but GIs nonetheless.

We settled into the familiar routine. The whole camp fell in love with Christine and a hardcore of victims followed her around wherever she went. The humid weather had the effect of making Don and Lyn almost serene. They bickered listlessly, but you could tell their hearts weren't in it. Pete started drinking, taking full advantage of 'Happy Hour' – all drinks ten cents – getting legless every night. This was not the familiar routine. But there were extenuating circumstances. Since Gwyneth and little Anthony had gone home, Pete had seemed rudderless and his level of tolerance had noticeably dipped. Easy-going by nature, he was now irritable and edgy. Lyn wasn't helping by endlessly niggling away at him about his drinking. Pete did his best to ignore her.

Every night we would arrive at the club at six. By six-thirty Pete would be drunk. By seven he would have disappeared. At midnight he would be returned to us, usually comatose, by two duty MPs. If we were lucky he'd play the first set. So for the rest of the night we needed a drummer. Luckily there was a drummer in the audience. Unluckily he could only play one song – 'Wipeout' by the Surfaris. This was fine when we were playing 'Wipeout' but not so good for the rest of the set. 'Summertime' was very odd with a galloping tom-tom beat. but we had no choice in the matter.

Then another drummer appeared. An English drummer. Our hearts leapt when he informed us that he was playing at a local civilian club for the month, but sank when he said his working hours coincided with ours. Except on a Tuesday. Tuesday was his day-off. And today was Tuesday. We tried him out. Unfortunately he was a jazz drummer who played everything at a slow, swing rhythm. This was as unworkable as the galloping tom-toms. Which was a shame because he was something of a character. He was a large, bluff, middle-aged, RAF type, of substantial girth, who sported a magnificent handlebar moustache. We

the blackjacks 111

immediately christened him 'The Wingco'.

'Hardly, old boy,' he said, twirling the end of his moustache. 'Hardly a Wingco.'

It turned out that he really had been in the RAF and he'd had a good war in Fighter Command. His party piece was twirling his sticks between each beat. At first it lit up his pedestrian style, giving it the illusion of flamboyance, but it soon paled and seemed to accentuate his complete lack of imagination. But on Tuesday he was ours. Unless we fancied 'Wipeout'.

One Tuesday we arrived at six. By six-thirty Pete was legless. By seven he had disappeared. We had to choose between the Wingco and Wipeout. We chose Wipeout. The Wingco didn't seem to mind.

'More time at the bar, old boy,' he said.

Two sets in, a black medic rushed up. He was a fan of the band so we knew him quite well.

'You'd better come quickly,' he said, visibly shaken, 'Pete's gone crazy in the oxygen room. That's fucking dangerous, man.'

I rushed off with him, without the faintest idea of what an oxygen room was, let alone how dangerous it might be. As we rushed along, the medic filled me in on the details. Drunk out of his mind, Pete had stolen a jeep and tried to drive home to Carmarthen. This was no surprise. It was a nightly occurrence. Every night Pete, drunk out of his mind, stole a jeep and drove around the camp at high speed, making occasional attempts to leave the post. Each time he was good-naturedly turned back by the gate MPs. They weren't too upset by his behaviour because, as far as they were concerned, it relieved the tedium of a sleepy posting. Tonight, for some reason, he had ended up at the Medical Centre, where the medic was on duty. He and Pete had talked normally until the topic of Don and Lyn arose. Pete seemed to snap. He got more and more worked up. The medic had tried to calm him down but Pete had broken away and locked himself in the oxygen room, which contained hundreds of cylinders full of oxygen as well as several others containing what the medic referred to as 'dangerous, volatile gases'.

'If he starts throwing them around, they'll probably explode,' said the medic. 'Then it's goodbye to the whole camp.'

We arrived at the Medical Centre. Two duty MPs were already outside, sitting in their jeep. They were pitifully glad to see me.

'Pete's gone apeshit.' they said. 'You'd better sort him out or he'll blow us all to hell.'

'Where is he?' I asked.

'Follow me,' said the medic. We all followed him into the Medical Centre and down a maze of corridors, stopping in front of a steel door.

'He's in there,' said the medic. Inside I could hear Pete cursing. Occasionally there was the clang of metal against stone. At each clang the Americans winced and backed-off slightly.

'Well, he's certainly started to throw the cylinders around,' I said. The two MPs shifted from foot to foot and the medic started to pray. 'Right,' I said, trying to sound confident, 'shall we get him out?'

'You're his friend,' said the medic. 'You get him out.'

'OK,' I said, trying to sound as if I did this kind of thing every day. Gingerly, I opened the steel door and peeped in. It was a long, flagstoned room with rows of five-foot high oxygen cylinders along either side. Pete stood in the middle of the room, with his back to me, surrounded by toppled cylinders. He was raging against the world in general and Don and Lyn in particular. He cradled a cylinder in his arms, like a sick animal.

'Pete,' I said quietly.

'Who's that?' he said, turning sharply and brandishing the cylinder, like a flame-thrower. 'Come on! Come on! Try and take it off me!' He shook the cylinder menacingly. 'Come on!'

'Pete,' I said, 'It's me – Deke.'

'Oh, hello Deke,' he said, lowering the cylinder.

'What's up?' I said.

'I've had enough, mush,' he said angrily. 'I can't take any more from Don and Lyn. If she orders me about once more I'll kick her fucking teeth down her throat. And as for Don, he's fucking useless. Fucking useless!' He punctuated the last word by hurling the cylinder across the room. It clanged across the flagstones, before bouncing into a rack of cylinders, scattering them like skittles. The sound was deafening. I instinctively ducked and covered my ears. Pete picked up another cylinder and resumed threatening.

'For Chrissakes, Pete,' I said, 'this is fucking dangerous. Be cool.'

'It's no good,' he said, 'I thought I could last till the end of the month, but I can't. I've tried. Honest to God, I have.'

I have to say that Pete's attitude was probably, at least in part, my fault. Since I'd been in the band I'd been poisoning his mind against Don and Lyn. It had started as a joke but, as so often happens, it had got out of control. Pete was a great drummer and, to me, it seemed criminal that he was wasted in a lousy band like this. That's not fair. It wasn't a lousy band, but the ageing process had taken firm hold and they were showing definite signs of atrophy. I was determined to set Pete free and I was on the brink of success. We had made plans to split and form a band of our own as soon as the tour was over. I, a conspirator by nature, could wait until Doomsday to strike but Pete, who had been in the Blackjacks all his working life, was getting edgy. Dangerously edgy, it would seem.

I spoke quietly to him, emphasising the benefits of procrastination and urging him to hold his nerve. Gradually he calmed down and I got him to lay down the oxygen cylinder. The medic, hearing the silence, poked his head around the door.

'Everything all right?' he enquired.

'OK,' I said.

'OK,' said Pete, now positively cordial.

The medic, reassured, came in and we started to chat. The talk was friendly and Pete was apologetic. The medic said he understood that Pete was under pressure but he hoped that in future his outbursts would not involve large cylinders of extremely dangerous gas. We were all relieved that the crisis had passed. Then the door burst open and Lyn came charging in, followed closely by Don. She was livid.

'Peter,' she said, sharply, 'what do you think you're doing? You're drunk again? Don't you realise that what you're doing reflects badly on the band? Now, pull yourself together and come back to the club.' She tugged at Pete's sleeve. He snatched it back.

'Don't touch me,' he hissed.

While Lyn had been talking Pete's face had been getting redder and redder. He was close to exploding, but he was making a gargantuan effort to hold his temper. Don didn't realise this and thought that what was needed was the firm smack of discipline.

'Now, come on Peter,' he said, 'you're being stupid.'

He grabbed Pete's collar and tried to drag him toward the door. Pete exploded. He leapt at Don and they grappled in the middle of the room. Being Welsh, I went to help my mate and grabbed Don from behind. Suddenly I was yanked backwards. Lyn, screaming abuse, jumped on my back, her talons locking on to my shirt.

'Take your filthy hands off Don,' she yelled in my ear. 'You're not fit to lick his boots.' She began to pummel the back of my head. I yelped when she bit my ear. The medic foolishly tried to restrain her. With a sideswipe, she knocked him flying across the room. He cannoned into a rack of cylinders and, like dominoes, they crashed on to the stone floor, the room's echo amplifying the already ear-shattering din.

The door opened and two duty MPs, presumably under the impression that war had broken out with Russia, marched in and surveyed the carnage with a practised eye. With the experience born of a thousand drunken brawls, they immediately focused in on the primal cause of the conflict, and grabbed Lyn. Even with two burly MPs pulling at her she refused to relinquish her hold on my shirt, so they pulled harder. And harder. Something had to give and it was my shirt. The buttons, like machine-gun bullets, ricocheted around the room. The medic gamely returned to the battle, this time selecting the safer target of Don, who was now flailing away at Pete. He held Don while the two MPs held Lyn.

'Quick!' he yelled to me. 'Get Pete outta here.'

And that's exactly what I did, but as soon as we hit fresh air the alcohol got the better of Pete. He hit an invisible wall and collapsed. As I bent over to pick him up I heard a drunken voice behind me.

'Want a hand, old boy?' It was the Wingco.

'Quick, Wingco,' I said. 'We've got to get Pete out of here before Don and Lyn kill him.'

'Piece of cake,' said the unflappable Wingco. After facing a sky full of the despicable Hun, Don and Lyn were minor aggravations. 'We'll use that jeep.' He pointed to the duty MPs' jeep parked on the forecourt, its engine idling.

'Good idea,' I said. 'Let's get him into it.'

The Wingco and I dragged Pete over to the jeep and bundled him into the back.

maybe i should've stayed in bed?

'I'll drive,' said the Wingco.

We stopped at the gate. I started to explain to the gate MPs why we were taking a jeep, the property of the US Military, off the base – a piece of France that was forever Manhattan – but I didn't have to. They knew all about the fracas and, realising the gravity of the situation, waved us through. As we drove off I could hear them whooping and cheering.

'Let's take him to the hotel,' I said.

The hotel was ten minutes away. It was the worst ten minutes of my life. The route took us through twisting French lanes in pitch darkness. It was an inky-black, moonless night and a light, summer drizzle had begun to fall. The Wingco regressed twenty years. Suddenly, he was flying a Spitfire again at hedgerow-level, chased by half the Luftwaffe.

'How do you turn the lights on?' he said airily, taking the jeep into a sixty-degree turn at seventy miles an hour, depositing half a tree in my lap.

'Slow down!' I screamed. 'For god's sake, slow down!'

But he didn't hear me. All he could hear was the delicious whine of a Rolls-Royce Merlin engine.

'Enemy coast ahead,' he muttered to himself.

Ten bowel-wrenching minutes later, we skidded to a halt outside the hotel. It had closed for the night and it was just a shape in the darkness. The Wingco switched off the engine. I sat there for a second, gathering my thoughts and rearranging my intestines while Pete snored peacefully in the back. The Wingco began to whistle 'Bless 'Em All'.

'Right,' I said. 'Let's get him into the hotel.'

We took an arm each and struggled to get him up the outside stairs to the balcony.

'He's heavier than he looks,' said the wheezing Wingco. We dragged him along the balcony and stopped outside our room. I let go of Pete's arm and fumbled in my pockets for the room-key. There was a sickening thud. It was Pete hitting the deck.

'I thought you had hold of him, Wingco,' I hissed.

'I thought *you* did,' said the Wingco, somewhere in the darkness.

I found the key, opened the door and switched the light on. We picked up Pete, dragged him into the room and put him on his bed. He lay on his back, gently grunting. I threw myself on my bed and let the relief flood through me. The Wingco flopped down into an armchair, pulled out a hip-flask and took a long swig.

'Ah, mother's milk,' he said, offering me the flask. I declined. We sat there in silence. Then Pete started to make strange gurgling noises. Intestinal noises that seemed to come from deep down in his anatomy. They were the sounds of extreme digestive discomfort. He started to retch.

'Oh, no,' I said, 'he's going to puke.' I searched around the room for a bowl of some sort. There was nothing. Pete's body began to heave and he started to eject geysers of brown vomit vertically into the air.

'Oh, no,' said the Wingco, turning green.

the blackjacks

I ran to the wash-stand, grabbed a towel and threw it over Pete's face. It stemmed the flow, or, rather, diverted it. It now ran down the side of Pete's face on to his pillow. Behind me, the Wingco started to retch. To be fair to him, he tried to reach the door, spewing what looked like fruit salad all over the carpet. He turned as he reached the door.

'Sorry, old boy,' he said, wiping his mouth, 'I'm not very good with this kind of thing. I've got to go.' And he ran into the night. I know he ran because I heard him falling down the balcony steps.

I sat on my bed and waited for the tide of vomit to ebb. When it had, I removed the towel and cleaned Pete up. I tried to get some of the fruit salad off the carpet but it had assumed all the properties of mercury. I sprayed the room with a whole can of Pete's after-shave and went to bed.

I was shaving when Pete woke up in the morning.

'Welcome to the vomitarium,' I said.

He sat up in bed and surveyed the disgusting spectacle that was once our room.

'You want to learn to control your drinking,' he said.

We went down for breakfast. Don and Lyn were already there. I had expected post-mortems, recriminations and ructions, but it was as if nothing had happened. Breakfast was cordial, the afternoon relaxed, and the gig was dynamite, as it so often is after a major band upheaval.

But now the end was in sight. We had a week to go. Everybody was on their best behaviour. Don and Lyn were excessively polite to Pete, who didn't stop drinking but he slowed down, stopping this side of rat-arsed. I was de-mob happy so it didn't bother me. Don and Lyn were civil but cold. If they hadn't actually sent me to Coventry, they had had certainly reserved my ticket, booked a bed & breakfast, and sent my luggage on ahead. Christine, who got on with everybody, was just sad to see grown-ups acting like children. I tried to explain to her that all male musicians were petrified adolescents and, as such, incapable of mature thought, but she, being a woman, thought that was just a pathetic excuse to justify an almost pathological desire to avoid responsibility.

'You're perfectly capable of mature thought,' she said, 'you just don't want to admit it. Because once you do, you'll have to face up to life. Just because you know how to play a guitar doesn't mean the world owes you a living. Now and again you have to put your guitar down, come in from the playground, and clean around the toilet bowl. Talent isn't a sick-note, to be presented every time you are confronted with inconvenience.'

Well, I didn't think she'd understand, her being a grown-up. Grown-ups, I find, have little facility for abstract thought, preferring to dwell on the silly little realities of existence.

Toward the end of the month I had one of the most depressing days of my life. One night at the club I was approached by a corporal. He asked me if I could spare an hour the following day to meet the Colonel's son.

'Why?' I said.

'Because the Colonel's son plays the guitar and the Colonel wants you to tell him if the kid's any good.'

'Do I have to?' I said, sensing a minefield ahead.

'In this man's army, you don't say no to a colonel. I'll pick you up at three.'

The following afternoon, at three o'clock sharp, the corporal picked me up at the hotel and we drove to the Colonel's house, a rambling old mansion about ten miles off-base. He was waiting for us at the front door. He was a big man with a bullet head and a pot belly, dressed in a red lumberjack shirt.

'Thanks for coming, son,' he said, shaking my hand vigorously. 'The boy's round back. Follow me.' He led us around to the back of the house. 'The boy wants to be a guitar-player so I bought him some equipment, but I don't know a goddamn thing about music so I need somebody to tell me if I've wasted my money.'

As we rounded the house, my heart sank. Set up on a patio, arranged like an advert in a guitar catalogue, was a top-of-the-range Fender Showman amp, surrounded by three brand-new Fender guitars on stands; a sky-blue Jaguar, a white Jazzmaster and a salmon-pink Stratocaster.

'Junior,' shouted the Colonel, and his son waddled out from the house. He was a ruddy-faced teenager with a crew-cut, wearing an identical lumberjack shirt to Dad, and he must have weighed twenty stone. 'Show him what you can do, boy,' said the Colonel.

The boy picked up the Jazzmaster, plugged in, and began to play. The sun moved behind a cloud. Cows in an adjoining field ran away from the sound and milled about in the furthest corner of their field, and birds began to drop from nearby trees, fluttering briefly on the ground beneath before stiffening into death. A distant dog began to howl. The corporal, standing to my right, averted his eyes and shuffled uncomfortably. The Colonel, standing to my left, looked at me, then he looked at the boy, then back at me, I strained to look inscrutable. Then the Colonel started waving his hands in the air and shouting.

'JUNIOR! JUNIOR! THAT'S ENOUGH, GODDAMN IT.'

Junior stopped playing. There have probably been more profound silences in this world, but you'd have to go to a Tibetan monastery to find them. The sun came out, the cows edged warily back to the centre of their field, the birds set about burying their dead, and the distant dog fell silent.

'Well,' said the Colonel, looking me steadily in the eye, 'whatcha think?'

I racked my brain for ambiguities with which to fob him off. Something that would imply that Junior had the potential to be the greatest guitarist in the world, without actually saying that the boy should be killed immediately, and his body taken to some distant land, far from human habitation, and burned, along with his clothes and belongings, with instructions to stay with the pyre until absolutely certain every scrap is reduced to ashes.

'Very nice,' I said. 'He'll go far.'

Yeah, if you believe that Darwin made a spelling mistake in 'The Origin Of Species' and what he meant to write was 'the survival of the fattest'.

'OK,' said the Colonel, apparently satisfied. 'The corporal will take you back to your hotel.'

the blackjacks

'Can I have a quick go at the guitars?' I asked.

'Of course,' said the Colonel, suddenly remembering his manners. 'Do you guys want a beer or anything?'

I asked for a Coke and the corporal had a beer. The Colonel went off to get them. I picked up the Strat. It was shop-fresh and beautiful. Junior offered me his lead. I plugged in and played a chord. It wasn't even in tune. By the time I'd tuned up, the Colonel was back with our drinks. I played 'Wildwood Flower', a finger-picking classic. We'd been doing it in the set, so it was a work in progress. I played it every time I picked up a guitar. The Colonel stopped in his tracks and listened. When I finished, he turned to his son.

'Junior,' he said, 'You got no future as a guitar player. I think you'd better join the army like your old man.'

Junior, his world shattered, hung his head.

'I'm a professional musician,' I said. 'I'm supposed to be good. Junior's got a long way to go.'

'Yeah,' said the Colonel. 'I'll take the guitars back to the shop tomorrow.'

All music should have a purpose. A lullaby is designed specifically to put a sprog to sleep; a work-song is sung to keep those convicts swinging those pickaxes productively; and a requiem is written to mourn the passing of a patron and the end of funds until the next rich sucker comes along. In this case, we have a perfect example of music as a deterrent. I'd saved the Colonel some money; I'd stopped the boy from inflicting further damage on music, an art form I'm particularly fond of; and I'd secured, at least in the short term, the peace of mind of the local fauna. The birds seemed to sing a little sweeter when we left. I was in reflective mood as we drove back to the hotel.

'All those beautiful guitars,' I said. 'What a waste. What did you think, corporal?'

'I come from a pig-farm in Iowa,' he drawled, 'and I got pigs that can play guitar better than Junior.' He paused for effect. 'Ain't much in it when it comes to weight, though.'

The last day arrived. The camp buzzed with excitement. Everybody was coming to the gig. Even the gate MPs had their duty roster staggered so that they could catch at least one set. Our arrival onstage was greeted with sustained cheering. Each song was greeted with rapture. Black GIs cheered the white songs, white GIs cheered the black songs, and the master sergeants danced around the foyer. And when Christine sang they all held their breath. By now, every man in the camp had proposed marriage to her; some more than once; some on a daily basis. Every man-jack of them was filled to overflowing with unrequited love and Cupid's arrows darkened the sky over Bar-le-Duc, turning it into an Agincourt of the heart. She had received so many proposals she was now turning them down in batches. She would gather them into groups of twenty or so, telling them she was genuinely touched by their offers but, although she was fond of each and every one of them, she was not 'in love' with any of them. They would hang their heads in sorrow, then quietly trudge out of the room, passing the next batch of hopefuls coming in. But after an hour or two of mooning about they would – thanks, no doubt, to the common bond of mutual rejection – recover their

maybe i should've stayed in bed? 118

equilibrium and start bragging again. They hadn't, after all, been rejected by any old inamorata, they had been rejected by the sweetheart of the regiment.

The evening flew by, kept aloft by hot thermals of affection, and everything went well until five to twelve. The strict midnight curfew imposed by the High Command was inviolable – the word 'approximately' does not appear in US Army codes of conduct. Before we did the last number I thanked everybody for being a wonderful audience, praised them for being exemplary hosts, and expressed the hope that our paths would cross again in the near future. Then, overcome with genuine emotion, I made a ghastly mistake.

'We've got one number left,' I said. 'Any requests?'

The white GIs leapt to their feet, shouting for 'Wipe Out', and the black GIs jumped up, shouting for 'Can I Get A Witness?' They started banging the tables and it quickly became a contest as they tried to out-shout each other. The master sergeants suddenly appeared and began to patrol the central aisle, I had brought an evening of blissful catharsis to the brink of a race riot. I stood in the midst of the turmoil and shit myself. A decision had to be made. I turned to the band. They all stared at me with baleful eyes and raised eyebrows, that said, 'Don't look at us, you prat. You fucked it up – you sort it out.'

'Can I Get A Witness?' I shouted, for no other reason that I preferred it to 'Wipe Out', which is such a tedious song to play.

We launched into 'Can I Get A Witness'. The black GIs bellowed with delight, congratulating each other with soul handshakes. As one, the white GIs sat down and glowered. Half the place was dancing and the other half was thinking about burning crosses. The black GIs began to taunt the white GIs, who started flexing their shoulders. The master sergeants faced the black GIs and drew their batons. I looked at the clock above the foyer door. It was two minutes to twelve. I turned to Pete and Don.

'Wipe Out', I yelled. 'Change to "Wipe Out".'

Pete started the galloping tom-tom beat and Don and I joined in on the riff. Suddenly all the white GIs jumped up and started dancing and, just as suddenly, all the black GIs sat down and glowered. The white GIs began to taunt the black GIs and the master sergeants turned to face them, tapping their batons gently on the palms of their hands. I looked up at the clock. Thirty seconds to midnight. Close enough. I made a cut-throat sign to Pete and Don, and we finished with a relieved flourish. The end of the song seemed to catch everybody by surprise and although there was some sporadic clapping they were more interested in glaring at each other than applauding the band. There were a few minor scuffles but the master sergeants, with genial malevolence, nipped them in the bud. Order was restored and the audience began to leave. As we packed the gear, one of the master sergeants walked past the stage.

'That was close,' I said.

'Just another Saturday night,' he said, shrugging his shoulders. 'Just another Saturday night in Bar-le-Fucking-Duc.'

We carried the gear to the foyer and Don went to pull the Bedford around to

the blackjacks

the main doors. He returned, white as a sheet.

'The whole audience is standing out front,' he said. 'They're not aggressive but they're very quiet.'

As we carried the first pieces of gear out of the door, they began to clap and cheer. When Christine came out they went apeshit. They milled around her, giving her slips of paper.

'This is my address and phone number back in the States. If you should ever change your mind…'

As we were about to leave, the Wingco appeared.

'Just thought I'd come and say goodbye, old boy,' he said, shaking my hand. 'The place won't be the same without you.' There might have been a tear in his eye but I can't be sure because my vision was ever-so-slightly blurred at the time.

As we drove off, Christine stuck her arm out of the window and waved goodbye and, even above the chug of the Bedford, we could hear a collective groan. A few GIs ran alongside for as long as they could, but they knew the dream was over. It was time to wake up and face an unforgiving future in a cold, bleak world without Christine in it. Christine herself, pockets filled with slips of paper, was blubbing copiously.

'They were all so sweet,' she said.

I can't remember the journey home but that in itself speaks volumes. I do remember having a quiet word with Pete about forming a band. That was next on the agenda. But I'd only been home for ten minutes when Martin Ace phoned. The Jets were playing in the Park Hotel in Swansea that night and would I like to come? Yes, I would. It'd be nice to see the boys again.

17
the jet set

When I arrived at the Park Hotel the Jets were already playing. The place was packed and I elbowed my way through the crowd to the bar. Under normal circumstances – a Llanelly boy barging his way through a Swansea crowd – this would have been suicidal behaviour, especially here, where the clientele was almost entirely made up of Swansea villains and their molls; not the sort of people who would take kindly to being elbowed aside. But I, as a well-known musician, was given, by the tacit approval of all concerned, special dispensation to continue breathing. So instead of finding myself lying in a pool of blood in the gutter outside, I was greeted warmly and asked repeatedly what I was drinking. Somebody bought me a pint and I settled down to watch the band. And when my glass was empty, a full one appeared in its place.

The Jets' line-up had changed since the last time I'd seen them. Plum and Martin were still there but John P and Billy Doc had gone. In their places were Alan Popham, who I didn't know, on guitar, and the fearsome Beau Adams, formerly of the Meteorites, on drums. There are certain musicians in this life who are touched by the wings of angels. They are few in number – Elvis Presley, John Lennon, Jimi Hendrix, Johann Sebastian Bach, Karlheinz Stockhausen, Zappa and Beefheart, and that's about it – but they form a tidal wave of genius, crashing through the labyrinth of our petty preconceptions, leaving us lesser mortals foundering in their wake. If, when history has run its course, these immortals decide to provide a soundtrack for Armageddon and they need a drummer, then there is only one man for the job – Beau Adams.

Beau was the perfect drummer. A revolutionary who questioned all the long-established wisdoms of his trade, deconstructed them, and rebuilt them into a dazzling firework display of innovation. I will give you one illustration. His cymbals were upside-down and he crashed upward. Think about it, ye drummers – that cuts out a whole arm movement.

The Jets were in their element, and every song exploded with the sheer joy of existence. They took my breath away. By the time they finished I was as pissed as seventy-three parrots, and duly lapsed into unconsciousness. I can remember lying on the pavement outside the Park Hotel, surrounded by the Jets. I could hear their voices, muffled in the alcoholic distance. But I did hear Alan Pophams's voice as clear as a bell.

'I suppose this means that Deke's back in the band and I've had the sack?'
'That's about it, Al,' said Plum.
So, when I woke up, I was back in the Jets again.

the jet set

And that was the end of the Blackjacks. Well, it wasn't the end of the Blackjacks; they carried on for years but without my involvement – an arrangement with which Don and Lyn, I'm sure, were semi-ecstatic. It also meant that forming a band with Pete was out the window. I felt terrible about letting him down, but evidently not terrible enough to honour our agreement. You can rely on me to let you down.

The Jets rehearsed at the Tivoli Ballroom in Mumbles, a regular gig for both the Corncrackers and the Jets. It was run by 'Duke' Mackay, a local business man and *bon viveur*. If there was a pie in Mumbles, Dukey had his finger in it. The Jets were his favourite band so we had the run of the place.

'I think he was a bit of a millionaire on the quiet,' says Plum. 'He drove a red TR4 and Jenny, his girlfriend, was a mod type, all mini-skirts and mascara. She was a bit of a snob and a bit of a dancing teacher. She used to sit on the boys' laps and make them hard. She used to squirm about on your dick. Dukey'd walk past and say, "Ooh, look at Jenny sitting with the boys again." He didn't give a fuck.'

The Jets believed that music should be played in the deep end and there was no cobbling a set together from common, 12-bar ground. The first three numbers I was expected to play were 'You're Gonna Lose That Girl' by the Beatles, 'Make It Easy On Yourself' by the Walker Brothers, and 'My Prayer', which Martin sang, *à la* PJ Proby. By the time we knocked off for the afternoon my head was spinning.

The Jets' heavy gig sheet meant that picking me up and dropping me off in Llanelly would be a major inconvenience so I moved up to Swansea, staying with Martin at the Glanmor Post Office, where his mother was the postmistress, She was a fabulous woman with a stiletto intellect and a bone-dry sense of humour and, suddenly, I could see where Martin got the withering look that so unnerves new acquaintances, making them think that what they've just said is the most stupid thing that has been uttered in living memory.

Once in a while, Martin's Auntie Gladys came to stay. A widow, she was a portly woman of pensionable age. When she arrived she wore a long, black, go-to-chapel overcoat and a black hat which, from certain angles, looked like an eagle's nest. Her only accessory was a shiny, black handbag that looked like an artillery shell with handles. She wouldn't take her hat and coat off for about three days and, even then, had to be prised out. I held her down while Martin got the coat off, but the hat, locked in place by thousands of hair-grips, proved impossible to shift. Underneath the coat she wore a permanent floral-patterned pinafore, which I suspect she was born in. She wouldn't be parted from her handbag for a second, even taking it into the kitchen when she made a cup of tea. She'd sit for hours at the living-room table, arms crossed, telling us scandalous stories, almost gothic in construction, about people we didn't know.

She'd usually stay for a fortnight, during which time some of her friends would come to visit her. All widows, they always came alone and they all wore identical black ensembles, a mirror-image of Auntie Glad. Seen together, they would look like a mysterious religious sect, possibly the Hassidic Baptist Grandmothers. They would each come in and scrutinise the room, taking a cursory inventory of its contents, before sitting down on the edge of a chair, bolt upright with their handbags in their laps. Auntie Glad would make a pot of tea and they would sit there looking at each other. Long moments of silence were interrupted by brief interludes of gossip, when highly sensitive information about mutual acquaintances was exchanged in low, confidential tones, which dropped to a whisper when a particularly shameful item came onto the agenda. When the matter under discussion was deemed too awful for words, the salacious details were just mouthed theatrically. Auntie Glad and her friends were expert lip-readers.

One day, Auntie Glad's friend, Blodwyn, came to see her. During a silence that seemed to go on for days, Martin, trying to get a party spirit going, joined the conversation.

'Would you like me to take your coat, Blod?' he enquired.

Blod's head turned slowly in Martin's direction, as if she was fearful of disturbing the eagle nesting in her hat. Speaking slowly in a low voice, she answered.

'I won't take my coat off, thank you, Martin. I'm waiting on death.'

Living in Swansea meant that I had a whole new circle of friends. I was introduced to several members of the local Constabulary. Basil and Wally were long time friends of the Jets, and they came to every gig that duty allowed. If they were on traffic duty, the Jets' van would be given immediate right of way, its passing marked by a sharp salute. If they were on night duty, patrolling the town centre, Martin would make a flask of tea, get in the van and take it down to them. Very welcome, I imagine, at two o'clock on a winter's morning. If they were on the Post Office beat and they saw a light still burning, they would call in for a cup of tea and a chat.

The high-water mark of Basil's career, he told us, had come on the roof of a large warehouse in Swansea docks. Investigating reports of a man acting suspiciously in the vicinity, Basil spotted movement on top of a warehouse. He climbed up the fire-escape and spotted the intruder trying to prise open a skylight. Basil tip-toed up behind him.

'Freeze,' he shouted.

The burglar was rushed to the cardiac unit at Swansea General and Basil was awarded a commendation.

'I'd always wanted to say "Freeze" in the line of duty,' said Basil,

Basil was a gifted singer-songwriter with a high, edgy voice. He wrote one or two songs for the Jets. I can still remember some of his lyrics:

Oh baby, never mind,
Oh baby, never mind,
Now that I have you.

Simple at first glance but, I think you'll find on further investigation, eloquent.

Basil was shortly to become the most hated man in Swansea. He rose through the ranks to become the head of the drugs squad. He was ruthless in the pursuit of the marijuana-smoking classes. of which I was one. And so was Martin. By then *the jet set*

we were in Man, a band renowned for its ostentatious drug intake and, although we spent most of the year away on tour, we were in town long enough to expect, by the law of averages, a visit from Basil. But it didn't come. We seemed to have immunity. We often speculated about what might happen if Basil appeared on our doorstep, but considered the matter to be academic. We knew he wouldn't bust us.

The years passed and Basil continued his war on drugs, while we remained convinced of our impregnability. Then, one summer evening, Martin and I were lounging around the living room of 129 Hannover Street, where we were living at the time. The Morris girls were out – Martin and I married sisters; Fran was my wife and George was married to Martin – so we had the place to ourselves. The weather was sublime and we'd left all the doors open, including the front door. I was sitting in an armchair, rolling a joint. I had an LP sleeve on my lap and I'd already stuck the skins together. The dope – a quarter of Nepalese temple-ball – lay on the arm of my chair, next to a torn-up cigarette packet. Martin was sitting opposite me in another armchair, finishing the tail-end of the previous joint. The air was thick with marijuana smoke. We heard footsteps coming down the passage. We looked up to see Basil, looking like Sam Spade, filling the doorway.

'Good evening, gentlemen,' he said, 'Long time, no see. How's tricks?' He strolled over to the settee. 'Mind if I sit down?'

We gestured our assent. The conversation that followed was friendly but guarded. I missed most of it because I was wrestling with my criminal soul. Should I grab the dope and stuff it down the side of the chair? No, because Basil would notice and, more importantly, it would be tacky; conduct unbecoming a gentleman smoker. But what if he hadn't seen it? Making a lunge for the dope might just draw his attention to it. He must have seen it, though. He's the head of the drugs squad, for god's sake – it's his job. I considered eating it but it was too big. Even if I'd managed to swallow it, I'd have had the whirling pits for about three years. Just then, a breeze wafted through the front door, nosed its way down the passage, crossed the living room, and whisked the five-skinner off the LP sleeve. It fluttered to the floor, where it twitched nervously. Basil must have seen that. I was sweating now and I could hear my pulse racing. I might as well confess my guilt and take my punishment like a musician. I looked up at Martin.

He was lolling back in his armchair, crossed legs stretched out, taking huge tokes on his joint and blowing smoke rings into the air. In between puffs, he and Basil chatted amicably. I relaxed a little, but not much.

'Still write songs?' said Martin.

'No,' said Basil. 'Don't have the time anymore.'

'Why?' said Martin. 'What are you up to these days?'

'I'm the head of the drug squad.'

'Never,' said Martin. 'Well, it's nice to see you getting on in the world.'

Basil snorted with laughter.

'Remember you used to bring me a flask of tea when I was on night duty down on the Kingsway? Good times. How's Auntie Glad?' he said wistfully.

Martin made coffee and we talked about old times. I almost forgot about the

maybe i should've stayed in bed?

dope. Almost. After three-quarters of an hour, Basil stood up.

'Well,' he said, 'much as I've enjoyed our conversation, duty calls.'

He walked toward me, leaned forward, and picked up the dope. He looked me steadily in the eye. My stomach began to churn.

'See this?' he said, holding up the dope. 'If this was cannabis I'd have you both down the station before you could say Elliot Ness.' With a certain delicacy of movement, he put the dope back on the arm of the chair and walked toward the door. In the doorway, he turned around. 'See you, gentlemen,' he said with a mischievous grin. 'It's been a real pleasure. Take care.' And he was gone.

'See,' said Martin, 'I told you Basil would never bust us.'

'I had one or two doubts,' I said.

'Nah,' said Martin. 'Sweet as a nut.'

It was one of life's cruel ironies that we were responsible, in part, for Basil's downfall. We decided to have a Christmas fancy dress party at Hannover Street. The girls liked fancy-dress parties. Invitations were to be sent out. Should we invite Basil? His previous visit had been encouraging. Bravado said yes, and the invitation was sent out.

The party was in full swing when Basil arrived. The butler took his coat. Well, I took his coat. It had been suggested, by Martin and George, that it would be a triffic wheeze if I dressed up as a butler and greeted the guests. It would be even better, they added, if Fran were to dress up as a maid and serve drinks. Fran and I were, at first, doubtful.

'This is just a scam to get Fran and me to do all the work while you two swan around doing fuck all, isn't it?' I said.

'The thought never crossed my mind,' said Martin, seemingly appalled.

'What are you going as?' said Fran.

'Lord Nelson and Lady Hamilton,' said Martin, snapping to attention and bowing slightly. George assumed a regal aspect.

'Which is which?' I said.

I showed Basil into the lounge. Martin, in the full dress uniform of an Admiral of the Fleet, greeted him and gave him a guided tour of the drinks table. Pointing out various punch bowls, he said, 'That's spiked... that's spiked... that's not spiked... that's spiked...'

I took Basil's overcoat to the bedroom and threw it on the bed with the other coats. Then the bloody doorbell rang again.

Basil mingled. He knew everyone. At one time or another he had bust most of them. The conversation was a little brittle at the outset but then the drugs took hold and things mellowed somewhat. Then a guest arrived in some distress.

'Basil's just bust me,' he said, handing his coat to the butler. 'A quarter of Red Leb. I'd just bloody scored it.' He shook his head sadly.

'Basil's here,' said the butler.

'He can't be.' said the guest. 'He only bust me ten minutes ago.'

'He must have come straight here, then.'

'Then he'll still have the dope and the charge sheet on him,' said the guest, brightening up no end.

the jet set

By now a little crowd had gathered in the hallway. There followed an animated discussion during which we reviewed our options. With due deliberation and careful consideration of all the available facts we came to the unanimous decision that we should do something.

'His overcoat's in the bedroom,' said somebody. 'Maybe the dope's still in one of his pockets?'

'Too easy,' said someone else. 'He'd keep it on him.'

'Maybe not. He didn't know he was busting someone who was on their way to the same party.'

'Do us a favour,' said the guest, glimpsing a whiff of redemption, 'nip upstairs and have a look.'

Somebody – I can't, for the life of me, remember who – nipped up to the bedroom, found Basil's coat and went through the pockets. And there, in the inside pocket, was the Red Leb. It was removed and, in due course, returned to its rightful owner, who then joined the party. He was seen, some time later, engaged in a long and apparently genial conversation with Basil, smiling smugly, with the Red Leb snuggling righteously in his pocket.

During the course of the evening Basil was offered several spliffs. Each time he declined graciously. But he did give the punch a hammering. And after a while he probably couldn't remember which punch was spiked and which wasn't. This is pure conjecture on my part, but when he left he was rather glassy-eyed and unsteady on his feet. But he looked OK, although the fixed grin was a little disconcerting.

The next part of the story is based entirely on hearsay. It is alleged that the head of the Swansea Drug Squad wrapped his car around a lampost. Subsequent blood tests revealed that he had vast quantities of lysergic acid diethylamide surging through his bloodstream. That, and the missing evidence, did for him, and he was busted back to constable. He was next seen on crowd duty at the Vetch Football Field. The crowd erupted into violence and the fighting spilled onto the pitch. Basil was spotted, well away from the heart of the action, cornering a small boy who eventually broke down in tears. He left the police force and got himself a proper job. He became a private detective, specialising in divorce cases. And a very successful one, I am led to believe.

One of the first gigs I did with the Jets was at the Regal, Ammanford, supporting the Who, who had just become flavour of the month – in London, that is. In Ammanford, where the citizenry were only interested in alcohol and violence, visiting musicians, be they famous or obscure, were regarded as merely the latest batch of sacrifices to arrive at the amphitheatre to face the local lions. In other words, legitimate targets.

There were two stages at the Regal, one at either end of the hall. We set up on one, and waited for the Who to arrive. They were seriously late and we were already playing when they finally appeared. There were only about twenty punters in and most of them were fighting or vomiting. The Who took one look at them and beat a quick retreat to their dressing room and locked themselves in. And I don't blame them. Their roadies set up their gear an while we finished the set.

maybe i should've stayed in bed?

When we'd dried off and changed, Martin suggested a visit to the Who's dressing room to welcome them to the Principality. I went with him. He was wearing a fawn duffle coat with the hood pulled down over his eyes. We arrived at the Who's dressing room and knocked on the door. We heard a bolt being drawn back and the door opened an inch. A suspicious eye gave us the once-over.

'What do you want?' said an apprehensive voice.

'We're the support band,' said Martin, 'and we've come to say hello.'

The door shut. Then it opened again and a different eye gave us the once-over. The it shut again. Then it opened again, this time wider, and Roger Daltrey gestured us in. They each nodded a guarded welcome. They all had coiffured mod hairdos and they all wore T-shirts with aircraft roundel motifs on the front. They were skittish and nervous, obviously looking for axes cunningly hidden in the folds of our clothes. We were disappointed. We were expecting hard cases, because their publicity spin made much of the fact that they hated each other and could barely be in the same room together without resorting to fisticuffs. But in the flesh they seemed perfectly civil to each other. Maybe they had been brought closer together by the shared experience of facing imminent obliteration at the hands of one of Ammanford's death squads. Intrigued, Martin brought the subject up.

'Why aren't you all fighting?' he said. 'You're supposed to hate each other. Go on. Start fighting.'

They looked sheepish and shuffled their feet, making don't-believe-everything-you-read-in-the-papers noises, while exchanging glances that seemed to say, 'Careful boys, we are in the presence of great and volatile evil.' Just then, their roadie stuck his head round the door.

'You're on,' he said.

'How many's in?' said Daltrey.

'About thirty,' said the roadie, 'all pissed out of their brains.'

'OK,' said Daltrey, his shoulders dropping. 'Let's get it over with.'

They filed past us with looks of utter dejection on their faces.

'Break a string,' said Martin.

When they'd gone, we went out into the hall to watch them. The audience did not cluster around the front of the stage like normal audiences would do, preferring to lurk around the edges of the hall, presumably because they needed to be near a radiator in case they lost their equilibrium – easily done with a belly full of Barley Wine – and needed something solid to hold on to. So Martin and I had the hall to ourselves. We stood right in front of centre-stage, about ten feet back. The Who plugged in and, standing well back from the front of stage, started to play. The first number was 'Dancing In The Street', and they were terrific. They may have been shitting themselves but you couldn't hear it in the music. Every now and again Keith Moon caught our eye and nodded nervously, no doubt keeping a weather eye open for that cleverly concealed axe. We were inscrutable, especially Martin with the duffle coat-hooded eyes. At the end of the song we ostentatiously clapped and Moon, realising that we were not cobras but grass snakes, burst out laughing. The next song he went up a gear and started making outrageous faces. The rest of the band, taking their cue from Moon, started to burn. Daltrey started swinging the microphone around his head, Townshend began wind-milling, and Entwistle smiled occasionally, which, I was told, was a sure sign that things were going rather well. By the end of the set, even the citizenry of Ammanford had lurched to he front of the stage and were dancing or fighting to stay upright without support; although which, it was hard to tell. Those who could still move their arms gave the Who the best applause they could muster.

We gave the Who ten minutes to change and went to see them, this time with Beau in tow, bringing his camera with him. On the way I was side-tracked by one of the local amazons, almost too drunk to speak, who was, she said, interested in exploring the boundaries of carnality with an out-of-towner who could play a musical instrument. I told my compadres I would join them shortly and the amazon and I went off in search of a secluded place. We found an anteroom next to the Who's dressing room. It was full of cleaning equipment and a gymnasium bench ran the length of one wall. Custom-built. We closed the door behind us, settled down on the bench, and commenced to fornicate. Two minutes in, just when it was getting steamy, the door burst open and Keith Moon bounded in, brandishing Beau's camera. Behind him, in the open door, stood Martin and Beau, grinning like idiots, although what they found amusing was beyond me. Moon took a photo of me and the amazon and, cackling maniacally, ran back out and closed the door behind him. It had happened so fast that, for a second, I thought I'd imagined it. In fact, I don't think the amazon would have noticed anything had it not been for the flash, which galvanised her into action. She pushed me off on to the floor and, adjusting her dress, read me the riot act. Fortunately, most of it was in Welsh so I didn't get the precise details about my shortcomings, so to speak, as a human being. I tried to explain to her that in the coming years Moon would cause so much mayhem that this incident would pale into insignificance as soon as the first Rolls Royce was driven into the first swimming pool, but she wasn't having any of that. She belted me across the side of my head knocking me into a pile of mops and buckets. Then, pausing only to spit at me, she flounced out.

Martin, who has seen the resulting photograph, says that he can only remember one thing about it. My glasses were on the skewiffe.

Sunday gigs were proving hard to find for the Jets so we went to Dukey and suggested a regular gig in the little-used bar upstairs at the Tiv. He could, we further suggested, call it 'Sunday Night at the Tivoli'. He went for it and it soon became a regular watering-hole for local musicians and their girlfriends. One night, halfway through a song, violence erupted.

'I pushed half-a-grapefruit in Martin's face,' says Plum, 'and he hit fuck out of me.'

Blinded and in pain, Martin lashed out at Plum, but between each punch he played a bass note and the song continued. Plum, who had adopted a foetal position, couldn't get to the microphone to sing, so I took over the vocal and we didn't miss a beat. The audience loved it and after the set Dukey suggested we make it a regular part of the act, even offering to buy the grapefruit, but Martin, for some reason, wasn't too fond of the idea.

For the next six months the Jets played every gig in Wales, and then played them again. And again. We decided we had gone as far as we could go in the motherland. It was time to burn our boats. It was time to break out. We decided to move to London and starve. The Bystanders had done it very successfully. We would blitz the London agents. We were a good band. We'd get loads of work. Beau wasn't too sure. He had a wife, Moira, and son, Anthony. He didn't like being away from Moira and Anthony for too long.

'It won't be for long,' I said. 'Once we get a few gigs up there, we'll get a flat and then Moira and Anthony can move up. It shouldn't take more than a month.' Optimism, damn optimism, has always been a fatal flaw in my character. Beau wasn't convinced.

'We've got to go,' said Martin. 'There's nothing for us in Wales. We've got to go to London and get a record deal.'

'OK,' said Beau, with zero enthusiasm.

Mike and me – Tenby, '62.

Mike, me, Gene Vincent and Jinks.

Mum and Dad.

The first gig at the Carbay Club. Mike (left), me (below)...

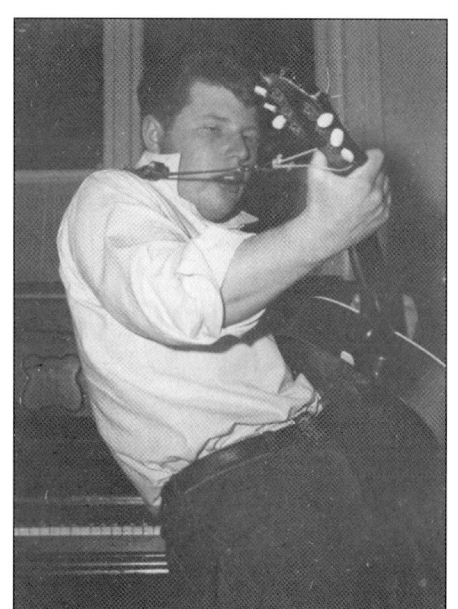

...and the British Legion. Geoff (above) and Hugo (left).

All pictures courtesy of Ron Bevan.

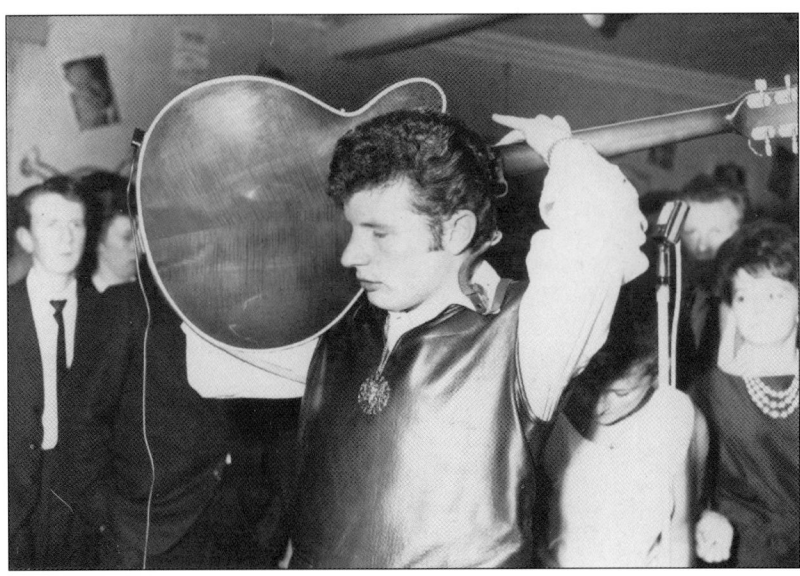

Top: the next incarnation of the Corncrackers –
me, Keith and Wes.

Above: At the L-Club. (Ron Bevan)

The Corncrackers in the North Dock, Llanelly. (Ron Bevan)

The Mansel Hotel today is now a listed building, so it has hardly changed since the days of the L-Club, which was situated first floor left. (Mary Hodge)

The ambulance outside the L-Club. (Ron Bevan)

The Jets – Plum, Billy Doc, John P and Martin.

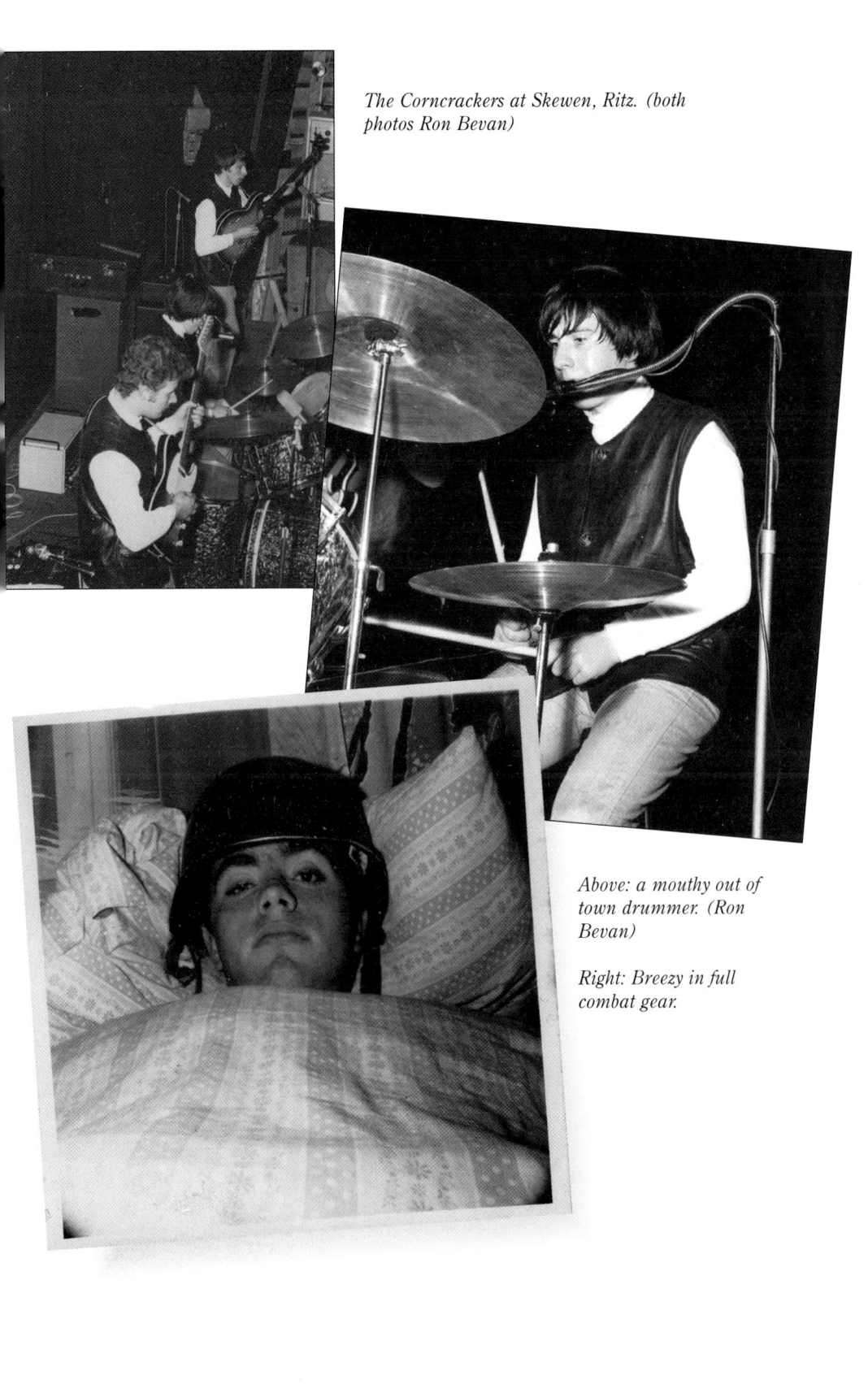

The Corncrackers at Skewen, Ritz. (both photos Ron Bevan)

Above: a mouthy out of town drummer. (Ron Bevan)

Right: Breezy in full combat gear.

Me and Pete on the banks of the Loire.

In festive mood in Ardon – Christine, Little Anthony, Pete and me.

Role reversal – Pete puts an amiable drunk to bed.

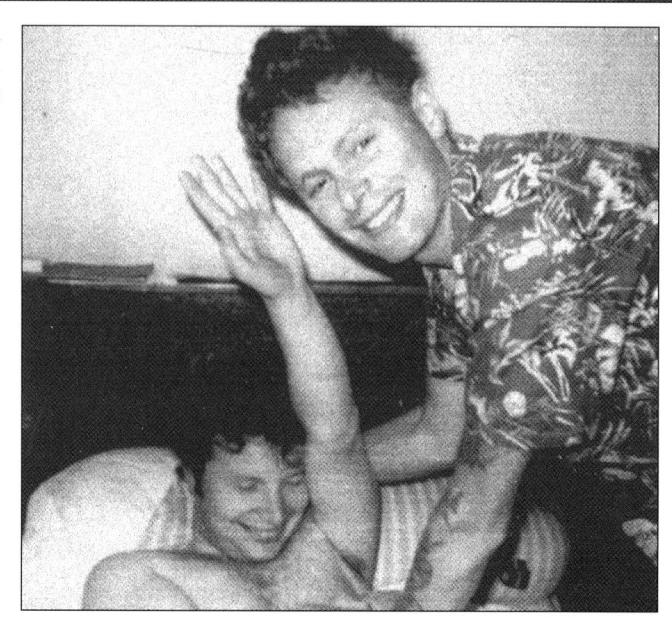

18
taking london by storm

We decided to change the name of the band. The Jets was a much-used band name and, if we were going to make it in London, we needed a name that would make agents jump up and down. We decided on 'The Smokeless Zone' because none of us smoked. We could just as easily have become the Gormless Zone. We set a date to leave and refused to accept any Welsh dates beyond that time. As the date grew closer, Beau seemed to wilt. When the day arrived we got in the van and went to pick him up. It was a tragic scene, like one of those ghastly Victorian paintings – probably called 'Off To War' – wherein a soldier carrying a huge kit-bag is leaving for the front, while his wife and children cling to his legs, weeping uncontrollably, pleading with him to stay. But no man can turn a deaf ear to the bugle's call. Except for Beau. We had to drag him into the van and sit on him until we got way past Cardiff.

We had a plan. We would sleep in the van until we got a flat. And we'd get a flat as soon as we got some gigs. We had a Thames van. Not the biggest van in the world, especially now that there were five of us. We had a new roadie, Keith Rogers. Keith was a Llanelly mod, with all that that entails. He was part of a clique of mods; sallow youths who minced around in their burgundy-red leather coats, thinking they were God's gift to women. Keith was acutely aware of fashion trends. He was allergic to certain clothes. He once sent a date home to change her shoes because he wouldn't be seen dead with a girl who wore shoes like that. A woman, to Keith, was a fashion accessory. Sartorially, he considered us to be a lost cause. He would dissolve into fits of giggles every time we held forth on the subject. We met him at a gig and adopted him, liberating him, we thought, from the straightjacket of style. But Keith wouldn't be seen dead in a straightjacket unless, of course, it was a Ben Sherman straightjacket. We endlessly took the piss out of him and he loved every minute of it. He was moderately pleased about going to London and talked of little else.

His first gig was at the Glen Ballroom in Llanelly. His mod friends gathered at the front of the stage and cheered his every appearance. We added to the festivities by calling him onstage every ten minutes or so, on the flimsiest of pretexts, on the basis that any applause is better than none. At the end of the evening we went for a meal at the Thistle Grill, the Glen Ballroom's restaurant, while Keith and Stuart Hickman got the gear in the van (Stuart Hickman was Keith's mate and he was even more fastidious than Keith when it came to fashion. Keith was a mod but Stuart was an ascetic. His nickname – don't ask me why? – was 'Knickers', which Keith pronounced as Knickwahs. He too was our roadie for a brief period, until coming home from a gig at three in the morning and then getting up again at six to go to work got to him. He would change into his working clothes as soon as he got home from a gig and sleep on the couch. His mother would wake him at six and he would get up and walk straight out of the door. Something had to give. Incidentally, Keith's nickname was 'Scruff', but we called him 'Steaming Stonker', which seemed far more appropriate. He was famous for it).

The van was parked outside the main entrance, in the stark light of the Glen's neon sign. Getting the gear into the van was not a simple matter because the van had been commandeered by Beau. He was tucked up in the back, banging the life out of a married woman from Carmarthen, whose husband, if my memory serves me, was sitting at the next table to us in the Thistle Grill. As Keith and Knickwahs lugged the first piece of gear onto the pavement, they saw an agitated policeman nosing around the van, which was rocking violently. He put his ear close to the side of the van and listened intently. Keith and Knickwahs approached.

'Anything wrong, officer?' asked Knickwahs.

The policeman jerked to attention. He turned to face Keith and Knickwahs, worry written across his face.

'I think there's an animal trapped in there,' he said, pointing at the van, 'and it's not very happy. Put your ear to the side of the van. You can hear it snarling. It sounds like a big bugger.'

Keith and Knickwahs put their ears to the side of the van.

'Sounds like a big dog to me,' said Keith. 'Maybe an Alsatian.'

'Sounds bigger than that to me,' said Knickwahs, helpfully. 'It could be a goat.'

'Look, you stay here,' said the policeman, 'and I'll nip back to the station and fetch some help.'

The police station was next door to the Glen so they didn't have much time. They alerted Beau and his consort to the possibility that they might be arrested for gross indecency on the Queen's highway, and Beau, not a man easily deflected, dragged his married woman across the road to Peoples' Park. Keith and Knickwahs made themselves scarce, hiding in a nearby bus-shelter.

The policeman returned with two colleagues, both in shirt-sleeves, and each in turn put his ear to the side of the now-empty van. They had a whispered conversation. They put their ears to the van again. Suddenly, one of the shirt-sleeves started barking loudly and the other two policemen jumped out of their skins. They burst out laughing and, shoving each other playfully, made their way back to the police-station, making farmyard noises. One of the noises was uncannily pig-like.

London did not welcome us with open arms and sleeping in the van didn't work out too well. Wherever we parked for the night the police moved us on, so we went further and further out of London searching for a reclusive little niche. We eventually found one; the huge car park at Sandown racecourse. Apart from a car or two, it was deserted and we found a well-aspected pitch under a tree. The van was a little crowded at night. The roof-rack held our luggage but, even so, five people and the gear was a trifle congested. Everyday we drove into London and

taking london by storm

went to see every agent who advertised in the Melody Maker. They all expressed polite interest in the band but, naturally, they wanted to hear us first. Were we, they asked, doing any local gigs? No, we said, that's why we'd come to see them. We were hoping they could get us some. No, they couldn't, they said, not without hearing us first. After two weeks of this we found it hard to sustain our resolve although, on the plus side, we did become expert at circular argument. But we weren't going to give up and suffer the ignominy of returning home like whipped dogs, with our reputation between our legs.

After a day of tramping around London we would dine in style at the hot dog stand on Chelsea Bridge. Nothing so nourishes a man, weary from back-breaking toil, than a cup of British standard tea and a dog with onions. Then back out to Sandown. Sandown Racecourse car park was a refuge. A haven of stillness in a world of flux. Except on race days, of course, which we never saw coming. We'd just wake up, rub the sleep from our eyes and, still in our underpants, climb out of the van to find ourselves in the middle of a cavalry-twilled, tick-tacking, binoculared nightmare. The van was surrounded by Jags and Daimlers and Bentleys, and the piece of grass where we traditionally emptied our bowels every morning was now covered by a picnic cloth, and surrounded by champagne-drinking yahoos. Our sudden appearance caused them no end of mirth but we didn't mind because we knew whereupon they sat.

But after a week we'd had enough. We needed a bath. We threw ourselves on the tender mercies of Chris Farlowe and the Thunderbirds. The Thunderbirds were regular visitors to Swansea. We'd met them at one of their gigs and offered them lodging, which they accepted and, from then on, every time they came to Swansea, they'd stay with us. Now we were on their patch, we hoped they would return the favour. We went around to Farlowe's 'drum', as they say in 'the Smoke'. His mum made us a cup of tea while Tubby, as he was known to his associates, rang around the rest of the band. All offered accommodation and we were dispatched to the four corners of London. Some stayed with Tubby, some with Dave Greenslade, the organist, and some with Albert Lee, the guitarist, who lived out in Blackheath. I stayed with Albert. He showed me a few licks, which I'm still trying to play, and gave me a couple of prehistoric BB King albums. Our welcome was immaculate and Thunderbird hospitality was second to none. Thus refreshed, we gathered ourselves for the next onslaught on the commanding heights of the music industry, but it all came to nothing.

Beau developed a mysterious illness. It was a sort of a headachey, backachey, stomachy kind of thing, hard to pinpoint, but devastating in its effect.

'I think I've got some sort of virus,' said Beau, weakly, as if fighting to cling on to the last vestiges of life. 'I think I'd better go home.'

We urged him to stay a little longer and he reluctantly agreed, but the following morning he was gone. He had hitch-hiked back to Wales. We followed him.

The following week the Herald Of Wales ran the headline: SICK DRUMMER FORCES JETS TO LEAVE THE LONDON SCENE.

maybe i should've stayed in bed?

Once home, Beau made a remarkable recovery and pronounced himself fit and ready to gig, Plum spent a day on the phone and our gig-sheet was restored. We were back on the treadmill. But our London jaunt wasn't in vain. A couple of weeks later Jack Fallon phoned up. He ran the Cana Variety Agency, one of the agencies we had visited. Were we interested in a month's residency at the Top Ten Club in Hamburg? Yes, we bloody-well were.

The Top Ten wasn't just another club, it was an icon. The Beatles had played there. As far as I was concerned, this was confirmation of my worth. I was on the right road. This was a major stepping stone across the river of success. Soon I would be famous. It was only a matter of time.

We were due to start on the 1st June and finish on the 30th. We would be paid 3,500 Deutschmarks for the first two weeks and 3,000 for the second two. I assumed there was some logic behind this although I failed to spot it.

Jack Fallon booked us into Brentford FC clubhouse the night before we were due to leave, partly to break the journey, partly to give us some travelling money. We went up a couple of days early to sort out the final details with him. Beau was happy because Moira and little Anthony were coming along. I don't know if this was because Beau couldn't bear to leave them for a whole month, or because Moira didn't trust him to go to the corner shop to get a pint of milk. This time we arranged to stay with the Cheating Hearts, a Welsh band already living in London. Their singer, Jerry Braden, now known as Owen Money, had once been in the Bystanders, but he had struck out on his own and formed the Cheating Hearts. There would plenty of room for us, we were assured over the phone. We arrived and were shown to our room. There should have been a couple, but some people had arrived unexpectedly. They weren't exaggerating. It seemed as if half of Wales had come to stay. People milled about the hallways and landings, discussing the issues of the day. The kitchen was like the trading floor of the Stock Exchange and the queue for the bathroom went out of the front door, down the street and past the tube station. Getting into the toilet required brute force, ruthlessly applied. I made enemies then who are still my enemies today.

The following day we went to see Jack Fallon at his house. It was a well-aspected house in a leafy suburb. He showed us into a room with veranda doors that opened on to a superbly manicured lawn. In the corner of the room was a double bass. Martin headed straight for it. It was beautiful.

'I used to be a bass-player,' said Jack. Some bass-player. We later found out that he was a massively respected musician who had played in the Ted Heath Orchestra. There was an organ in another corner and we were soon jamming. Jack made us tea and we played until about six, when he called it a day.

'I've got to go out,' he said. 'I've got John Mayall's Bluesbreakers on at the Refectory. Do you want to come?'

The Refectory was a pub in Golders Green. The Bluesbreakers were in the middle of a hot streak. Eric Clapton was in the band and he was dynamite. He played with passion in those days, before he went all mobile phone.

The following day we played at Brentford and the day after left for Hamburg.

19
what a show! what a show!

The journey seemed to take about two years. We finally arrived on the Reeperbahn around midday, bleary-eyed and stiff. The Reeperbahn, a long, wide boulevard, is in the St Pauli precinct of Hamburg, which comprises the docks and its environs, including the red light district. I had profound expectations. I expected a glittering Sodom, a Teutonic Tombstone, a Delphic oracle auguring the total breakdown of social constraint. I assumed it to be one of Nature's portals to unfettered hedonism, where I could learn what secrets lay in the darkest corners of the human soul. That's what I expected.

What I got was surely the bleakest place on this earth. It was shabby and tawdry, seedy and tacky. Clutches of self-conscious men strolled down the wide pavements, fending off the advances of strip-club doormen, each convinced that their club provided the dirtiest show in town. Now and then, an impossibly floozy woman hurried past, on her way, no doubt, to do the afternoon shift at the Sex Palace – 'the Sexiest Girls in the Sexiest Show in Hamburg, six shows a day, seven days a week'. The bracing sea air was laced with exhaust fumes and bratwurst. There were three kinds of shops on the Reeperbahn – dens of iniquity (strip-clubs or sex shops), weapon shops (which sold anything from flick-knives to low-calibre hand-guns), and schnell imbisses (fast food outlets). This said a lot about the local clientele. They obviously needed sex without complication, the means to dispatch one of their fellow human beings into the next world at a moment's notice, and a pizza.

The Reeperbahn must have brought a glow of civic pride to the heart of the Hamburg citizenry.

We found the Top Ten Club nestling in between a schnell imbiss and a gun shop. It was owned by Peter Eckhorn, who had inherited a strip club from his father and turned it into a rock'n'roll institution. It predated its main competitor, the Star Club, but now the two clubs were neck-and-neck and locked in fierce rivalry. The Beatles had played both, including a marathon 100 night residency at the Top Ten five years earlier. We were met by the Top Ten's manager, Ricky Barnes, a hard-bitten Scot with an acerbic manner. He had come over to Hamburg in the fifties as a sax-player with King Size Taylor and the Dominoes. When they broke up he stayed in Hamburg, married a prostitute, and ended up managing the Top Ten. He had a fearsome reputation as a sax-player but he no longer played, although, he told us, he still had his sax.

'Bring it along to the club,' said Ace, 'and have a blow with us.'

'You must be fucking joking, laddie,' he sneered. 'I dinna play anymore.

maybe i should've stayed in bed? 134

Besides, I don't know how good you are. I dinna work with shite.'

He took us to the club office and checked our work permits were in order. When he got to Martin's permit, he looked up.

'Marrrtin Ace? You should have put your real name down, laddie, not your stage name. What's your real name?'

'Martin Ace,' said Ace.

'Nobody's called Marrrtin Ace.'

'I am,' said Ace, producing his passport. He handed it to Ricky Barnes.

'Good God,' he said, shaking his head, obviously not convinced.

'What time do we start playing?' said Plum.

'Seven o'clock. Hour on, hour off, until I tell you to stop. You're on with Sol Byron and the Senate, a Scottish band. They'll do the other hour.'

He showed us to our sleeping quarters. They were in the next building. We had to go out of the club entrance, across a courtyard, through a door, and up two flights of stairs. We had the whole floor to ourselves. It was a labyrinth of spacious rooms with single beds dotted here and there, plus the odd table and chair and a washroom – a barracks. Ricky Barnes regretfully informed Beau that only band members and crew were allowed use of the barracks so Moira and Anthony, and by implication Beau, would have to sleep outside in the van.

'This is also your dressing room,' said Ricky Barnes. 'You'll have to go through the crowd to get to the stage. It's a bit of a trek but it's all right, unless you're pissed out o' yer fuckin' mind, Jimmy. Which you won't be because, if you're too pissed to play, I'll sack youse.' He cackled to himself.

I picked a bed. On the wall next to the bed was a large smudge, about a foot across.

'What's that?' I asked Ricky Barnes.

'That's the bed John Lennon used to sleep in when he played here. First thing every morning, as soon as he woke up, he spat at the wall. We keep it for sentimental reasons.'

I was definitely on the right road. It was only a matter of time.

We all went straight to bed. We were fighting to stay awake. Sitting in a Commer J2 van for twenty-two hours has that effect on the human body. It was dark when I woke. Through the walls I could hear the not-so-distant pounding of drums. As my eyes grew accustomed to the gloom I could pick out the dark patch on the wall. I summoned up a quantum of gob and propelled it into the darkness. I heard it hit the wall with a satisfying splosh, which, it seemed to me, had the ring of destiny to it.

After a shit, a shave and a shower I was ready to take on the might of Germany. And so were the rest of the Smokeless Zone. And so was Keith. It was the first time he'd been abroad and he was twice as excited as the rest of us put together.

We trouped downstairs, through the Top Ten courtyard, into the Reeperbahn. And there it was – the jewel-encrusted temple of depravity I'd fondly imagined. All the lights were on and the wide pavements now teemed with people; gangs of boisterous Germans shouted to each other over the din; red-eyed drunks tottered in and out of the melee, seemingly oblivious to the surrounding chaos; and well-dressed young couples, always arm-in-arm (safety in numbers?), out on a let's-go-and-see-the-animals date. Tomorrow we'll go to the zoo.

We went next door to the schnell imbiss, sat at the central bar and ordered. Martin and Plum had played in Germany before – a couple of months in a club in Dortmund – so they could speak some German. They guided me and Keith through the menu. While we were eating, the world turned Scottish. Sol Byron and the Senate arrived. They had got here just after us and were staying on the floor above us. There was much Celtic bonding. Sol Byron and the Senate were famous in Scotland, having been the house-band on Stramash, a Scottish TV rock show. They surveyed the menu with increasing bewilderment.

'Ha'e ye no got any haggis there, Fritz?'

'What the fuck is strammer max?'

'Fuck this, I'm away hame.'

On our advice, they all ordered currywürst mit pommes frites.

'Gi' us a beer there, Helmut,' said a Scotsman to the waiter, a hollow-cheeked, darkly-stubbled individual in a white coat.

'My name is Lupo.' he said, eyes expressionless. 'I am not a German, I come from Yugoslavia.' This impassioned statement of identity was delivered in a flat monotone, as if reciting the menu to a five-year old child.

'OK, Lupo,' said the Scot, 'gi' us another o' them curry things and a double portion of chippies while you're there.'

Lupo shrugged his shoulders. It wasn't that important.

We later discovered that Lupo was a Hamburg institution. He had worked in this imbiss for twenty years, and during that time he had seen everything; at least twice. Nothing bothered him. He was phlegmatic to the point of comatose. He remembered the Beatles and, in his more voluble moments, would mumble the odd, skeletal anecdote. We hung on his every grunt.

Now we were fed, we hit the town. Lupo recommended the Blockhaute, on the Grosse Freiheit, just down the road from the Star Club. Off we went. The Blockhaute was rustic in design, log cabin, circa 1840. The clientele was an even mixture of German carousers and British musicians. Hamburg was rich in rock'n'roll clubs so that, at any given time, there were about thirty or forty British musicians in town, and they all ended up in the Blockhaute. I assumed that it occasionally closed for an hour or so, maybe twice a year, to let the cleaner in, but I never saw it happen. No matter what time of day or night a lost soul arrived at its portals, it was open for business. I remember going in that first night, but I don't remember coming out. The next morning I woke up in my bed, in the early stages of rigor mortis but still, mercifully, above ground. I dragged myself out of bed. There was work to be done. Unforgiving work.

We, along with the Senate, spent the afternoon down in the club preparing for the first night, sorting out the gear and trying to plan the changeovers. Delicate Celts, some still drunk from the night before, shuffled past each other, voices low and hoarse. forcing their bodies into some semblance of movement, when all they

maybe i should've stayed in bed? 136

really wanted to do was lie down and go to sleep. All except Ace, who has the constitution of a small herd of buffalo. Ace has never had a hangover in his life. I have seen him at five in the morning, obliterated by substance abuse, seemingly heading across the Great Divide, but at nine he's up, boiling himself an egg and singing Buddy Holly songs. It is extremely unnerving. He moved among we purgatorians like an archangel, dispensing bonhomie and universal energy in equal amounts.

'Who the fuck is he?' said a Scottish voice, 'Captain Fantastic?'

The schedule for the evening, and indeed the whole residency, was long-established and carved in granite. Ricky Barnes ran through the nuts and bolts. He'd obviously said it a million times before.

'The firrrst band goes on at seven. They play for three-quarters of an hour. Then there's a quarter-of-an-hour changeover. Then the second band plays for three-quarters of an hour. Then there's another quarter of an hour changeover. Then the firrrst band goes on again. This will continue until I tell you to stop. Am I going too fast for youse, laddie?'

The question was directed at a dozing Scotsman, who jerked awake and said 'Aye' a few times. Ricky Barnes shook his head and continued.

'You will take it in turns to open. Is that clear?'

Grunts of assent.

'Who do you want on first?' said Sol Byron.

'I dinna give a fuck,' said Ricky Barnes.

We tossed for it. We lost and the Senate put us in to bat. Even at seven, the club was almost full. We made our way through the crowd to the stage, plugged in, introduced ourselves, and struck up. The audience listened attentively, watched carefully, and applauded warmly, just like a good audience should. One thing was apparent – they were here for the music. There were one or two borderline psychotics, drunk beyond belief, looking to cut somebody's throat, but they were usually members of the Senate, waiting to go on. We went down a storm. As we picked our way out through the crowd, all trying to pat us on the back, we passed Ricky Barnes, leaning on the bar. We raised a collective eyebrow.

'Nay sa bad, gentlemen,' he said. 'Nay sa bad. Now, don't be late for the second show. You will be back here at quarter to nine sharp, ready for the changeover. Understood?'

'Understood,' said Ace. 'By the way, have you got your sax with you?'

'Bugger off, you bloody Welshman,' he said, but Martin had disappeared into the crowd.

We took our guitars upstairs and went back down the club to hear the Senate. They were a big band; guitar, bass, drums, keyboard, a two-man brass section, and Sol Byron out front at the microphone. They were great. If there's one thing the Scots know about, it's how to make a big band work. It promised to be an enjoyable month.

That first night we continued playing, on and off, until the early hours. At three o'clock, as soon as the crowd fell to single figures, Ricky Barnes called it a day and

what a show! what a show!

we all went to bed. Except Ace, who went back out on the town.

We soon settled into the Top Ten routine and I began to enjoy life in Hamburg. We started to get to know the ex-pats. There was a substantial conclave of British musicians resident in Hamburg who had come over with visiting bands and, rather than return home to boring old Britain, had chosen to stay on. They gave us some insider lowdown on how to get the best out of the place. Particularly interesting was the advice on domestic alternatives.

There were two ways of doing it. You could either continue to stay at the Top Ten, or you could move out and shack up with one of the local girls. There were advantages and disadvantages to both methods. If you shacked up with one of the local girls they would, for the month, feed you, clothe you, house you, buy you drinks, buy you drugs, and cater for your most outlandish sexual requirements, and you didn't have to put your hand in your pocket for the whole time. So far. so good, but those who chose this route appeared, over subsequent days, to undergo some sort of personality back-somersault, becoming slightly introspective, as if seeing something disconcerting for the first time. They began to wear the most astonishingly inappropriate clothes. This was unavoidable because if somebody, upon whose limitless generosity you now depend, insists on buying you bright red dungarees, how, in the name of reason, can you refuse to wear them?

'Why don't you wear those lovely red dungarees I bought you, meine liebling?'

'I thought I'd wear something else tonight, meine shatz, and save the red dungarees for a special occasion. What do you think?'

'OK. Wear the yellow, PVC boiler-suit, instead.'

And that was the problem. You had to take the whole package. There was no escape. Which was why I stayed put at the Top Ten; that, and the fact that I was terrified of the local girls. They seemed so worldly-wise, so direct, so imposing, so adult. It meant that I had to buy my own food and drink, but at least I didn't have to wear red dungarees.

Everyday, we ate at the Chug Oo or the Ning Po, two Chinese restaurants in the back-streets just off the Reeperbahn. The food was good and served in huge quantities, but the pungent, stale aroma that emanated from the kitchen seemed to explain the lack of cats and dogs in the St Pauli district. Most of the clientele were strippers, catching a snack between shows, and transsexuals, doing whatever it is transsexuals do. The door would open and a tall, statuesque woman, dressed to kill, would sashay in, sit down, and order her food in a voice that sounded like Lee Marvin with laryngitis. But this just added to the atmosphere of decadence we were beginning to love and, like Kublai Khan, on honeydew we fed.

But after a week of Chinese food, we began to mutate. Our conversations took on a Confucian dimension. We began to understand the concept of permanent revolution and found ourselves fighting off an almost irresistible urge to open a laundry. Postcards home took ages to write because it was hard not to succumb to a powerful inclination to write backwards. Martin became fairly fluent in Mandarin, but we put this down to his facility for language, rather than his Orientalisation. On the fourth day, Ricky Barnes overheard one of us bemoaning the incontrovertible fact that we hadn't had a tidy cup of tea since Dover.

'Oh, I forgot to mention it,' he said, 'Youse can get a full English breakfast at the Seamans' Mission, any time of day.'

'Haven't you got to be a sailor to get in?' we asked, our pulses galloping.

'No,' said Ricky Barnes. 'There's a special arrangement. Any British bands that play the Top Ten Club or the Star Club can eat there too. But if you're a British band and you play in any other club, the Crazy Horse, for instance, they won't let you in.'

'Why's that?'

'Who fucking knows? Tradition? It was like that when I got here, ten years ago. Just go down there and tell them you're the band from the Top Ten and they'll let you in, nay bother. And it'll only cost you a couple of marks.'

'Where is it?'

'It's right in the middle of the docks.'

The Seamans' Mission provided refuge for the British sailor in Hamburg. If he had a few days to kill he could, at an impossibly reasonable rate, sleep in a feather bed that wasn't subject to the rolling of the tides. If he was stranded and fiscally scuppered – easily done in Hamburg – he could always get a bed and a full English breakfast for as long as it took him to sort out his affairs.

It wasn't easy to find. Nobody we asked had heard of it. We found it by accident. Drawn to it, you might say. It was a long red-brick building with white sills and lintels, municipal in aspect, and only identifiable by the tiniest of brass plaques, just visible next to imposing mahogany double-doors. They were open and we went in. Outside, it was Bradford Town Hall, inside, it was the Royal Yacht, Britannia; dark oak-panelled walls, gleaming brass fittings, and thick maroon carpeting that muffled every footfall into a whisper.

It was staffed entirely by white-jacketed, bow-tied stewards, all retired British sailors, who treated everyone who came through the doors as if they were officers. At the reception desk we said the magic words, 'Top Ten Club'. We felt a little silly because we fully expected the receptionist to say, 'Pardon, sir? Is sir feeling under the weather? Would sir like to sit down for a moment?' But no. The receptionist, a dead-ringer for the old man of the sea, simply came out from behind his desk and beckoned us to follow. He showed us into a large, high-ceilinged, dining room, containing some twenty tables, each with pristine, white, linen table cloths, heavy, silver cutlery, and bone china crockery, bearing the monogrammed crest of the Mercantile Marine. Along one side of the room were a series of tall windows, giving a panoramic view of the docks and bathing the room in daylight. We selected a table near a window.

A steward glided silently to our table and took our order. We ordered a full English breakfast, and Martin, almost as an afterthought, asked for a glass of proper milk.

'Is it proper milk?' he said.' It's not that terrible German condensed stuff, is it?'

'It's proper milk, sir,' said the steward, smiling slightly. 'Would you like a full pint or a half?'

'I think I'll have a pint,' said Martin, rubbing his hands together with anticipation.

The Germans don't understand milk. They seem pathologically opposed to certain micro-organisms and go to great lengths to eradicate them. Milk coming straight from a cow is, to them, a seething cauldron of bacteria, falling over themselves in a headlong rush to enter and pollute the German bloodstream; so it is pasteurised, sterilised, fumigated, ultra-heated, and then pasteurised again. The most that can be said for the finished article is that it is a white liquid.

A couple of minutes later we were driven to the brink of madness by the smell of bacon being fried. We were dribbling uncontrollably by the time it arrived. I suppose there have been better breakfasts served elsewhere, possibly in some far off Elysium, but not on this earth. Bacon, egg, sausage, mushrooms, fried tomatoes, fried bread, toast and butter, and a bottomless pot of tea. All it lacked was HP sauce.

'HP sauce, sir,' said the steward, placing a bottle on the table.

Martin's pint of milk, served ice-cold in a beer glass, was a thing of great beauty. I was tempted to order one myself, but I still had some serious tea-drinking to do.

Honesty compels me to confess that a tear came to my eye. The pursuit of happiness is regarded, by all free men, as an inalienable right; indeed some of the more primitive nations on this earth have felt obliged to write it into their constitutions. It has often been said that if you can't find happiness, you're just going to have to learn to be happy without it. Now, I had found happiness. Fleeting to be sure, but happiness nonetheless. Enough to confirm that, in spite of overwhelming evidence to the contrary, it does exist. And it resides in a pot of tea. I poured a cascade of the brown ambrosia into my monogrammed cup and ascended, even unto Paradise. When we were done, we sat back and watched huge freighters passing through the harbour. Bliss. The Seamans' Mission was indeed a sanctuary for the tortured soul, lost in a foreign land. We would come here every day.

Two or three times a week we spent the afternoon in the club, learning new songs. Halfway through the month, the Beatles released a new single – 'Paperback Writer'. We bought it on the morning of its release, learned it in the afternoon, and played it that night. The crowd went ape-shit. Even Ricky Barnes was impressed.

Playing five hours a night in front of an audience sharpens the musical intellect to a razor-edge, adding dexterity to flair, and frightening the vocal chords into hair-trigger readiness. The band gets tight as fuck. Everything becomes easy. Telepathy becomes a factor. Solos become more adventurous, their execution unencumbered by thought. Flaws in technique are cruelly exposed and quickly rectified. And with so much time to fill, the imagination must reign supreme or you will perish in the fires of repetition.

Civilians often wonder about the hypnotic lure of the stage. They could never, they say, get up on a stage in front of all those people. It would be far too nerve-wracking. Wrong! When things are going right, an almost monastic calm prevails.

The cares of this lousy world fall away. Toothaches and migraines disappear, only, it has to be admitted, to return with renewed vigour when you walk off the stage, but, for the duration of the set, you are freed from the bondage of pain. Even when things go wrong, it is exhilarating, because you know that whatever happens you can handle it. You have that extra yard of pace. You are match-fit.

But even Agamemnon must have needed the occasional pick-me-up. So, if you found yourself flagging, all you had to do was nip down to the toilets, situated in the bowels of the Top Ten, and have a word with the toilet attendant, an old woman sitting at a table just inside the entrance, smiling broadly as she listened to the satisfying clink of pfennig on saucer. She would discreetly sell you enough Preludin to replenish your creative juices and keep you awake for the rest of your life.

One night, deep into the month, we made our way down the stairs from the barracks to do the ten o'clock set. Plum led the way, Martin followed and I brought up the rear. Beau was already in the club. We made our way through the throng of people milling about at the club entrance. Suddenly a stocky, blonde man stepped out of the crowd and stuck a shotgun into Plum's back.

'Stick 'em up,' he said.

Plum froze. Martin, coming behind, raised his bass in the air, like an executioner's axe, preparing to decapitate the gunman. Just as he was about to strike, the gunman turned around and smiled broadly.

'Hi,' he said cheerily, 'I'm Tony Sheridan.'

'You were nearly the late Tony fucking Sheridan then, pal,' said Martin, dancing on the balls of his feet, all fired up.

'It was just a joke,' said Sheridan, sliding the shotgun inside his coat. 'I hear you're a good band. I thought I'd come up for a jam.'

'We'll see,' said Martin, lowering his bass. 'But behave yourself. OK?'

'OK,' said Sheridan.

I had mixed emotions. Sheridan, a Hamburg legend, had been a seminal figure in the birth of the Beatles, providing them with their first recording experience as his backing band. On the one hand, an association with Tony Sheridan would look rather impressive on the CV – an uncanny echo of the Beatles. On the other hand, he appeared to be a borderline simpleton with psychopathic tendencies. But then most guitarists are. I decided to give him the benefit of the doubt. Always a mistake. We went onstage and he headed for the bar. Half-an-hour later he presented himself at the front of the stage and asked if he could play.

'OK,' said Martin.

He climbed on to the stage and the crowd went wild. I offered him my guitar but he brushed it aside.

'I'm playing drums tonight,' he said. His breath was pure alcohol. He picked his way through the gear to the back of the stage, stood over the drums, and held out his hand. 'Sticks,' he demanded. Beau sat firm and stared balefully at Sheridan.

Now then, Sheridan was known as a singer-guitarist but, for all we knew, he was also a drummer. And it was just possible that he was one of those musicians who can still function musically despite being in an alcoholic stupor. I've known a few of them in my time. The crowd were baying for Sheridan. We had to make a decision. We shrugged our shoulders in Beau's direction and he, with a great show of reluctance, got off his stool and handed over his sticks. Sheridan took them and sat down. He didn't adjust the kit, which was a bad sign, because I've never yet come across a proper drummer who didn't, when playing somebody else's kit, spend a couple of minutes making microscopic changes – a millimetre forward, a millimetre back – to the position of every hittable thing within his scope of vision.

'What shall we do?' said Ace, leaning toward him and eyeing him suspiciously.

'Anything,' said Sheridan.

'Some Other Guy?' said Ace.

'Great,' said Sheridan. 'Whan – tooo – threee – farr!'

Instinctively we started. Sheridan couldn't play the drums. Not even close. He thrashed away with total abandon, showing no evidence of form, structure or rhythm. Three verses in, things were going badly. We stubbornly stuck to the song while Sheridan seemed to be playing free-form jazz. Before we got to the solo, Ace waved us to a halt. Sheridan, oblivious, carried on for about twenty seconds, then suddenly stopped.

'Wash'a mattah,' he said.

'You're pissed,' said Ace.

'Yeah?' said Sheridan, apparently genuinely surprised.

'Yeah,' said Ace, 'and you're no drummer, so fuck off and let us get on with the set.'

The crowd, now silent, listened avidly to the exchanges.

'Lesh doo 'nuther one,' said Sheridan. 'Whan-too-threee-farr!' He launched into a drum pattern that would have baffled Copernicus.

'Whoa, whoa, whoa!' said Ace, climbing on to the drum rostrum and snatching the sticks from him. At first Sheridan didn't notice and flailed away regardless. Then he stopped, turning his hands over and over, looking for the sticks.

The crowd cheered.

'Oi!' said Ace, fists clenched. 'If you don't fuck off, I'll beat the fuck out of you.'

The crowd cheered again.

Sheridan thought it over. He looked at Ace, on the balls of his feet again, ready for action. Then a shaft of light obviously pierced the alcoholic gloom. He stood up.

'OK,' he said, seemingly hurt to the quick. He stumbled off the stage and elbowed his way through the cheering crowd, who back-slapped him all the way out of the club. Things settled down and we finished the set to thunderous acclaim. As the cheering died down, a lone German voice piped up:

'What a show! What a show!'

On our way back to the barracks we passed Ricky Barnes, leaning on the end of the bar.

'What a prat,' we said.

'That's Sheridan for you,' he said. 'But dinna jump to conclusions. He's great when he's sober.'

The following night we made our way to the stage for our first set. It was always quiet for the first set and there were maybe thirty punters in, standing in clusters around the bar. One of them was Sheridan, holding what appeared to be a glass of orange juice. He waved and walked over to us.

'Fuck off, Sheridan,' said Ace.

'Hear me out,' said Sheridan, a picture of contrition. 'I know I made a twat of myself last night but I'm sober now.' He raised the glass of orange juice as irrefutable proof. 'Let me have another blow. I'll play guitar this time. What do you say?'

Maybe it was pride. Maybe he didn't want us to leave Hamburg thinking Tony Sheridan was a burnt-out lush. Whatever it was, he seemed so sober and penitent, we relented. Ace leaned toward him.

'OK,' he said, 'but one fuck-up and you're off.'

'I won't fuck up,' said Sheridan, taking the hangdog-look into new panoramas.

I handed him my guitar. Plum and I, now surplus to requirements, went and sat at a table near the stage. This is the life, I thought – somebody else doing the work and me getting paid. Sheridan and Ace plugged in and, after a brief discussion with Beau, launched into the first number, 'Workin' In A Coalmine'. Sheridan's guitar-playing was sparse and precise and his voice was strong and clear. Ace, who can tell class from shite in a micro-second, was dancing by the third note. Urged on by Ace, Sheridan started to burn.

'He's a bit sharp,' said Plum.

'You could cut your hand on him,' I said.

He did six songs, one of them 'Nobody's Child'. It is a mawkish, self-pitying whinge of a song but Sheridan sang it with such emotional power that I found myself wondering whether he really was an orphan. I started to feel sorry for him. It didn't last long. As so often in my life, cynicism rode to my rescue. Once again, on the brink of emotional incontinence, the misanthropic cavalry came over the hill, sabres rattling and bugles blaring. He was only singing a song, after all. He finished his set and, to a spattering of applause, bowed briefly and left the stage. Where he'd stood was a pool of water.

'Urgh!' I said, strapping on my guitar. 'What's that?'

'He was sweating like a pig,' said Ace.

Sheridan sat at the bar, still nursing his orange juice, while we finished the set. Afterwards we walked over to him for an apres-gig post-mortem.

'Fucking brilliant, pal,' said Ace. We chorused our agreement.

Sheridan was modest. He knew how good he'd been and he didn't need to underline it. He didn't react to our thinly-veiled suggestions that we go into a studio together and make a little bit of history, so we stopped fishing and talked shop. I asked him something I'd been dying to know.

'Was the shotgun loaded?'

'You bet it was,' he said. 'Do you think I'd be mad enough to walk around

what a show! what a show!

Hamburg with an empty shotgun? I wouldn't last five minutes.'

We talked for a while, then he made his excuses and left. On the way back to the barracks we passed Ricky Barnes.

'I told youse,' he said, 'When he's sober he's fuckin' great but he's his own worst enemy.'

'We suggested making a record together,' I said, 'but he didn't seem interested.'

'He wouldn't be,' said Ricky Barnes, 'Nobody wants to know about him anymore. He fucked up, big time.'

Ricky Barnes told us the story of Sheridan's downfall. Riding on the crest of the Beatles' wave, he had played a gig in Munich, the capital city of Bavaria. Bavaria was the crucible of Hitler's Aryan dream and it is still a stronghold for right-wing imbecility. Beneath the perilously thin veneer of civilisation lurks a dark and insidious loathing of all things liberal. The rolling farmlands provide a breeding ground for sleek, urbane politicians who parade their bigotry like campaign medals. Time alone may rid us of these festering sores on the body politic, but I seriously doubt it. Time can only do so much.

So Sheridan entered the wolf's lair. The audience, three thousand strong, awaited him. The gig started well and he soon had them in the palm of his hand. He finished his show with 'What'd I Say', the Ray Charles song. By the time he got to the audience participation section, performer and audience were one.

'YEAH-EAH-EAH,' he shouted.

'YEAH-EAH-EAH,' aped the crowd.

'WHOAH-OAH-OAH,' he shouted.

'WHOAH-OAH-OAH,' yelled the crowd.

'OOH-OOH-OOH,' he shouted.

'OOH-OOH-OOH,' screamed the crowd.

They were in a frenzy. It was then he made his big mistake. He snapped to attention and threw his right hand upwards in a Nazi salute.

'HEIL HITLER!' he shouted.

There was total silence.

Sheridan had to be escorted out of the building by a small squad of Munich's finest, who had been on security duty at the gig. While most of them would probably have agreed with the sentiment expressed by Sheridan, they weren't too pleased about having to protect an uppity Britisher from a three thousand-strong mob of their fellow countrymen, howling for blood. The resulting publicity was, it has to be admitted, slightly hostile, and Sheridan had to go into hiding. A few months later he emerged, watchful and skittish, like a lone antelope walking past a pride of hungry lions. It was then, I assume, that he started carrying the shotgun.

'They didn't seem to hate him last night,' I said. 'They went wild.'

'Oh, they still love him in Hamburg,' said Ricky Barnes. 'They probably thought it was hilarious.'

While we're on the subject of fascism, Ace bought an Iron Cross. It was an impulse buy. He'd spotted it in the window of the gun shop across the road from the Top Ten and bought it for sartorial reasons. A month or so earlier we'd played Aldershot, and Ace had bought, in a second-hand shop, the full dress uniform of a 2nd Lieutenant of the Parachute Regiment. It was black with a red stripe running down the side of the trouser-leg. It could have been made for him. He wore it, against Queen's regulations, with the trousers tucked into black riding boots. The Iron Cross, worn on a red ribbon around the neck, would set it off nicely. And indeed it did, but it immediately transformed the uniform into that of the Waffen SS, and turned the riding boots into jackboots. Onstage that night, he wore the full ensemble. The bucolic good-nature of the Top Ten audience wore a little thin and Ace had to endure much barracking. He gave as good as he got. He always does, but... He wore it a few times just to show that he couldn't be intimidated, then put it away.

One night, a German TV film crew arrived. They were making a documentary about the Beatles and they needed some footage of the Top Ten today. Could they film some of our set? Silly question number one. Another rung on the ladder to the stars.

Keith, meanwhile, was getting down to some serious shoplifting. Naturally, he specialised in fashion crime. His modus operandi was seemingly foolproof. Wearing his parka, he'd enter a men's outfitters. He'd select a few items from the racks and take them into the fitting room, where he'd take off his parka and put on all the clothes. Then he'd put the parka back on and stroll out of the shop, an accomplished thief with an apparent weight problem. So successful was he, he became reckless. He began to steal things he didn't want. But he seemed to lead a charmed life. He entered a state of judicial nirvana. He was criminally invisible. Kleptomanically sublime. His ill-gotten spoils, thrown into a corner of the barracks, grew substantially every day and he soon began to steal suitcases.

On the penultimate night we held an end-of-residency party in the barracks. The official starting time was the last note played by the last band. As providence would have it, we were the last band on. Ricky Barnes, all heart, gave us special dispensation to finish at three in the bastarding morning. We downed tools and headed for oblivion. The Senate had flagrantly ignored the starting gun and were already kilted-up and halfway there. By the time we got up to the barracks they were already whetting their claymores and talking Bannockburn trivia.

As you would expect, self-control was an abstract concept. The proceedings were dominated by manly pursuits. Rudolph, the head bouncer, a genial psychopath, challenged all-comers to an arm-wrestling contest. We queued up to be humiliated. The Senate went first. They didn't last long. When Rudolph had laid waste to the pride of Caledonia, he turned his attention to the sons of Glyndwr. We fared no better. Plum was the last to go. Rudolph, grinning broadly, gripped Plum's hand and, looking him straight in the eye, began to apply his considerable strength. But Plum held firm. Rudolph's smile began to fade. He began to frown. He redoubled his efforts but Plum, poker-faced, was immovable. The minutes ticked by. Rudolph's face moved from lobster pink, through post office red, into

what a show! what a show!

cardiac-arrest crimson. Their locked arms began to quiver. Almost imperceptibly, Rudolph's arm was forced backwards. He began to sweat. He still held Plum's gaze but he knew he was beaten. The assembled Celts bayed for Teutonic blood. Suddenly, his face contorted with pain, Rudolph caved in. To great cheers, his arm crashed back on to the table. He and Plum stood up, their eyes still locked. A silence fell on the room. Then Rudolph laughed and held his hand out. Plum, still impassive, took it, and they shook hands. We all cheered. Rudolph put his arm around Plum's shoulders and, whispering Germanic niceties in his ear, steered him toward the nearest beer crate where, like two gladiators who have survived a particularly stressful day in the arena, they set about drinking themselves into unconsciousness.

At the time, the Top Ten was undergoing some renovation and our side of the building was scaffolded. All we had to do was open any window and there it was. As dawn broke, shadowy figures could be seen swinging, like Celtic orang-utans, from platform to platform. No one, as far as I know, was killed.

About five o'clock an unseemly scuffle took place, Beau, rightly or wrongly, suspected that Moira and Bob, the Senate's sax-player, were getting a little too friendly for comfort. I'd like to inform you of the outcome but, just as it was getting interesting, I lost consciousness. I was not alone. Keith, who had been drinking steadily since six o'clock the previous evening, spent the entire party, comatose, in the toilet.

The last night was a rather subdued affair. Drained of emotion and still a little hung-over, everybody tip-toed through the evening, trying very hard not to make any sudden movements. Except, of course, for Ace who, seemingly immune from the ravages of alcoholic excess, still exhorted us on to even greater deeds and legendary exploits.

'Where the fuck does he come from?' said an awe-struck Scottish voice. 'Fucking Mars?'

As we came into the club for the eleven o'clock set, Ricky Barnes emerged from behind the bar, carrying his sax. We whooped with delight. Finally we were, it seems, good enough to play with the great Ricky Barnes.

'Where do you think you're going?' said Ace.

'You've been pestering me for a month to have a blow with you,' said Ricky Barnes. 'Well, tonight's the night.'

'I don't know about that,' said Ace, shaking his head doubtfully. 'Do you think you're good enough?'

'Fuck off, Marrrtin,' said Ricky Barnes, and headed for the stage. We followed. As he climbed on the stage the crowd erupted. They understood that this was a long-overdue blessing from above. Nobody could remember the last time Ricky Barnes had brought his sax to the Top Ten. Our applications for membership of the Honorary Company of Angels had been processed and accepted. We decided to put him through his paces. We gave him solo after solo, egging him on all the way. He stood there, legs apart, and honked. I was sure I'd heard better sax-players but, for the life of me, I couldn't remember when. Maybe on Little Richard records? Or Jim Horn on Duane Eddy's stuff? If Lord Byron had played the sax, this is what he would have sounded like. He stayed on for the whole set. When we came off we were wild-eyed and buzzing, Ricky Barnes more than most. We made our way to the bar but Ricky Barnes was ambushed by the Senate, who'd stayed to watch the show. They crowded around him and took it in turns to shake his hand. When they finally let him go, he walked over to us.

'Nay sa' bad, gentlemen,' he said, grinning like an idiot, 'nay sa' bad. What are you drinking?'

This was overwhelming. Not only had we been honoured with his musical presence, we were now being offered a drink on the house. I expect this is how C.B. Fry must have felt when offered the throne of Albania. We sat at the bar and talked shop.

'I wanted to have a chat with youse,' said Ricky Barnes, 'because I won't see you tomorrow before you go. I want you back here before the end of the year. Maybe November? Are you free in November?'

'Yes,' we chorused.

'I'll give Jack Fallon a ring and fix it up. OK?'

'OK,' we chorused.

'Right,' he said, draining his glass. 'I've got work to do. I'll see youse later.'

The following morning, after a perfunctory sleep, both bands gathered outside the Top Ten and loaded our gear into our respective vans. Keith's luggage was our main problem. He seemed to have stolen every item of clothing in St Pauli. We got most of it in, but he had to ditch two suitcases. He gave one to a passing down-and-out who would, no doubt, turn heads tomorrow on the Reeperbahn with his new, mod wardrobe.

Davey, the Senate's guitarist, was in sombre mood.

'Leave my gear out,' he said, 'I'm staying in Hamburg. I'm joining Lee Curtis and the All Stars.' Nobody seemed surprised. Lee Curtis was often in the Top Ten and he and Davey had become firm friends.

We said our goodbyes, promised to keep in touch, and drove off, the Senate to their next German residency and us back to Wales. Davey stood on the pavement outside the Top Ten, next to his amp, guitar and suitcase and waved us off.

20
a few swansea stories

We played our first gig back home at the Tivoli Ballroom in Mumbles. After a month of playing five hours a night, going back to an hour-long set was a doddle. The Tivoli was a cavernous, old ballroom and at the end of the night we carried our equipment on the long trek from the stage to the foyer, ready for loading. There were still a few bouncers about so we didn't mind leaving it unattended while we schlepped back for the next instalment. When it was all in the foyer, Plum went to fetch the van. We sat on the gear and waited. Suddenly Beau frowned.

'Where's my snare drum?' he said. We searched through the gear but there was no sign of it. 'Somebody's nicked it,' he said.

'Maybe one of the bouncers is taking the piss,' said Martin.

We asked around but nobody'd seen it.

'I'll phone the police,' said Beau. He used the phone in the box office, while we listened from the foyer.

'I'd like to report the theft of a snare drum,' he said. 'A snare drum... S-N-A-R-E... it's about a foot across and about four inches deep... no, it's not in a case... it's just the drum... yes... from the Tivoli ballroom... my name is Ken Adamson... yes, Beau... yes, the Jets... no, Plum's not here at the moment... OK... Thank you very much.' He returned to the foyer. 'They'll keep an eye out for it, but they don't hold out much hope.'

Plum came back.

'Beau's snare drum's been nicked,' I said.

'You're joking,' said Plum. 'Let's go and look for the bastard who did it. He can't have gone far.'

'Forget it,' said Beau. 'He's probably miles away by now.'

We put the gear in the van and drove back along the Mumbles Road into Swansea. The Mumbles Road is about two-and-a-half miles long and follows the coastline almost all the way. There are few buildings to speak of, except Swansea University which is set back off the landward side of the road. Apart from that, it is open terrain. About a mile along the road, the van's headlights picked out the back of a man, dressed in a white shirt and dark trousers, walking unsteadily. Under his right arm he was carrying something shiny. As we approached he stuck out his thumb.

As we drew level with him, Beau started jumping up and down.

'He's got my snare drum,' he shouted.

Plum braked sharply and pulled the van over to the side of the road. We waited for the hitchhiker to catch up. He arrived, breathless.

maybe i should've stayed in bed?

'Where are you going?' said Plum.
'Swansea,' said the hitchhiker.
'Get in,' said Plum.

Martin opened the side door and the hitchhiker climbed in. He handed Beau the snare drum while he did so. When he was seated he took it back.

'Thanks, boys. I thought I'd have to walk all the way home.' His speech was slurred and he was reeking of alcohol. We drove off.

'Drummer, are you?' said Martin.
'No,' said the hitchhiker, holding up the drum, 'this belongs to my mate. He's a drummer.' He belched loudly.
'Where've you been?' said Martin.
'The Tivoli,' said the hitchhiker
'Oh, who was on?' said Martin.
'The Jets,' said the hitchhiker.
'Any good?' said Plum.
'Great,' said the hitchhiker. 'They're my favourite band.'
'Mine too,' said Martin. 'They should get a new bass-player though. Martin Ace is useless.'
'No, he isn't,' said the hitchhiker. 'He's great. They'd be lost without him.'
'I am Martin Ace, you twat,' said Martin.
'You're not,' said the hitchhiker, trying to focus his eyes in Martin's direction.
'Yes, I am,' said Martin, 'and you've just stolen my drummer's snare drum. And that's him sitting next to you.'

The hitchhiker swivelled in his seat and peered at Beau.
'Good God,' he said. 'Beau Adams.'
Beau glared at him.
'I'm sorry, pal,' said the hitchhiker, fear crossing his face. 'I don't know why I did it. It was just lying there and I picked it up. I'm sorry. I'm pissed as fuck.' He lapsed into silence.

'What shall we do with him?' said Plum.
'Let's kill the bastard,' said Beau.
'Good idea,' said Martin. 'We could dump his body in the university grounds. They wouldn't find it for weeks. And nobody would suspect us.'
'Steady on,' said the hitchhiker, suddenly fearing for his life. 'I didn't mean any harm. It was just a spur of the moment thing. Honest.'

Beau snatched his snare drum back.
'Let's kill him anyway,' he said, coldly,
'It would be justifiable homicide,' I said. 'According to international law, the theft of a musical instrument is regarded as a crime against humanity. What do you think, Dermot?'
'I agree,' said Dermot.
'I've got a better idea,' said Martin. 'Let's drop him off down the Gower.'

The Gower peninsula, for the geographically dismal, juts out of the Swansea Bay into the Bristol Channel. It is the lower lip of the cow's head that is the map of Wales. It is a nature reserve and, as such, outside the clutches of rapacious, short-sighted, property speculators who would destroy all that is precious in this world for the sake of filthy commerce. There are places in the Gower that can still be considered remote.

'Aw, come on, boys,' said the hitchhiker. 'Don't leave me down there. I'll die of exposure.'

'Too good for you,' said Beau.

'I agree,' said Dermot.

We headed for the Gower. It was a clear, moonlit night and we drove in silence, as if to emphasise the gravity of the crime and the sentence passed. We stopped at the most inhospitable place we could find. There were gorse bushes in all directions, as far as the eye could see,

'Get out,' said Martin, opening the side door. The hitchhiker, by now resigned to his comeuppance, got out and stood at the side of the road, looking sheepish. 'And if I ever see you at another Jets gig I will personally beat the fuck out of you. Understood?'

The hitchhiker nodded and we drove off.

'All right, Beau?' said Plum.

'No,' said Beau. 'Let's go back and kill him.'

'I agree,' said Dermot.

Dermot had been around for years. He was a pale, dark-haired, hollow-cheeked Englishman who, for some unfathomable reason, had chosen to live in Wales. He was a one-arm bandit maintenance engineer by trade, and he was lodging with Plum. He didn't say much, preferring to sit on the sidelines, smiling enigmatically. A passer-through might conclude that here was a man who had seen everything and done everything at least twice and now looked on life's inescapable tragedy as a tedious charade, worthy of nothing more than a fleeting smile. The truth was that he was pissed. Dermot liked to drink. He slept very little, judging that such an activity would cut into his drinking time. He told us nothing about his past so he was full of surprises. It was a good two years before we realised he could play guitar. There were always guitars lying about but Dermot never showed the slightest interest in any of them until, one day at rehearsal, he picked one up and played a beautiful classical piece. We were stunned. He showed Martin and me how to play it. He didn't know what it was called and neither did we, but we can still play it today. I never saw him pick up another guitar. He was exceedingly accident-prone and a simple fall would often result in torn fingernails and severe bruising. Some part of his body was always bandaged-up and you could usually find a sticking-plaster somewhere or other. My favourite Dermot story happened before I joined the Jets.

They had met some Norwegian sailors, in port for a few days, at a Swansea gig. They stayed in the club till the early hours, seeing how much they could drink without dying. One of the sailors was the ship's cook and he invited everyone back to the ship for breakfast. The invitation was graciously accepted, The full

maybe i should've stayed in bed?

compliment – Plum, Martin, Dermot, Peter Williams, Big Johnno, and the three Norwegians – piled into Peter Williams's car and Dermot's van, a brand new, small, yellow Bedford, owned by his boss, Ron Bateman. When they arrived at the ship, the tide was out and to get to it they had to walk down a near-vertical gangplank. Dermot, naturally, fell down it. Once on the ship, they headed for the galley. The cook produced several bottles of Blue Bols, to keep them occupied, he said, while he made a twenty-four egg Spanish omelette. As the evening progressed, Martin kept falling over. He was convinced they had put to sea.

'I thought we were going to Norway.'

He stumbled over to the nearest porthole and looked out, expecting to see billowing seas. Instead he saw the stationary dock.

'You know what it's like, when you think everything's moving and it's not.'

As the first, tentative shards of daylight shone through the porthole, Dermot stood up. Sort of.

'I'd better go,' he said. 'I've got work in the morning.'

'It is the morning,' said Martin.

'We'd better go, too,' said Plum.

'You must wait some minutes,' said the cook. He disappeared into the bowels of the ship. He returned carrying a catering-sized block of cheese which he presented to Plum as a token, he said, of enduring friendship between Norway and Wales; hands across the sea and all that stuff.

The boys thanked the Norwegians for their hospitality and made their way up on deck. The tide was now at full flood and the ship was high in the water, so to disembark they had, once more, to climb down a near-vertical gangplank. Dermot was the first to go, still expecting, not unreasonably, to go up what he had earlier fallen down. He stepped out into fresh air and plunged, head first, down the gangplank. Halfway down he tipped off into the sea and was only saved from certain drowning by the chain handrail which, even in a drunken stupor, he had the sense to hold on to. Martin and Plum followed him down and hauled him back on to the gangplank. He stood for a moment, swaying, then tumbled downwards again, ending up in a crumpled heap on the dockside. Martin picked him up and dusted him down.

'I'm all right,' said Dermot, and walked straight toward the dockside. Just as he was about to step off into the harbour, Martin grabbed him and pulled him back. He fell backwards, landing heavily and whiplashing his neck. At first Martin thought he was unconscious, but he immediately got up and walked towards his van.

'Dermot,' said Martin. 'Do not drive! You're fucking pissed.'

'Naw,' he said, 'I'm all right,' He got in his van and revved the engine. Everybody pleaded with him to stop but he drove off, so they climbed into Peter Williams's car, pausing only to put the catering-sized block of cheese into the boot, and followed.

To get out of the dock and back to town they had to turn left, but Dermot drove straight on, toward some railway lines. When he reached them he turned left at a

a few swansea stories

level crossing and drove on to the track. The rear axle jammed on top of the rails and the van ground to a halt, back wheels spinning off the ground. Dermot sat in the van with his foot on the accelerator, doing, he thought, sixty miles an hour.

'The twat's driven straight on to the railway line,' said Martin. 'Let's go and rescue him.'

They pulled up at the level crossing and Martin got out, walked up behind the van, and tapped gently on the passenger window. Dermot was concentrating on the way ahead. When he saw Martin he did a double-take. Keeping one hand on the steering wheel, he reached over and opened the passenger door.

'Quick,' he shouted, 'Get in. Get in. We're doing sixty miles an hour.'

Martin got in and, for a while, they sat there, while Dermot revved the engine, still concentrating on the way ahead.

'Dermot,' said Martin finally. 'Where the fuck are you going?'

'Home,' said Dermot, eyes glued to the windscreen. 'I've got work in the morning.'

'Dermot,' said Martin, 'you aren't going anywhere. You're stuck on top of a railway line. Your back wheels are off the ground.'

Dermot opened his door and looked back at the spinning wheels.

'Thank fuck for that,' he said, 'I thought there was something wrong with the van.'

'Stay there,' said Martin, 'and we'll lift you off. And turn the engine off, for God's sake.'

Dermot didn't hear him and continued revving the engine.

They lifted the van off the rails and, when the spinning wheels touched the ground, it shot forward and crashed into a points-changer, catapulting Dermot forward into the windscreen. The engine stalled and began to hiss. They helped him out and he sat on a railway sleeper, rubbing a nasty bruise on his forehead.

Martin checked the van over. There was an almost perfect vee in the front.

'Ron Bateman'll play fuck about this,' said Martin.

'No, he won't,' said Dermot, 'I'll get it fixed before he sees it.' They pushed the van over to the side of the railway lines and abandoned it. 'I'll pick it up tomorrow,' said Dermot.

They all piled into Peter Williams's car and drove home. On the way they picked up a no-waiting sign, as you do, and put it in the back of the car. On Walter Road they were flagged down by a policeman.

'Are you going anywhere near Sketty?' he said.

'Yeah,' said Peter Williams, 'that's where we're going.'

'Good,' said the copper. 'Give us a lift up.' He squeezed into the car and sat next to the no-waiting sign. 'Been out for a drink, have you, boys?' he said.

Plum and Dermot were the last to be dropped off. Plum opened the boot to get his cheese, but it was gone.

'Big Johnno's pinched my fucking cheese,' he said.

Plum unlocked the front door and they tip-toed in.

'It's not worth going to bed now,' said Dermot. 'I might as well go straight to work. Get an early start. Get the van fixed. A couple of pints at lunchtime and I'll be set up for the day.'

So Plum, and the no-waiting sign, went to bed. Dermot got the van fixed and Ron Bateman didn't find out what had happened until years later, when Martin told him the story.

'Noooo,' he said. 'Not Dermot. He'd have told me. Honest as the day is long, Dermot.'

One night, about four o'clock in the morning, the phone rang in the Ace Post Office. Martin was asleep upstairs. He went downstairs and answered it. It was Dermot.

'Martin,' he said. 'Where are you?'

'Dermot.' said Martin, 'I'm at home. You just phoned me. Where the fuck do you think I am? I'm on the end of the phone. What do you want?'

'I've lost the van,' said Dermot. 'Can you remember where I left it?'

'No, I can't. You were the one driving it.' Martin went through a list of possible locations, none of which rang Dermot's bell. Finally, he gave up. 'Look,' he said, 'come up to the Post Office and we'll sort it out. Where are you?'

'I'm in the phone box outside.'

Martin drew back the curtains and there, in the phone box, was Dermot. He waved.

'Dermot,' said Martin, 'why did you phone me? Why didn't you just knock on the door?'

'Well, I didn't want to disturb you,' said Dermot.

The phone box outside the Post Office began to assume iconic status. We acquired a new road-manager. His name was Mike and he was a television engineer, who just appeared one day and started helping out.

'He used to put plugs on for us,' says Plum. 'He'd open up the amps and squiggle about with the valves. He assumed the mantle of Mr Fixit.'

He had a girlfriend called Judy.

'She was like a lollipop on a stick,' recalls Plum. 'She was a bit of a roly-poly bird with long, thin legs.'

Beau took a fancy to her. She fluttered her eye-lashes and the game was on. There followed months of speculation. Will he? Won't he? Mike, a really nice chap, suspected nothing. He worshipped Beau and even wore gloves when he handled his drums. One night at the Tivoli, the band left straight after the gig, leaving Mike to pack the gear. Ominously, Beau stayed behind to help. Plum saw him the following day.

'Did you walk Judy home last night?' he said.

'Yes,' said Beau.

'Any good?'

'Shagged her.'

'You didn't shag Mike's bird?'

a few swansea stories 153

'Well, she was asking for it.'
'Where did you shag her?'
'In the phone-box outside the Post Office.'

In the summer of '66, Dermot died. He was at a party in the Langland Bay Hotel, sitting on the parapet of a balcony, pissed as a newt, talking to a few friends when, without warning, he leant backwards and disappeared over the edge. He fell thirty feet and was killed instantly. His funeral was held at the Roman Catholic church in Glanmor. It was packed. Everybody liked Dermot. Dermot's close relatives, who we'd never met, were already in the church when we arrived, sitting on the front pew. We shuffled into a pew near the back. I was sitting next to Terry Williams, who was by then the Jets' drummer. Terry didn't like funerals; he felt queasy just going into a church. We stood up to sing a hymn. Terry began to sway. Suddenly there was a disturbance on the front pew. It was obviously too much for one of Dermot's relatives. A man, head bowed, was helped unsteadily from the church and as he passed us, he raised his head. A chill ran through my bones. It was Dermot. Terry immediately passed out and collapsed in a heap at my feet. Still shaken, we helped Terry out of the church and sat him on a low wall, a few yards away from Dermot's ghost, also recovering. When Terry came to, the first thing he saw was Dermot, who smiled wanly at him. Terry passed out again.

'Who are you?' I said.
'I'm Dermot's twin brother,' he said, weakly.
'I didn't know Dermot had a twin brother,' I said.
'Well, Dermot didn't say much,' said his brother.

We got Terry to the nearest pub as quickly as possible. After a couple of drinks he was set up for the day.

One afternoon we played a Christmas gig at Cocket School in Swansea. We were welcomed by the headmistress, a portly woman with a booming voice, dressed in a Santa Claus outfit. She showed us to the main hall where we were due to play.

'There's no stage,' she honked through the thick, white beard, 'so you'll have to play on the floor. If you need anything, ask the caretaker.'

The caretaker, a balding, sallow man dressed in a brown overall, skulked up to us.

'This is a newly-laid parquet floor,' he droned, 'so you can't hammer nails into it.'

'So, how am I going to anchor my bass-drum?' asked Beau.

'Not my problem,' said the caretaker, despondently.

School caretakers are always despondent. They are semi-tragic figures who exist in that terrible twilight world between teachers, who consider them a necessary evil, and pupils, who see them as figures of fun. This one seemed to be a paradigm of the breed.

'Have you got any clothes line?' said Beau.

'There's some in the boiler-room,' said the caretaker, 'What do you want it for?'

maybe i should've stayed in bed?

'I want to hang out a bit of washing,' said Beau, looking upwards to the heavens, hoping for a little salvation. 'What do you think I want it for? I'm going to tie my bass-drum to that radiator.' He pointed to a radiator fixed to the wall just behind our playing area.

'You can't do that.' said the caretaker. 'You might damage it.'

'Well, it's either that or the nails.' said Beau.

Life for a caretaker is a series of petty accommodations.

'All right,' he said grudgingly, showing no signs of movement.

'Well, can you get it?' said Beau, tetchily.

The caretaker sighed deeply. He looked at Beau and, for an instant, a vivid look of pure hatred flashed across his dull eyes. Then he sighed again and trudged off. Ten minutes later he was back with the clothes line. He handed it to Beau. 'I want it back afterwards,' he said petulantly.

Under the caretaker's hawk-like gaze, Beau tied one end of the clothes line to his bass-drum and the other end to the radiator. He gave his bass-drum a couple of fearsome thumps. The caretaker winced, but the radiator held.

'Like a rock,' said Beau.

The radiator held until the middle of the third song, when it broke free from its brackets. Beau's bass-drum shot forward and the radiator skidded along behind, gouging out two parallel grooves in the parquet floor. The caretaker, who had been standing on guard next to the radiator, dropped to his knees and began to sob.

It took us a minute or two to reorganise, then we were off again. It wasn't easy for Beau. With every beat, the bass-drum, now unsecured, edged forward, and he spent most of his time hauling it back whenever there was a stop in the song. Thus engaged, he didn't notice the headmistress, still dressed in the Santa Claus outfit, tip-toeing up beside him. I have no idea what she wanted. Maybe she wanted to know how much longer we were going to play? Maybe she wanted to inform us what time the raffle would be drawn? Maybe she just wanted to wish Beau a Happy Christmas? Whatever she wanted, she tapped him on the shoulder.

Beau jumped out of his skin. Wild-eyed, he turned and came face-to-face with Santa Claus.

'Fuck off!' he screamed.

The headmistress went as white as her beard. Then she tip-toed backwards the way she'd come, like a courtier leaving the presence of an emperor. Beau, huffing and puffing, went back to work.

While we packed the gear, I got into conversation with the caretaker. He was not a happy man. He told me that working at the school was like a jail sentence, because all the kids would sneak up behind him, tap him on the shoulder, call him a twat, and run off. And there was nothing he could do about it, except report it to the headmistress, which he hated doing; he said it was fucking horrible going to tell her that 'a bunch of kids just called me a twat.' One boy threatened to kill him. 'I'm not having that,' he said, and went to see the headmistress. She called the boy's father in for a meeting in her office. The boy showed no remorse and repeated his threat to kill the caretaker. The boy got expelled. But, even without the psychos, his life was hell. He puts something down and they pinch it. In the summer, the school kitchen windows were left open and the kids put all the plugs in the sinks and turned on all the taps, flooding the kitchen. He said he hated every second of the day.

We sent Beau to get the gig money from the headmistress. assuming that the evening's events had given him a psychological edge. We didn't want to get saddled with a repair bill for a damaged radiator; the municipal mind is so unbending when it comes to matters fiscal. She did bring up the subject but Beau brushed it aside with an end-of-discussion gesture. I suppose it could have been interpreted as a throat-cutting gesture, but only by a terrified spinster in a life-threatening situation. She paid up without further discussion. We waved goodbye to the caretaker, fixing new radiator brackets on the wall, but he didn't wave back.

If schools were a pain in the neck to play, then church halls were a sexual minefield. Every church hall had a vicar, and every vicar, in true Anglican tradition, had doubts. We played at St Somebody-or-other's Youth Club.

'I was changing into my stage clothes,' remembers Martin, ' and I only had my shirt on. I was just reaching up to get my trousers off the peg, when I felt a hand on my back. "Fuck off, boys," I said. I thought it was one of the boys fucking about. It was getting a bit whatshisname so I turned around and it was the vicar, frothing at the mouth.'

I always feel irritated in the presence of the clergy. It irks me to talk to people whose entire life is based on a fallacy. I believe it is my duty, as a born-again atheist, to shake the foundations of their faith. It is easily done. One question is usually enough – 'Where did Noah get the kangaroos from?' They just don't think these things through.

But if they thought I was a difficult customer, they were lucky they weren't dealing with 'Micky the Fringe'. Fringy, the guitarist with the Echoretz, was a militant atheist, who became so incensed by the stupidity of the clergy, he would often resort to physical intimidation. He wouldn't actually beat them up, but he did have a few up against the wall.

'Why isn't there any mention of dinosaurs in the bible?', he would yell into their faces.

However, the high-water mark of Fringy's agitprop was political rather than spiritual. He was thrown out of Ely Conservative Club, where he was playing, for throwing a pint of beer at a framed photograph of Winston Churchill.

Fringy can come to my funeral, any day. It'll be a secular funeral, of course. Any priests spotted in the vicinity will be chased off with sticks. I'd like to be buried at sea. It would be a dignified affair. As the funeral barge left the harbour, a riderless, white horse, with boots reversed in the stirrups, would gallop along the jetty, while Elvis Presley's 'Hound Dog' blared out from strategically-placed tannoy speakers. The media scrum would be kept at a respectful distance by a ten-foot high barbed wire fence. I did briefly consider Byron's blueprint for Shelley's send-off – a funeral pyre on a lonely beach – but rejected it on the grounds that it wasn't quite poetic enough.

maybe i should've stayed in bed?

We met the Marauders in a car park. The Marauders were, arguably, the best band to come out of the beat boom. At three in the morning, coming back from an out-of-town gig, we pulled into a transport café. There was only one other vehicle in the car park, another group van. As we went in, they were coming out.

'Who are you?' they said.

'The fucking Jets,' said Plum. 'Who are you?'

'The fucking Marauders.' came the answer.

'Fucking hell,' said Plum. 'We do one of your songs.'

'That's What I Want' by the Marauders is one of the great unsung songs of the beat era. One day, some record executive with a brain – and there must be one out there somewhere – will re-release it, although it will probably get lost in today's conveyor-belt, lowest common-denominator, anally-retentive music scene. Unless some Tarquin in Ad-land decides to use it to sell Volvos.

Music isn't what it used to be. Today in the Swansea area there are five or six bands; in 1966 there were hundreds. True, they all played the same songs, but they stood there in the spotlight, night after night, convinced they played them better than anybody else. A band could stand or fall by their version of a rock'n'roll standard. 'My Babe', for instance, was a barometer by which a band's worth could be accurately gauged. Rivalry was intense. If a band did an unusual cover, a week later everybody would be doing it, either better or taking the piss.

And every tit-bit of gossip – who was leaving what band and who might be joining in their place – was rigorously catalogued by Beaterama, the weekly music column in the Herald of Wales, gleefully written by Con Atkin. Con was an unusual hybrid – a journalist/drummer. Most drummers can't read, let alone write, and, in my experience, journalists have no sense of rhythm whatsoever. As a drummer, Con had once played with the Raiders from Cardiff, a band with a fearsome reputation; the brain-child of Dave Edmunds, they were the prototype for Love Sculpture. Con used to tell a great story about Jimmy Witherspoon, who was, for the illiterate among you, one of the greats. He was the most sophisticated of blues singers. So sophisticated, in fact, that the jazz fraternity were forever trying to claim him as their own. Crap! He's ours.

Witherspoon was booked to play the Glanmor Jazz Club. He was the biggest act they'd ever booked and a gala night was planned. But, his agent informed the committee, there was a catch, Witherspoon didn't travel with a band so he'd be singing with the houseband. Would that be OK? Yes, it would, gulped the committee. The houseband – a collection of ageing alcoholics, social misfits and borderline psychotics – were summoned. Con was the drummer. The gig was three weeks away so they had plenty of time to get nervous. On the big night, rigid with fear, they reported for duty. They had a few drinks, just to relax a little. By the time Witherspoon walked in, about two minutes before show-time, the place was packed, and the houseband were relaxed as newts.

'What's the set?' said Con.

'Don't worry,' said Witherspoon. 'I'll count you in, you just play a groove, and leave the rest to me.'

a few swansea stories

'OK,' said Con.

'By the way,' said Witherspoon, 'the first number's kind'a slow.'

And indeed it was. It was the slowest song Con had ever heard. He didn't even know there was a tempo down there. Witherspoon was introduced to ecstatic applause, followed by hushed expectancy. He turned to the band and began the count.

'One,' he said.

An age passed. The houseband looked at each other, shrugging their shoulders. The pianist took his pint off the top of the piano, had a sip, and put it back. Would 'two' ever come?

'Two,' said Witherspoon.

Con was desperately trying to establish some sequential relationship between 'one' and 'two' before 'three' arrived, but the void stretched out before him. The bass-player started to shake and the sax-player began to sob quietly.

'Three,' said Witherspoon.

Panic set in. They all looked at Con who, as the drummer, was supposed to understand these things. Con looked glumly ahead.

'Four,' said Witherspoon.

Time stood still. During the next few seconds. they had to start playing and they didn't know when; or how fast; or, they suddenly realised, what key they were supposed to be in. Miraculously, they all came in together, but at different speeds and in different keys. The crowds' collective jaw dropped and Witherspoon turned around, eyes wide open with surprise; Con swore he saw a look of fear flash across them. Then Witherspoon burst out laughing. He waved his arm in tempo and the houseband struggled to slow down. He shouted out the key and gradually, one by one, they arrived in tune. Witherspoon slowed them down until they reached their limit. When they could go no slower, he began to sing.

'He was fucking great,' said Con. 'Well, he was a proper singer, wasn't he?'

Witherspoon, once he realised the limitations of the houseband, delivered a set of shimmering emotion. Con came offstage drained but elated.

'It was a great feeling,' he said. 'I'll take it with me to the grave.'

Which he did, poor bastard, a few years ago. Why do they always take the good ones?

Con picked up most of his Beaterama copy in the Orient, a curry-house just across the road from Swansea railway station. It was a late-night meeting place for jobbing musicians. After a gig, musicians, girl friends, ancillary staff and hangers-on, would meet to chew the fat, literally so in the case of the Orient, where the clientele shared the common western perception that what they were eating was not, as the menu claimed, beef or pork or chicken, but local cats and dogs, and mice caught in the kitchen. But at two o'clock in the morning, a mongrel rogan gosht didn't even touch the sides.

The road outside was jammed end-to-end with group vans and an endless trail of roadies traipsed in and out every five minutes checking them; an enterprising thief could have ended up with enough gear to fill ten pages in Exchange & Mart.

If a suspicious character was spotted lurking in the vicinity, the whole restaurant would rush out, knives and forks in hand, and surround him. He was then mercilessly interrogated at length. Usually it was just a drunk on his way home, but you can't be too careful. There can be no-one lower on the evolutionary scale then a guitar thief. I am against capital punishment because the police and judiciary, surely professions that most attract the simpletons in our society, are incapable of logical thought, and seem hell-bent, with all the fervour of the semi-moronic, on prosecuting the innocent and acquitting the guilty. Detection is too important to be left in the hands of the police, and justice is too important to be left in the hands of the judiciary. But when it comes to guitar thieves, hanging's too good for 'em. If they're allowed to live then who knows where they'll end up. I wouldn't be surprised to find that General Pinochet started out stealing guitars.

Inter-table banter at the Orient was fierce and taking the piss, especially in the hands of Martin and Plum, became a surgical skill. Communal activities included drinking contests, always won by Plum, and fart-lighting, a hangover from the Age of Enlightenment. Eating habits were noted and, in the fullness of time, exploited. Breezy, for instance, would always order the hottest curry available – probably a spaniel tindaloo – and two glasses of coke. He'd eat the first half of his curry before draining the first glass of coke, then, sweating profusely, he'd attack the second half. This completed, he'd drain the second glass and sit back, contented; if Breezy could ever be described as contented. As soon as the meal arrived he would, leaving it to the very last minute, run to the toilet to piss away a couple of pints of lager to make room for the upcoming feast, leaving his curry unattended. While he was gone, I drank one of his cokes and filled the empty glass with vinegar (all Welsh curry houses have a vinegar bottle on every table). Breezy returned and began to eat. As he approached the halfway point a hush fell on the restaurant. Which would he drink? The coke or the vinegar? Suddenly he put down his spoon, grabbed the glass of vinegar and downed it in one. Nothing. He picked up his spoon and ate another mouthful of curry. Then it hit him. He began to retch violently. Everybody got out of his way as he ran for the toilet, spewing as he went. Twenty minutes later he was back, pale-faced but purged, intent on revenge. He demanded to know who had done it. I blamed Plum. Plum blamed Martin. Martin blamed Beau, and the blame went around the Orient until it came back to me. But there was not enough evidence for conviction – unlike the police, we human beings need concrete proof – and the matter was dropped. Breezy, with murder in his eyes, went home, but he was back the next night eating a Pekinese madras with two cokes. But from then on, he went to the toilet as soon as he ordered his meal, closing the window of opportunity. If he reads this book – which I know he will because I've promised him a copy – he will finally know the truth and, I have no doubt, wreak his terrible revenge. But I'm not worried. Time has given me the moral high-ground on this one. Years later, when I was living in Shepherds Bush, Breezy came to stay for a few days, during which time he got pissed and capriciously vomited over a white shag-pile carpet I had in the bathroom. I was tempted to tell him about the Orient incident there and then, but it might have interfered with his flow of guilt and given him succour in his darkest hour.

21
the hottest ticket in K-town

We were booked to play the month of August at the Club Studio 45 in Kaiserslautern, Germany. It was a Jack Fallon gig. He was turning out to be a sweetheart. Kaiserslautern is fifty miles south-west of Frankfurt and it took us two days to drive down there in blistering summer sunshine. We arrived, hot and sticky, the day before we were due to start. It was early afternoon but the club was open. It was a long, narrow cellar with a small stage at the far end, where a band's gear was set up. Out of the baking sun, the club was refreshingly cool and smelled of disinfectant. We were greeted by a stocky, old woman with a mop and bucket. We enquired as to the whereabouts of the owner but she spoke no recognisable language. She did, however, repeatedly point upwards at the ceiling. We took this to mean that the boss was upstairs. We found a door behind the bar which led to a flight of stairs and shouted a few hellos. We heard a door slam, some shouting, and the sound of footsteps. We waited.

Two men emerged. The first was a wiry, grey-haired, bantam-weight, bustling with energy. At his elbow was a dark, shambling hulk of a man with dull eyes and a five o'clock shadow that would frighten the life out of any self-respecting razor.

'Christ almighty!' said Plum. 'It's Popeye and Bluto.'

Popeye walked toward us and held out his hand.

'Hello,' he said. 'I am Chico. I am boss.' He made an expansive sweeping gesture that spun through 360 degrees. 'I own club. And this…' He jerked his thumb toward Bluto, 'is Antonino. He is my man.'

Antonino grunted suspiciously.

'You want drink?' said Chico.

'Yes,' we croaked.

'Antonino, give them drink.'

Antonino, in a permanent sulk, poured our drinks, while Chico, in perpetual motion, put us in the picture.

'You start tomorrow. The band tonight is Quiet Few. They are from England too. They have been here for month. They are very good band. You must be very good too. You will stay in hotel. Antonino will take you there after drink. OK?'

'OK,' we said. 'By the way, Chico, we are not from England. We are from Wales.'

'Is not the same?' he said.

'Is not the same,' we said.

He seemed disappointed.

'I have told efferybody you are from England,' he said. 'I have put it on all the posters. It is too late to change.'

'It's not important,' said Martin. 'We're just correcting a misconception. Everybody in Germany thinks we're English. It's as if you came to Britain and, just because you spoke with an accent, people thought you were…' He searched for a suitably obscure nationality. '…from Yugoslavia, for instance.'

'I am from Yugoslavia,' said Chico, frowning. 'You can tell where I come from just by looking?'

'It's a knack,' said Martin.

'And where do you think Antonino comes from?' said Chico, clearly intrigued.

Martin took a long, hard look at Antonino.

'Italy?' he said.

'That's right,' said Chico excitedly. 'How do you know that?'

'Because his name is Antonino, you prat,' said Martin, patiently. 'If his name had been Adolf I would have said he was a German.'

'But you know I come from Yugoslavia.'

'It was just a guess,' said Martin.

But, beyond reason, Chico was impressed.

After our drinks Antonino took us over to the hotel which was within walking distance. Dragging our suitcases behind us, we followed him. He didn't offer to help. We tried to draw him into a little small-talk, but with no success. The most we got out of him was a grunt or two. The hotel wasn't bad. We even had single rooms. Antonino handed us a fistful of room-keys and, his mission completed, turned to leave. Before he left we asked him what time the club was opening. He shook his head. We asked him again. He shrugged his shoulders.

'What – time – does – club – open?' said Plum.

With an air of supreme resignation, Antonino fished around in the folds of his jacket and produced a dog-eared, pocket dictionary. He began to thumb through it slowly, mouthing the word 'what' to himself. After what seemed like a fortnight he stopped at a page and frowned. Using an index finger the size of a telegraph pole, he went down the list of words. Then he stopped. The ghost of a half-smile passed across his lips.

'Ah, che,' he said. Then, mouthing the word 'time', he started to thumb through the dictionary again.

'This could take all night,' said Plum. He waved his hands in the air. 'Forget it, pal. We'll just come over later.'

Antonino continued to thumb through the dictionary, this time mouthing the word 'forget'. We picked up our cases, went to our rooms, and got our heads down for an hour or so. It was dark when we awoke. We had a shit, shower and shave, and headed for the club.

It was buzzing when we got there. The crowd were mainly pissed Germans, with a substantial smattering of American GIs. You could tell they were GIs because they had crew-cuts and wore ghastly leisurewear. The Quiet Few were in full flight. They were truly terrible. Chico elbowed his way through the crowd and gestured toward them.

'They are great, no?' he shouted above the din.

the hottest ticket in K-town

'No,' we chorused back.

He laughed and clapped his hands.

'Are you this good?' he shouted.

'Don't be a silly Yugoslavian,' said Plum, putting his arm around Chico's shoulders and kissing him on the cheek. 'Now, how about buying the Smokeless Zone a drink?'

We spent the following afternoon setting our gear up while the Quiet Few took theirs down. Their bass-player seemed semi-detached from the rest of the band. He rarely talked to them and they rarely talked to him. He hung about as we set things up. He was small and pear-shaped with wispy blonde hair. He spoke in a Birmingham monotone and seemed profoundly depressed; suicidal even. He was, he said, leaving the band.

'Musical differences,' he droned.

'What? You want to play music and they don't?' I said.

'Something like that,' he said flatly. He was, he said, going to stay in Germany for a while. Maybe join a German band? Maybe marry a German girl? Maybe stay here for good? 'There's nothing left for me in Britain,' he said, almost to himself. 'I might as well try Germany. It can't be any worse.'

We were all feeling depressed by now.

'By the way,' he added, 'I haven't got anywhere to stay tonight, I've been kicked out of the hotel. Can I sleep in your van?'

'Yes, of course,' we said. Well, you've got to have some feeling for your fellow man when he's on his uppers.

'And would you mind if I kept my bass and amp in the van, too? It'll only be for a few days. Just till I get myself sorted out.'

'All right,' we said, reeking of tolerance.

'And would you mind parking the van around the back of the hotel? It's shady there and the sun won't wake me up in the morning.'

'How does "fuck off" sound?' we said.

Compassion is such a transitory emotion.

Our first night was great. The place was jam-packed and jumping. Chico was beside himself.

'You are the greatest group in the world,' he said, eyes brimming with tears.

'Oh, I bet you say that to all the bands,' said Martin. 'Now, fucking shut up and buy the Smokeless Zone a drink.'

The ex-bass-player from the Quiet Few appeared, as from nowhere, like a troubled spirit searching for eternal rest.

'Very good,' he said, brow furrowed, obviously wrestling with some terrible soul-shaking dilemma. 'Seeing you has made me realise what a useless musician I am. I think I'll give up the bass and try another line of work.'

'Good idea,' said Martin.

We got back to the hotel, ready for bed. We gave the van keys to the ex-bass-player of the Quiet Few – who we now called 'Quiet' – and off he went. We'd parked the van on the east side of the hotel, in perfect position to catch the first

maybe i should've stayed in bed?

mysterious rays of sunlight that announce the dawn of a new day; about five-thirty in the morning, according to our calculations. More importantly, it was just below the windows of our rooms so we could keep an eye on it. We didn't want the van to get stolen, did we?

The following morning Martin got out of bed, threw the curtains back, and checked on the van. It was still there. Then his eye caught movement in the back. He opened his door and shouted down the corridor.

'Come and see this, boys!'

In our underpants, we emerged from our rooms and shuffled sleepily down to Martin's room. He beckoned us over to the window.

'Look at this,' he said. We looked down and tried to focus our eyes. Then they cleared.

'He's having a wank,' said Plum. 'Quiet's having a wank. The dirty little bastard. I'm not clearing it up.' He looked at his watch. 'Five marks says it'll all be over in two minutes.'

We laid our bets, picking our estimated times. After one minute and fifty-five seconds Quiet started to thrash about.

'Thank you, gentlemen,' said Plum, 'you can pay me when you get your trousers on.'

We settled down into our new routine – get up, watch Quiet having a wank, lose five marks, have some breakfast, hang about a bit, go to the club, play all night, have a bite to eat in the Italian restaurant next door, go to bed, get up, watch Quiet have a wank…

We started to meet the locals. We seemed to be very popular with the black GIs. They all wanted to come up and sing with us. The trouble was that they all wanted to sing 'Stormy Monday Blues'. Some were great and some were next-to-useless, but playing the same song over and over again got tedious for us and the audience, so we had to insist upon some programme variety. We banned the singing of 'Stormy Monday Blues' altogether. Except when Dave wanted to sing it. Dave was born to sing it. The lyrics have a poetry to them that has rarely been equalled. Byron for sure. Maybe Shelley.

They call it Stormy Monday,
Lord, but Tuesday's just as bad.

Dave, a tall, hawk-like man, was always dressed in an immaculate white shirt, a serious, slim-Jim tie, with matching tie-pin and cuff-links, dark trousers and patent-leather shoes. When Dave sang the word 'Lord' his voice swooped down into a beautiful dark-brown bass-note that sent a shiver down your spine, and straight back up again.

One of the white GIs made a lasting impression. Dressed like a backwoodsman, he would, given the slightest excuse, eat a pint glass without apparent discomfort. Martin, who likes this kind of thing and can take the top off a beer bottle with his teeth, tried it, but soon gave up.

'Didn't like the taste,' he said.

There was a shy German lad, muscular and blonde, who always wore a red-

the hottest ticket in K-town

checked lumberjack shirt. His name was Gerhardt and he became our unofficial road-manager, fetching drinks and replacing broken strings. He could get morose on occasions, but he had good cause. He was in dispute with his wife, from whom he was separated, over the custody of their son. In similar circumstances we'd all become morose on occasion, so we sought to lighten his tragic burden by taking the piss out of him. It seemed to work.

Then there was Ingrid; twenty-five stones of pulsating oestrogen. At first we gave her a wide berth but then Plum discovered her father owned an off-licence and it all changed. From then on Ingrid's approach would be heralded by the distant sound of clinking bottles and she would burst into the dressing room carrying about twenty carrier bags full of free hooch.

But there was a price to be paid. One night I got back to my hotel room to find her, totally naked, reclining provocatively on my bed. I did what any red-blooded, penis-led, hair-trigger male in musk would do in similar circumstances – I ran like hell.

Ingrid didn't speak to me for a week and, worse, cut my drinks ration. The only benefit I seemed to derive from the situation was that I learned how to apologise in German.

There was Paul Titse, who claimed to be the principal dancer at the Stuttgart Ballet. He came to see us every night and we got to know him quite well. After a week or so, he invited us back to his flat for a meal. We accepted and, one night after the show, we walked to his flat through old Kaiserslautern. It had been raining and the shiny cobbled streets, overhung by Hansel and Gretel buildings, glinted in the streetlights. He was excited and talked endlessly, in near-perfect English, about the band. He had, he said, been thinking of our future. How would it be if he were to manage the band in Germany? He'd never managed a band before but he had plenty of contacts in the business and saw no major problems ahead.

'It can't be that different from ballet?' he said, exhibiting the blind optimism of the unsuspecting.

'Just a minute,' said Martin, poking him in the chest with a friendly finger. 'How do we know you're a real ballet dancer? We've only got your word for it.'

'I'll show you,' he said, taking off his jacket and handing it to Martin.

He raised himself onto his toes, took a deep breath, and bounded down the street, pirouetting across the cobbles and leaping majestically into the lamplight. Stripped of music it became pure athletics, and the only sound to disturb the stillness of the night was the scuffling of his feet. When he reached the end of the street, he turned around and came back toward us in, what I believe is called, a travelling spin. A little pas-de-deux with a lampost, two or three aerial splits, and he landed in front of us. He threw his arms up dramatically and raised a questioning eyebrow.

'There's no two ways about it,' said Martin. 'The man's a ballet dancer.'

His flat was just like you'd expect the flat of the principal dancer with the Stuttgart Ballet to be. Dark, stained floorboards and white walls, sparsely furnished and discreetly lit. The only relief from the ascetic were the violently-coloured African artefacts. He put some weird classical music on the record-player, placed the biggest bottle of alcohol we'd ever seen on the table and disappeared into the kitchen. Plum and Martin eyed the bottle.

'It's Bacardi,' said Martin. We'd never seen Bacardi before. He read the label. 'It's white rum,' He unscrewed the top, filled one of the crystal-glass tumblers provided, drank about a third and sat back. 'Very nice,' he said, smacking his lips. 'Very nice, indeed.'

I went over to his record-player and looked at the album sleeve.

'Bartok,' I said.

'Not Brigitte Bartok?' said Martin.

I got down on my knees and scanned his record collection, housed in a minimalist mahogany cabinet. Naturally they were in alphabetical order. I read them out loud.

'Berlioz, Mussorgsky, Ravel, Stravinsky'

(I've always been rather ambivalent about Stravinsky. I like him in spite of his atonality. Because the fact remains – any fool can write atonal music.)

'Any Buddy Holly?' said Plum.

The meal was cordon-bleu class. Each flavour complemented its neighbour and the spices and herbs were subtly insistent and aromatically seductive. It was like tasting food for the first time.

'Have you got any tomato sauce?' I asked. He didn't have any. So much for culture.

After the meal, we put some Ravel on the turntable, gave the Bacardi a hammering, and talked until dawn. Or the end of the Bacardi. Whichever came first. When it was time to leave, Paul waved us off.

'It's going to be great,' he shouted at our disappearing backs. 'You're going to be as big as the Beatles. Bigger!'

'That'll be the day,' said Martin.

'He's full of it, isn't he?' said Plum.

'Nice chap, though,' I said.

'Mad as a hatter,' said Beau.

The following night he arrived at the club, full of enthusiasm. He'd made a few phonecalls to his business contacts. They'd expressed polite interest in the band but no demi-semi-commitments had been suggested. But he was optimistic. It was early days yet. On each subsequent night he'd arrive, still positive, but slightly less optimistic. After a week or so his attitude had become infected with doubt.

'I don't know what's the matter,' he would say. 'They all listen politely but they won't do anything.'

'Welcome to the music business,' I said.

After a couple of weeks he gave up.

'I tried my best,' he said.

'We know,' said Plum, patting him gently on the back. 'We know.'

The month passed slowly, which was fine because we were enjoying ourselves.

the hottest ticket in K-town 165

The crowds were large and enthusiastic, the club owner was deliriously happy, the weather was fabulous, and we were getting paid. What more could a man want? This, we all agreed, was the life. Then we woke up one morning and the van was gone. Immediately suspicion fell on Quiet.

'Maybe's he's just moved the van around to the shady side of the building,' I said.

'And maybe he's halfway to Berlin by now,' said Plum

We walked around the hotel but there was no sign of the van. We had a brief group meeting and formed a lynching party.

'They must have some rope in the hotel,' said Beau. 'I'll go and ask.'

As he turned to go, Quiet came around the corner.

'Where's our bloody van?' said Beau, moving menacingly toward him.

'I don't know,' he said. defensively, curling up in a semi-foetal position. 'When I came back last night it was gone. I thought you'd moved it, so I slept in the club.'

'Oh, fuck,' we said.

'We'd better tell the Polizei,' said Plum.

'Bollocks!' said Martin. 'My passport was in the van.'

'And so was my bass and amp,' said Quiet, mournfully. 'Maybe it's Fate telling me to find another line of work.'

'Fuck your bass, and fuck your amp,' I said. 'And I think Fate might have a point.'

But it was obvious that Quiet was innocent. It wasn't his fault but we blamed him anyway, just because he was there. He was, without doubt, one of life's scapegoats so we were, to be fair to us, engaged in a little positive reinforcement. We were sure that, in retrospect, he would, one day, appreciate it.

Martin phoned the Polizei and gave them all the details. They were polite but they didn't seem too hopeful about the chances of recovery. Still, they said, they would keep an eye out for it.

That night at the club we asked around but nobody'd seen it. As the evening progressed the true horror of the situation began to assert itself. I was still kidding myself that somebody had just borrowed it, but the truth, as it always does, finally elbowed its way to the front of my mind. Things always take a while to sink in with me. But if the van had really been stolen, we were fairly and squarely in the shit. I assumed it was insured although, from choice, I am not a party to such things. I have always held to the belief that administrative matters tend to sully the artistic soul. But, knowing what I know about insurance companies, I would imagine that any compensation would be payable only after due process had run its interminable course, which could, and probably would, take years. In the meantime, we'd have to buy a new van. That would knock a huge hole in our liquid assets.

'By the way,' I said to Martin, 'I need new strings.'

'We can't afford them,' he said.

'But what if I break a string? I've got to have a spare.'

'Well, don't break a string then,' he said. 'You can have one spare set, OK? I'll send Gerhardt down to the music shop in the morning. Oh no, I can't. The van's been stolen. He'll have to get the bus. By the way, where is Gerhardt?'

We froze. Gerhardt, you will remember, was our unofficial road-manager. He never missed a night. We asked around but nobody'd seen him. One of the barmaids said she had seen him last night at closing time. Yes, he'd seemed a little edgy, but he was a nervy kind of guy, wasn't he? And he did have personal problems, didn't he? Two and two began to move inexorably toward four.

'Gerhardt's nicked the van,' said Plum. 'The bastard.'

'I never liked him,' I said.

Does anyone know where he lives? Does anyone know where his wife lives? One of the barmaids did. She and Plum went off to do some detective work. They were back in twenty minutes. There was no answer at Gerhardt's poky little flat but his wife was at home. She'd seen him last night. They'd had a blazing row and Gerhardt had stormed off into the night, muttering darkly.

'He might be at his mother's house,' she'd added helpfully. He wasn't. His mother hadn't seen him.

'There's no two ways about it,' said Martin. 'Gerhardt's nicked the van.'

Gerhardt, the bastard, had indeed nicked the van. In a post-marital rage, consumed by pain, he had stumbled into the darkness and with his soul in turmoil had, understandably, wanted to get as far away from this shitty, little town as quickly as possible. And who can blame him? As a man, I found his behaviour entirely justifiable. I just wish he hadn't picked our van in which to do it.

The days went by and the end of the month loomed large. In a minute the gig would be over and we'd have to move out of the hotel, which meant finding somewhere else to stay while we found a new van. There was no word from the Polizei, but no news, we told ourselves, was good news, and we – mainly me – still treasured the gossamer thread of hope that the van was still in one piece and it was a only a matter of time until it was returned to us. But, just in case, we pooled our money into a central fund and battened down the fiscal hatches.

Chico came to the rescue. He was, he said, going home to Yugoslavia at the end of the month so we could stay in his flat above the club for as long as we needed. Of course, Antonino would be there keep an eye on us. Would that be all right? Yes, Chico, it certainly would.

Then the Polizei phoned to say they'd found the van, abandoned on an autobahn, two hundred miles away. Was it all right, we asked, holding our breath?. No, actually, it wasn't. Gerhardt had driven it into the ground. The engine had seized up and the big ends had gone. The police would tow it back to Kaiserslautern but then it was our problem. We could have a new engine put in, but that would mean getting one sent out from Britain. That would cost a fortune. It would be cheaper to buy a new van. We put the word out, especially among our American friends. They said they would keep an eye out for one.

When the van arrived back in Kaiserslautern we went to see it. It stood, like the bleached bones of a long-dead buffalo on the African savannah, in the corner of a police compound. We patted it gently and talked to it in soothing tones, absolving

the hottest ticket in K-town

it from any blame whatsoever arising from the incident. Martin climbed in and gave it the once-over.

'My passport's gone,' he said, 'but Quiet's bass and amp are still here.'

'Let's smash them up,' I said.

'No,' said Beau. 'Let's sell them.'

'I'll have to go to the British Embassy in Frankfurt to get a new passport,' said Martin. 'That's more money down the drain.'

The policeman at the compound gate was very helpful and told us there would be a storage charge of five marks per day until the van was removed, payable on a monthly basis.

Quiet was delighted with the return of his bass and amp. He saw it as another message from Fate, this time telling him to devote, to the exclusion of all else, the rest of his life to music. We tried to convince him that to do so would inflict irreversible damage on the performing arts, but he wouldn't have it.

'I've got a lift to Berlin in the morning,' he said. 'I'll find a band there.'

And that was the last we saw of him. For all I know he became the bass-player with the Berlin Philharmonic, but I doubt it. Someone with his almost supernatural lack of musical talent was destined to end up in some inferior profession like accountancy, or management, or the priesthood.

The last night at the club was an absolute hoot. Halfway through the first set we noticed five scowling figures standing, mob-handed, at the side of the stage. They all had long hair and black leather jackets. They looked like a band. They watched us for a while and made it fairly obvious that they didn't think much of what they saw, talking amongst themselves, laughing and shaking their heads. They watched us for a few numbers then disappeared into the crowd. We finished the set and headed for the bar, where we found the five scowlers arguing with Chico.

'What's up, Chico?' said Martin.

'This is the group I've booked to play at the club the month after next, but they have arrived a month early. I tell them the club is closed next month. They are very upset because they have come a long way. But is not my fault. I tell them they will have to come back next month, but they want to play tonight. They are crazy.'

Just then the head scowler stepped forward.

'Vee are the Black Stones,' he said in a thick German accent. 'Vee are the best band in Chermany and vee must play.'

'OK,' said Martin. 'You can use our gear.'

'OK,' said the head scowler. 'Vee show you how good vee are.'

They walked to the stage with an arrogant swagger, picked up our instruments and plugged in. The head scowler was the singer. He grabbed a microphone and addressed the multitude.

'VEE ARE THE BLACK STONES,' he shouted, 'AND VEE ARE THE BEST BAND IN CHERMANY. NOW VEE SHOW YOU HOW TO PARTY, YES?'

Polite applause.

They roared into their first number. I think it was the Rolling Stones' version of

'It's All Over Now', but it was hard to tell. The singer sang the words if not the tune, while the rest of the band seemed to be playing a different song altogether. The crowd watched open-mouthed. They finished the song and launched into the next number. God knows what it was, I think I heard the singer yell 'Go Johnny, Go!' at one point but I can't be entirely sure. They did another three or four unrecognisable songs then, mercifully, left the stage, punching the air with delight and hugging each other, despite a total lack of audience reaction. They made their way back to the bar, where we were still standing with Chico.

'What did vee tell you?' said the singer. 'Are vee not the best band in Chermany?'

We tried to keep a straight face but it was impossible. Chico was close to tears, but he pulled himself together.

'You are the worst band I have ever heard,' he said.

'You didn't like us?' said the singer, stunned.

'No,' said Chico.

'But vee come back to play here next month,' said the singer.

'No, you don't,' said Chico. 'You're fired.'

He dissolved into uncontrollable laughter, and so did we. The Black Stones milled about in some distress. They began to argue amongst themselves. Suddenly the singer whirled around, spitting with rage.

'Vee go now,' he said, 'but one day the Black Stones will be ferry vamous and you will be ferry sorry you treated us badly.'

We roared with delight, and the Black Stones stalked out of the club,

The following day, Chico, still laughing, paid us off and left for Yugoslavia. We moved out of the hotel and into his flat. Antonino watched our every move. Once we were settled in, he turned the fridge off and went to leave.

'Don't turn the fridge off, Antonino,' said Plum. 'The food will go off.'

Antonino pulled out his pocket dictionary and began thumbing through it. We waited patiently.

'Chico spreche,' he said. 'No electreeceety.'

'That doesn't mean the fridge, you prat,' said Plum. 'And we've got to have the lights on at night.'

Antonino shook his huge head.

'Chico spreche,' he said, and left.

We turned the fridge back on and got on with our lives. The first priority was to buy a van. The American connection seemed to be the most promising, but it was also the most elusive. Now that we weren't playing at Club Studio 45 every night, we wouldn't have GIs on our doorstep. We'd have to seek them out. We'd have to go to Johnny's Keller. We'd heard some of the black GIs talking about it. Johnny was a black ex-GI who had stayed in K-town when his tour of duty ended. He'd married a German girl and opened a blues club, which, by all accounts, was a piece of Germany that was forever Harlem. We got there about nine. It was a long, dimly-lit cellar, honeycombed with alcoves. There was a bar along one side and, somewhere in its murky recesses, lurked a stage. There was a huge Wurlitzer

the hottest ticket in K-town

juke-box just inside the entrance. The only white record on it was the Righteous Brothers singing 'You've Lost That Loving Feeling'. The first person we saw was Stormy Monday Dave.

'Are you guys playing here?' he asked.

'No,' we said. 'We just want to buy a van.'

'You should play here,' he said. 'I'll have a word with Johnny.' He took us to meet the man.

Johnny was a big man, about sixty years-old, who spoke slowly with a deep musical voice. He exuded a polite dignity that you wouldn't care to fuck with in a dark alley. He listened while Dave told him how great we were. If he was impressed, he didn't show it. Finally, he spoke.

'I don't think so,' he said. 'I don't book bands without hearing them first, but the houseband's looking for a stand-in drummer for a couple of weeks. Who's your drummer?'

'I am,' said Beau.

'You interested?' said Johnny.

'Yes, I am,' said Beau. 'By the way, what happened to the last drummer?'

'He got stabbed,' said Johnny.

'Who stabbed him?' said Beau.

'The piano-player,' said Johnny.

The following night Beau played with the houseband. At first he was treated with suspicion, him being an uppity white boy but halfway through the first song he was made an honorary negro.

After the gig Johnny approached us.

'Are you as good as your drummer?'

'We're all right,' said Plum.

'OK,' said Johnny. 'I'll give you a try on the weekend. You free Friday?'

'We're free everyday,' said Plum.

'OK,' said Johnny. 'It's a date.'

'You don't know anybody who's got a van for sale, do you?' said Plum.

'Nope,' said Johnny, 'but I'll keep my eyes open. Now, gentlemen, what would you like to drink?'

We walked back to the flat with a lightness of foot. There was a ray of light shining into our darkness. Oh joy of joys, oh dream of dreams – a gig. Any extra money would help. We naturally assumed that Beau would put his earnings with the houseband into the communal pot, but he refused. There was a little t-t-tension in the air. Then Beau put the matter to rest.

'I've got a wife and child to think about,' he said. Which was fair enough, although we found it almost impossible to get around the concept of a wife and children.

'Beau was an unheard of quantity,' says Martin. 'We were in a band with somebody who had a wife and kid. Totally unheard of.'

'And he was a bit… I wouldn't say tight…' says Plum. '…careful.'

Martin went into the kitchen to get a beer.

maybe i should've stayed in bed?

'The fridge is off again,' he said.

'It's bloody Antonino,' said Plum. 'He waited until we'd gone out and then came back to turn the fridge off. What a twat.'

Our first gig at Johnny's Keller was a stormer. The audience went wild and Dave came up to sing 'Stormy Monday'. After the first set we went to see Johnny.

'What do you think, boss?' we asked.

'Not bad, gentlemen,' he said. 'Not bad.'

We started the second set with our tails up. Then we made a mistake. We played 'Ubangi Stomp', the Jerry Lee Lewis song.

Parted the weeds and looked over the swamp,
And I seen them natives doing the Ubangi Stomp.

It is not the most enlightened opus in the rock'n'roll songbook, but what had seemed like a harmless tune in Club Studio 45 was, here, extremely offensive to all concerned. But we didn't twig it. We played it with our usual innocent abandon. When we finished there was a stony silence. We shrugged our shoulders and moved on to the next song. After the set Johnny called us over.

'Don't play that song again,' he said, pointing at the skin of his hand, 'It ain't nice.'

'OK,' we said.

We thought we'd blown it, but at the end of the night Johnny paid us and re-booked us for the following Friday. And, he said, we could leave our gear in a back room. As we left, Johnny was standing by the exit.

'Night, now,' said Martin.

'Night, now,' repeated Johnny wistfully. 'Man, I haven't heard that since I was stationed in London during the war. You'd be walking down the street in the black-out – it was pitch-black so they couldn't see us anyway – and you'd hear footsteps across the road, Somebody'd say, "Night, now." And I'd say "Night, now" back.'

We left him gazing into the far distance, thinking, no doubt, about yesterday's ghosts. The first thing that hit us when we got back to the flat was the smell.

'Antonino's turned the bloody fridge off again,' said Plum. 'I'll slaughter him tomorrow.'

When Antonino arrived the next morning we were still in bed. He turned the fridge off and sat at the kitchen table. Plum was the first up. At first, he tried to be reasonable, which woke the rest of us up. He was still trying to be reasonable when we'd dressed and got to the kitchen. He was standing with both hands planted on the table, staring at Antonino, who was looking through his dictionary. Every now and then Antonino would look up and say, 'Chico spreche.'

'I know Chico fucking spreche,' said Plum, 'but Chico's not here now so...'

Suddenly Antonino lumbered to his feet and slammed his fist on the table.

'CHICO SPRECHE,' he shouted. He pointed at the door. 'YOU GO.' His face turned purple. 'YOU GO. NOW!' He lumbered toward the door, knocking over several items of furniture on the way. When he reached the doorway he turned to face us. 'YOU GO, NOW,' he yelled, with murder in his eyes, 'ANTONINO SPRECHE!' Then he was gone.

the hottest ticket in K-town

'Well, that's fucked it,' said Plum.

'He'll be all right,' said Martin. 'He'll calm down. He'll be all right tomorrow.'

'I don't think so,' said Plum.

That night we went down to Johnny's Keller to drown our sorrows. Not only were we vanless, we were in serious danger of being homeless. During any musician's life there are moments when he is deprived, by circumstance or foolishness, of a bed for the night. No problem. Sleep in the van. But we haven't got a van, stupid.

We threw ourselves on the mercy of the United States of America. After all, their motto is: Give me your hungry and homeless, etc, etc, etc… I paraphrase, of course. But they semi-came through. A couple of GIs said that some of us could stay at their barracks. It would mean waiting until lights-out, climbing over an eight-foot high, guard-dog patrolled, perimeter fence and sleeping in the toilets. It would also mean waking up a half-an-hour before reveille, climbing back over the eight-foot high, guard-dog patrolled, perimeter fence, this time in broad daylight, and making a run for the nearest cover, in this case a clump of bushes a hundred yards from the fence.

'Luxury, mate,' said Martin. 'Sheer luxury.'

But they could only take two. Any more, they said, would be too much of a risk. They would be committing a serious breach of US Army regulations and should things go wrong, they would be for the high-jump.

'This man's army don't take kindly to that sort'a thing,' said Stormy Monday Dave. 'No, sirree.'

'Well, that's two sorted out,' said Martin. 'What about the other two?'

'Well, they could stay at the Mission,' said Dave. There were murmurs of agreement from the other GIs.

'What's that?' I asked.

'It's the Catholic Mission for Waifs and Strays,' said Dave. 'It's about a mile away and it's run by a bunch o' nuns. They take care of hobos and such. You can sleep there for free but they kick you out pretty early in the mornin'. But they give you a bowl of soup and they don't turn nobody away.'

'Very reassuring,' I said. 'I'll stay there. I don't think I could climb an eight-foot fence, especially in the dark.'

'Neither could I,' said Beau. 'I'll sleep at the Mission.'

'OK,' said Martin, 'Me and Plum'll stay at the base.'

'That's settled then,' I said.

'Just a minute,' said Martin. 'We may be a bit premature here. Maybe Antonino's calmed down.'

'I don't think so,' said Plum.

I didn't think so either. Martin is a force-of-nature optimist, who believes that brick walls are temporary set-backs, obstacles are challenges, and mountains are there to climb. I, on the other hand, am an elemental pessimist, who believes that brick walls are insurmountable barriers, obstacles are a cause for retreat, and mountains are no more than very nice scenery.

maybe i should've stayed in bed?

We got back to the flat about four in the morning, rat-arsed and teetering on the brink of oblivion, and went straight to bed. Martin and I were bivouacked in the lounge, he on a chaise longue, and I on a camp bed. I was just dropping off when I heard scuffling. I looked over in Martin's direction. As the first light of dawn seeped through the curtains I could see his silhouette. He was standing on the chaise longue, naked, legs apart, head thrown back, like an Arapaho prince preparing for battle, about to sing his death song. Primordial mist rose from his feet. It was a vision of dauntless courage in the face of terrible odds, and I watched in wonder. Then I realised what he was doing. He was having a piss. And he was pissing on his own bed, and what I had thought was primordial mist was piss-steam. He finished, let out a moan of content, and lay back down, snuggling up in the urine-drenched blankets. So I did what any friend would do in similar circumstances, I went to sleep.

I dreamed I was in a cavernous, white-tiled toilet. Urinals stretched as far as the eye could see. The door opened and famous men, in single file, trooped in – Fidel Castro, Lawrence of Arabia, Alfred Hitchcock, Alistair Sim, Paul Robeson, and a fearsome-looking chap wearing Greek armour whom I assumed was Leonidas. They each took their places at a urinal. Then, as one, they pulled their todgers out and began to sing: 'They call it Stormy Monday, Lord, but Tuesday's just as bad.' The pianist in the corner was playing the wrong chords and I told him so in no uncertain terms. but he just sat there smiling. Paul Titse wasn't much help either; he was pirouetting around the piano, and far too engrossed to talk to me. When I turned around all the famous men had turned into Gerhardt, and they were approaching me slowly, holding their todgers in front of them, like check-shirted zombies. They shuffled inexorably toward me. I tried shouting for help but my voice wouldn't work. I tried to adopt a boxing stance but my limbs were as lead. I dropped to my knees and began to sing my death song. They stood over me, blocking out the light. Then, as one, they began to piss on me.

I sat bolt upright in bed, dripping with sweat. Martin was in the kitchen boiling his morning egg, singing 'Raining In My Heart'. I got up and dressed as quickly as possible because the lounge smelled like a Paris pissoir. I joined Martin in the kitchen.

'You were out of it last night,' I said. 'You got up, pissed on your bed, and then lay back down in it.'

'Thank god for that,' he replied. 'I thought you'd pissed on me in the middle of the night. At least it was my own piss.'

'Antonino will hit the roof if he goes into the lounge. The smell is awful.'

'Then we'll just have to keep him in the kitchen,' said Martin, buttering his soldiers.

By the time Antonino arrived we were all in the kitchen, in various stages of breakfast. One thing was immediately clear – he hadn't calmed down; the low brow was furrowed, the eyes dark and smouldering, the hands clenched tightly. He pointed at the door.

'GO,' he roared, 'YOU GO NOW. ANTONINO SPRECHE!'

the hottest ticket in K-town

There was no reasoning with him. We tried and failed. So, while he stood in the kitchen, arms folded and incommunicado, we started packing. We put our luggage in the hallway and waited while he checked the place over, room by room, just in case we'd stolen or broken anything. Finally, he reached the lounge.

'Maybe he won't smell it,' I said.

We heard a roar. It was the roar of a dumb beast in inconceivable agony.

'I think he has,' said Martin.

Grabbing our luggage, we tumbled out of the door, down the stairs, through the club, and into the street. We stopped about a hundred yards down the road and sat on our luggage, gasping for breath. We looked back at the club. Antonino stood in the doorway, face scarlet with rage, shaking his fist at us and shouting what I imagine were Italian terms of endearment. I managed to pick out one word, 'fanculo', which I think means 'you will be much missed'.

'We're well out of that,' said Beau.

We spent the afternoon bivouacked in a nearby park. At six, we headed for Johnny's Keller. We put our luggage in the back room with the gear and waited for the club to fill up. At eight o'clock our GI saviours arrived, and we worked out a plan. At the end of the night Plum and Martin would go back to the base with them and Stormy Monday Dave would take Beau and me to the Mission. They advised us to leave our luggage at the club. It would, they said, be difficult enough just getting Plum and Martin over the perimeter fence, without them dragging two large suitcases behind them. Stormy Monday Dave agreed and recommended that Beau and I do the same, because they wouldn't let us leave our cases at the Mission during the day, so we'd have to lug them around town until they let us back in the following night.

'Just take a toothbrush,' he said.

At closing time Stormy Monday Dave drove Beau and me over to the Mission in his sky-blue Pontiac convertible with zebra-skinned upholstery. Before we left we said our goodbyes to Plum and Martin. We shook hands with them and wished them good luck. It was like a scene from 'Cockleshell Heroes'.

The Catholic Mission for Waifs and Strays was a 14th century abbey, gothic in aspect, set back from the road, and surrounded by a high, stone wall. Dave pulled the car up in front of large wrought-iron gates, secured on either side to ten-foot high crumbling pillars. On top of each pillar was a stone eagle, frozen in threatening pose. The gates looked locked but when Beau tried them they reluctantly opened with a low moan.

'When you get to the abbey go around the back,' said Stormy Monday Dave. 'That's where the entrance is. You can't miss it. It's the only door there.'

'You're not coming with us?' I said.

'Nope,' he said firmly. 'This is as far as I go. There's graves and shit in there.'

Beau and I started up the tree-lined drive. The Pontiac's headlights lit up the first fifty yards but beyond that there was profound darkness. Behind us, Stormy Monday Dave began to sing softly.

'I put a spell on you because you're mine,' he sang, doing a passable impression of Screaming Jay Hawkins, to whom he bore more than a passing resemblance.

Beau and I entered the darkness. There was a little moonlight, but not much. We heard Stormy Monday Dave drive off. We were alone. The sound of our feet crunching on the gravel seemed obscenely loud in the stillness of the night.

'If we stick to the drive we should be all right,' whispered Beau.

We walked for what seemed like centuries. Suddenly, we were walking in bracken.

'Beau,' I said, trying to sound brave and cheerful, 'where's the fucking drive gone?'

'I don't know,' said Beau. 'It was here a minute ago.'

We back-tracked. More bracken. We were lost, but we could see a solid black shape in the distance.

'That must be the abbey,' said Beau. 'Let's head straight for it.'

Almost immediately the bracken cleared and our footfalls sounded firm.

'Whoagh,' screamed Beau. There was a scuffling noise.

'Are you all right?' I said.

'I fell over something,' said Beau, breathing heavily. 'Oh, no,' he sobbed, 'it's a grave. I just fell over a fucking grave.'

I walked toward the sound of his voice. My leg hit something unyielding and I pitched into the blackness.

'Aargh,' I shouted.

There was metallic clattering as I landed. Stagnant liquid splashed all over me and a sharp pain shot up my spine.

'Are you all right,' said Beau, somewhere to my left.

'No,' I said. 'I think I've broken my neck. And I'm soaking wet.'

I lay there, afraid to move. Something was pressing into my back. I fished it out. Even in the pitch darkness I could see its dull shine. I had landed on a long-abandoned, memorial flower vase. Judging by my dripping state, it must have been full. I picked a few rotting flowers off my clothes. I smelled like a sewage farm.

'Can you move?' said Beau. 'We've got to make it to the abbey.'

'I'll try,' I said heroically. I stood up, broad of shoulder, narrow of hip. and marched toward the sound of the guns.

I've always been good in a crisis. I'm just the kind of chap you'd want with you when the chips are down. Through my veins runs the same blood that drove Owain Glyndwr to become the blueprint of the perfect guerrilla. The same blood that impelled Prince Madoc to discover the Americas, two-and-a-half centuries before the charlatan claims of Columbus. The spirit of Rorke's Drift saturates my bones. I am, after all, a man of Harlech.

'Oooph,' I yelled, and fell over another grave. The air left my body. 'I give up,' I gasped. 'Leave me here. You can arrange to have my body sent back to Wales tomorrow. Now go. Think of yourself. Just tell them back home that I didn't let them down. I died a noble death.'

'Faawgh,' said Beau, as he fell over another grave.

We gradually threaded our way through the graveyard and made it to the abbey. We picked our way along the walls until we reached what we assumed was the back. We could just make out a heavy wooden door. We stood in front of it.

'What's that smell?' said Beau, sniffing the air. 'It's you. You smell like a toilet.'

'It's all right,' I said, 'it's only stagnant water. You'll get used to it.'

There was a bell-pull to the right of the door. We pulled it. Nothing. We pulled it again. Nothing again. We banged on the door. Still nothing.

'It's about two o'clock,' I said. 'Maybe they've knocked off for the night.'

'Nuns don't knock off,' said Beau impatiently. 'They're married to God. That's a twenty-four hour job.'

Then we heard movement behind the door. We heard a reluctant bolt being drawn. We heard the jangle of keys. There was a loud click and the door edged open. Silhouetted in dim light was a cowled figure. It was a nun.

'Excuse me, sister,' said Beau cheerily. 'We were told that we could get a bed here for the night. Is that right?'

She beckoned us in. We followed her down a corridor, lit by a naked, twenty-watt light bulb. On either side were cell doors, each with an observation hatch. She stopped at one, rifled through her bunch of keys, selected one, and unlocked the door. She gestured us in. It was a small, semi-dungeon containing two beds, each with a thin mattress and a single folded blanket. The only item of furniture was a shabby wooden table, on which was placed a white china jug full of water and a washing bowl. Under the table was a chamber pot. The room was lit by another naked, twenty-watt light bulb. When we were in, she closed the door behind us and locked it.

'Well, this isn't too bad,' said Beau, selecting a bed and testing the springs. He lay down. 'Turn the light out, wuss,' he said.

I looked around.

'There's no light switch,' I said. But he was asleep.

We were woken at five o'clock by the rattle of keys, and a nun threw the door open. Whether it was the same nun as the night before I had no way of knowing. If God is indeed married to them all I have no idea how he tells them apart. Well, I expect that's the price you pay for being a serial bigamist.

'What a wasted life,' I said, almost to myself.

'Oh, I don't know,' said Beau. 'They seem quite happy.'

'But it's a happiness based on delusion,' I said.

'Happiness is happiness,' said Beau. 'It doesn't matter what it's based on.'

'Yes, it does,' I said, feeling combative. 'It's better to be miserable for the right reasons than happy for the wrong ones.'

'Speak for yourself,' said Beau, putting his jacket on. 'Surely, it's better to believe in it, just in case it's true.'

Beau was always something of a religious zealot.

'Think about it,' he added, fixing me with a steely gaze, 'it might save your soul.'

'I don't have a soul,' I said.

'Anyone can see that,' said Beau, nudging me in the ribs with a friendly elbow. I obviously underestimated Beau's capacity for belief because years later he

maybe i should've stayed in bed?

emigrated to Australia and became a Jehovah's Witness.

'By the way,' he said, 'I don't want to get personal, but don't you think you'd better have a wash before breakfast. You still smell like a toilet.'

'I had a wash last night before I went to bed.'

'Well, I think you'd better have another one,' he said. He waited while I had another wash; in semi-freezing water, I may add. It didn't help. I still smelled like a toilet.

'Right,' said Beau, when I was done. 'That'll have to do. I'm going for breakfast. Coming?'

'OK,' I said, and followed him out the door.

From the other cell doors emerged down-and-outs of all shapes and sizes. In a silence broken only by the odd clearing of the lungs, they shuffled down the corridor. They obviously knew the way so we followed them, and ended up in a long, high-ceilinged hall with an altar at the far end. Above the altar was the statue of a larger than life-size, weeping Madonna, arms outstretched, welcoming the sad cases to a free nosh.

We each took a bowl and spoon from a table just inside the door and took our places at long, rough wooden tables which ran the whole length of the hall. When we were all seated, teams of nuns bustled in, carrying tureens. A murmur of expectancy ran through the hall. The nuns placed three tureens on each table and disappeared. We served ourselves. I assumed it was soup, but it could have been mud. I ladled a divot into my bowl and poked it with my spoon. It had the consistency of engine oil and contained a few UFOs – unidentified floating offal. I tried a spoonful. It tasted like John Innes, Number 2. Mercifully, the taste was masked slightly by a soapy bouquet.

'Not bad,' said Beau, wolfing it down. I pushed my bowl away, Beau helped himself to seconds.

Ten minutes later, we were back on the street. Our fellow dossers shuffled off in different directions, without so much as a goodbye. I looked at my watch. It was only six o'clock in the bastarding morning. We'd arranged to meet Plum and Martin that night in Johnny's Keller, so we only had twelve hours to kill. We wandered aimlessly around the town. About midday I began to wish I'd eaten the infernal breakfast gruel. By four I was suffering from severe malnutrition. When Johhny opened the Keller at six, we were waiting outside. He let us in.

'How did it go?' he said.

'Not bad,' said Beau.

'Fucking terrible,' I said. 'We were up at five. We've been wandering around town all day. And we're bloody starving.'

But Johhny wasn't listening. He was sniffing the air and frowning.

'I gotta get my toilets cleaned up,' he said.

'It's all right,' I said. 'It's me.'

Plum and Martin arrived.

'Any shape?' asked Plum.

'Not bad,' said Beau.

the hottest ticket in K-town

'Fucking terrible,' I said. 'They got us up at five. We've been wandering around town all day. And we're bloody starving.'

But Plum and Martin weren't listening either. They, too, were sniffing the air.

'Is that you?' said Martin, looking at me. 'You smell like a toilet.'

'At least I don't piss in my own bed then sleep in it,' I said bitterly.

'Fair point,' said Martin.

'Anyway,' I said. 'How did it go with you?'

'It was like a James Bond film,' said Plum. 'We did a lot of running.'

'We had to sleep in the toilets so we didn't get much shut-eye.' said Martin. He put his arm around my shoulders. 'You wouldn't have lasted five minutes, Deke,' he said. 'You'd still be half-way up the perimeter fence.'

'We've got some good news,' said Plum, 'and some bad news.'

'Gimme the good news,' I said. 'Quickly.'

'We've got a van.'

'Oh, thank god for that,' I said, relief flooding through my body. 'I don't think I could spend another night in that bloody nunnery. What's the bad news?'

'We won't be able to pick it up for a fortnight.'

'Why not?'

'Because it's owned by a sergeant's wife whose husband has just died, She's going back to the States in a fortnight but she needs it till then.'

'That's rather selfish of her,' I said. 'Does she want to sell it or doesn't she?'

'That's the deal,' said Plum. 'And we've got just enough money to buy it, but not enough for petrol home, so any money we earn goes in the pot. Everything. So no more frittering away money on things like food, OK?'

I felt myself losing weight as I stood there.

'What kind of van is it?' asked Beau.

'It's a Ford Ranch Wagon,' said Plum. 'It's a huge estate car. Big enough for all the gear. And we can all sit in the front at the same time, if we want to.'

During the next fortnight we did another two gigs at Johnny's Keller. This time even Beau's money went in the pot.

'We can pick up the Ranch Wagon tomorrow,' said Plum, as we met at Johnny's Keller for another night of treading water.

'Brilliant,' I said. I do like it when escape is on the agenda.

'But it's going to cost us more than we thought,' he continued. 'The sergeant's widow has upped the price. Not by much, but enough to cause us problems. We'll still have enough money to buy the car but not enough for petrol and ferry tickets. But Stormy Monday Dave says he can rob us a few cans of petrol from the motor pool. It'll have to be late at night, but it should be all right. I don't know what we're going to do about the ferry tickets but we'll work something out.'

'Bless you, my son,' I said.

The following morning Beau and I said goodbye to the nuns. They seemed genuinely upset. One or two of them gave me letters to post and I reaffirmed an earlier promise to another to send her a copy of *Lady Chatterley's Lover*, in a plain-wrapper, of course. I kissed her on the cheek and she giggled like a five-year-old.

maybe i should've stayed in bed?

We arrived at Johnny's Keller at six. The Ranch Wagon stood outside. It was like a sky-blue shark with chrome teeth. But what impressed me most was a three-inch high model of Batman, standing, hands on hips, on top of the dashboard, looking out at the road ahead.

'We've got to be outside the perimeter fence at the base at two o'clock tonight to pick up the petrol,' said Martin.

We spent the night in Johnny's Keller, saying goodbye to everyone. Johnny gave us drinks on the house and we all went up and had a blow with the house band. At one-thirty we drove to the base. Johnny waved us off.

'If you're ever in K-town again,' he said, 'call in. I'll always give you a gig. But don't play that song again. It ain't nice.'

At two o'clock, lights switched-off, the ranch wagon swished to a stop alongside the perimeter fence. As our eyes became accustomed to the dark we could make out the shapes of nissen huts. We waited. What if something had gone wrong? What if Stormy Monday Dave had been caught red-handed? What if…?

'I can see someone,' said Martin.

Something moved in the darkness. It was a figure and it was carrying something. It was Stormy Monday Dave and he was carrying two jerry-cans.

'This is as much as I could get,' he whispered through the wire. 'It should be enough to get you home.'

It was a struggle to get them over the fence but we did it without serious injury. We put them in the back of the ranch wagon and thanked Dave. He waved our thanks aside.

'I'll never sing "Stormy Monday Blues" again without thinking about you guys.' There was a catch in his voice. 'Now, get lost,' he said. 'I'm on duty in four hours.' And he was gone.

We drove about half-a-mile down the road and pulled into a lay-by to put the petrol in. Martin opened a jerry-can. He frowned.

'It doesn't smell like petrol,' he said, sniffing the opening. He dipped his finger in and examined it. 'It's bloody oil,' he said. 'Try the other can.'

We did. It was the same.

'The twat's given us two cans of engine oil,' said Plum. 'What the fuck are we going to do now?'

'We'll go back and change it,' said Martin. 'I know which barracks he sleeps in. I'll nip over the wire and wake him up, He can change it for some petrol.'

'That's a bit risky,' I said.

'What choice do we have?' said Martin.

We drove back to the perimeter fence and Martin shinned over the wire. We passed him the two jerry-cans and he disappeared into the darkness. Again we waited. After half-an-hour we were nervous wrecks. Then we saw movement in the gloom. It was Martin and Stormy Monday Dave. He couldn't apologise enough. He was, he whispered, an asshole. Grunts of assent all around.

'I can't change the oil for petrol,' he said. 'It'd be too risky to break into the motor pool twice in one night, so,' he fished around in his pockets, 'the guys took

the hottest ticket in K-town

up a collection.' He held out a wad of banknotes. 'This should be enough to get you to the ferry.'

We were genuinely moved. We asked him to thank all the guys and tell them it was just a loan. We promised to send the money back as soon as we got home. It was a solemn promise. We crossed our hearts and hoped to die. Stormy Monday Dave opened his mouth to speak but Martin held up his hand.

'No speeches, please,' he said. 'Anyway, we'll probably be back in half-an-hour. You've probably given us 2,000 Japanese yen.'

'No, it's OK,' said Stormy Monday Dave, wincing slightly. 'It's all in dollars.'

'No D-marks?' said Martin.

'No,' he said, 'just dollars.'

'Never mind,' said Martin. 'They'll probably take dollars.'

We stopped at the next filling station. Martin went in and spoke to the cashier. He returned, looking glum.

'They won't take dollars,' he said.

There was universal cursing.

'Only joking,' he said.

'Just put the fucking petrol in the fucking car,' I said. 'It's four in the fucking morning and I want to go home.'

'No sense of humour, that's your trouble, Leonard,' he said.

We reached the ferry about two in the afternoon. The next sailing was at six o'clock. We parked at the ticket office and Plum and Martin went in. They were back in five minutes.

'We haven't got enough money for the tickets,' said Plum. 'We're fourteen marks short. Anybody got any secret cash?'

Nobody did.

'I'm going for a walk,' said Martin. 'I'm going to do a bit of begging.'

An hour later he was back.

'No luck,' he said.

Just then a scruffy chap carrying a haversack walked around the corner of the ticket office and went in.

'There's our man,' said Martin, and followed him in. They came out together, chatting amiably. They walked over to the ranch wagon.

'This is Tony,' said Martin. 'He's going to lend us enough money to get home, if we give him a lift to London.'

At ten o'clock the following morning we arrived back in Swansea, penniless and knackered, but extremely relieved.

22
the decline and fall of a sky-blue shark

Three days after we got home we played the Glanmor Jazz Club in Swansea. Originally the Glanmor Club – a grey-walled, semi-gothic mansion at the end of a long driveway – had been a social club, probably used by rotarians or some other pointless civic organisation. In the dim and distant past, the local jazz society had rented the function room and it soon became known as the Glanmor Jazz Club. But time and fashion had turned it into a rock gig. Only the name betrayed its scurrilous past. It was always a pleasure to play there because the committee were an affable bunch who took the view, rare in committee-land, that audiences were not captured prisoners-of-war to be watched at every turn, but paying customers upon whom depended the well-being of the club. There were few rules of conduct and after-hours drinking was positively encouraged. The gig finished at eleven but we rarely left before two or three.

After the gig Beau went into a huddle with Plum. Five minutes later Plum walked over to me and Martin.

'Beau's handed in his notice,' he said.

I was stunned but Martin and Plum were sanguine. They'd seen it coming for months.

'I think that K-Town was the straw that broke the drummer's back,' said Martin.

'I was surprised he came to K-Town in the first place.' said Plum.

'I didn't see this one coming, at all,' I said.

'You don't see Christmas coming, Leonard,' said Plum, giving me an affectionate hug.

'So, who are we going to get instead?' I said.

'Terry, I think,' said Martin.

'Brilliant,' I said.

Terry Williams was the drummer with the Comancheros, a young band from Swansea with whom we had shared many a stage. They were all good musicians but Terry was exceptional.

'I'll go and ask him,' said Martin. 'He's in the bar.'

Five minutes later he was back.

'He said yes.'

'Problem solved,' said Plum.

Rehearsals, conducted over the next few days, were brief and painless. Terry knew most of the numbers. He'd seen us often enough.

The ranch wagon caused quite a stir on the streets of Swansea. Plum took to driving it up and down the Kingsway, wearing an arab headdress and dark glasses.

the decline and fall of a sky-blue shark 181

A rumour spread, I don't know how, that a Saudi sheik had bought a house on the Gower. There was even speculation that oil had been discovered near Worm's Head. Property prices soared. However, not everyone was impressed. One day Plum stopped at a zebra crossing to let a gang of schoolgirls across.

'Ooh, look,' said one, 'a cowing sheik.'

Fairly soon the horn developed a fault. It was a horn with a swagger. When pressed it would emit a strident blare that seemed to say – 'I am an American dream. Listen to me, ye mighty, and despair.' But it took to going off on its own, and not at full power. Just a quiet 'barp' now and then. Like a sly fart. At first it was just an occasional occurrence but soon it was happening every thirty seconds. It began to threaten Plum's image, if not his sanity.

'I'd be driving along thinking, "Look at me. I'm driving a big American car" and it would go "barp".'

We slipped back into the old routine. Three or four gigs a week. The money came in very handy. After a week or two we were back on our feet again. Of course, we didn't pay back the GI loan; we always meant to send the money back to K-Town but we never quite got around to it. Something always cropped up. This time, because we needed money to get to Hamburg. The next Top Ten stint was less than a month away. We were looking forward to pulling up outside the Top Ten in the ranch wagon. Even Ricky Barnes would be impressed. Well, perhaps not. You can only push the bounds of possibility so far.

The following month we were back at the Glanmor Jazz Club, showing off our new drummer. It was a great gig and afterwards we celebrated its passing in the bar. About one o'clock Cracky and I, who both lived in Llanelly, decided we wanted to go home.

Cracky – Graham Dean-Jones – was, to say the least, a local personality. Cracky's the name, unfettered hedonism's the game. Slightly older than us, he'd been the first beatnik in Llanelly and something of a childhood hero for me. It was rumoured that he suffered from lung problems and only had a short time to live. This rumour was reinforced by his tendency to cough up blood in public. We assumed his lust for life was the last hurrah of a condemned man. He managed several Llanelly bands, including the Spartans and Headline News, he drank pints of vodka & tonic, and smoked personally monogrammed cigarettes.

So Cracky and I wanted to leave, and Plum was our lift home. But Plum, already semi-pissed, didn't want to go just yet. He was, he said, just warming up. Cracky and I insisted. An ugly exchange followed.

'Right!' said Plum, suddenly slamming his glass down on the bar 'Let's go. I'm losing valuable drinking time here. Give us a couple of bottles for the journey, Cliff,' he said to the barman.

We piled into the ranch wagon. Cracky sat in the front and I sat in the back. Plum, bottle of beer in hand, crunched the ranch wagon into gear and we skidded out of the car park, barping gently. The Ford Ranch Wagon, if required, could be a powerful machine, combining speed with stability, strength with elegance; but Plum could also be a powerful beast, combining impatience with ill-temper, hot blood with alcohol. The wheels left the road on the brow of every hill and during cornering G-forces came into play. It was a miracle we got out of Swansea alive. Lougher Bridge, which spans the estuary that divides the counties of Glamorgan and Carmarthenshire, is long and straight, then the road turns sharply left into Bynea. It is a notorious accident black spot. As soon as Plum reached the bridge, he put his foot to the floor, and by the time we reached the turn we were doing eighty. Halfway through the bend the sky-blue shark, tyres screaming, went into a tail-spin.

'Fuck,' said Plum.

The ranch wagon, spinning wildly, went sideways into a powerline pole, sheering it off about three feet from the ground. The street lights went out and the remainder of the pole, still attached to the overhead wires, swung out into the darkness. Then, almost in slow motion, it swung back in toward the car.

'Oh, Christ!' said Plum.

With an explosion of sound it hit us head-on, shattering the windscreen and burying itself in the dashboard, sending the Batman figurine bulleting past my ear. The horn gave a last plaintive barp and then silence. Cracky began to moan.

'Is everybody all right?' said Plum, picking pieces of glass off of his clothes.

'I'm all right,' I said, 'but I don't know about Cracky.'

'I'm all right,' said Cracky, holding his shoulder, 'but I think I've broken my arm.'

'What's that hissing sound?' I said.

'It's the powerline wires,' said Plum. 'They've come loose and they're all lashing about. Be careful when you get out.'

I handed Plum his bottle of beer, which had landed in my lap, making me think for a moment that I'd pissed myself. He drained what was left in the bottle and tossed it out of the window.

'Oh, shit!' he said, suddenly remembering there were drink-driving laws. He began collecting the other empty beer bottles, now strewn over the floor of the car, and started throwing them as far from the crash as he could. I helped Cracky out. He was obviously in some pain. I led him away from the car, dodging the hissing wires. which were sparking like fireworks. I sat him on a nearby wall. Just then a car pulled up and the driver wound his window down.

'Cracky,' he shouted, 'is that you?' It was one of Cracky's beatnik friends.

'Yes, it is,' said Cracky. 'Do me a favour. Take me to hospital.'

We got Cracky into the car.

'Can you give me a lift home?' I said.

'Yeah. Get in.'

'Hang on,' I said, 'I'll just get my guitar.'

I'd just remembered my guitar. It was in the back of the ranch wagon. For all I knew it was in bits. I ran back over, yanked the back door open, and opened my guitar case. The Tele was all right, apart from a bent machine-head.

'We're taking Cracky to hospital, OK?' I said to Plum.

'OK,' said Plum. 'I'll wait for the police to come.'

the decline and fall of a sky-blue shark 183

We got Cracky to hospital and the medical profession swung into action. X-rays revealed that Cracky had a broken collar-bone. They kept him in overnight and I went home.

Back at the crash Plum sat on the wall and waited for the police. A drunk walked past. He burst out laughing.

'You were lucky to get out of that alive,' he said, nodding towards the mangled ranch wagon.

'Yes,' said Plum. 'I'm a lucky man.'

'Yes,' said the drunk, putting his hands in his pockets, 'you were lucky to get out of that alive, that's for sure.'

'Yes, I was,' said Plum, starting to boil.

'Yes,' said the drunk, laughing as if his life depended upon it, 'you were lucky to get out of that alive.'

Plum was about to strangle him, when a woman ran across the road toward him.

'Are you the driver?' she asked.

'Yes,' said Plum.

'Yes,' said the drunk. 'He was lucky to get out of that alive.'

'Would you like a cup of tea?' asked the woman, ignoring the drunk. 'I live just across the road. I expect you'll want to make a few phone-calls.'

'Brilliant,' said Plum. He followed the woman across the road. 'Keep an eye on the car,' he said to the drunk.

'There's nothing like a cup of tea at moments like this,' said the woman, as they entered the house. 'I've put the kettle on.'

'I don't suppose you've got any beer?' said Plum.

The police never did arrive. Plum phoned the Jazz Club and got Cliff, the barman, to come and pick him up. Twenty minutes later he arrived and drove Plum back to the Jazz Club. They waved goodbye to the drunk as they left.

The following day the police phoned Plum and asked him to bring his licence and insurance down to the station. This he did. They asked him what had happened. Plum said he had lost control of the car in the rain and they accepted his explanation. But I don't remember any rain and neither, I suspect, does Cracky.

The following day, the Evening Post carried an accident report headlined – WAGON CRASH CUTS OUT STREET LIGHT FOR HALF A MILE. It appeared to be a fairly accurate account of the proceedings but it did contain one glaring factual error. It said that Cracky was twenty-three years old. Cracky's never been twenty-three. Ever.

23
cool hand plum – stealing by finding

So, we were about to leave for Hamburg but we didn't have a van and we didn't have enough money to buy one. The Corncrackers came to the rescue. They were playing an American Army base in Nuremberg for the month of November and they offered to drop us off in Hamburg on the way over and pick us up on the way back. It would be a massive detour for them but they didn't seem to mind. It would also be a little cramped – eight musicians and two sets of gear in a Commer J2 van? – and a little chilly, because the heater, naturally, was broken, although it could still blow out cold air quite effectively. But none of this seemed important because we were young and fearless and stupid.

The Corncrackers had resolutely remained a trio but now they confronted the might of the US Army who, as a matter of policy, insisted that every band they employed had a lead singer. So the Corncrackers were forced to hire a singer for the month. Everybody good was working so they hired a local lad named Mike Fortune. He wasn't a professional musician and he was taking a month off work to do the gig. He wasn't much good and by all accounts he was a pain in the neck, but a singer is a singer. The rest of the band – Wes, Keith and Brian – were resigned to the upcoming horror.

We left on a cold October morning. All the gear and luggage was crammed into the back and we sat on two bench seats running down either side of the van. There was room for three in the front but the one in the middle had to sit on the engine cowling, which was uncomfortable but warm. The cowling proved vital for the preservation of life and we each took turns to sit on it for half-an-hour before returning to the arctic wastes of the back. If we didn't, body-heat became a distant memory. You sat there and suffered, enduring the three-and-a-half hours that elapsed before it was your turn to sit on the cowling again.

By the time we got to Cardiff everybody wanted to kill Mike Fortune. It wasn't that he was loud or obnoxious or unpleasant in any way, although he did like a good whinge, but he was, like all amateurs, fascinated by the professional mind. So he questioned us, relentlessly, about our motivation, our attitude, and the apparent lack of any desire for security in our lives. Martin, who was sitting directly opposite him, took the brunt of it and soon withdrew into sarcasm.

We arrived in Hamburg, tired, stiff and cold. We unloaded our gear into the Top Ten and said goodbye to the Corncrackers,

'See you on the way back,' said Mike Fortune.

'I think I might get the train home,' said Martin.

We carried our luggage up to the barracks, commandeered our usual beds and

cool hand plum-stealing by finding

went to sleep. We were woken by the sound of cursing Scottish accents. Someone was dragging what sounded like military equipment up the stairs to the barracks above. I swear I heard the sound of hoofbeats. I got up and went to the toilet and on the way stuck my head around the door overlooking the stairs.

'Y'all right, Jimmy?' said a voice. It was not an enquiry, it was a demand,

'Fine,' I said, offering my hand. 'I'm Deke from the Smokeless Zone. We're the other band. We're Welsh.'

'Thank fuck for that,' said another voice. 'I could'na stomach spending a whole month wi' a bunch o' English wankers.'

'We're the MI5,' said another voice. 'We're Scottish.'

At least one of the bands at the Top Ten was always Scottish. I expect it made Ricky Barnes feel at home. The MI5, a five-piece, played abrasive Scottish rock. We introduced them to the delights of Hamburg. We took them to the Seamans' Mission, the Chug Oo and the Ning Po and, of course, the Blockhaute. They thought they were in heaven.

One night Tony Sheridan walked in. He was ostentatiously sober. We invited him to join us onstage but he politely declined.

'I want to talk to Martin,' he said. He and Martin went into a huddle. They talked conspiratorially for about ten minutes, then shook hands. Sheridan left and Martin walked back over to us.

'What was that all about?' said Plum.

'Sheridan just offered me a job,' said Martin. 'He's going to Vietnam and he needs a bass-player. That's a hell of an idea.'

'What are you going to do?' I asked, fearing the worst.

'I don't know,' said Martin. 'He wants me to listen to his band with the old bass-player so that I can hear his stuff. He's arranged a rehearsal tomorrow afternoon in the club.'

The following afternoon Martin went down to the club.

'They were fucking brilliant,' he recalls. 'He was doing his own songs and I can remember thinking that if he was still with the Beatles they'd probably be even better. I thought "yes", but I said to him, "It's a big step for me. I've got to think about this one." He was cool.'

Over the next few days Martin was quiet, often lost in thought. Then he made up his mind.

'I'm going to Vietnam with Sheridan,' he said.

'OK,' we said.

'I'm going to phone him,' he said, and off he went.

'I suppose we'll have to get another bass-player,' said Plum, without enthusiasm.

'It won't be the same without Ace,' said Terry.

'Fuck!' I said.

Ten minutes later he was back.

'The job's gone,' he said. 'By the time I'd thought about it, they'd got somebody else.'

maybe i should've stayed in bed?

Half of me was delighted but the other half was as disappointed as Martin. It sounded like a great adventure. For the next few days Martin was in sombre mood. We caught the mood and nobody said much. Then, about the middle of the month, all hell broke loose.

One night, about four o'clock, everybody was having a drink in the Blockhaute. Plum was talking to Tuan, the bass-player of the MI5. They noticed a noisy German standing by the bar.

'He was a loud-mouthed twat,' says Plum.

He was also drunk to the point of oblivion and he was looking for something in his wallet. As he did so, a thick wedge of Deutschmarks fell out. He was too drunk to notice at first and it lay on the floor for some time.

'There's about 2,000 marks there,' said Plum.

'At least,' said Tuan.

The drunk noticed the money and picked it up. He stuffed it back into his wallet and carried on drinking. A little later, Plum and Tuan went to the toiletten. As they got there the door burst open and the loud-mouthed German barged past them, still doing up his flies.

'Nazi bastard,' said Plum.

'Bomber Harris was right,' said Tuan.

The toiletten was empty but there, on the floor, was the loud-mouthed German's wallet. Without a word spoken. Plum and Tuan split the money up and tossed the wallet into a urinal.

'We didn't even have the sense to hide it,' says Plum. 'We just flung it,'

Ten minutes later there was a disturbance at the bar. The loud-mouthed German was arguing with the bartender and waving his empty wallet in the air. In German bars you order a beer, the bartender makes a tick on your beer-mat, and you pay up at the end of the night. It was paying-up time and the loud-mouthed German couldn't find his money. He started shouting.

'Polizei! Polizei! Heiligger Rauch! Ich must der Polizei fetchen. Meine geld hast gestolen been. Donner und Blitzen!'

The bartender calmed him down and Plum and Tuan exchanged knowing smiles. They were still smiling when, twenty minutes later, four members of the Hamburg Polizei walked in. We all cheered. One of the Polizei went over to the bar and had a brief conversation with the bartender and the loud-mouthed German. Then he called for silence and made a little speech. We all cheered again.

'What did he say?' I asked Martin.

'He says there's been a robbery and the suspects are in here. We've got to line up against the wall because we're all under arrest and they're going to take us down the police station.'

'All of us?'

'Looks like it.'

We all lined up against the wall.

'This is a lark,' I said to Plum, but he didn't answer. In fact, he didn't look too well at all.

cool hand plum-stealing by finding 187

We were shepherded out onto the street by the Polizei, waving their batons theatrically and shouting 'Raus! Raus!' We started whistling 'Colonel Bogie'. Waiting for us were three police cars and a large police van; I suppose you'd call it a Schwarz Maria. Those that couldn't be wedged into the back of the van were herded toward the police cars. Plum was among these. As soon as he got into the police car he stuffed his wedge of money down the side of the seat. It was a mistake. One of the Polizei saw him, leaned into the car, and reached down for the money.

'Gott in himmel!' he said, holding up the bundle of banknotes. 'Was ist dis?'

'I was really stupid,' says Plum. 'I could have said it was mine. I could have said it was the band float. They couldn't have proved differently. It was only money.'

We were driven straight to the Hamburg nick – an imposing building on the Reeperbahn just across the road from the Top Ten – and searched. When it was Martin's turn he spread-eagled himself against a wall, They were not amused.

'Look,' said Martin, as one of the Polizei went through his pockets, 'I don't know why I'm here. I don't know what you're looking for.'

'Vee are looking for ze rest of ze money,' said the copper.

'What money?' said Martin.

When they had searched us all, we were unexpectedly released. We gathered on the pavement outside the nick, about twenty of us, and picked through the bones of the matter. Speculation was rife.

'What the fuck was that all about?' asked a Scottish voice.

'It'll flit yer graw,' said another.

'Pardon?' said Terry.

'Where's Plum,' said Martin.

'Where's Tuan,' said Big Alan.

'They've kept them in,' said Martin. 'Something must be up.'

'I'm not looking forward to telling Ricky Barnes tomorrow,' said Big Alan.

'I hope Tuan hasn't got his gas-gun with him,' said Wee Alan.

The following afternoon two delegations of musicians, one from each band, sat together in the Top Ten, waiting for Ricky Barnes to arrive. How would he take the news?

'He's gonna go ape-shit,' said Big Alan. 'Totally ape-shit.'

'Totally ape-shit,' repeated Wee Alan. 'Don't forget, he's Scottish. Ape-shit isn'a the right word.'

And he was right. Ape-shit wasn'a the right word.

At first Ricky Barnes listened quietly while we outlined, to the best of our knowledge, the previous night's events. Then he stood up and took a deep breath.

'ARE YOUSE FUCKING MAD?' he said. 'ARE YOUSE TOTALLY FUCKING INSANE? HOW FUCKING OLD ARE YOUSE? YOUSE ARE ALL A BUNCH OF STUPID LITTLE WANKERS. WHAT ARE YOUSE?'

'A bunch of stupid little wankers,' we chorused.

'I'VE A MIND TO SACK ALL OF YOUSE. THERE'S PLENTY OF BANDS IN HAMBURG QUEUING UP TO PLAY HERE. FUCK, THEY'D PLAY HERE FOR

NOTHING. I'M PAYING YOUSE BASTARDS AND THIS IS THE THANKS I GET.'

Then he really let rip. I missed most of it because his Scottish accent got thicker and thicker until it became like a foreign language but, judging by the flushed faces of the MI5, he was getting rather personal. Suddenly he turned toward us.

'Now what the fuck am I going to do about youse?' he said, reverting to English. 'These wankers,' he jerked his thumb toward the sheepish MI5, 'can play as a four-piece, but youse can'na play as a three-piece. You're going to need a singer.'

Oh Gawd, I thought, not the old three-piece argument again.

'Of course we can play as a three-piece,' I said, 'I've played in a three- piece for most of my musical life.'

Why didn't I keep my big mouth shut?

'And just how much of your fucking musical life do you think you've got left, laddie?' he snarled. Then he said something really personal about my mother.

'OK,' I said, 'you've convinced me. We need a singer.'

'Right,' he said. 'I'm going over to the nick to see if I can get those two tosspots out.'

He walked purposefully out of the club.

'Well, that was'na too bad,' said Big Alan.

'Aye,' said Wee Alan, 'we're still alive.'

Ricky Barnes was back in half-an-hour.

'They're keeping them in the nick,' he said. 'They say the fucking stupid buggers robbed a German citizen in the Blockhaute last night. They'll be released on the day youse finish and they'll have twenty-four hours to get out of Germany. If they don't, they'll be re-arrested and charged with robbery. Either way they'll get a hefty fine, which you,' he pointed savagely at each one of us, 'will have to fucking pay.' He composed himself. 'Now I'm going to ring Jack Fallon. He can fly out a replacement singer for youse Welsh bastards.'

'What if he's no good?' said Martin.

'I don't care if he sounds like a dying fucking swan, laddie,' said Ricky Barnes, 'you'll take what you fucking get. And what's more,' he added with a certain amount of glee, 'his air-fare'll come out of your fee. Both ways.'

This would be, on top of Plum's fine, a crippling financial blow. We'd be lucky to come out of this with any money at all.

We played the next two nights as a three-piece. I thought we were rather good but Ricky Barnes, on principle, thought we were shite. On the third day Plum's replacement arrived. His name was John Walker. He was a singer with Long John Baldry's Steam Packet. He'd only been in the band for a couple of months, replacing Rod Stewart, who had gone on to more lucrative pastures. They were off the road for a while and he'd jumped at the chance to go to Germany for two weeks. He was pure London. His hair was spiky and he wore a calf-length, tan suede coat and flared trousers. We thought he looked like a pansy. He moved into

cool hand plum-stealing by finding

the barracks. As he unpacked we gave him a gentle grilling about the Steam Packet but he didn't give much away, probably because, being a new boy, he didn't know much, Martin christened him 'Short John'.

We didn't have time for any rehearsal so we went through our set list, searching for common ground. He knew most of the songs. It just depended on how good he was. That night we found out. He was great, in a sub-Rod Stewart sort of way. He had a big, shouting, blues voice and, although he minced around the stage in a most alarming fashion, it could have been worse.

Hamburg scared the shit out of him. It was his first time abroad and he treated everything with suspicion. The ordering of food was an agonising experience and no amount of reassurance would convince him that it was safe to eat. The Hamburg girls, with their kamikaze directness, filled him with terror and he was convinced, after only one meeting, that Ricky Barnes was the anti-Christ. He was a lost ship, adrift on treacherous seas. After each set he scuttled back to the safety of the barracks.

But within a week he had shacked up with a Hamburg prostitute, he was eating bockwürst by the handful, and he was doing some serious drinking. Now we only saw him at showtime. He would stumble into the club, a mysterious smile on his face, clamber on to the stage and sing like an angel. He would still make occasional visits to the barracks, usually to pick up a change of clothing. It was on one of these occasions that things turned nasty. He had left his toiletries on a shelf next to his bed. Among these was a bottle of Brüt. We'd never seen it before and asked what it was. It was, he said, a new fragrance that was all the rage in London. As soon as he left we'd all take a splash and top the deficit up with water. This worked for a few days until chemistry intervened. Terry had a splash and went to top it up, but as he added the water the Brüt suddenly turned white. He hurriedly replaced it back on the shelf and made himself scarce. The next time Short John arrived at the barracks he rummaged around in his case, looking for something. Suddenly he noticed the Brüt.

'Ere,' he said. 'Who's been putting milk in my Brüt?'

We feigned innocence.

'Do you know how much it costs?' he said.

We shrugged our shoulders.

'Well, it's too late now,' he said. 'It's fucked.' He threw the bottle in a wastepaper basket. 'Thank you very much,' he said and stomped out.

Terry fished the Brüt out of the bin, took the top off and sniffed it.

'It still smells all right to me,' he said. And we all had a splash.

The last night started out in a subdued fashion, except for Short John who sang as if it was his last gig on this earth. We, on the other hand, were somewhat preoccupied. We didn't know what was going to happen to Plum and Tuan. Would the Polizei deliver them to the Top Ten in time for us to leave in the morning? The Corncrackers were due to pick us up first thing tomorrow and any delay would be disastrous. Would they keep Plum an extra few days, just to fuck us up? All the balls were in the air.

maybe i should've stayed in bed?

Then Plum walked into the barracks. It was a huge relief and there was much back-slapping.

'You look like death.' said Martin, 'as if you'd just spent two weeks in a German jail, not knowing what the outcome was going to be.'

Plum told us the gory details.

'I've never been in jail before,' he said, 'let alone a German jail. They were all hardened criminals in there. One day we were walking around the exercise yard. There was a new prisoner there, a big fat guy, and somebody asked him how long he was in for. "Fünfzehn jahren," he said. He'd just come in to do a fifteen-year stretch. I shit myself.'

He and Tuan were brought before a court, provided with translators, and charged with stealing by finding. They were found guilty, fined a large sum of money, and given twenty-four hours to get out of Germany.

'I wouldn't mind going straight away,' said Plum.

'You can't,' said Martin. 'We're on in ten minutes. Get your skates on.'

For the rest of the night Plum and Short John shared the singing duties, each trying to out-sing the other. It was brilliant. At the end of the night both bands started packing up their gear. Tuan had also been released and the return of the prodigals was a cause for great rejoicing. A mood of contentment took hold. Then Ricky Barnes walked up to the stage. He looked balefully at Plum and Tuan.

'Fucking wankers,' he said. 'Do you know how much I had to pay to get you two tosspots out of jail? You don't want to know. Come up the office. You've still got about two Deutschmarks in the kitty – between youse.' He wasn't exaggerating. We ended up with about ten pfennigs.

We said goodbye to Short John because we wouldn't see him in the morning. He was due to fly out the next afternoon but he said he might stay in Hamburg. We strongly advised him not to do so. I believe, although I'm not certain, that he returned to England and the Steam Packet.

The following morning the Corncrackers were late – snowdrifts near Cassel. We'd been kicked out of the Top Ten and when they arrived we were sitting on the gear which was stacked in the club entrance. We were freezing. The Corncrackers bounced out of the van dressed in full US Army winter combat fatigues. Mike Fortune was absent. He was probably sitting in the van.

'Where's Mike Fortune?' said Martin, hope springing eternal.

'He couldn't face the long journey home,' said Breezy. 'He caught a train back yesterday.'

Martin did a little dance.

The journey home was a nightmare. The van was colder than ever, thanks to a hole that had appeared just under the accelerator pedal, although the Corncrackers were positively snug in their combat gear; one of the perks of playing US Army bases. It took two days to get home. The weather was ghastly and we were delayed by floods and blizzards, causing us to miss the ferry by ten minutes. We had to wait twelve hours for the next one. Once back in Britain, the gear-box went and we had to nurse the van home in third-gear. Hills were a

cool hand plum-stealing by finding

problem, particularly Chepstow Hill. We had to reverse up it with both bands pushing,

'This is a bit like that scene in "Ice Cold In Alex",' said Keith.

'More like "Nanook of the North",' said Breezy.

We arrived back in Swansea in a black mood. We dropped Martin off at the Post Office. He stood on the pavement with his suitcase.

'I'm leaving the band,' he said. 'We're going round in circles and we're not making any money. I've had enough. I'm jacking it in.'

'So am I,' said Breezy, from the back of the van.

24
'lectric is it?

To paraphrase the sublime Oscar: it could be said that one band breaking up may be regarded as a misfortune but two bands breaking up looks like carelessness. The local press stoked up the rumours. Martin, they said, was quitting the business for good; Plum and Terry were forming a new band with Breezy; I was returning to the Corncrackers; Breezy was going back to school; and Martin was joining the Corncrackers as vocalist. When the smoke cleared the new lie of the land became apparent.

Plum joined the Jug & Bottle Set; Martin and Terry joined the Bobcats, a band built out of the remnants of the Blackjacks; Breezy went back to school; and I did indeed return to the Corncrackers.

During my absence the Corncrackers had established several useful London connections. They had played a club in Bognor Regis and had been spotted by an associate of Shel Talmy, the recording manager of the Kinks. He was involved with a band called the Untamed, managed by Ken Chapman, who were in the throes of breaking up. They had lost their drummer, bass-player and guitarist, leaving only a keyboard-player and Lindsey Muir, the singer and *force majeure* of the band. Talmy recommended the Corncrackers as replacements. So the Corncrackers joined the Untamed. They dyed their hair blonde and made two singles – one a cover of the Pete Townshend song 'It's Not True' – and embarked on a tour of Britain. But within six months things turned sour. The band seemed to be making money but none of it reached Keith, Wes and Breezy. They complained to Chapman but were fobbed off with the usual managerial codswallop. Things came to a head at a gig in Cheltenham. There was an argument, Lindsey Muir had a nervous breakdown, and that was that. But the time was not wasted. They now had a little black-bookful of contacts and in no time at all the Corncrackers had a formidable itinerary, most of it across southern England.

Almost immediately things started to look up. I don't know how or why, but we had a recording audition for EMI Records at Abbey Road Studios. I don't know who fixed it up. It just seemed to come out of the ether. One thing I do know was that they wanted us to record a song called 'Cara Mia', which was one of the highlights of our set; a corny, Italian love song, it was one of those songs that catapult people out of their seats and propel them, wild-eyed and gyrating, toward the dance floor. We had found the song on a Jay & the Americans EP (For those too young to remember, EP stands for Extended Play. They were a halfway house between a single and an LP. That stands for Long Playing Record. Remember them? EPs were the same size as a single but they contained four tracks. They also

The Jets – Plum, me, Martin and Beau.

The first rehearsal at the Tivoli.
Below: Plum. Right: Me.

Martin – My Prayer?

Martin and me – taking five in the sun.

(All photos Beau Adams)

Leaving for London – Martin, Keith Rogers, Beau, me, Plum and Kit, a wellwisher.

"Taken as we left for London"

"Kit."

Above: Supper at Chelsea Bridge – Plum, me, Martin and Keith.

Right: Martin at Sandown Racecourse.

(Both pics Beau Adams)

*The Top Ten Club.
Right: The Sign.
(Beau Adams)*

*Above: Me.
Right: Martin and Plum.*

*Ricky Barnes in the barracks.
(Beau Adams)*

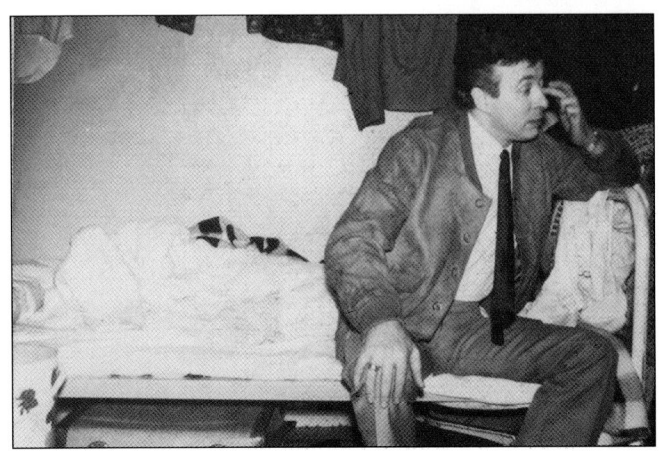

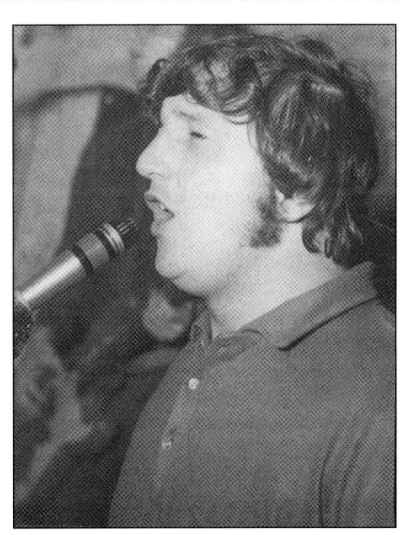

*Top and left:
The Smokeless Zone in K-Town.*

Above: Plum in Johnny's Keller.

Above: Plum – Hamburg-bound and seasick.

Above: Terry joins the band.

Right: The Corncrackers again.

THE DREAM

Representation:
JAY-VEE ENTERTAINMENTS LTD.
1 KINGS LANE, HIGH STREET, SWANSEA
Tel. Swansea 53695 - 53693

Right: The Dream – an explosion in a frilly shirt factory.

Wimpy (above)…and Jeff (below).

Maybe I should've stayed in bed.

The Dream at the Jazz Club: Ace strips for action.

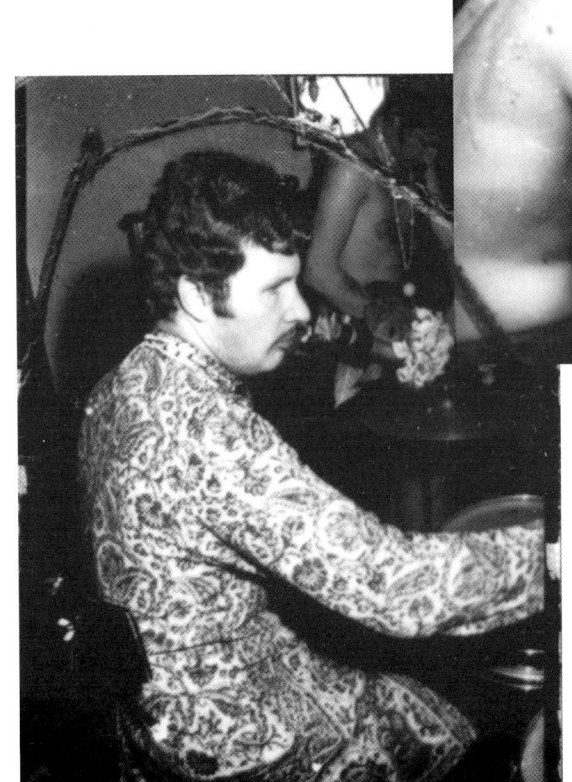

The vandal in charge of the scandal. (caption by Spiv)

Josef Stalin on the drums.

had a shiny, picture sleeve. I mourn their passing, as indeed I mourn the passing of vinyl).

Jay & the Americans, with their strident harmonies bolted to irresistible danceable rhythms, turned us around. We learnt all four songs on the EP. 'Living Above Your Head' was our favourite but the citizens of Rome, as it were, demanded 'Cara Mia'. Somehow EMI, two hundred miles away in London, got a whiff of this. They summoned us to Abbey Road Studios to record 'Cara Mia' and one other song; they didn't care what it was. A possible flip side? So for the occasion I wrote a song called 'Rusty Silver Spoon', a vicious satire on the aristocracy.

We were booked in at ten o'clock on a Sunday morning, a terrifying time for a musician. Musicians are nocturnal creatures who only function in artificial light. Daylight, it has to be said, has little to offer the artistic soul. A 2000 kilowatt follow-spot, on the other hand, illuminates not just the stage but the darkest corners of the musical id. It is my contention that musical faculties are only fully activated during the hours of darkness. During the daylight hours musicians are sluggish and behave in a churlish manner. Fingers, fairly crucial to a guitar-player, are stiff and unwieldy, and a voice which just the previous evening was soaring and full-throated now, with the rising of the sun, croaks and hisses like an asthmatic door-hinge. But when the trumpets sound, the musician must gird his loins and march toward the sound of the guns. And this we did, taking Sherlock with us as road-manager.

We went up the day before and booked into the Madison Hotel, or the 'Mad House' as it was commonly known. The plan was to get up really early in the morning, walk over to Hyde Park, and do a bit of singing to wake the voice up. We arrived at the Madison at six in the evening, booked in, and went out for a quiet meal. We agreed an early night would be advisable but it didn't quite work out like that. Most of us got back to the Madison around three in the morning but the police didn't bring Sherlock back till around four. They were under the impression that he was a Chinese drug dealer wanted on slavery charges. To be fair to the police, Sherlock does have a slight Oriental aspect. We explained to them that Sherlock was a harmless boyo from the valleys, up for the day from the land of our fathers and, as such, no threat to the security of the state – he just happened to look like a dodgy Chinaman. The police reluctantly accepted our explanation and left, but not before giving our room the once-over, presumably hoping to find slave girls or drugs. Luckily we didn't have any slave girls hidden in the wardrobe and we hadn't yet started taking drugs. We got to sleep about six and we were up at seven-thirty.

We had a quick breakfast and headed for Hyde Park. It must have been winter because the grass was covered in a light, overnight frost. For an hour, muffled up against the chilly morning, we sang to the startled ducks, trying to jar our artistic souls into life. Then we got in the van and drove to Abbey Road. Apart from milk-floats the roads were deserted and we were there in twenty minutes. At reception a sleepy security guard directed us to Studio One. It was huge and we stood for a

maybe i should've stayed in bed? 194

while in awe. This was the studio used by the Beatles. There were no two ways about it, we were on the ladder. It was just a matter of time.

It was still only ten o'clock and already we felt as if we'd been up for days. It took a while to get the gear in. We had to carry it up innumerable flights of stairs and down endless corridors. When it was done we collapsed on the studio floor, fighting for breath. We set up in the middle of the studio. A chap in shirtsleeves appeared and miked everything up. The control room was high to our right and we could see shadowy figures moving about behind the perspex window. Then a voice crackled over the tannoy.

'Would you like to come up to the control room? The stairs are through that door to your left.'

We shuffled through endless corridors and climbed innumerable flights of stairs and finally got there. The voice introduced himself. He was a famous producer whose name escapes me for the moment, but we'd heard of him. He was very friendly and we relaxed a little. Although we had no yardstick by which to judge such matters, the recording seemed to go well. We played the songs and they recorded them. We sang the vocals and, although they got a little hoarse toward the end, nobody complained. When it was over we were invited back to the control room to hear the mix.

During the mix, the control room door opened and George Martin walked in. He indicated, by gesture, to the producer that he was just fetching something. He crossed the room and picked up a sheaf of manuscripts from the top of the console and, still miming an apology, tip-toed out. At the door he paused and listened. George Martin, the man who produced the Beatles, was listening to our music. In a perfect world he would have waited until the end of the song and then, in a quiet voice, heavy with the gravity of the moment, he would say:

'This is the moment I have waited for all my life. I have found the best band in the world. I thought the Beatles were the best but I was wrong. Compared to the Corncrackers they are but shadows on the face of destiny. I will immediately ditch them and devote the rest of my life to your service. Here's a million pounds, just in case you need some petty cash.'

In the real world he remained motionless for a minute, then smiled, nodded approval, and left. But that was vindication in itself. He hadn't laughed. He hadn't vomited. This was praise indeed.

'Well, what do you think of it?' said the producer, when it was mixed.

'It sounds great to us,' we chorused.

'OK,' he said, 'I'll play it to the high-ups and if they approve it'll be released as a single. OK?'

'OK,' we said.

'Thank you, gentlemen,' he said. We shook hands and left.

When we got down to the studio Sherlock had packed all the gear and was starting to lug it down to the van. Guilt dictated that we help him. Muttering about the damage that it might cause to our artistic souls, we picked up the lightest bits of gear we could find and joined the long trek, up innumerable corridors and down endless flights of stairs. I deposited my first load, the hi-hat stand and the small tom-tom, at the van and made my way back to the studio. I came to the foot of a flight of stairs and looked up. Sherlock was standing at the top holding one of my amps; an airforce-blue Vox AC30.

'Come on, Sherlock,' I said. 'Pull your finger out. I've got a life to live.'

'Shut it, Leonard,' he said. 'Somebody's got to carry the heavy stuff.'

Then he seemed to do a little dance. His hips swivelled and his knees bent. I thought he was fucking about until I saw the terror on his face. Suddenly, his legs buckled and he fell forward. My amp, my beautiful amp, flew into the air. It bounced halfway down the stairs with a splintering crash and took off once more, headed for me. I, coming from Scarlet country, did an elegant side-step and the amp flew over my shoulder and landed with a sickening thud behind me in the stairwell. There was silence.

'Oops,' said Sherlock, sprawled over the top steps, clinging to a hand-rail. 'Sorry.'

'Oops?' I said. 'OOPS?'

He came down the stairs slowly. He put the amp the right way up and inspected it.

'It looks alright to me,' he said sheepishly.

'It's an electrical appliance, isn't it?' I said, grabbing him by the throat, 'and it is in the nature of electrical appliances that we won't know whether they're still working until we've plugged them in, will we?'

'It'll be alright,' said Sherlock, as any convicted murderer would claim innocence just before ascending the scaffold. 'You'll see.' he added, none too convincingly.

We finished loading the gear and headed back to Wales, feeling demi-semi-satisfied with the day.

The next gig, two days later, was at Pontyberym Welfare Hall, a cavernous, old, municipal shed, famous, at least in Pontyberym, because John Wesley, the itinerant, 19th century evangelist, once preached there. Of course, he preached in similar places all over Wales so it's no big deal. We decided to get there early to test my amp and rehearse a few new songs. We arrived at four in the afternoon. The cleaning lady let us in and we set up on the large stage. At the time I was using two AC30 amplifiers linked up, so if the damaged amp didn't work I still had a spare. We plugged the amp in and it worked fine. We marvelled at the indestructibility of the Vox AC30 amplifier. Not even Sherlock, a barbarian amongst barbarians, could so much as scratch it. I rigged both amps up and sat on top of them as we ran through the chords of the first number – an Everly Brothers song called 'You've Got The Power'. Then we moved on to the vocals. Holding my guitar by the neck, I leaned over to grab my microphone stand and the world turned upside-down. As I gripped the stand, electricity surged through my body, catapulting me backwards over my amps. My arms crossed, pulling my guitar and the microphone stand, now locked in my hands, in against either side of my neck. I lay there, unable to move, throbbing with electricity. I tried to let go of the guitar

maybe i should've stayed in bed?

and microphone stand but it was impossible. I became aware of a burning smell. I looked up at the ceiling, seeing each knot in the wood with incredible clarity. I felt I was made of electricity. It seemed to go on forever. I prepared myself for death.

Suddenly, it stopped. It was the most beautiful feeling in the world. I became aware of voices raised in panic. Keith and Wes dragged me out from behind the amps to the front of the stage and began pummelling my body. I'd just been electrocuted, for Christ's sake, and now they were beating me up.

'He's still alive,' said Keith, hitting me on the chest.

'Thank God for that,' said Wes, and disappeared.

'Stop hitting me,' I said to Keith. 'I thought you liked me?'

'Your clothes are on fire, you twat,' said Keith. 'I'm putting them out.'

I lay there, smiling with relief. It was all over and I was still alive. Wes returned carrying a glass of water. His hands were shaking and the water splashed all over me. The cleaning lady, mop in hand, appeared at the front of the stage. She looked me up and down.

''Lectric, is it?' she said.

'No,' I snapped. 'Pissing gas.'

Wes and Keith started giggling.

'I think he's all right,' said Wes, with relief. He handed me the glass, which now contained about a quarter of an inch of water, and I sat up and looked down at my clothes. They were still smoking. So was my guitar. So was the microphone stand. They helped me to my feet, gently shepherded me outside into the van. and drove me to the nearest hospital. The doctor said I was lucky to be alive.

'How long was he electrocuted for?' he asked Wes and Keith. They looked at each other and shrugged.

'About ten seconds,' they said.

'Another few seconds and he'd have gone,' said the doctor, 'but because he pulled his arms up to his neck all the electricity went around his shoulders, bypassing his heart. He's a very lucky man.'

Keith and Wes had saved my life. As soon as Wes realised what was happening he'd rushed across the stage and yanked my leads out. At the same time Keith had run in the opposite direction and pulled out the mains plug.

I was treated for burns to both sides of my neck, burns to the palms of my hands and the inside of my fingers, and general lacerations. The lacerations had been caused by my guitar strings. Where I was holding the guitar-neck, the strings were soldered to the frets, slicing them in half; the resulting string-ends had whiplashed my face. The gig was cancelled. I sat in the van, swathed in bandages – looking like Karis, high priest of Isis – while the gear was loaded. We drove home.

'I'm giving up the guitar,' I said, my voice muffled by the bandages. 'It's too fucking dangerous.'

'It wasn't our fault,' said Wes. 'I checked our plugboard and it was all right. It must have been a faulty mains system in the hall.'

'It was probably the same mains system that John Wesley used when he was here,' I said. 'I bet he had a shock or two as well.'

'It wasn't anything to do with the mains system,' said Keith. 'It was Sherlock's fault. Don't forget, he was the one who dropped your amp down a flight of stairs at Abbey Road.'

'The bastard,' I said, thinking about it for the first time. 'Do you think he did it on purpose?'

'Probably,' said Wes. 'He's never liked you. By the way, your guitar neck is fucked, The strings are soldered to the frets and the fingerboard is all scarred from the string-ends. And there's deep grooves cut in the scratch plate. You're going to have to get a new neck.'

'That is the least of my worries,' I said. 'In fact, I don't have any worries at the moment. I'm still above ground, and that's enough for me. But I do have one suggestion.'

'Fire away,' said Keith.

'I suggest we never play Pontyberym again. Ever.'

'Agreed,' said Wes.

'You've got the power, Deke,' said Keith, I assume humorously.

A few days later I confronted Sherlock with charges of attempted manslaughter. He brushed them aside.

'It was probably a loose connection,' he said.

Sherlock is one of life's loose connections.

25
here come the drugs

After a week or so, when the burns had healed a little, I noticed a loss of feeling in my left hand. So I got a rubber ball and squeezed it for a week or two and the feeling came back, which was just as well because there was an avalanche of new work, some of it in London. While we were there, I went around the music shops looking for a new Telecaster neck. I couldn't find one so I bought a Stratocaster neck instead. There were differences. It was narrower, so the strings converged slightly toward the nut. It took me about half a song to get used to it.

We played Billy Walker's Uppercut Club, a vast aircraft hanger in East London; we supported the Turtles in Blaizes, a tiny basement full of London's nouveau-hip; and we picked up a semi-partial-intermittent-residency at the Speakeasy.

The Speakeasy was famous for being the late-night watering-hole for the music business. On any given night the big names would be out in force, drinking gallons of Tequila Sunrise and talking shop. Legendary jams were supposed to have occurred there. One night Stephen Stills and Jimi Hendrix went head-to-head and, rumour had it, Stills came out on top. I didn't believe that. Stills is no slouch, but no-one, with the possible exception of me, could get the better of Hendrix. The Speakeasy paid peanuts but, if you wanted to be spotted, this was the place to play.

The playing times were half-hour on, half-hour off, all night from seven till four. People didn't start coming in till eleven so the first three sets were played to a virtually empty club. We viewed these first three sets, sans audience, as paid rehearsals; a chance to try out new numbers, adjust arrangements on existing songs, and generally fuck about.

On our first gig we started at seven on the dot. There was only one person in the club, a man sitting way back in the Speakeasy gloom. We played the first song and the figure in the darkness applauded enthusiastically. We turned toward him and bowed ostentatiously. We played another song and once again the figure in the darkness applauded. He was a wonderful audience and we told him so. He was, we said, the largest audience we'd played to in some time. We invited him to clap along with the songs – on the off-beat of course; to clap along with the on-beat, we reminded him, was, in the words of Duke Ellington, considered to be an act of aggression. We advised him not to get too close to the stage, fearing he would be injured in the crush. After the set, on our way to the bar, we took a detour past our audience's table. All the tables were lit by candles in transparent, orange, glass bowls and, as we approached, our audience leant forward into the amber light. My heart stopped, my mouth went dry, and I broke out into a cold, cold sweat. It was Jimi Hendrix. He was dressed in *the* black, military jacket. He stretched out a huge, boney hand.

'Far out, man,' he said.

'Thank you very much,' we said, lining up to shake his hand.

We made our way to the bar and tried to compose ourselves.

'How,' I said, pouring a large brandy down my throat, 'am I supposed to play guitar in these circumstances? It's like trying to make a human being out of a lump of clay in front of God. If there is a God, which I seriously doubt.'

Half-an-hour later we were back on the stage. The place had filled up a little but Hendrix watched our second set from the same table. This time I pulled out all the stops. Well, you would, wouldn't you? Your mortal soul would demand it, wouldn't it?

By the fourth set, the place was packed and you couldn't turn around without falling over somebody famous. The were a couple of Kinks present and Graham Nash held court near the bar. I went up to him and reminded him of our previous meeting. He was aloof and indifferent. And why not? He was the great Graham Nash and I was, at best, a footnote in the history of the performing arts. We ignored him and the rest of the audience and continued to play for the benefit of one man. He was no longer at his table but we caught the odd glimpse of him as he did some serious mingling.

At the end of the night we packed up our gear and the crowd thinned out. Hendrix, apparently by tradition, was the last to leave, accompanied by a tall, Nordic blonde. As he walked out of the door he turned and waved goodbye to us. Grinning like synchronised swimmers, we waved back. Wes picked up the money and we drove back to Wales.

I considered the evening to be another vindication of my existence. I had, in effect, been judged by the highest court in the Cosmos. Hendrix, surely a man at the pinnacle of human achievement, had not run screaming into the streets with his hands over his ears. He had listened. It's as if Michaelangelo had said, 'Nice sketch, Deeko.'

Back in Swansea, we supported Tom Jones at the Brangwyn Hall, The bill also included Welsh showbiz personalities Kim Cordell and Johnny Tudor, and the Dunvant Male Voice Choir. The show was compered by Alun Williams, a highly-respected journalist and well-known voice on BBC Radio. It was a gala event and the audience were mainly civic dignitaries togged out in their Sunday-best. We were on second after the Dunvant Male Voice Choir, who sat, *en masse*, on tiered seating along the back of the stage. While we stood in the wings waiting to go on, we listened to the awesome beauty of one hundred and twenty full-throated Welshmen, dressed in blazers and aided only by a pre-gig pint or two, wrenching the last shards of simmering passion from mystical and ancient harmonies. Harmonies that unlock wistful longings in the Celtic breast, exposing long-hidden yearnings for a time when wizards and dragons and giants walked the land; a time when a man could paint his body blue and dance among the wooded glades and mist-fingered crags of Cambria without feeling one stone short of a circle.

With the spirit of Owain Glyndwr coursing through our veins, we walked on stage and opened up with Neil Sedaka's 'Breaking Up Is Hard To Do'. We started with an acappella section accompanied by handclaps. We encouraged the audience to sing and clap along. Suddenly, from behind us came a thunderous sound. The choir were singing and clapping along. They drowned us out, PA and all. It was a physical force and it nearly blew us off the front of the stage. The rest of the set was something of an anti-climax.

In fact the whole evening was something of an anti-climax until Tom bounced onto the stage. He was greeted by a blizzard of knickers thrown onto the stage by the civic dignitaries' wives who'd turned, in the heat of the moment, from snobby little matrons into sex-hungry tigresses. I didn't see any of them take their knickers off so I assume they brought a spare pair with them. Tom ostentatiously picked up one or two and used them to wipe the sweat off his brow before throwing them back into the audience. The wives went ape-shit while their husbands, faces flushed with embarrassment, looked like they wanted to die. Who says the masses have no feeling for art?

One good thing about the evening was that we were billed in the programme as EMI recording artists. It wasn't true but it looked good. Worryingly, things had been rather quiet on the EMI front. Finally they let us know that they had decided not to release 'Cara Mia' as a single. However, they wished us well in the future. We took it on the chin – one door shuts and another one opens. We had a recording test for CBS Records coming up. We went to London, brim-full of hope. Two weeks later they turned us down – one door shuts and then another one shuts. We were getting depressed, Keith more than most. He said he was leaving the group to form his own band, provisionally called Dark Albert. Wes and I started looking for another drummer. Martin and Terry had just come back from a tour of American bases with the Bobcats. We offered Terry the job. He accepted on condition that Martin came too. But, Wes pointed out, we already had a bass-player. That was OK, said Terry, Martin could assume the role of general dogsbody, playing guitar, tambourine, and anything else that took his fancy. This sounded fine. So Martin and Terry joined the Corncrackers. We decided to change the name of the band. The search for a new name began.

We were beginning to feel the balmy breezes of psychedelia blowing across the Atlantic. Music was changing and we changed with it. We bought the 'Freak Out' album by the Mothers of Invention which, apart from rearranging my tonal imperatives, made me realise what a poxy, little, anally-retentive musician I was.

We began a search for the inner self. We read Carlos Castaneda, R.D. Laing, Timothy Leary, and Lobsang Rampa (who we later discovered was a bus conductor from Birmingham).

Our mode of dress was changing. We started wearing kaftans and bells. There was no way you could buy a kaftan in Llanelly so my mother made one for me, using some old, flowered curtains she had left over from doing the house. Perfect domestic camouflage; if I stood perfectly still next to a window I could escape detection for hours, thereby avoiding the ever-present threat of being coerced by my mother into painting the fucking living-room ceiling again.

Out in the real world, psychedelic one-upmanship flourished. There was an

here come the drugs

unofficial competition over who had the largest bell hanging around their neck. I found a three-inch circumference bell made out of whatever bells are made out of. It looked great although its weight meant that I walked with a permanent stoop. It emitted a fearsome clang so you could hear me coming from the other side of the Bristol Channel. We grew moustaches. I hoped it would make me look like John Lennon but I looked more like Joseph Stalin. We let our hair grow. I had a great deal of trouble with this. I had naturally curly hair. I hated it. Any attempt to grow it long resulted in outcrops of hair jutting out from my head at startling angles. I looked like someone recently released into care in the community. I was often asked if I had remembered to take my medication.

I painted Egyptian hieroglyphics all over the body of my Telecaster. Close up it looked fantastic but from a distance it just looked grey, so I painted a large French flag over most of them. It still looked murky so I painted a portrait of Napoleon Bonaparte, looking miserable as sin, in front of the flag. Bonaparte always looked miserable. I pictured him at what was possibly the lowest point in his life; the moment when he probably said, 'Bugger moi! It's bloody Blücher.' For some unfathomable reason it worked. The Telecaster looked magnificent. Not traditionally psychedelic, it's true but enough, I thought, to distort the consciousness of a casual observer. Logic, you will have no doubt noted, had very little bearing on my thought processes. Very few things did.

We started smoking dope. Again I had trouble. I didn't smoke. Smoking is something I came to late in life. In those days I found it nauseous so I couldn't have a joint. But everyone around me was giggling and talking rubbish and I wanted to be a gibbering idiot too. The worst part of it was being constantly told, by every dope-smoker in the vicinity, that I was missing out on the second-best feeling in the world. Just what I wanted to hear.

Then I went to see Plug – a Llanelly drummer playing with Screaming Lord Sutch and the Savages – who had a flat in Deptford. He had a bottle of tincture of cannabis. I had a swig or two. Bloody nirvana, mate! I had the lot – universal, unconditional love for my fellow man; ultra-sensitivity to sound, preferably communal humming; the unshakeable conviction that I and my companions were the funniest people on this earth; the munchies; slight and fleeting paranoia; the munchies again; the compelling urge, fortunately resisted, to go outside and look at the stars; and the conclusion, sombrely arrived at, that deep down in the darkest and murkiest corner of my soul, in that part of you wherein resides your essence, the universal me wanted to be somebody else; and, of course, the munchies again.

I had an uncontrollable urge to write a song. I couldn't wait to see what sort of music my newly expanded mind would come up with. But there were no musical instruments in the flat. It was, after all, a drummer's flat. Drummers' flats are pockets of pure rhythm from which pitch is banished. They get very edgy in the presence of melody and anyone with a facility for producing it is regarded with suspicion, bordering on paranoia. And, worst of all, they keep tapping on the table, paradiddling away as if their life depended upon it. On the upside, there is no shortage of creature comforts and the fridge contains enough food for a second

maybe i should've stayed in bed?

Berlin air-lift, should one be required. In short, a wasteland for the musical mind but paradise if you've got the munchies.

Incidentally, you don't need a musical instrument to write a song. Indeed the best songs, I find, are written totally in the head. That way your imagination is not shackled by the habit and custom of your technique. When you pick up your instrument – piano-players think metaphorically here – your hands go to familiar positions and for the songwriter these warming-up exercises become jumping off points for new songs. And that's fine, but their direction is now determined, and channelled, by the limitations of your technique. Without an instrument imagination is uncluttered by technique because technique is purely a physical matter. It is a means, not an end. In my head I can play like Hendrix but when I pick up a guitar and really play, it still, depressingly, sounds like me. However, once you have the complete song in your head, keep repeating it until it is firmly lodged in the tonal memory. Then, and only then, pick up your instrument to work it out. If you go too early and the structure is not fully formed, your technique will do its level best to override your memory and, as you soar into the creative sky, it will clutch at your feet, peevishly trying to drag you back to earth and tedious reality.

Back in Llanelly, tincture of cannabis was hard to come by, so I had to put my drug-taking on hold. This didn't work, because now I understood. Now, I knew what they were all talking about. And they were playing it down. It was even better than they said it was. I steeled myself and took the next joint offered me. It was disgusting and I coughed for about two hours, but I got stoned. I considered it a price worth paying.

We rented a communal flat in Mirador Crescent in Swansea. The front door was always open. In the day we slept, but at night we daubed our faces with day-glo paint and held parties in the dark. We played Hendrix's 'Are You Experienced' album over and over again. At least we did when Frank wasn't hogging the record-player. Frank was one of our many flatmates and he was obsessed with Bob Dylan; everybody else was shit. Day after day, he would crouch in front of the record-player, playing all his Dylan albums in chronological order. Any attempt to elbow him aside, to try and get some Hendrix on the turntable, would be greeted with snarling, spitting, and threats of extreme violence. What was the point, Frank reasoned, of listening to Hendrix when you could be listening to 'The Master'? He even started talking with a Dylan-like, sing-song lilt to his voice.

'Do you want a piece of toast, Frank?' you'd ask.

'She's a junkyard angel and she always makes me toast,' he'd reply.

'Is that a yes or a no?' you'd say, through gritted teeth.

'All I really wanna a do is have a piece of toast.'

He slept with his eyes open and snored fiercely. The snore was a hellish amalgam of revving outboard-motor and the death rattle of a regimental sergeant-major, punctuated by Dylanesque grunts. When Frank went to bed early, we would take parties of visitors to his bedroom to watch him for a few minutes; that's all they could take, before rushing to the toilet to retch their guts up. I have heard a

here come the drugs

rumour that Frank went on to make a fortune by whipping blokes for money, but that may just be wishful thinking on my part.

We got ourselves a new manager. Tony Court, who had been Billy Doc's predecessor on the early Jets' drumstool, now ran a music agency. He already represented the Eyes of Blue and the Jug & Bottle Set. He shared an office, above Wilkes' Garage, with Brian Curvis, the boxer; it was just a room with two desks in it and they shared the rent. We outlined our plans for the new band, he got suitably enthused, and we struck a deal.

We threw ourselves into rehearsals. Among the songs we included were – 'Magical Mystery Tour', 'The Letter', 'Most Likely You'll Go Your Way', 'Jacky', 'McArthur Park', 'Pledging My Time', 'So You Wanna Be A Rock'n'Roll Star', 'Hey Grandma', and 'Sgt Pepper's Lonely Hearts Club Band (Parts 1 & 2).

We decided to have a 'freak out' section. If it was good enough for Zappa, it was good enough for us. We had no idea what a freak out was, so we made it up as we went along. We had a skeletal plan. Terry would play abstract rhythm patterns on the drums while the rest of us would put our guitars on top of our speakers with the volume turned up full, thus creating a background of howling feedback that would maintain itself, thereby freeing us to move amongst the audience encouraging 'happenings'.

And we found a name for the band – Dream.

26
the biggest freak out to hit south wales

We didn't have to worry about gigs because the Corncrackers gig-sheet was a magnificent thing. All Tony Court had to do was phone up the promoters and inform them of the name change. They weren't too keen on it. The Corncrackers' name was well-known, but nobody knew who Dream were.

'The Dream?' they'd say. You could almost hear them frowning.

'Not "The Dream",' Tony would say patiently. 'It's "Dream". There's no "The". It's not a noun, it's a verb. It's a command.'

Now, without being unkind to promoters as a breed, most of them, it is universally acknowledged, wouldn't know what a noun or, for that matter, a verb is, let alone tell one from the other. But Tony insisted and they reluctantly agreed, without really knowing what they had agreed to.

The first gig we did was at the Redcliffe Hotel on the seafront at Caswell Bay. The management were, understandably, a little jittery. A week earlier, the Herald Of Wales had announced that the gig would be the first 'love-in' in Swansea, predicting that thousands of flower-children would descend on the Redcliffe Hotel, turning it, they implied, into a hippy Sodom and Gomorrah (The word 'hippy' was increasingly being used to describe us, and our ilk. Those of us who seriously aspired to psychedelia hated it; we weren't 'hippies', we were 'heads').

We assured the management that, although we didn't quite know what we were going to do, whatever it was would be perfectly harmless. We could further assure them that it would not involve any damage to property, particularly to the Redcliffe Hotel.

An hour before we went on, the place was packed. Nearly everybody was wearing kaftans and beads, and most of them were carrying flowers. Curiously, they were all rhododendrons. I put this down to universal consciousness; that mysterious, invisible, spiritual thread that touches us all. There was a buzz of expectancy. We came on to rapturous applause. It was a magic summer night and, although you couldn't quite put your finger on it, there was, tangibly, something in the air.

As the end of the set approached, we, and the audience, were ecstatic. Then Martin shouted, 'FREAK OUT!' We put our guitars on top of our speaker cabinets, turned up all the volume knobs and, letting them hum, ventured into the audience. We had decided that, at this juncture in the proceedings, we would, in name of peace and love for our fellow man, throw things at the audience. We had buckets filled with confetti and thirty cans of Crazy Foam. Crazy Foam is one of Mankind's greatest achievements – you can make a real soap-suddy mess of someone, and

the biggest freak out to hit south wales

when they get fed up of it, they can wipe it off, leaving no damage to person or clothing; it could, however, fuck up your hair. The idea was to cover everybody with Crazy Foam then throw confetti over them. At first it was a little slow because we could only spray the front row while Martin threw handfuls of confetti at them. but when we threw cans of Crazy Foam into the crowd, things picked up and they began to spray each other. We moved through the crowd carrying the buckets, dispensing confetti. When the buckets were empty we returned to the stage and watched the carnage from a safe distance. It was amazing. The gig was playing itself. It was in full swing and we didn't have to do anything, so we lolled against our amplifiers, pointing out feats of derring-do amongst the audience. All except Terry, who was still going like the clappers. Keeping up a thunderous bass-drum tattoo, he offered me his sticks. Foolishly I took them. He leapt from behind the kit, grabbed one of the remaining cans of Crazy Foam, and disappeared into the audience, squirting indiscriminately.

I am no drummer. I am psychologically unsuited to play the drums. I have plenty of inspiration but very little stamina and, of course, I lack the bestial qualities so necessary in the make-up of a good percussionist. So I thrashed about, trying to be as abstract as possible. Fortunately Terry was back in about twenty minutes. He returned to the drum stool, we picked up our instruments, played a coda of blistering audacity, and left the stage. There was pandemonium. The crowd stomped and whooped and cheered while, back-stage, we were grinning like fools. The applause was relentless so we went back on and did a quick 'Hey Grandma'. This in no way satisfied them and they cheered on regardless. Then the hotel put the lights on and they reluctantly went home.

The management were stunned. The hall was a mess. It was ankle-deep in confetti mixed with rhododendrons crushed underfoot. There were great swathes of Crazy Foam, jagging across the room like snow-drifts, making the floor surface as treacherous as an ice-rink. One poor barmaid, collecting glasses, went flying, in gymnastic terminology, arse over tit. She skidded along for a yard or two before doing a back-flip and landing face-down in the soggy muck. She was rescued, with some difficulty, but not without humour, by senior management who led her, crying, back to the bar for a stiff brandy.

The management gave us a list of their grievances, which were mainly about the cost of cleaning the hall, which would have to be done that night because they had a wedding breakfast first thing in the morning. And what about the damage done to the hotel gardens? Apparently our audience had stripped the flower-beds bare and there wasn't a rhododendron bush left. So much for universal consciousness; it looked more like universal convenience to me. And, of course, there were the injuries to staff. Martin asked them how many punters had come through the doors and they grudgingly admitted they'd been full to capacity. Furthermore, they added, they'd had to turn people away in droves. And how were the bar-takings? Oh, the bar-takings were tremendous.

'Then what,' said Martin, 'are you fucking complaining about?

The next few gigs followed a similar pattern. The Herald Of Wales trumpeted

maybe i should've stayed in bed? 206

the arrival of 'Flower Power', but expressed some concern for the moral well-being of Swansea's young people. This was somewhat tongue-in-cheek. It was written by Gary Radd, the Herald's music correspondent. Gary Radd was, in fact, Con Atkin. Con, who had been writing for the Herald of Wales for years, changed his by-line every two years, so that readers would have someone new to hate. He came from journalistic stock. His elder brother was Leon Atkin, the journalist priest, famous for his mordant wit, who wrote syndicated religious columns for many national newspapers. Con shared his sense of mischief, and just a whiff of moral decline was enough to send him, cackling and rubbing his hands, to his typewriter, there to knock off five hundred words of outrage before you could say 'Morrel Pure Lard'. He finished his article on us by saying he would reserve his judgement until our up-coming gig at the Glanmor Jazz Club, when he would see for himself.

We arrived at the Jazz Club in the early afternoon to set things up. We were let in by the caretaker, who then disappeared into his cubby-hole for a siesta. We had the club at our mercy. We stripped the gardens of flowers, again rhododendrons, and decked out the stage. We stuck them onto the back wall of the stage with sticky tape and piled bunches on every flat surface. We ran lines of string, just above head-height, from one side of the stage to the other and hung flowers on them to form an overhead canopy. I'd never seen so much mauve in my entire life.

When the committee arrived they were appalled. We blamed the caretaker. He had, we said, given us permission. One of the committee stumped off to the caretaker's cubby-hole, woke him up and sacked him. So, we had to own up (we didn't want another caretaker loose in the community. Without supervision, they forget to take their medication and deteriorate rapidly into a spiral of despair, forgetting to perform even the minimal requirements of basic hygiene, and begin to suffer increasingly from paranoid delusions. Most of them end up in the Tory party). By way of mitigation, we explained that if we hadn't picked the flowers, our fans would have. We'd just done it first. They didn't see this as an explanation at all and stomped off, making huffing noises. Within ten minutes of the doors opening the audience were jammed-up and jelly-tight and the air hung heavy with the pungent smell of incense and marijuana. Everybody carried flowers taken, this time, from nearby private gardens. More complaints. In the afterlife we will, no doubt, spend eternity running a never-ending gauntlet of homicidal gardeners.

The gig was damn-near perfect. On the shout of 'Freak Out' we immediately threw cans of Crazy Foam into the crowd and let them get on with it. We had solved the confetti problem; Martin now blew it over the heads of the audience, using a vacuum-cleaner. Instant mess. We compounded the mess by throwing the stage flowers into the audience. Once more I went on to the drums, liberating Terry from the shackles of his trade. No longer content to spray the audience with Crazy Foam, he had, for the last few gigs, taken to playing my guitar. Now, Terry will be the first to tell you that he is no guitar-player but that matters little to the true artist in the steely grip of inspiration. He proved to be quite good in a cubist sort of way. At the climax of his guitar spot he would play the guitar with his teeth. This, as anyone who has tried it will tell you, is not the easiest thing in the world

the biggest freak out to hit south wales

to do, and can, if not conducted with accuracy, lead to chipped fillings followed by dreadful toothache. To prevent tooth damage he had tried holding a plectrum between his teeth but had found that, in moments of psychedelic abandon, he had a tendency to swallow it. He returned to the chipped fillings.

Martin had stripped naked, except for my seersucker shirt, which he wore as a loincloth (I don't know why I wasn't wearing it at the time. I don't normally take my clothes off in public). His body painted with flower designs, he presented himself to the audience in a Christ-like pose, arms at full-stretch, head thrown back. We left the guitars humming on top of the amps and left the stage. It was a good ten minutes before the audience realised we'd gone. When they did, they went ape-shit. A quick 'Hey Grandma' and we were gone. Pandemonium. The house-lights went up, breaking the spell, and the flower children wilted and went home. A delegation from the committee arrived in the dressing-room, in a foul mood. Who's going to clean up the mess? And where have all our rhododendrons gone? All the usual shit.

'How were the bar-takings tonight?' said Martin. But answer came there none.

On the following Thursday the Herald of Wales came out, and we'd made the front page. Over a ten-inch high photograph of Martin, wearing just my shirt knotted around his waist, ran the banner headline: FLOWER POWER. Alongside the photograph was an editorial, sub-titled: IT WAS INEVITABLE. It read:

It was inevitable. The flower children had to come as successors to the beatniks, the Teddy boys, and the mods and rockers.

It was inevitable, too, that this new teenage cult should reach Wales. Swansea had its first taste of organised Flower Power last week – and the centre pages of the Herald of Wales this week show what it was like.

This week the Flower Children will descend on Neath for a "Flower Power Festival."

Where next, and what next? That is the question.

The centre-page spread was headlined: THE FLOWER CHILDREN, and dominated by a terrifying half-page photograph of Terry, with face painted, playing my guitar with his teeth. There was a photograph of Martin holding up a vacuum cleaner, captioned: 'TURNING ON' – WITH A VACUUM CLEANER. There were a few photographs of the crowd, and one of me looking exactly like Joseph Stalin.

The article described us:

The Dream were dressed in full Flower Power outfits, and the music was purposely adjusted to transmit the psychedelic effect synonymous with "freak outs."

And the gig:

Confetti was strewn from end to end of the room.

And the audience:

In the middle of the dance-floor some kissed while others kept their eyes fixed intently on the strangely-clothed group. One well-educated and half-naked boy wearing coloured beads and bangles told me that he saw nothing wrong in making love when and where he pleased. His girlfriend agreed.

They interviewed the audience at some length:

'Bells, beads and flowers might be considered a sign of femininity, but to us,' said a boy wearing a black-flowered Mandarin coat with beads to match, 'they serve to counteract the hard, tough reputation of the male.'

'Drugs are a means to an end. Not something taken for kicks but an instrument used in the search for our true selves. But we can get high on just love alone, without the use of drugs.'

Some were almost evangelical in tone:

'The flower theory is the boost that religion has needed for some time. We do what we like when we like and achieve the same ends as the Church.'

My contribution was a subtle blend of unfettered ambition and simple-minded self-delusion, but, I think, capturing the spirit of the age:

'I think we're on to something big here. It will probably take some time to catch on among some but I think it will grip everybody eventually.'

All in all. it was a little cracker. As soon as it came out, Tony Court's phone started ringing. Everybody wanted to book us.

The following week the Herald of Wales printed a disclaimer from the Jazz Club, accusing us of cynically cashing-in on the latest trend, and adding that although their members, which were all they were concerned with, had thrown flowers, they were only entering into the spirit of the act. The club disassociated itself completely from any of the remarks made by the clientele and quoted in the article. It further reassured parents of teenagers in the 'Jazz Section' that nothing improper would ever be allowed to be carried on at the club and that they need have no fears for the moral well-being of their children. It was signed by WH Jones, on behalf of the committee of the Glanmor Jazz Club. It kept the ball rolling.

We even made it to the nationals. The Daily Mirror did a feature on Flower Power and we were mentioned. We had a paragraph to ourselves. I quote it in full:

By evening, drunk with sun, scenery and salt sea air, the holiday-makers come to the fun-spots of Swansea Town. At the Glanmor Club a group of flower children called the Dream made a hell of a noise.

'Biggest freak out to hit South Wales,' said a dazed onlooker happily.

Not much, but a start.

Meanwhile Plum, with the Jug & Bottle Set, was ploughing his own furrow. While we were all doing flower power and trying to be incredibly groovy and hip, Plum went for vegetable power.

'I took the heart out of a cabbage and put it on my head,' says Plum, 'and I made a necklace of spuds, turnips, carrots and onions and, at the end of the gig, I chucked them at the audience.' Give peas a chance?

Back in Dreamland, we were constantly augmenting the set. Martin found a child's wind-up toy that made a jangling sound, so we called it, imaginatively, 'the jangler'. He found a school bell, which he rang at opportune moments. Then he had an idea. What if he filled the upturned bell with methylated spirits and set it alight? – it would make the perfect torch. At the end of the set he could now present himself to the crowd, holding a beacon aloft, looking like the Statue of

the biggest freak out to hit south wales

Liberty. We tried it. It worked fine, except that he could only stand there for so long without looking a bit of a prat, so he took to spilling methylated spirits over Terry's cymbals. Terry would then whack the cymbal and the flames would shoot upwards. It could be dangerous. On more than one occasion Martin set fire to Terry's drumheads, which melted on contact with the fire, and once, in Brecon Town Hall, he spilled a fireball into Terry's lap. Terry, screaming in pain, leapt off his drum-stool and ran for the backstage toilet, beating the flames out with his hands. It went down well and Martin suggested we do it every night but Terry, for some reason, disagreed.

When we were due to play a gig, the local town council would go on red alert. Llanelly was a good example. We were due to play the Glen Ballroom. The Llanelly Star documented the preparations. Council gardeners, it said, were keeping twenty-four hour guard over their municipal flower beds, because they were afraid the cult of 'flower children' would lead to some of their choice blooms ending up in someone's hair.

The Glen Ballroom was the old Ritz Ballroom. Still owned by Dave Scott, it was now split in two; downstairs was a bowling alley and upstairs was a ballroom, where a revolving stage had been installed, framed by thick, powder-blue, velvet curtains. There was extensive carpeting, all of it red tartan, which we presumed was the long-lost Scott tartan. The revolving stage was, as all revolving stages are, an accident black spot. So many things can go wrong. PA speakers have to be some distance out from centre-stage to prevent feedback so they have to be on terra firma, while the microphones and PA amp have to be on the revolving section, so, as the stage goes around, you have to start with an instrumental to give the road crew a chance to plug in the speakers. You also have to end with an instrumental to give the road crew a chance to unplug the speakers. And if some idiot presses the revolve button in the middle of your set – not as unusual an occurrence as you might think – it's all over. I still shiver when I see a revolving stage.

It was not a particular problem for us because we were now in a position to demand that the revolving-stage be immobilised. Besides, it was beyond our road crew to execute the complicated road-managerial manoeuvres required in the turning of the stage.

Ladies and gentlemen! May I introduce you to Wimpy and Jeff Hurley – our road crew. Wimpy was tall and thin, slightly stooped in posture, with a grin that would have sent a chill through the heart of Uriah Heep. Jeff Hurley was diminutive in stature, with long, black hair like a Red Indian maiden and a braying, tenor laugh which, given a fair wind, could be heard by dogs in western France. They were all right when it came to carrying the gear but not so good when it came to plugging it in. As a road-crew they had few equals; many superiors but few equals.

One night, at Brett's Club in Oxford, the strobe-light made its first and last appearance. We had made our own strobe light. We had fixed a spotlight on top of an old hairdryer-stand we got from Wes's father. We cut a piece of hardboard into a circular shape about three-feet in circumference, cut a series of long, narrow slits around it, and attached a spindle to its centre. The designated operator could now hold the spindle against the hairdryer-stand and, by positioning the hardboard disc correctly and spinning it vigorously, create a reasonable strobe effect. Wimpy, to his utter disgust, was the designated operator.

A grumpy Wimpy stood in the wings next to the primed strobe light, waiting for the nod. On cue, he started spinning the hardboard disc, building up a head of steam. Suddenly, the disc came off the spindle and cartwheeled across the stage, knocking over microphone stands and nearly decapitating Wes, before crashing into the wings on the opposite side of the stage. Wimpy chased after it. With the disc tucked under his arm he trudged back across the stage, cursing under his breath. He got back to the hairdryer-stand and picked up the spindle. It was broken in two. Forced to improvise, he started waving the disc back and forth in front of the light. The effect was less than strobe-like. He kept going for a while then, obviously reaching some watershed in his life, he kicked over the hairdryer-stand, hurled the disc into the audience and stomped off to the dressing room. And that was the end of the strobe.

The 'thunder-sheet' also made only one appearance. We had decided we wanted the sound of thunder during a particular song. We had a vague picture in our minds of a BBC sound-effects man shaking a metal sheet over his head, so we bought a sheet of aluminium from a local sheet-metal works. It measured eight-foot by three. We thought it would be fairly rigid but it bowed and bent easily. Much to our delight, it made a satisfying thunder-like rumble at the slightest touch. Again Wimpy, much to his horror, was the designated operator. He reluctantly tried it out during the soundcheck. It took him a while to get it over his head because it was awkward to hold, mainly because its edges were razor-sharp. Once aloft, it immediately drooped down in front and behind him. All we could see was a sheet of metal with a hand sticking out on either side.

'You're going to have to stand sideways-on to the stage,' said Martin, 'so that you can see the signal.'

Grudgingly, Wimpy shuffled around into a sideways position.

'Go!' said Martin.

Wimpy began to shake the thunder-sheet, a little half-heartedly we thought, but even at half-power it sounded like thunder. It echoed around the hall most impressively.

'Good,' said Martin. 'We'll use it.'

Wimpy gave Martin a filthy look and lowered the thunder-sheet, gingerly, to the floor.

'The edges are really sharp,' he said, rubbing his hands.

'Don't worry,' said Martin. 'If it works all right we'll get you a pair of gloves. Now put some welly into it tonight. OK?'

We told Wimpy to stand in the wings, out of sight of the audience, and, at a given signal, shake the thunder-sheet as if his life depended on it. The audience would hear the thunder without knowing where it was coming from. As we

the biggest freak out to hit south wales

approached the point in the set where it was required, we could see Wimpy struggling to get the thunder-sheet above his head. Finally, he was set. We gave the signal and Wimpy began to shake. We couldn't hear a thing. What had sounded like thunder in a quiet hall was, with the band in full flight, totally inaudible.

'Louder!' we shouted. 'Faster!'

We could see his arms going up and down like pistons and the thunder-sheet was undulating furiously, but we still couldn't hear a thing. Wes, standing nearest to Wimpy, slid his microphone in front of the thunder-sheet. Still nothing. We tried dropping the volume but you still couldn't hear it. We let Wimpy carry on for a bit, just to see if it had a cumulative effect, but it didn't.

'Faster!' we shouted. 'Louder!'

Suddenly, Wimpy threw the thunder-sheet down, kicked it a few times, and stormed off. We didn't see him for the rest of the set but after the gig we found him in the dressing-room, cursing and whimpering in equal measure and shaking violently.

'We couldn't hear bugger-all,' we complained.

'I CAN'T HEAR YOU,' shouted Wimpy, banging his temple with the heel of his hand. 'MY EARS ARE STILL RINGING.'

'WE COULDN'T HEAR BUGGER-ALL,' Martin shouted back, throwing in a bit of sign language

'WELL, IT WAS BLOODY LOUD UNDERNEATH IT,' shouted Wimpy. 'AND LOOK AT MY HANDS.' He held out his hands for us to see. They were cut to ribbons and dripping with blood.

'DON'T WORRY,' shouted Martin. 'IT'LL BE ALRIGHT WHEN YOU GET THE GLOVES.'

'NO, IT BLOODY WON'T,' he shouted bitterly, 'I'M NOT DOING THAT AGAIN.'

And no amount of persuasion, threat or bribery would get him to change his mind. So that was the end of the thunder-sheet. Wimpy had the shakes for three days before steadying out but, even to this day, he has a tendency to shout.

The gig at the Glen Ballroom was eventful. We walked onstage to rapturous applause. We were pleased to see that the audience had ignored council warnings about flower stealing and everybody was wearing a flower somewhere or other. There can't have been a municipal bloom left within a five-mile radius of Llanelly. It was like playing at the Chelsea Flower Show.

A line of bouncers ringed the front of the stage, arms linked, protecting us from the audience, whose behaviour was judged, by Mike Monkton, the manager, to be highly unpredictable. Martin was in prime form but about halfway through the set he got a little too exuberant with the meths and set the blue velvet stage curtains on fire. Two bouncers with fire extinguishers rushed on and, after a brief but valiant struggle, managed to control the blaze. The bouncers along the front of the stage seemed to be enjoying it, even when we brought out the Crazy Foam. They were stuck directly in the line of fire and so got the worst of it. but they took it with good humour, although there was a rather sinister glint in their eyes. At the finale,

Martin, centre-stage, presented himself to the crowd, wearing only a white loincloth. The loincloth was at eye-level to the central bouncer. He looked up at Martin. Then he looked back at the loincloth. Then he reached forward, grabbed the loincloth and yanked it off. Martin, suddenly naked in front of the multitude, cupped his genitals with both hands and leapt behind my amp, shouting for Wimpy to fetch him a pair of trousers. Wimpy, pretending to examine a perfectly good jackplug, chose not to hear him, so Martin had to run across the back of the stage, from amp to amp, to the privacy of the dressing-room. The crowd cheered wildly and so did the bouncers. It was a highly successful gig. The following week, the Llanelly Star quoted Mike Monkton. He said:

'It was the most amazing and extraordinary experience I have ever had in the business.'

Knowing Mike Monkton, I seriously doubt it. Mike Monkton, a Londoner, had been the manager of the Glen for some time. He was a seen-everything, done-everything entertainments manager. An urbane bantamweight with black, curly, brilliantined hair, I never saw him without a dinner jacket and bow tie. He was parachuted in by Dave Scott to provide the ballroom with professional management. Rumours abounded that he was a homosexual. We were in no position to judge because we had no experience of homosexuality. If there were any gays in the town, which there must have been, they stayed firmly locked in the closet. To have emerged would have been suicidal. The very best they could expect was wall-to-wall bum-boy jokes and the very worst doesn't bear thinking about.

The Llanelly bouncers were an amiable mix of ex-boxers and psychopaths. By common consent, the hardest of them was Maldwyn, a small, wiry man, the wrong side of fifty. He was chronically short-sighted and wore thick pebble-glasses, which he took off in the event of a fight, thus rendering himself virtually blind. But a helpful colleague would point him in the right direction and off he went. He was deadly and even the sight of him taking off his glasses was enough to stop most brawls. Some years later he was forced into retirement when his sense of direction deserted him and he began to inflict terrible damage on innocent passers-by.

The final time we used the methylated spirits was at the Eriskay Ballroom in Ammanford, recently opened by Bill Leslie, a genial, Llanelly-based Scot. Bill, a seemingly sensible chap, was regarded as courageous, even foolhardy, for even thinking about opening an entertainments centre in a war zone. Llanelly may not have been the most enlightened place on earth but compared to Ammanford it was Shangri La. We approached the gig with some trepidation. It was one thing to spray an audience of like-minded, marijuana-addled druggies with Crazy Foam, it was quite another to spray a bunch of swivel-eyed psychopaths who probably hadn't tasted blood for a week or two.

Everything went well until Martin did his Statue of Liberty bit. As he stood on the edge of the stage holding up the school bell full of burning meths, a stocky, red-headed moron, wearing a crumpled suit, emerged from the audience and jumped up beside him. He grabbed Martin's up-raised arm. The burning meths spilled out of the bell and ran down their interlocked arms.

the biggest freak out to hit south wales

'Get off, you fool,' shouted Martin. 'You'll set us both on fire.'

Maybe the moron didn't hear Martin's warning, or maybe Martin's voice was just another voice among many in his head, but he was single-minded. He tightened his grip on Martin's arm and stared, wild-eyed, at the bell. The flaming meths started dripping onto Martin's body, naked except for the loincloth. He had no choice. He tipped the bell forward, emptying the entire contents over the moron, who was enveloped from head to foot in flames, like a protesting Buddhist monk. He let go of Martin's arm and ran screaming from the stage, through the audience and out of the nearest exit. We finished the set and headed for the dressing room. Bill Leslie followed us in.

'Now that's what I call entertainment, gentlemen,' he said.

Martin checked himself for injuries but, apart from superficial burns, he was all right. We speculated on the fate of the moron.

'Went and jumped in the nearest river?' suggested Martin.

Naturally, after a show like that we were re-booked immediately.

On Saturday, August 24th, we played with the Eyes Of Blue at what was billed as a 'Giant Flower Power Freak Out' at the Empire Ballroom in Neath. The Eyes Of Blue were the new incarnation of the Mustangs. They were now a six-piece. Gary Pickford-Hopkins had joined as a second singer and Phil Ryan, a famous local keyboard genius, gave them a symphonic dimension.

We always enjoyed playing with the Eyes because they were a cracking band but this time they had an added new dimension. They had a dry ice machine. It was the first we'd seen. At selected moments in their set, mist billowed, with primordial grace, around the feet of the musicians. We decided to get one. They were fairly expensive to buy so we decided to make our own. How difficult could it be?

Wes went through the yellow pages and found a firm who supplied dry ice to industry. We didn't know how much we'd need so he ordered a hundredweight block. On the morning of the next gig it was delivered to Wes's barber shop. It was huge. The delivery men tried to get it into the shop but it got wedged in the doorway.

'Leave it for an hour or two,' they said. 'It'll melt a bit and you'll be able to get it in.'

But until then customers, if they wanted a haircut, had to climb over it. I couldn't imagine anybody wanting a haircut that badly.

At gig-time we loaded it into the back of the van. It took four of us and when we'd finished our hands were numb and a frost had appeared on my moustache. We also bought four large, black, rubber buckets. The idea was to fill the buckets with boiling water and then drop large chips of dry ice into them. We stationed them at the side of the stage. Wimpy spent most of the run-up to the gig in the wings, boiling endless kettles of water to fill the buckets. While each kettle was boiling he would attack the large block of dry ice with a hatchet, trying to knock off usable chunks. But dry ice, Wimpy soon discovered, is virtually indestructible. The hatchet just bounced off the ice, sending jarring waves of pain up his arm.

'Fuck this,' he said, throwing the hatchet down.

'Try a more sideways motion,' said Wes, miming a karate-like sweep of the hand.

Wimpy reluctantly picked up the hatchet, braced himself, and slashed sideways at the ice. This time the hatchet just glanced off the block, sending a lethal spray of ice-splinters bulleting in all directions. We retired to the other side of the stage and, from a safe distance, shouted encouragement and advice. Wimpy, understandably, lost control. Screaming obscenities, he attacked the ice, flailing away with some venom. Faced with such savagery, the ice put up only token resistance and began to fissure. In his frenzy Wimpy kicked over a kettle of boiling water, which sloshed around his feet, causing him to make little yelping noises. The ice soon crumbled, and Wimpy of the Antarctic stood, soaking wet but triumphant, surrounded by broken ice. He was sobbing quietly.

'I'm not doing this every night,' he said.

'Oh, it'll get easier the more you do it,' I said. 'After a couple of gigs you'll do it without thinking. It'll become second nature to you.'

'Fuck off, Leonard,' he said.

Obviously he still had doubts.

By the time we started the set, everything was ready to go. The buckets were full of boiling water and there was a shoulder-high pyramid of ice chunks, in assorted sizes, ready for the drop. Wimpy stood, cold and wet, ankle-deep in slush, poised, like a bedraggled vulture, to create primordial mystery.

During the freak-out section we gave him the signal and he dropped the first chunk of ice into the first bucket. There was a brief puff of mist and the water froze. Wimpy frowned. He dropped the second chunk of ice into the second bucket. Another puff of mist. This one, like the last one, refused to behave like dry ice at all, preferring to lurk around the bucket for a few seconds before disappearing. The third, as you would expect, was no different except that, this time, Wimpy grabbed a nearby amp-cover and attempted to fan the mist across the stage. But by the time he had picked up the amp-cover the mist had gone. He was snarling now. It was the snarl of a man who has just realised that what he is doing is utterly pointless but he has to keep doing it just in case, by sheer accident, it starts working. The fourth chunk of ice flew straight at Wes who ducked, avoiding certain decapitation. Afterwards, Wimpy denied attempted murder, maintaining that the chunk of ice had slipped out of his wet hands, but we recognised a straightforward case of roadie rage when we saw one. The audience, of course, remained blissfully unaware of these proceedings. In the dressing room we conducted a post-mortem.

'What we need is a constant spray of hot water over the dry ice,' said Martin, 'and a fan to blow it across the stage.'

'What we need is a proper dry ice machine,' snapped Wimpy, wringing out his shirt.

'Too expensive,' said Wes.

'Potassium nitrate and sugar,' said Martin. 'We'll mix it up in a bucket and set fire to it. It makes great smoke.'

the biggest freak out to hit south wales

'Isn't that gunpowder?' I said.

'No,' said Martin. 'Gunpowder is potassium nitrate, sulphur and charcoal. This stuff doesn't explode, it just smokes. We used to make it at school.'

Ah, the benefits of a public-school education. It isn't all premeditated sadism and mutual masturbation, you know.

Before the next gig Martin mixed up a batch of potassium nitrate and sugar. We couldn't use the rubber buckets because they'd melt so we each had instructions to bring as many saucepans as possible to the gig. We raided our mothers' kitchens and came up with about twelve assorted sizes. We placed them in the wings. Martin poured a heap of smoke mixture into each, according to size. This time Wimpy, at a given signal, would light each one and stand well back. He wasn't too keen at first but, after a Chinese-burn or two, he soon came around to our way of thinking. At the appointed time Martin yelled 'Freak Out!' and signalled Wimpy, matchbox at the ready, to light up. Wimpy, straining like a greyhound in a trap, dropped a lighted match into a large saucepan.

You wouldn't describe it as an explosion – more like a low, dull 'phutt'. There was just enough time to see a look of abject terror take possession of Wimpy's features before he was enveloped in a dense cloud of white, acrid smoke. And this was no ordinary white, acrid smoke. It was a malevolent force of nature, dedicated to searching out every crevice in existence. Within seconds it had filled the stage and was making for the audience. In two minutes it had filled the hall. We couldn't see a thing and, more importantly, we couldn't breathe. We stopped playing. There was an amazing sound; it was the sound of four hundred people coughing their guts up. People ran out of the building and threw themselves on their knees in the car park, vomiting. The saucepan was still belching smoke so we made a run for the car park to join in the vomiting. Wimpy, who had taken the full force of the blast, was in bad shape. His skin was red and shiny and his hair was singed and crinkled. He had lost the power of speech so he mouthed obscenities at us. We wrapped him in a blanket and sat him in the van. We stood and watched the club as smoke mushroomed out of the windows and doors. A committee-man stumbled up to us, red-eyed and sweating.

'How long will this bloody thing last?' he wheezed, before his chest went into spasm, giving way to a real chest-rattler.

'Not long now,' said Martin, lost in thought. 'I think I got the mixture wrong. A bit more sugar, I fancy.'

The next gig we tried the new mixture and it worked a lot better. We still smoked the hall out, but at least people could breathe. Sort of. Wimpy, who still smelled of burnt hair, refused to have anything more to do with the bloody smoke so Jeff Hurley was offered a straight choice – fill the breach or face the sack. It was touch and go for a while but he finally agreed. At the next gig, he stood well back from the saucepans of death and hurled little bits of burning toilet paper at them. Once one was lit he considered his duty done, whereupon he retired to the dressing-room, growling.

A few days later we supported the Who at Swansea University. We went on just before them. We used a lot of smoke because it was a big hall. When we'd finished you couldn't see your hand in front of your face. The Who refused to go on until the hall was cleared of smoke. We thought they were making a fuss about nothing. All the windows were opened. This had the effect of driving the smoke up into the rafters, where it lurked menacingly, showing no signs of dispersing. It was enjoying the gig, thank you very much. It didn't want to go out into the cold, cold night. But after half-an-hour it was deemed clear enough for the Who to play, which they did, breaking off occasionally for a sternum-shaking cough.

The last time we used the smoke was at an open-air, council-run, free gig in Singleton Park, Swansea, on the coast road to Mumbles. I hate municipal gigs because you have to wait three months to get paid. By the time the paperwork is finished and the cheque arrives, you're probably in another band. That said, it was a cracking gig. It was the first summer of love and the flower children were blossoming and putting the fear of God into anyone in authority. Swansea Parks and Leisure committee, in a state of high panic, summoned every park attendant in the greater Swansea area to Singleton Park, They were each deployed to defend a designated area of the park. The punters – or 'los punteros' as the Spanish say – drifted in and, in a disorganised sort of way, organised themselves into hit-squads. One group would attack one end of a flower bed, attracting the attentions of the park-keeper who would gallop off after them, leaving the other end of the flower bed undefended, allowing another group to nip in and strip the area of flowers. Once serious operations were underway, there were red-faced park-keepers running up and down in all directions.

We discussed the use of smoke at an open-air gig, in broad daylight, with the wind coming straight off the sea.

'It'll just blow away,' said Jeff, 'and I'd be risking my life for nothing.'

'Well, we might as well as not,' I said.

'OK,' said Jeff, shaking his head. 'There's no wings on the stage so where shall I put the bloody saucepans?'

'On top of the van?' I suggested. The van was parked alongside the stage.

'Oh, great!' said Jeff. 'I'm going to look like a right prat standing on top of the van surrounded by bloody saucepans. Thank you very much.'

I find such loyalty in a subordinate rather touching.

We passed the van as we went on. Wimpy was on the ground filling the bloody saucepans with smoke mixture before handing them up to Jeff, who was kneeling on the roof of the van. We tried to engage them in light, humorous banter but they were extremely offensive. By the time we reached the freak out section, Jeff was standing on the roof of the van, matches in hand, surrounded by the bloody saucepans. On cue, he lit the first. The smoke went straight up in the air. So did the second. And the third. When they were all lit, a thick column of smoke rose vertically into the Swansea sky. Jeff, at the epicentre of the vortex, was no longer visible. We finished the set but the column continued to rise, mushrooming out at the top. I'm told that nervous people in Port Talbot, just across the Swansea Bay, alerted the emergency services, under the impression that Swansea had been the

the biggest freak out to hit south wales

victim of a surprise Soviet nuclear strike.

It took about twenty minutes for the smoke mixture to burn out. Gradually, as each saucepan fizzled down to nothing, Jeff became visible again. He was standing rigidly, legs apart, with blackened face and frizzed hair. We helped him down. He couldn't talk because he was gulping in lungfuls of glorious sea air. When he could talk again he was most unpleasant. We allowed him a little time to go through his lexicon of foul language then, when he was spent, ordered him back up on the roof of the van to collect the bloody saucepans, which he did without a shred of enthusiasm. Suddenly we heard his machine-gun laughter.

'Mah-ha-ha-ha-ha-ha-ha!' A pause. 'Mah-ha-ha-ha-ha-ha-ha!' He was obviously delighted. 'The bloody saucepans have been welded to the van,' he said. 'They're stuck fast. Mah-ha-ha-ha-ha-ha-ha!'

We tried to get them off but, fused in the white heat of psychedelia, they had become part of the van roof. So that was the end of the smoke. And, of course, we had to drive around in an extremely silly-looking van. It was nigh-on impossible to feel dignified while riding in that van. One by one, the bloody saucepans fell off of their own accord, but two particularly stubborn ones were still there when the van had its final brush with destiny at the scrapyard.

Our next attempt at spectacle was even more dangerous, and a product of chance rather than design. We played at a school. The gig was in the main hall and we changed in the gymnasium.

'Brilliant,' said Martin, taking off his jacket.

Martin sees a gymnasium much as Attila the Hun saw Rome. He has to conquer it, even humiliate it; probably another public school legacy. He throws himself at each individual apparatus with reckless gusto, testing it to destruction, before moving on to the next. Undiminished by effort, he continues until his back locks. This time the rowing-machine did for him. He was just going under Hammersmith bridge, two lengths ahead of Cambridge, when L4 and L5, two fairly crucial vertebrae in the lumbar region, decided to call it a day. He gingerly limped to the nearest bench and lay down, where he stayed until showtime, groaning softly to himself.

Robbed of any further entertainment we were thrown back on our own resources. We started looking in cupboards. I found one full of cricket equipment. I put on a pair of batting gloves and picked up a bat. I was just rehearsing the sublime cover drive that would bring up my 100 against the Aussies at the Gabba, when there was an fearful crash. Terry had opened a high cupboard and about thirty swords had fallen out on top of him. To avoid the cascade of sword-points, he jumped backwards, with a balletic leap that Errol Flynn would have been proud of, twisting and turning as he did so, thereby avoiding serious injury but sustaining a nasty graze on his shin.

'Christ!' he said. 'My life flashed before my eyes, then.'

We helped him put the swords back.

'They wouldn't miss two,' he said, looking furtively around. 'There's no point in having one sword, is there? It'd be like having one tennis racquet.'

maybe i should've stayed in bed? 218

The gig was memorable only for Martin, who limped on, stood statue-still for the whole set, then limped off.

Terry brought the two stolen swords – épées, I believe they're called – to our next rehearsal. Taking a sword each, Wes and I went at it. But not for long. Wes, being a barber by trade, was practiced in the art of wielding cutting implements and I was soon fighting for my life. I saved myself by using the old Welsh trick of begging for mercy. I handed my sword to Martin, who instantly became Scaramouche, adopting an *en garde* posture while testing the blade by swishing it sharply through the air.

'Mmm,' he said, 'I haven't done this since boarding school.'

They teach 'em to fight, but they don't teach 'em to think.

Wes and Martin circled each other, probing for an opening. Suddenly Martin lunged forward, driving Wes back. There was a furious exchange of thrusts and parries. Then Wes, summoning up all his hairdressing skills, gradually drove Martin back to the centre of the rehearsal room, where they broke off and began circling each other again.

It was entertaining for the first hour or so but then it began to get a little tedious. Terry and I sloped off to the pub. We came back an hour later and they were still at it, so we went back to the pub. After last orders we strolled back. As we approached the rehearsal rooms we heard the 'pok-pok-pok' of blade striking blade.

'They're not still at it?' said Terry.

Inside the rehearsal room it was like some Napoleonic hell. Wes and Martin, stripped to the waist, dripping with sweat and breathing heavily, were still circling each other. Occasionally one of them would take a huge, agricultural cleave at the other, usually falling over themselves in the process. The cleavee, as it were, waited until the cleaver had regained his feet, then they resumed circling.

'Shall we call it a day?' I said.

Wes and Martin each raised an eyebrow.

'It's up to you,' said Martin.

'It's up to you,' said Wes.

'That's settled then,' said Terry.

'Well, I enjoyed that,' said Wes, putting his shirt back on.

'So did I,' said Martin, towelling himself down. 'Shall we put it in the set?'

'Good idea,' said Wes.

Terry and I exchanged rueful glances. After scant discussion, it was agreed that, at a suitable point in the set, Terry and I would play some dramatic music while Wes and Martin staged a duel.

'There's got to be a winner,' said Martin, 'so somebody's got to pretend to lose.'

'Don't look at me,' said Wes, bristling.

'Take it in turns,' said Terry.

'OK,' said Martin. 'Who's gonna be the first to lose?'

'Don't look at me,' said Wes, bristling again.

'Toss for it,' I said.

And so it went on. While Wes and Martin worked out the order of battle, we put the gear back in the van.

'Good rehearsal, gentlemen,' said Terry.

The next gig we tried it out. Terry and I hated it but Wes and Martin loved every second. They had tossed a coin for the dubious privilege of dying first and Martin lost. His death scene was tragic. He lay on the stage, propped up on one elbow, head thrown back, and with a languid sweep of his arm seemed to perfectly capture the death throes of a noble man, killed in a just but hopeless cause. He was a long time dying. Just when you thought he was slipping off, he would rally long enough to squeeze out one more tortured gesture. The emotional impact was slightly diminished by the huge winks he gave the audience at moments of great poignancy. Finally, to cheers, he expired, but before rigor mortis could set in he was back on his feet and bowing. But it worked. We decided to keep it in the act.

It lasted four gigs. Each night, as Martin and Wes got more adept, it got nastier and nastier. Back and forth across the stage they fought, asking and giving no quarter. It was like being in a band with Errol Flynn and Basil Rathbone. I stood as far back as possible with my back against my amp, hoping to avoid injury. On the fourth night Wes drove Martin across the stage in my direction. As he passed me he swung his sword in a huge arc, obviously with the intention of decapitating Martin. I felt the wind of the passing sword whip across the top of my head. A tuft of hair wafted down on to the stage. That's funny, I thought, it's the same colour as my hair.

'MY FUCKING HAIR!'

And that was the end of the swords. Today my hair, tomorrow my throat.

So now we had to find something to replace the swords. We decided to move into film. At the time, when the technology was in its infancy, this meant an 8mm projector, situated in the midst of the crowd, projecting on to a large white sheet hanging behind the band. But who was going to work the projector? Wimpy told us to fuck off, so it seemed like a job for Jeff.

'So,' he said, beginning to boil, 'I've got to stand in the middle of the punters, have I?'

'On a chair,' we said, explaining that the projector would have to be above head-height with a clear view of the screen. This, we further explained, was the nature of projection, which, being subject to the laws of physics, seemed beyond our influence. 'The projector will have to be on some sort of raised platform,' we added, 'and you'll probably have stand on a chair.'

'So, I've got to stand on a chair in the middle of the punters and...' He went off on one of his rants. So that was settled.

We decided to show ten-minute, black and white, silent, edited versions of horror films. These were commercially available from specialist dealers. The houselights would dim, the film would start and we, the band, would provide the soundtrack. We started off with two films – the Hammer Films version of 'Dracula' and 'The Creature From The Black Lagoon'; the latter being the story of a slimy, black, lizard-like creature terrorising a small American town. They called in the

US Army who, with typical overkill, fired a nuclear missile at it. There were bits of the creature everywhere.

It was a roaring success. The audiences loved it and we, having to play ten-minute mood pieces, soon discovered the delights of band improvisation, when, ideally, nobody knows where they are. We added a third film – 'Tarantula'; the story of a giant spider terrorising a small American town. The US Army, with typical overkill, fired a nuclear missile at it. There were bits of spider everywhere.

Every now and again, just to keep the audience honest, we'd play the films backwards. They seemed to enjoy it even more. Our foray into the cinematic arts was regarded by all as a success. Everybody loved it except Jeff, who, he said, had to stand 'in the middle of a room full of scrotums'.

Occasionally, on a long trek, we'd take a third road-manager, usually Mike Brewer. Mike, a Llanelly boy, was a much misunderstood individual. For some unfathomable reason, the local constabulary seemed to think he was less than law-abiding and subjected him to constant harassment. Mike always maintained it was a case of mistaken identity, claiming that all those church roofs had been stripped by a long-lost twin brother.

On the road, he was often mistaken for one of the band and asked for his autograph. He always signed, justifying his actions on the grounds that he had records out. Police records, to be sure, but records nonetheless.

'Besides,' he added, 'it makes a nice change from people asking me for my fingerprints.'

He came with us on one of our recording tests. While we listened to the mix, we left Mike to pack the van. After the session, we said our goodbyes and left. As we drove off, the recording engineer came running after the van, banging on the side. Breathlessly, he explained that several microphones had gone missing and may have been put in our van by mistake. Could he possibly have a look in the back?

'Of course,' we said. 'Open the back, Mike.'

Somewhat reluctantly, we thought, Mike climbed out and opened the back doors. The engineer bounced around, looking over his shoulder.

'There they are.' he said.

'Oh, I thought they were ours.' said Mike.

'He's new,' we said. 'He still doesn't know what's ours and what's not.'

The engineer gathered his precious microphones to his chest and walked back to the studio. We looked at Mike.

'It was a mishap.' he said.

We called him Batman, because he didn't go anywhere without robbin'.

27
'you will arrive!'

We went up to London to audition for a big-time continental agent who, it was rumoured, could offer work all over Europe. The audition took place in a huge church hall. There were about fifteen bands and each was allotted a postage stamp-sized area of floor space. We all set up and checked the gear. There was a cacophony of dweedling as fifteen lead guitarists tested out their favourite licks; there was the ever-present, urgent thunder of fifteen drummers paradiddling furiously; and the building shook as fifteen bass-players played the Lucille riff. Word circulated that the agent was about to arrive. A nervous silence fell in the hall, all eyes fixed on the entrance. We heard footsteps approaching. Suddenly, the door burst open and the big-time continental agent strode in. It was Ricky Barnes. He was accompanied by two men wearing sheepskin jackets, carrying briefcases. They walked to a table and chairs set up centrally and unpacked their briefcases.

'Right,' said Ricky Barnes, rubbing his hands together. 'My name is Ricky Barnes and if you're really good I might give youse a job. When I call out the name of your band you will play two numbers. Then the band leader will come to the table to be told the results of the audition. OK? Let's get on with it.' He rummaged through some papers, obviously searching for the name of the first band. He looked up and was about to announce it when he saw us, leaning nonchalantly against our amps, grinning like fools. His face broke out in a rare grin and he walked over to us.

'What're youse fuckers doing here?' he said. 'No other fucker'll book youse, I expect.'

We hugged and shook hands and had a little chat about the old days.

'So this is an audition for the Top Ten?' said Martin.

'Aye,' said Ricky Barnes, 'but there's no need for you to audition. Och, you can come over at any time.' He looked at the piece of paper in his hand. 'What are you called these days?'

'Dream,' we said.

He scanned the list,

'You're number nine,' he said. 'I'll try and call you earlier. Now that you're here, you might as well play.'

He walked back to the table and the bands began to audition. Each one seemed to be worse than the one before. As the afternoon progressed, Ricky Barnes got more and more depressed. He slumped in a chair, shaking his head. Then he shouted out, 'Number seven, Dream.' We did 'Keep a-Knockin'' and 'McArthur Park'. When we finished we walked over to Ricky Barnes.

maybe i should've stayed in bed?

'Well?' said Martin.

'It's a pleasure to hear you play again,' he said, 'especially after all the crap I've had to listen to today.' He looked dolefully round the hall. 'It breaks my heart, Marrrtin. It breaks my fucking heart. Just give me a call if you want to come back to the Top Ten.'

But we never did. We kept his offer in the back of our minds, to be taken up if things got a little slow, but things were looking up.

We played a gig with the Amen Corner, who were doing very well. They'd had a couple of records in the charts and they'd just moved into a mansion in Epsom, originally built as a wedding present for Sophia Loren by her groom-to-be, Carlo Ponti. So beautiful was the house, it attracted the attention of those driving by, who could just glimpse it through the trees. At about eight o'clock one morning – an unconscionable time for a musician – somebody started banging on the front door. Dennis, the drummer, bleary-eyed and dressed only in his underpants, answered the door.

'Yes?' he said tetchily.

'Hello,' said a bearded man, 'my name is Stanley Kubrick and I'd like to hire your house for some filming. Name your price.'

'What's the time?' asked Dennis.

'Eight o'clock,' said Kubrick.

'EIGHT O'CLOCK?' said Dennis. 'FUCK OFF!'

And he slammed the door and went back to bed.

That must be the equation – two hit records mean that you can tell Stanley Kubrick to fuck off; five hits mean you can tell the Queen to fuck off; ten hits and you can tell the world to fuck off. There's an inherent flaw in this. I don't need a hit record to tell the Queen to fuck off.

Anyway, the Amen Corner recommended us to Ron King, their manager. We called him and he offered us a gig at his regular, all-day, Sunday bash at the Town Hall in Romford for twenty-five quid. It was a long haul so we left at ten in the morning. When we arrived, at six, the gig was in full swing. The posters outside were a little puzzling. They proclaimed a 'Grand Audition' but mentioned no band by name. We went inside and found Ron King.

He was everybody's caricature of an East End villain. As broad as he was tall, he barked orders at his associates in an abrasive cockney drawl with the ease of one born to command. He looked, and acted, like Napoleon in a mohair suit. We introduced ourselves.

'It's an audition night and the winning band will get a prize of twenty-five quid,' he said. 'You'll go on last and win first prize. OK?'

'OK,' we said. 'What's the scam?'

'The scam is this,' he said, smiling. 'I get free bands all day. It doesn't matter if they're useless because they're only on for half-an-hour. But I need a top-of-the-bill act so they go home with good music in their ears. If you're as good as the Amen Corner say you are, you can do this every Sunday. OK?'

'OK,' we said.

One of Ron King's associates, an ex-heavyweight boxer, judging from his flattened nose and cauliflower ears, showed us where to get the gear in. All Ron King's associates appeared to be ex-boxers. They all exuded that supreme self-confidence that only comes with the knowledge that should things turn nasty they, without a shadow of a doubt, were perfectly capable of dismantling your body and re-assembling it in the shape of a table lamp. We explained that we had to erect a projector in the middle of the crowd.

'I'll put Ernie on it,' he said. He snapped his fingers and Ernie, a middle-weight, appeared. He and Jeff disappeared into the crowd. Jeff said afterwards that he and Ernie had built a platform out of trestle tables. Jeff stood behind it on a chair. As he climbed up on the chair he realised that he was about a foot too far to the right.

'Fuck,' he said, 'I'm about a foot too far to the right.'

Ernie bent down and, one-handedly gripping the chair by a leg, picked it and Jeff up, and moved them a foot to the left.

After our set we were proclaimed winners of the audition and presented with twenty-five quid. As we came off Ron King bounded up to us.

'You're just the band I've been looking for,' he said. 'Come into the office tomorrow and we'll discuss your future. Come about six. It'll be quieter then and we can talk.'

We had planned to drive straight home so that Wes wouldn't miss a day at the hairdressers, but this was deemed important enough, even by Wes, for the supreme sacrifice. This could be our big chance, to be grabbed with both hands. We drove across town and booked in the Madison Hotel. The following evening, just before six, we arrived at Ron King's office in Denmark Street. All the staff had gone home. We sat in his office and prepared to discuss our future. Ron opened the bowling.

'I'm emigrating to Australia,' he said, 'and I want you to come with me.'

I was initially disappointed. I didn't want to be famous in Australia. I wanted to be famous in Britain. And America. But I listened.

'There's a fortune to be made out there,' he said. 'You're a great band, We could take the place by storm. Leave all the arrangements to me and I'll promise you that when you get there, YOU WILL ARRIVE!' He laughed out loud. 'Believe me,' he said with relish, 'YOU WILL ARRIVE!'

The phone rang and he picked it up.

'Hello? Issa nobody 'ere,' he said in a thick Italian accent, 'Efferybody has gone home. I am the cleaners. Call back tomorrow.' He put the phone down. 'YOU WILL ARRIVE!' he shouted, thumping his fist down in his desk, 'YOU WILL ARRIVE!'

We said that it was a big step and we'd need a little time to think it over.

'Of course, you do,' he said, 'but I'm leaving in two months time so I'll need to know fairly soon. In the meantime, you can do every Sunday at Romford. OK?'

'OK,' we said.

'And remember,' he said, 'YOU WILL ARRIVE!'

In the van on the way home the discussion polarised. Martin wanted to go, now, this minute. Terry was cautiously tempted. I was emphatically indecisive and

maybe i should've stayed in bed?

Wes didn't want to go, period.

'I've got the shop to think of,' he said.

We argued our corners for most of the long journey without approaching, let alone reaching, a common position. We did, however, agree that we should continue to play Romford every Sunday. A gig's a gig. Every Sunday we set off on the interminable road to Romford and every Sunday Ron King fleshed out his plans for invading Australia. And every Sunday we told him we hadn't made up our minds yet. This state of affairs persisted for about six weeks until one Sunday we arrived at Romford to find the Town Hall boarded up. We made a few phonecalls. Suspicious voices asked us why we were interested in Ron King's whereabouts, not that they knew anyone called Ron King anyway. We finally got a result.

'He's gorne to Australia, mate,' said a voice that could have belonged to Bill Sykes. 'Fings were getting a bit hot.'

He'd gone without us. I felt rather wistful. I knew we'd never have gone to Australia but somewhere, way down in my soul, I'd wanted to. It would have been a great adventure.

28
the end of a perfect dream

During this period we were in and out of endless studios, doing recording tests for several interested companies. Although we were getting used to working in a studio, nothing ever happened. We were either turned down flat or recalled for further tests. I began to despair of ever making a record. All I wanted was to make one record. Then I could, quite happily, walk away from the business and get on with my life. It would only take one record anyway. Record shops would have to open twenty-four hours a day to cope with the demand. People would be killed in the rush to buy it. Martial law would be imposed. We would be bigger than the Beatles.

A TV series came and went. Ronnie Williams, part of the Ryan and Ronnie comedy-duo, was producing a new pop show for BBC Wales. He wanted us to be the resident band. We did several tests for them. They hummed and hawed for a few months then cancelled the show. Now, I was getting edgy.

We played a gig in Merthyr Town Hall with the Bystanders. They too had embraced psychedelia. They wore kaftans and dragoon jackets. Moustaches had been grown. They were doing very well. They lived in London. They had a recording contract. They were in the game. They were in the arena. They were a further reminder, if one were needed, that we still had a long way to go.

We got some surprising teenage publicity. We played with the Herd, a pop band fronted by Peter Frampton; they were the flavour of the month. They were one of those pretty bands so beloved of magazines aimed at the pubescent female. So popular were they that Fabulous 208, the Radio Luxembourg-sponsored glossy weekly, invited them to edit an edition. One of the features was about the best band they had played with recently. They chose us. We were rather chuffed until they told us we were chosen because we were the last band they'd played with and, as such, the only one they could remember. We went up to Fabulous 208's London office for a photo-shoot and an interview, stopping off on the way at Bona Clouts, the hippest clothes shop in London, to deck ourselves out in the latest clobber. At the interview, we were charming and lied about our age.

In the resulting edition we had a page to ourselves, most of which was taken up by a large photograph of us looking like an explosion in a frilly-shirt factory. In the accompanying article the Herd praised us to high heaven.

'They were quite exceptional and I'm afraid they quite put us to shame,' said Andrew Steele, their drummer. Well done, son.

I was brutally honest when asked about our recording prospects, admitting there were none. And our studio experiences, although limited, were not encouraging. 'When we were good,' I said, 'something went wrong with the engineers and when the engineers were good, we mucked it up.'

The article came and went without apparent benefit. Nobody offered us a recording contract.

We played a gig at the Cavern in Liverpool. The Beatles had long gone but there was a definite itch to the place. Just standing on the stage gave me the 'cryd' (pronounced creed), which is Welsh for that moment when the hairs on the back of your neck stand on end. I stood on the same spot I'd seen John Lennon stand in photographs. Walking with giants.

The Iveys were playing just down the road so they came to see us. They were a Swansea band. regulars on the Welsh gig-circuit, who were about to change their name to Badfinger. They were blissfully unaware that they were on the threshold of a whirlpool journey that would begin with a liaison with the Beatles and end in the consuming fires of corporate avarice. And in between, they realised the ultimate songwriter's dream – they wrote a standard. Well, Peter Ham and Tommy Evans did. 'Without You' is one of those songs that will be a hit for somebody-or-other every five years or so for the rest of Eternity. But they were screwed, literally, into the ground. Pete and Tommy were driven to take their own lives because the legal straightjacket in which they found themselves was so constricting that it destroyed virtually every facet of their lives. If their suicides were a gesture, then they were futile, because the intended targets, the anonymous parasites who feed off passing talent, have no concept of culpability. They have no concept of morality. Their only bench-mark is money; their only interest its accumulation. They don't care about anything else. So the golden geese have topped themselves. So what? There'll be another one along in a minute. Sometimes I wish I believed in God. It would be a comfort to know that the fires of Hell await the despicable maggots of this world. Then Satan, instead of tormenting misinformed atheists, would be performing a public service. But Pete and Tommy can rest in peace, secure in the knowledge that they have left an indelible mark on the never-ending tapestry of rock'n'roll. I, on the other hand, will be lucky to leave a smudgy fingerprint.

After the gig we drove straight back down to Wales. Just as we got to the border, on a dark and deserted country road, we were pulled over by a police car. Two policemen got out, flicked on their torches, and walked toward us. Those in possession of dangerous drugs put them in their mouths. Griff, our driver, wound down his window.

'What can I do for you, constable?' he asked, trying to smile and manoeuvre his dope around his mouth at the same time.

One of the coppers, a sergeant, walked to Griff's window and shone his torch into the van. We sat there, looking guilty.

'Where you going, lads?' he said, speaking with a Liverpool accent.

'Wales,' we chorused.

'Mmm,' he said. 'And where are you from?'

'Wales,' we chorused.

the end of a perfect dream

'And what's that?' he said accusingly, pointing his torch at a pile of leads and a fuzz-tone lying on top of the dashboard. At first we didn't see what he was driving at.

'They're two guitar-leads and a fuzz-tone,' said Griff. 'They're faulty. I left them out of the leads box so I can take them home and fix them.'

'It's not bomb-making equipment then?' said the sergeant.

'Pardon?' said Griff.

'It's not bomb-making equipment then?' he repeated slowly.

'No, it's two guitar-leads and a fuzz-tone.' Griff picked up the fuzz-tone for the sergeant to see. The sergeant backed off.

'Put it down,' he said in his best I-mean-business voice.

'See,' said Griff, holding it up and pointing at it, 'it says "fuzz-tone" on it.' You could see the sergeant wasn't convinced.

'What's this all about,' said Martin, leaning over from the passenger seat.

'That Free Wales mob have blown up two local reservoirs,' said the sergeant. 'We're looking for a van-load of Welsh terrorists. Seen anybody of that description?'

'We're a band and we've been playing in the Cavern,' we said.

'Good cover,' he said, unimpressed.

'Look in the back,' we said. 'It's full of guitars and drums.'

'We will,' said the sergeant. 'We will.'

They kept us for two hours. They made us take all the gear out of the van and explain what each item was. They made us unscrew the backs of the amps and they made Terry take off all his drum-heads. They spent a good hour or so examining the leads box, which, after a while, even started to look like bomb-making equipment to me. As dawn broke we were all sitting at the roadside, on bits of dismantled gear, watching them testing Terry's drumsticks, looking, no doubt, for secret compartments full of Semtex.

'There's no two ways about it,' said Martin to the coppers, 'we're a fucking rock'n'roll band.'

The police car radio, which had been buzzing away in neutral, crackled to life. The other copper walked over and listened. Then he walked back over to us.

'They've got them,' he said to the sergeant. 'Caught them in Ellesmere Port, just about to blow up another reservoir.'

'Great,' said the sergeant. But he didn't mean it. He wanted it to be us. He brushed down his uniform, straightened his cap, and turned toward us.

'Well,' he said, without enthusiasm, 'I suppose that lets you off the hook. Sorry to have bothered you. Thank you for your co-operation.'

He waved his hand in the general direction of the peak of his cap; we assumed this was a reluctant salute. In silence, we watched them walk back to the police car and drive off. We took our dope out of our mouths. Nobody said anything. The first rays of sunlight glinted over the eastern horizon and the dawn chorus was tuning up. It was going to be a beautiful day.

'Let's go and blow up a fucking reservoir,' said Martin.

maybe i should've stayed in bed?

The following day I had a phonecall. It was the Bystanders. Vic Oakley, their principal singer, was leaving the band and they thought they might replace him with a guitarist. Would I be interested in the job? Yes, I fucking would. That's what I thought, but that's not what I said. I asked if I could have a couple of days to think it over.

There were complications. I'd fallen in love with Frances Morris, a Llanelly girl, and the last thing I wanted to do was to move up to London. True. it would only be a temporary separation, because once I'd settled in she could follow me up, but any separation, however fleeting, was unthinkable. This was not, I decided, the moment to be torn apart by circumstance. After a couple of days, I phoned them up and turned them down. But as soon as I put the phone down, a part of me was sorry.

A week later the Herald of Wales got the story – 'DREAM GUITARIST QUITS TO JOIN BYSTANDERS' screamed the headline. I phoned them with my denial. The following week the headline was – 'NO BREAK-UP FOR US, SAY DREAM'. The following week the headline read – 'IT'S NO SHOCK – THIS TIME DEKE IS QUITTING THE DREAM'. Once again I rang in my denial. The following week the headline was – 'DREAM ARE IN TROUBLE'.

While all this speculation was running wild, it was psychedelia as usual for us. I told the band I was staying, and that was that. But the Bystanders offer kept nagging away. After a couple of months of shilly-shallying Fran and I reached a decision. It would be madness to turn down something I so obviously wanted to do, so I'd better phone the Bystanders to see if the job was still going. I picked up the phone.

'They've probably got somebody else by now,' I said, dialling their number.

'Hello,' said Ray, the bass-player.

'Hello, Ray,' I said. 'This is Deke. Is that job still going?'

'Yes, it is,' said Ray.

'Then I'd like to do it.'

'Great,' said Ray. 'Tomorrow we're starting a two-week residency in Manchester. Why don't you join us there?'

'OK,' I said. 'I'll need a few days to sort myself out.'

'Of course,' he said. 'See you in Manchester.'

I handed my notice in to the Dream. They weren't surprised, and wished me well. A couple of days later, I said goodbye to Fran and caught the train to Manchester. This time I really was on my way to the stars. It was only a matter of time.

29
outro

And where are they now?

Llanelly – or rather, Llanelli: Throughout this book I have used the anglicized version of the town's name because it was the one in use at the time. Now we have reverted, quite rightly, to the original Welsh spelling. OK – it doesn't register on the Istanbul-Constantinople Scale, but we do our best.

Llanelli is a shadow of its former self. The town has been unfortunate in its choice of public officials. They have been, almost to a man, people of low calibre with a breathtaking lack of vision. Committee-men elevated way beyond their capabilities, who were only too eager to drop their trousers for any out-of-towner waving a chequebook. To be fair, the electorate didn't have much choice. Llanelli is, by divine right, a Labour town, and it didn't matter what name appeared on the council ballot paper – if they were Labour, they got elected. It is often said about safe Tory seats, that if the local association put up a pig's bladder on a stick, it would be guaranteed a seat in Parliament. The same was true for Llanelli Labour councils. There was no opposition. Llanelli Tories are figures of fun, somewhere on the social scale between village idiots and arsonists. May I remind you that Michael Howard is typical of the breed.

Over the years successive councils have systematically destroyed the town. Llanelli was never a pretty town but it had a soul, and its architecture, although unremarkable, had a certain character and continuity. In the name of what these class traitors called 'progress', buildings of worth were torn down and replaced by a mishmash of featureless office blocks and pseudo-Victorian shopping precincts. The heart of the town was recently gutted so that Asda could build a superstore, and the shopping mall built to house it was inexplicably crowned by a huge, ghastly glass pyramid that now dominates the townscape. Paris has the Eiffel Tower, New York has the Empire State Building, and Llanelli has the Asda pyramid. God knows what concessions Asda were offered to locate in the town. The same thing happened twenty years ago. Tesco did a deal with the council to build a superstore in the centre of town. A site was chosen and all the surrounding properties were compulsorily purchased and duly levelled, including the Hippodrome Cinema where Charlie Chaplin and Marie Lloyd had once performed, and the Hodge Cycle & Model Shop. The building that rose from the rubble was a hideous lump of red brick and concrete that looked as if it had been designed by a chimpanzee (no insult intended to chimpanzees who, as a species, are far more intelligent than architects). Tesco stayed for two years then, when I assume their concessions ran out, moved to an out-of-town site, leaving the building empty for the next two decades (it is rumoured that part of the Tesco deal was a clause that ensured that the building couldn't be let to another supermarket chain for ninety-nine years. Can you imagine the depths of stupidity plumbed by the civic simpletons who agreed to that little iniquity?) The building has only recently been taken over by Agenda, an independent TV production company, who have, I believe, only created one local job – a bilingual receptionist.

The Law Courts – a drab, grey concrete eyesore that looks like an upside-down beer crate – are particularly offensive because they stand on the site of what was once the Bullring, where we used to meet after school.

The High Street, once the commercial heart of the town, is now a sad collection of electrical appliance stores and charity shops.

Llanelli is now a cultural wasteland. The Odeon is the only cinema left. It now a multiplex showing exclusively mainstream films targeted at children. There are no book shops in Llanelli (true, there is a W.H. Smith, but since they decided to turn themselves into a stationery shop, the book section gets smaller and more mainstream). There are no French restaurants, no Greek, no Italian. Not even a Pizza Hut. There used to be a froth of Italian cafes in the town – Rabiotti's, Strinatti's, Allegri's, Bracci's, Chiffo's, Florini's, and the Mayfair – but now you'd be hard-pressed to find one. There are no museums, no art galleries, and no theatres. We do have an amateur dramatic society but they only put on Chorus Line-style crap. But one thing, above all, illustrates the artistic depths into which Llanelli has sunk – there are no rock gigs in the town. If you fancy an evening of live music, you have to go to Swansea. Carl, at Brannigans, runs an anybody-can-get-up-and-play, acoustic evening but the council constantly try to revoke his licence because of noise complaints. For acoustic guitars? There is nothing to do in Llanelli except get drunk.

They've even fucked up the beach – the only place of sanctuary in the town. Not satisfied with nature's bounty, they decided a bit of landscaping was called for, bringing in tons of battleship-grey rocks that looked as if they were made of polystyrene. These they placed in artistic positions along the beach. The next tide immediately rearranged them. Now, we don't have a beach – we have a moonscape. But when the sun sets over Llanelli Sound at the end of a cloudless day, sending a jagged shaft of blood-red light from outer space, across the surface of the sea, to your feet, it is nigh-on impossible not to feel a frisson of love for this lousy little town. Spiritually refreshed, you walk up Queen Victoria Road back to town and the first thing you see is that bloody Asda pyramid.

There should be retrospective legislation in place that would hold those responsible for civic vandalism to account. You'd think the local press would do a little crusading on behalf of the townspeople, but the Llanelli Star is – how can I put this kindly? – supine. Unquestioning of authority, it is content to print pictures of Rotary Club dances. 'Go and see your MP,' I hear you say. No point. Our MP is Denzil Davies (Labour: maj 12,000,000,041). He is known in Llanelli as 'The Invisible Man'.

But now things are changing. Boundary changes now mean Llanelli no longer has a council. Administration has moved to Carmarthen. The word is that they will preserve the old-world charm of Carmarthen, and turn Llanelli into a giant shopping precinct. Well, what did you expect? Also it probably means that Prince Phillip Hospital – named after one of the great medical philanthropists of our time – might

outro

be closed. Should you then need emergency treatment, you will first have to drive twelve miles to the nearest hospital in Swansea. If it's a life or death situation, you might as well cut out the middle man and ring up Arthur Cambrey Funeral Services to order the coffin.

That said, it might be a blessing in disguise. Recently a surgical team at Prince Phillip Hospital was suspended – no doubt on full pay – for taking out the wrong kidney from a 70 year-old man. They took out a perfectly healthy kidney and left the diseased one in place. They were probably cutting corners in order to keep up with management targets. The patient was rushed to a Swansea hospital. He was dead within the month. In a world where justice prevailed they – management and medical staff – would be hung, drawn and quartered, and dumped in the sewerage system where they so obviously belong, but in the real world they'll probably lay low for a while, get a gentle rap on the knuckles from the General Medical Council, and be back to butchering within the year. Only one thing's for sure in this town – Arthur Cambrey will die a rich man.

Mike Rees – singer and founder member of the Corncrackers. After leaving Swansea University, Mike, with a metallurgy degree under his belt, went to Canada for two years, taking any work he could, before travelling down through the States en route to South America. He had a yen to see Patagonia, the southern tip of Argentina, where there is a large Welsh-speaking community. He got no further than Mexico because all the roads had been washed away by a hurricane. So he went back to Canada and got a boat, via Japan and Hong Kong, to Australia, where he worked for a year as a metallurgist. The British Lions were touring New Zealand so he went down there for the duration of their tour. Then he caught a boat to Singapore. and travelled up through Malaya, Burma, Nepal and India, where he got caught up in one of the periodical Indo-Pakistan wars and had to get out quickly. He travelled up through Pakistan, Afghanistan and Iran, before doubling back to Turkey, from where he got a flight home and got a job painting lamp posts for Swansea Corporation. It was then our paths crossed again. I was coming out of 129 Hanover Street one morning, when I saw Mike halfway up the lamp post opposite. We had a remember-the-old-days conversation and went our separate ways. He got engaged but asked his fiancée if she minded postponing the wedding for six months so he could go to South America first – the yen to see Patagonia just wouldn't go away. She agreed and Mike caught the next boat. He got a job 'making bricks with the Indians' in a place called Treorchy (yes, there is a place in Argentina called Treorchy, and I'd like to think they have a male voice choir, I wouldn't mind hearing them sing Cwm Santa Cruz). After six months he made his way home through Brazil, Paraguay, where he was briefly thrown in jail for vagrancy, and Bolivia. Back in Wales he finally got married and had two beautiful daughters, Rhiannon and Manon, He entered the teaching profession and is now deputy headmaster of Begyn Primary School in Llanelli. 'They may shoot the sheriff,' he says, 'but they never shoot the deputy.'

Geoff Griffiths – drummer and founder member of the Corncrackers. After leaving university Geoff went to work as a research & development analytical chemist at the

Wellcome Trust, rising to become the Head of Molecular Spectroscopy (spectrum analysis of the light and radiation from any source, dummy) and, naturally, a Fellow of the Royal Society of Chemistry. After twenty-six years, he retired. And for most of those years he didn't so much as touch a drumstick – shame on you, Geoffrey; molecular spectroscopists are ten-a-penny but a good drummer is as rare as an in-depth interview with J.D. Salinger. But, after sixteen years or so, he got the itch to play again. I've got a recent tape of his band, Bad Batch (a group of chemists. d'you think?), and that old signature snare-drum technique still jumps out at you. He spends his retirement playing golf and tennis although, as a former Dyfed Singles Champion, I suspect that 'playing' is something of an understatement. It seems appropriate to end Geoff's section with a Bill Tilden quote. Tilden, an American, was seven-times Wimbledon Singles Champion in the '20s and would have won another seven if his career had not been cruelly cut short by homosexual innuendo. In his day he was unbeatable and he knew it. He said: 'There is no need to look at your opponent – if he's good. you know where he is, and if he's no good, it doesn't matter where he is.'

Hugo Griffiths – reluctant guitarist with the Corncrackers. Hugo now lives in Cardiff.

Ron and John Bevan – Corncrackers' first transport supremos and official photographers. Ron, who took many of the photographs in this book, joined the Royal Air Force and became – what else? – a photographer, working in aerial intelligence. And that's about all I can tell you. I tried to prise a few more details out of him but he couldn't tell me anything because it would contravene the Official Secrets Act, to which he is a signatory. He did tell me his postings included Singapore, Cyprus, Germany, Aden and North Africa, and that he ended his days teaching in the RAF School of Photography, but that's all. After twelve years he left the RAF and became a pharmaceutical rep for a while before becoming a freelance photographer. (Today Ron appears to be happy but I know his soul is scarred. He has to live with the knowledge that he is responsible for one of the greatest crimes against humanity ever committed – he taught me to drive. There are plaster-casted, whiplashed motorists all over the civilised world who have just cause to hunt him down with extreme prejudice. If only they knew his identity – which they do now. Now that this information has come to light I fully expect the Automobile Association to issue a fatwa, declaring him an enemy of motoring and urging any motorist who sees him to take appropriate action.)

John joined the Navy where, during the '70s, he established the record for the deepest simulated dive in a pressure chamber, earning himself a place in the Guinness Book of Records. He left the Navy and joined Shell as a diving consultant. He left to form his own company, Submex, which provides divers for the oil business, and wrote 'The Professional Diver's Manual' which is regarded as the bible for the industry. He was in charge of the investigation into the deaths of World War Two British sailors in the North Sea and involved in the raising of the Mary Rose, at one point escorting Prince Charles down to inspect the submerged hull. (Johnny bach, you missed a golden opportunity to strike a blow for republicanism. All it would have taken was a firm tug on his air-pipe and you would have spared the country years of listening to his blinkered, sanctimonious, blue-blooded tripe.) Another of John's books, 'The Origins of the Diving Helmet', earned him his PhD.

As a diving consultant he is often employed in the film world, advertising and mainstream TV. He recently appeared in the Hale and Pace show, during a sketch about underwater childbirth. This was, no doubt, a long-overdue attempt by Hale and Pace to finally inject some humour into their dismal little show.

John and I have many things in common, but one thing is particularly striking. I, too, am in the Guinness Book of Records, as one of the least successful recording artists of all time, although the criterion used by the ultra right-wing McWhirter brothers was, to say the least, questionable. They decided that the least successful artists of all time – and the list included Big Bill Broonzy – were those who'd only spent one week in the top fifty album charts. In 1973 my album, 'Kamikaze', scraped in, qualifying me. According to the despicable McWhirter brothers, if I'd sold fewer records and failed to make the top fifty I would not have qualified, thereby escaping the ignomy of being branded a failure by one of the bestselling books of all time. So, if you adhere to McWhirter logic, it follows that this sorry mess is all your fault, dear reader – you bought too many of my records, thus ensuring my public disgrace.

And where are the McWhirters now? Well, there's only one left. The IRA got the other bastard (It's only a job half-done, gentlemen.). Either together or separately, they founded the Freedom Association, a ragbag of authoritarion dimwits who form an inoperable cancer on the body politic of British society, and by their every word and deed prove themselves to have the collective IQ of a small carrot. But they are dangerous because stupid people will take them seriously and there are enough stupid people in British Isles to make that a worrying prospect, bearing in mind the British public gave Thatcher three general election victories. In conclusion, may I say to the remaining McWhirter, and I think Big Bill would agree with me on this – fuck right off.

Allan 'Lewie' Lewis – Corncrackers' road manager and disgruntled policeman. Lewie did indeed resign from the police force and get a proper job. He went to work for Rowntrees for nineteen years, most of them as top salesman, rising to become National Sales Training Manager. He then struck out on his own and set up an interior design company specialising in refurbishing pubs. He went into partnership with with Alan 'Wimpy' Phillips, who you will remember as road manager for the Dream, and they opened twin nightspots in Station Road – Barnum's for the younger psychopath, and Bailey's for the more mature recidivist. Their business empire flourished for years until they split up (Caesar and Brutus spring to mind). Each now flourishes separately. Lewie now owns most of Llanelli and is probably approaching multimillionaire status. I saw him the other day at Enterprise House, his Llanelli office. We talked about old times, discussed the need for discipline in life (I couldn't get my head around that, at all), and ended up debating the possibility of an afterlife (Lewie maintained there was one – I said it would all go black). As I left I noticed some of the pictures on the wall. They were mostly photos of Lewie with prominent people. The two I remember were Prince Charles and Gareth Edwards. Normally I hate royalty but in Gareth's case I'll make an exception.

Billy 'Doc' Evans – drummer of the Jets. Billy died during the writing of this book and I've just come home from his funeral. He'd been ill for some time. About two hundred people turned up to say goodbye. The hearse was drawn by two magnificent black horses and after the service Plum and Martin sang 'Some Other Guy', Billy's favourite song. The preacher read out a piece written by Jenny, Billy's wife. The bit that stuck in my mind was this – Billy was English by birth, Welsh by choice. I didn't know he was English. A couple of months later Jenny arranged a gig to celebrate his existence, called 'Rock for the Doc'. We reformed the Jets and the proceeds went to the Renal Unit at Morriston Hospital. Why do they always take the good ones?

Pete James – drummer with the Blackjacks. When the Blackjacks broke up in '66, Pete embarked on what he calls the happiest days of his professional life. He went up to London to look for work and, as a drummer who could sight-read music, had little difficulty finding session work. And session work often led to tour offers. During the next five years he recorded and toured with Matt Monroe, Danny Williams, Dickie Valentine, Solomon King, Ricky Valance, Dorothy Squires, Lou Christie, Dusty Springfield and Diana Dors (beat that for a CV). Feeling the need for a change of pace, he returned to Wales and began a five-year residency at the Townsman nightclub in Swansea working for MD and organist Ron Williams (Terry's father). When this ended, he became the house drummer for Swansea Sound, the local radio station, playing live ads. He now runs a recording studio he built in Carmarthen. But drumming remains the passion. At the moment he is in the Earl Green Band, the only Welshman in a group of Texans, and has just guested on an as yet untitled blues album; fellow guests included Mark Knopfler and Georgie Fame. Gail, his daughter, is following in the family tradition. She is a stupendous drummer who, at the time of writing, is studying at the Institute of Percussion in Los Angeles, where she has just been awarded the accolade of Groove Stylist of the Year. The first non-American to win it and, more importantly, the first woman.

Peter has had a huge impact on my life – without him I wouldn't know what a triple paradiddle was.

Christine Corvette – singer with the Blackjacks. The break up of the Blackjacks coincided with vocal problems for Christine. During the last year of the band she had been experiencing increasing throat pains when she sang, particularly in the extremes of her range. She sought medical help. The diagnosis was a blow – corns on the larynx – and the remedies harsh. She had, she was told, two choices – surgery or give up singing for a year. She opted to take a year off. During that time, life conspired to deflect her from her chosen path. She got married and built a new life. By the end of the year her voice had recovered but her confidence had gone and she gave up professional singing. She still lives in Llanelli and now sings in old peoples' homes, accompanying herself on keyboards. I can think of worse ways to end my days than listening to Christine singing 'Summertime'. I'd like to think that one day

outro

Christine will return to the stage. If she doesn't, it would be an awful waste of a beautiful voice.

Keith Hodge – drummer of the Corncrackers. After leaving the Corncrackers Keith moved to London. He got a job as road-manager for the Nice, and sang on their first album, before joining the Attack. A year later he became the drummer of Screaming Lord Sutch & the Savages. A year after that he joined the Nashville Teens. All the while he was doing sessions with Joe Cocker, ELO, Renaissance, Rick Wakeman and Steve Howe.

He formed his own band, Mandragon, and came third, behind the Eyes Of Blue and Stray, in the Melody Maker Competition. He then joined the Jerry Donahue Band but was poached by Mickie Most for the Suzi Quatro Band. The week before their first single, 'Can The Can', reached number one, I lured him away to join my band Iceberg, thus scuppering his chances of unlimited wealth. On his departure from Iceberg he formed his own company, FRO Productions, and had Euro-wide hits with Zoë and Clare Severac.

He is currently working on a book, collecting B-movies, playing spasmodically with a blues band, improving his golf handicap and, I suspect, betting on the horses, a pastime in which, as I have said many times before, he can be said to approach genius (this last sentence is now redundant because Keith has fallen in love with Wendy, who has, as lovers so often do, transformed his priorities – the 1,500 B-movie videos are now in the attic and I fear for the safety of the golf clubs. On the plus side, Wendy is insisting that his appearancees on the musical stage be a little more frequent than 'spasmodic'. I would agree with that). My life is irrevocably entwined with Keith's because I have fallen hopelessly in love with his sister, Mary, so he is now doomed to spend every Christmas in my company. Every time he looks up, there I will be, peering at him over the turkey, a constant reminder of what life might have been had he escaped the Curse of the Leonards.

STOP PRESS: And with one bound he was free! The Curse of the Leonards, which once struck terror into the hearts of the unsuspecting, has, like most things associated with the name Leonard, proved to be nothing more than hot air. Seconds before this book was sent for publication, Keith hit the motherlode. When the accumulated items of his life were being moved up to the attic, Wendy noticed a rather colourful jacket. She enquired as to its origins. Keith told her that the jacket had been given to him by Keith Moon. (The genesis of this dated back to when Keith was drumming with the Untamed. They shared a producer and a record company with the Who and he and Keith became friends. One night Hodge was celebrating his birthday at the Speakeasy when Moon walked in.

'Nice jacket,' said Hodge.

'You like it?' said Moon. 'Have it.' He took it off and gave it to Hodge. 'Happy birthday'.)

'Do you want to keep it,' said Wendy, 'or shall I throw it out?'

'Don't throw it out,' said Keith. 'It might be worth a few bob.'

Intrigued, Wendy phoned up 'Find A Fortune', a populist TV show that specialises in asset valuation, to ask their opinion. The producer got really excited and Keith and

Wendy were invited on the show. The upshot was that, on air the jacket was valued at £25,000 and Keith nearly had a heart attack. After the show he was approached by Bonham's, the rock auctioneers, who suggested putting the jacket up for auction at the Hard Rock Café in August, where, they said, it should realise at least three or four times the initial valuation.

Naturally, Mary and I, watching on TV, were delighted at his good fortune. After the show we phoned up to offer our congratulations. He was flabbergasted but said his feet were still firmly on the ground and the money wouldn't change his life in any way, shape or form. He further added that he couldn't talk for long because he had a plane to catch.

If you'd like to ring him and add your congratulations, he can now be reached at Mustique 3162.

Tony 'Plum' Hollis – singer of the Jets. Plum's story is best told in his own words: I put my girlfriend up the duff. Or she said I did. She said I was responsible. I was working in a sheet metal works and she was working in the office. I was egged on – not that I needed much egging on – by Dai Abbot, the welder. He bet me I couldn't take her out, so I did. I started going out with her and doing all the usual things. Then she told me she was pregnant. Her mother came 'round the house. I was out and when I came home my mother said, 'What have you done now, you silly bugger?' So Cracky got me a job with Jimmy James & the Vagabonds and, fuck, I was gone. I shared a very small flat in London with Cracky. He was ill and went to hospital. I couldn't pay the rent so I did a moonlight and left all his stuff behind. He still plays fuck about that.

I went to work for Pete Brown's Piblokto. I left Pete Brown because he never fucking paid me. 'I'm going down to the accountants for money,' he'd say. 'Any money?' I'd say, when he got back. 'No, man,' he'd say, 'there's no money. Nothing's come in.' So I left and got a job with Wild Turkey. All the roadies used to meet on a Wednesday night in a pub in Putney. I was in there one night and Mick Lawford spotted me. I'll always remember Mick. He used to talk out of the side of his mouth. He used to wear a wig and he was hard as nails. He was a fucking maniac. He was the type of bloke who'd hit you with a hammer. He was working for Nigel Thomas, who managed the Grease Band. 'Ever been to America, Plum?' he said. 'No.' 'Like to go?' 'Fucking hell, yeah.' 'OK, you're going on Saturday night.' 'I can't do that. I can't just leave the boys.' But I talked to the boys and they said it was too good an opportunity to miss and wished me all the best. So I went.

We did a tour, then the Grease Band split up. They had a horrendous fight one night in Southport. Or Stockport? I remember there was a pier there. After the gig we were sitting in the dressing room and Henry McCullough had passed out in a chair. Alan Spenner was going to form a band with Chris Stainton, and he started talking about it because he thought Henry was asleep, but Henry was fucking listening all the time. He got up and ran at Stainton with a pint pot. There was a big fight and that was that. So I went to work for the Chris Stainton band. It was a brilliant band but they didn't have a singer, so we were advertising and auditioning. A guy came from Los

Angeles. I had to go and pick him up at the airport. He was a bit of a Rod Stewart lookalike and he was fucking awful. So everybody split. Nigel Thomas came over to me. 'I'm going now,' he said. 'Tell him he's rubbish and he's got to go home.' So they left me with this guy and I had to tell him. 'Look, man,' I said, 'I've got to take you to the airport. You don't make it.' He started ranting and raving. 'Where are they?' he was shouting. He wanted to kill them because they didn't have the guts to tell him face to face.

One day we were sitting in the rehearsal room, talking about singers. 'Why don't you ask Joe?' I said. 'Have you got his number?' They had, so we rang him up. I spoke to him and he agreed to join the band. I picked him up at the airport and that's when that saga started. It was incredible. I wish I'd written it all down. At one point we had Bobby Keyes and Jim Price, who'd just come off the Stones tour, Jim Horn, who played sax on all those Duane Eddy records, and Jim Karstein, who played drums on all those Everly Brothers records. I couldn't fucking believe it. Bobby Keyes was a methadone addict. He had this bent doctor and he used to bung him for a prescription. We were going somewhere and we missed a plane – the superstars could never get out of bed – so we hired a small aircraft. There was Keyes, Cocker, Stainton, Spenner and me. Bobby Keyes was trying to get Joe to inject mathadone and he was going to do it. I freaked, because Joe would take anything. He'd try any-fucking-thing. If you gave him a pile of horse dung and said, 'You smoke that, man, and you'll get off', he'd fucking smoke it. Once he smoked artificial flowers. He didn't have any dope so he took the leaves off, rolled it up and smoked it. 'Any good?' I said. He reckoned it was. When there were no drugs about they'd boil up benzedrine inhalers and drink the water. They were all wired up to fuck. One day, I read the contents. 'Look, man,' I said to Joe, 'it's not doing you any fucking good. It's one per cent strychnine. Fucking strychnine, man!' 'I thought I could feel something pulling at the heart,' he said.

We were in Adelaide, which is a bit like Llanelli. It's just a little back-town. We were in a motel called the Gazebo. We were big news. Fucking Joe Cocker and his entourage. There were forty-one of us on the road – a couple of bands and their women. This character turns up with a pillow-case full of grass. Thinking back on it, it was a plant. The seven superstars eke out this dope so they each had plastic bags full of grass. Normally I would have been en suite to Joe, in an adjoining room, but he had Eileen, his old lady, with him. Six o'clock in the morning there was a copper knocking on everyone's door. They went into Joe's room and woke him up. 'This is a bust,' they said. 'Where's the drugs?' 'Over there on the table,' said Joe, and went back to sleep. Cool as fuck. They searched our rooms. I didn't have any dope. If I'd wanted any smoke I'd just take some of theirs. It was the same with coke or anything. They had glass phials of coke – ounces of it. They'd get a mirror or a glass table, tip the lot out and blade it off. I went to pick some up once, at a flat in London. The guy had pounds of it. I shat myself. 'If somebody busted this place now,' I remember thinking, 'I'd go to jail for twenty years.'

All the superstars were busted and we were chucked out of Australia. We had a police escort to the airport and they put us on a plane. No matter where the plane

maybe i should've stayed in bed?

stopped we weren't allowed to get off. We tried to get off in Fiji but there were all these big policemen waiting. They let me off to buy some books and stuff. We came back to London and fell apart, Joe went on the piss, so I came home. I'd saved up a couple of quid so I went into partnership with a sheet-metal company. I've been through a few companies since then and that's what I'm currently doing – making stuff out of metal.

Graham Dean-Jones – bon viveur par excellence. Cracky got a job as road manager for Van Der Graaf Generator and went on to become personal assistant to Tony Stratton-Smith, their manager. When Tony died, Cracky became personal assistant to Steve O'Rourke, manager of the Pink Floyd. With the Floyd, he travelled the stadia of the world, performing his duties, which mainly centred around shipping the cars that Nick Mason bought back to Britain. He now runs a luxury car chauffeur service in Kent.

Brian Breeze – guitarist of the Corncrackers. After the Corncrackers Brian, a mechanical engineer by trade, slipped the surly bonds of reality, jacked his job in and joined Pete Brown's Piblokto. After recording an album and touring he returned to mechanical engineering, thinking, no doubt, that his creative juices had been satisfied. But no. The itch was still there. So, tragic creature, he phoned me up, looking for a gig. As circumstance would have it I was forming a band, which I intended to call Iceberg, and actively looking for a guitarist. You could call it synchronicity, although I suspect that Brian would consider the term philosophically invalid. Brian credits me with opening the valves of his heart and cutting him free from the shackles of conventional employment. I do my best, Brian. I do my best.

When Iceberg broke up he joined Maggie Bell. Then he was commissioned by Welsh television to write some music for one of their upcoming dramas, and the gates of a new career swung open. Most of the music you hear today on Welsh television is written by Brian. It could be said that he is, in an insidious sort of way, the most ubiquitous musician in Wales, He has also produced about twenty Welsh language albums. Then he became aware of something gnawing at his entrails. It was a yearning for knowledge. He returned to school. Breezy has always inclined toward academia. At the time of writing he is both teacher and student at Swansea University, running several courses on sound-engineering and doing a philosophy degree. A philosophy degree has inherent dangers. The brain can only take so much philosophy. You can saunter through Spinoza and dawdle through Diderot but by the time you get to Wittgenstein it's all over. One morning you will rub the sleep from your eyes and discover that your brain has turned to mush. A sane man would stop right there and get himself a job that makes no intellectual demands upon him whatsoever – the Church or politics would seem ideal – but should he choose to proceed he will, without a scintilla of doubt, end up stripping down to his underwear and telling dirty jokes at public functions. Such behaviour goes with the territory and is, to a certain extent, expected and accepted in professorial circles. So for pity's sake, Brian, let it stop here. No good will come of it and it is sure to end in tears. He won't listen to me, of course. He's got a mind of his own, that boy.

outro

I have a theory about Brian. I believe his parents were dyslexic and they meant to call him Brain. I asked him to sum up the achievements of his life in a sentence. 'Well,' he said, 'I've had several different cars, one of them light blue.'

STOP PRESS: Brian has just attained a First in Philosophy. Prince Charles was invited to present the current crop of degrees at Swansea University and duly arrived to do so. Brian did not attend the ceremony, preferring to accept his degree in absentia. This could be seen as an anti-monarchist boycott, but Brian prefers the word 'snub'. That's my boy!

Alan 'Wimpy' Phillips – road manager of the Dream. When I first met Wimpy he was working in his parents' newsagent shop on Swansea Road. It was on my way into town so I called in every time I passed. I was always welcomed until I persuaded him to be the Dream's roadie. Then it all changed. His mother, normally a well-balanced woman, turned on me, seeing me as a threat to Wimpy's future occupational stability.

'You're leading him into a life of razzmatazz,' she said, stabbing the air with a rolled-up Daily Mirror.

Well, somebody had to.

When the Dream broke up, Wimpy opened a booking agency and went into partnership with Allan 'Lewie' Lewis. He is now the biggest agent in Wales. I saw him the other day on Llanelli beach, watching the solar eclipse with his wife, children and grandchildren. I asked himself to sum himself up in a sentence. 'I'm an ageing theatrical agent,' he said, 'still looking for new talent.'

Jeff Hurley - road manager of the Dream. Jeff still lives in Llanelli. He is now a big wheel in the Trade Union movement (I knew he'd end up on the side of the angels), and his son is the bass-player with a heavy-metal band, so he obviously knows a thing or two about bringing up children.

Tony Court – early Jets drummer and manager of the Dream. Tony is now a Buddhist, and not your common-or-garden Buddhist either. From what I can gather he's very near the top of the tree and on first-name terms with the Dalai Lama, whom he meets once a year. I saw him a couple of years ago at a Dream reunion and he exuded happiness and self-fulfilment, much like he did when he was managing the Dream. Buddhism strikes me as being the only religion worth a damn because it is the only one with a sense of humour. The rest peddle their preposterous little dogmas as if their afterlife depended on it. May I offer a little advice to the spiritually committed? Whatever you do, don't die for your beliefs – they may be wrong.

Clive 'Wes' Reynolds – bass-player of the Corncrackers and the Dream. It doesn't matter where Wes is now. He has proved to be a substandard human being, unworthy of your interest.

Terry Williams – drummer of the Jets and the Dream. After the Dream Terry went on to play with Dave Edmunds' Rockpile, Man, Meatloaf, Dire Straits, Chuck Berry, Paul McCartney, Tina Turner, Ray Charles, the Everly Brothers, Tom Petty, Eric

Clapton, Keith Richard, Cliff Richard (shame on you, Tel), Hank B. Marvin (why, Tel? In the name of reason, why?), Billy Joel, Dion, Ronnie Wood, Bill Wyman, Nick Lowe, Graham Parker, Robert Cray, Steve Cropper, Bo Diddley, Carl Perkins, B.B.King, Albert Collins, Nils Lofgren, Tracy Ullman, Cindi Lauper, Natalie Cole, Terence Trent D'Arby, Joe Cocker, Al Green, Geraint Watkins, Yoko Ono and Bob Dylan. He returned to Man for a brief period but, softened by La Dolce Vita, he couldn't take the pace. Playing with the Manband is like taking part in the Krypton Factor whereas playing with Dylan is a piece of piss.

Martin Ace – bass-player of the Jets and front man of the Dream. Martin's career path has run almost parallel to mine. We both ended up in the Manband and we're still there. But while I spend my spare time drifting in and out of a drug-induced coma, Martin is almost pathologically active. (Once again the blame for that must lie squarely on the shoulders of the public school system; all those years of getting up at six in the morning and cold-showering in an atmosphere of barely-suppressed, latent sexual doubt are bound to have an effect.) For years, the main outlet for his energy was the magnificent Flying Aces but since they broke up he plays, both invited and uninvited, with any band that takes his fancy.

The bands close to his heart – of which there seem to be at least a mininum of six at any given time – include the Silverbirds and the Tydfil Thunderbolts (in the company of mysterious shamanic creatures called Cedric, Travis and Merthyr Tom); Marco di Maggio and the Italian Love Gods (a Sienna-based rockabilly band that could show Carl Perkins a thing or two); and the Crystal Blue Persuasions (a girl vocal trio that features Jo Ace, his daughter and my niece; Kate Leonard, my daughter and his niece; and Sadie Williams, Peter Williams's daughter and Katy's half-sister. Peter is Terry's brother. Are you following this?).

Martin has recently embarked upon a film career. His first screen appearance was in 'Twin Town', in which he plays the pivotal role of the Singing Sikh. His second screen appearance is in the soon-to-be-released 'Dad's Room', in which he plays the pivotal role of a tuba player. Jonathon Price is in it, so it must be a proper film. Now Martin's got this acting game down pat, I look foward to seeing his Coriolanus at the National.

Deke Leonard – agent provocateur and eminence grise. So, where am I now? Good question. I'll stick to the facts, as I so often do – I'm finishing off this bloody book.

THE BLOODY END